The Best Of
Alex
2013

D0731001

Charles Peattie & Russell Taylor

Masterley Publishing

The Best Of
Alex
2013

TWEET
TWEET
TROLL
TROLL

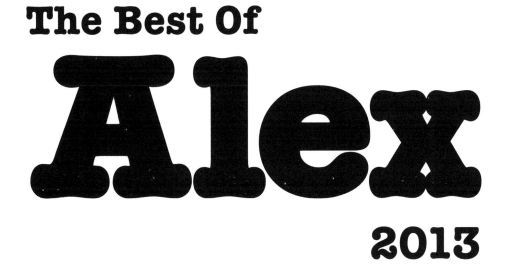

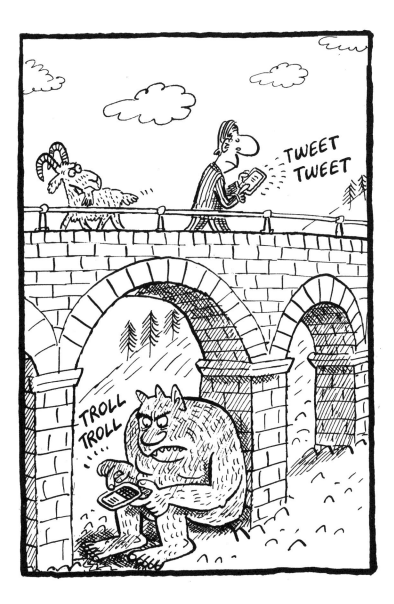

First Published in 2013 by MASTERLEY PUBLISHING

Layout and Artwork: Suzette Field
Additional artworking on *It's a Wonderful Crisis* by Agata Karpisz and Leonie Morris.

ISBN: 978-18537590-2-4

Printed and bound by CPI Group (UK) Ltd, Croydon, CR0 4YY

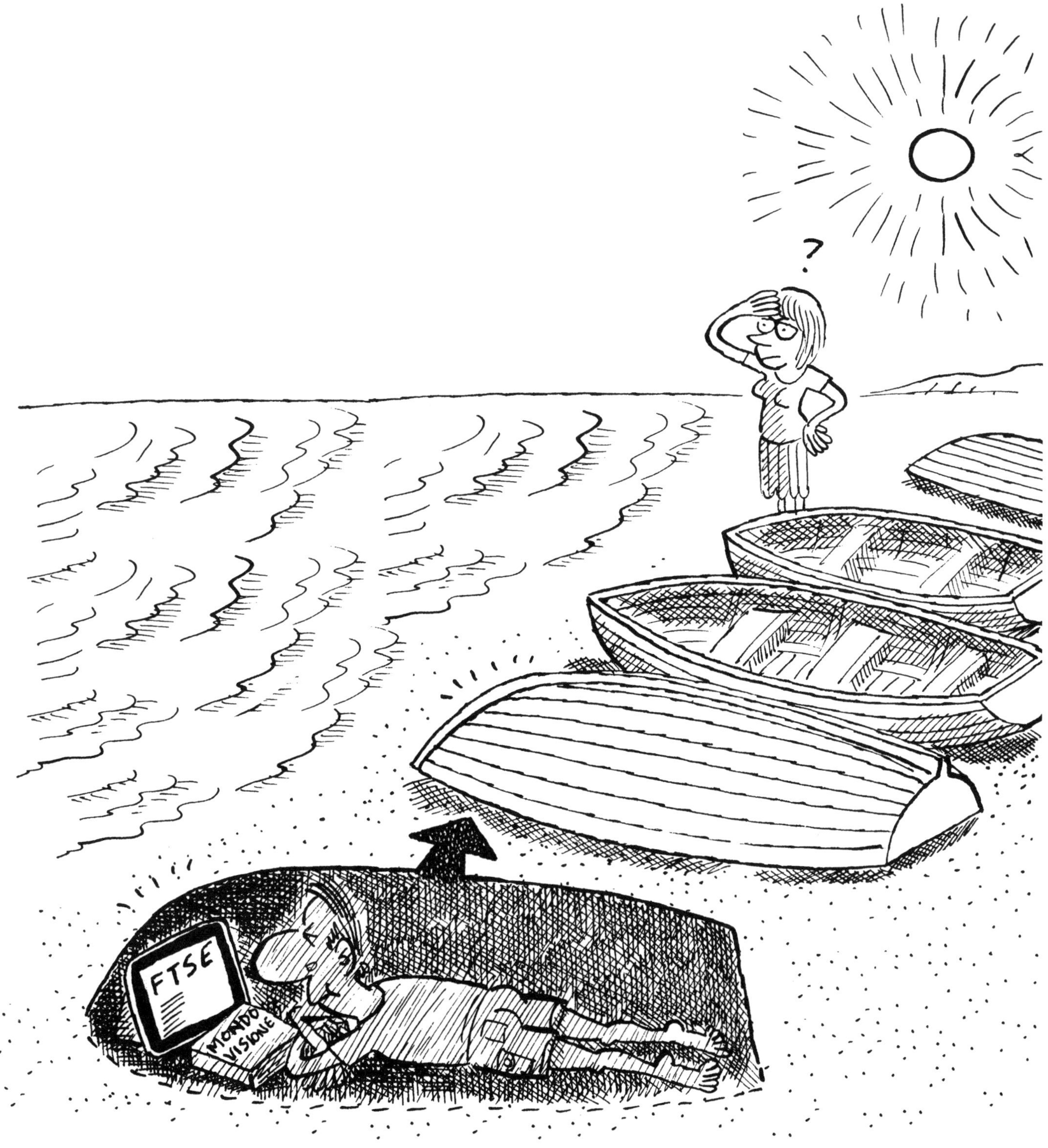
?
FTSE
MONDO VISIONE

Our usual gratitude goes to our generous sponsors.

FTSE Group (FTSE) is the world-leader in the creation and management of index solutions.

Mondo Visione provides vital knowledge about the world's exchanges and trading venues.

FOREWORD

If you were old-fashioned enough to have bought this book one of the country's few remaining bookshops and flicked through its pages before purchasing it you may have noticed that for the first time it boasts a full colour section. Yet despite this extravagance it still retails at its traditional stolid £9.99 (or rather cheaper if you are among the other 90% of purchasers who bought it on Amazon). In deciding to hold our prices at 2001 levels we are aware that we are failing in our duty to support the government in its mission to crank up the cost of living and inflate away as much of the national debt as possible. And of course Alex himself would be utterly appalled and embarrassed at having his 2013 yearbook listed at the same price it was at back in the days of the Enron collapse and the original model BlackBerry. We can only offer our apologies to both of them.

Still we hope you think our long-form story - It's a Wonderful Crisis - which ran in the Daily Telegraph over Christmas 2012 is a worthy addition to this annual. It has some elements which are perhaps a little atypical of the average investment banker's life. For example, Alex travels in time to visit his future and his past. But perhaps the idea is not so fanciful. As we write, the financial world is starting to behave as if it had been transported back to 2007: securitized debt products, leveraged buy outs and 100% mortgages and are back in fashion. Many people are once again acting as if there was no tomorrow, which, considering that national governments have run out of bail out money, this time round there might not be.

So is the global financial crisis actually over? Who knows? This is when it would be useful to have a time machine of our own, so we could sneak forwards a few months and find out what state the economy will be in by the time you are reading these words, comfortably ensconced in your smallest room on Boxing Day. Frankly we haven't a clue. Our only consolation is that we don't think anyone else does either.

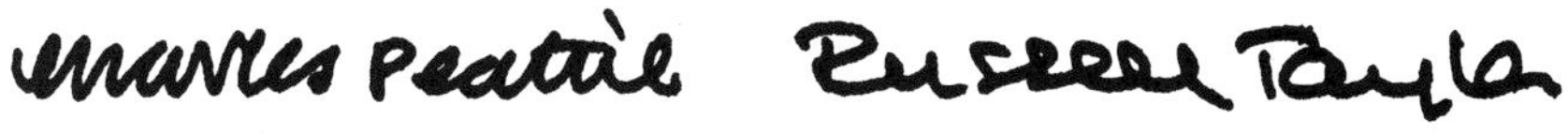

Charles Peattie and Russell Taylor

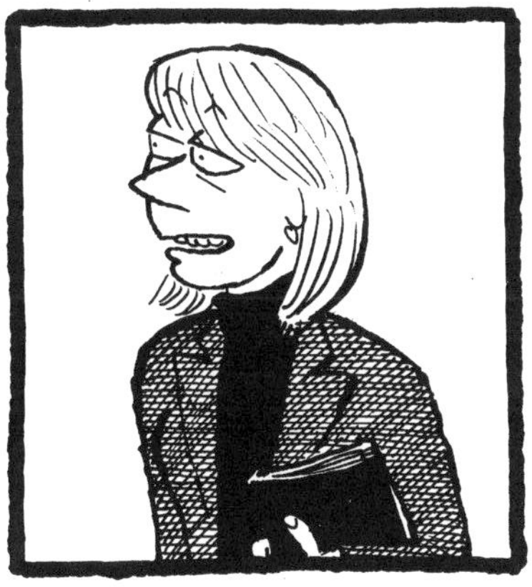

Penny - Alex's corporate wife

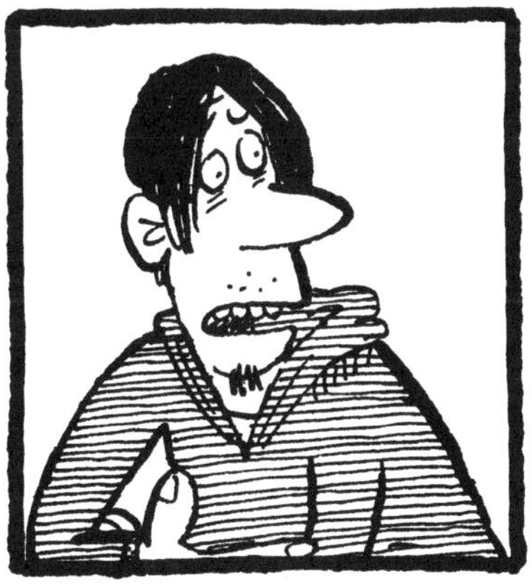

Christopher - Alex's unemployed son

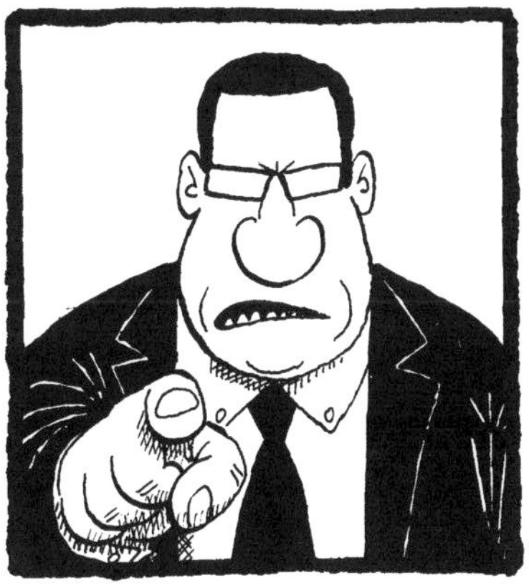

Cyrus - Alex's American boss

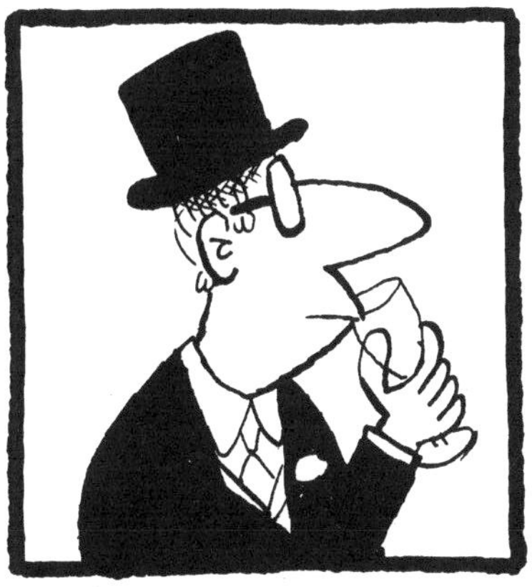

Clive - Alex's wimpish colleague

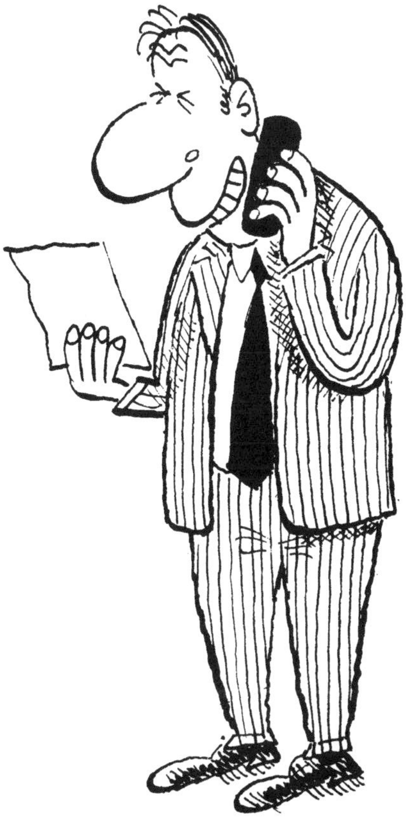

Alex
Devious investment banker

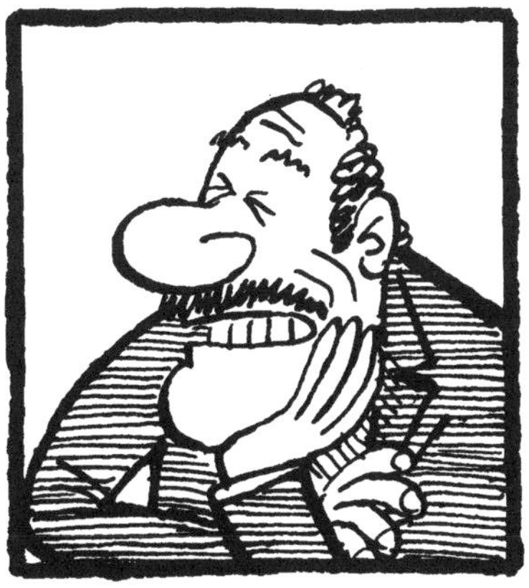

Mr Hardcastle - Alex's client

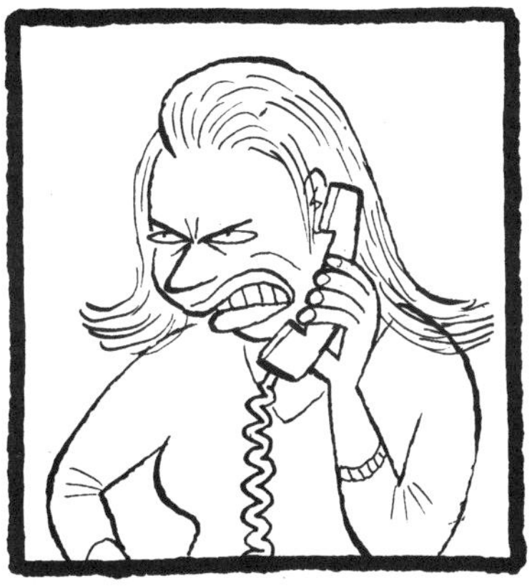

Bridget - Clive's fearsome wife

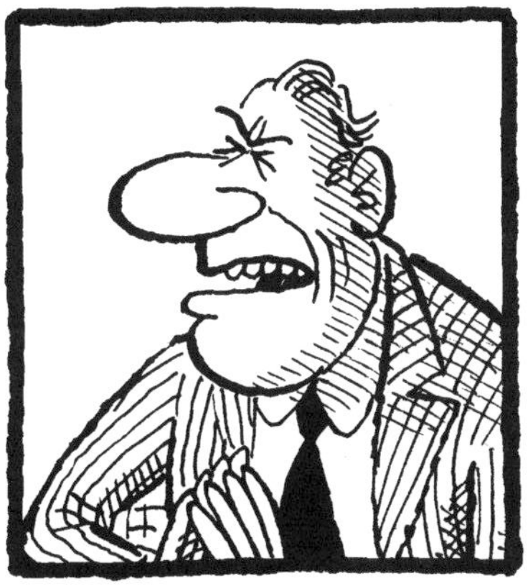

Rupert - Senior bank director

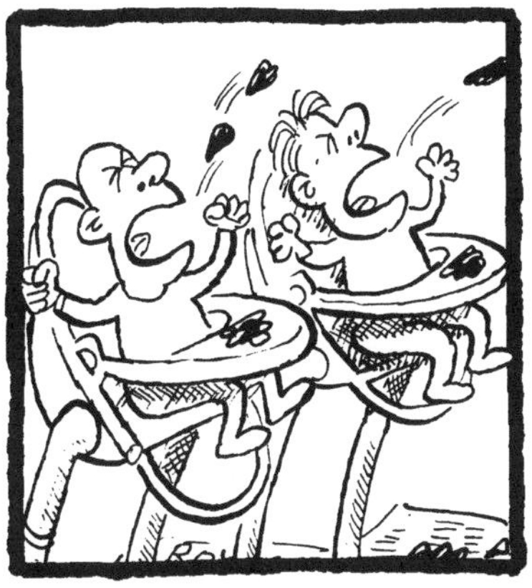

The Twins - Clive's recent offspring

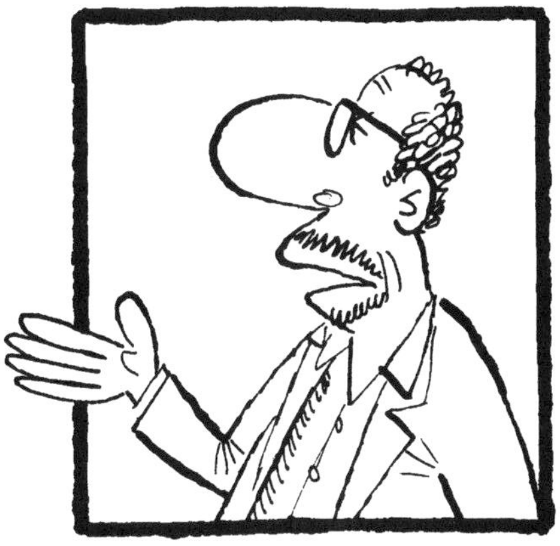

Greg - Alex's journalist brother

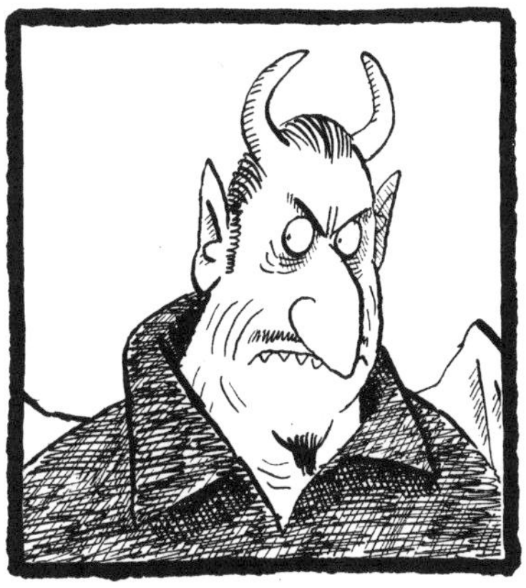

The Devil - Prince of Darkness

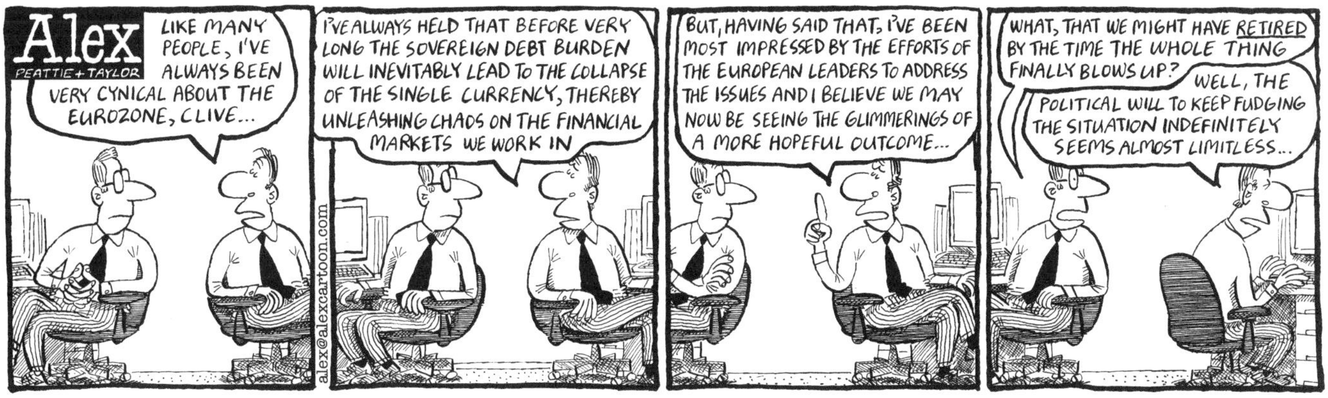
Alex
PEATTIE + TAYLOR
LIKE MANY PEOPLE, I'VE ALWAYS BEEN VERY CYNICAL ABOUT THE EUROZONE, CLIVE...
I'VE ALWAYS HELD THAT BEFORE VERY LONG THE SOVEREIGN DEBT BURDEN WILL INEVITABLY LEAD TO THE COLLAPSE OF THE SINGLE CURRENCY, THEREBY UNLEASHING CHAOS ON THE FINANCIAL MARKETS WE WORK IN
alex@alexcartoon.com
BUT, HAVING SAID THAT, I'VE BEEN MOST IMPRESSED BY THE EFFORTS OF THE EUROPEAN LEADERS TO ADDRESS THE ISSUES AND I BELIEVE WE MAY NOW BE SEEING THE GLIMMERINGS OF A MORE HOPEFUL OUTCOME...
WHAT, THAT WE MIGHT HAVE RETIRED BY THE TIME THE WHOLE THING FINALLY BLOWS UP?
WELL, THE POLITICAL WILL TO KEEP FUDGING THE SITUATION INDEFINITELY SEEMS ALMOST LIMITLESS...

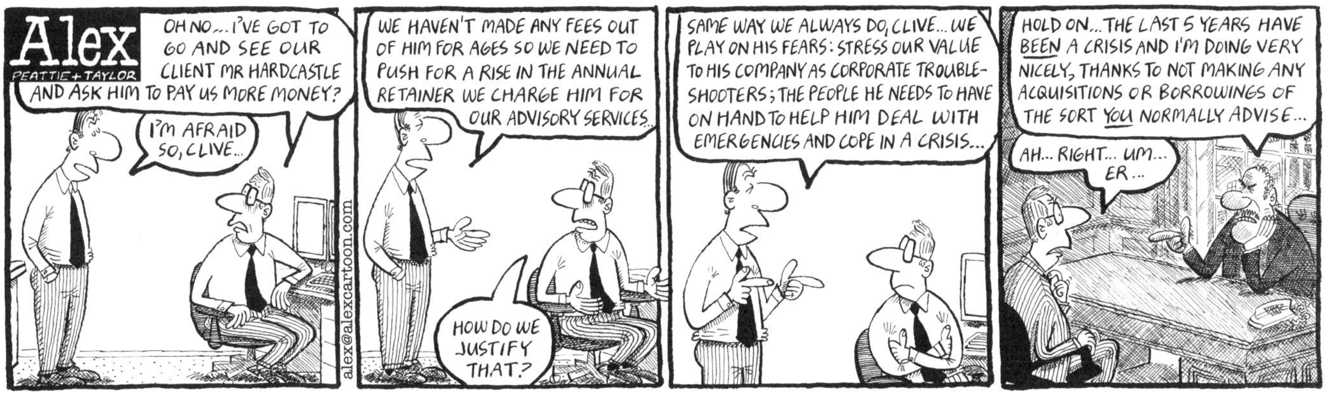
Alex
PEATTIE + TAYLOR
OH NO... I'VE GOT TO GO AND SEE OUR CLIENT MR HARDCASTLE AND ASK HIM TO PAY US MORE MONEY?
I'M AFRAID SO, CLIVE...
alex@alexcartoon.com
WE HAVEN'T MADE ANY FEES OUT OF HIM FOR AGES SO WE NEED TO PUSH FOR A RISE IN THE ANNUAL RETAINER WE CHARGE HIM FOR OUR ADVISORY SERVICES...
HOW DO WE JUSTIFY THAT?
SAME WAY WE ALWAYS DO, CLIVE... WE PLAY ON HIS FEARS: STRESS OUR VALUE TO HIS COMPANY AS CORPORATE TROUBLE-SHOOTERS; THE PEOPLE HE NEEDS TO HAVE ON HAND TO HELP HIM DEAL WITH EMERGENCIES AND COPE IN A CRISIS...
HOLD ON... THE LAST 5 YEARS HAVE BEEN A CRISIS AND I'M DOING VERY NICELY, THANKS TO NOT MAKING ANY ACQUISITIONS OR BORROWINGS OF THE SORT YOU NORMALLY ADVISE...
AH... RIGHT... UM... ER...

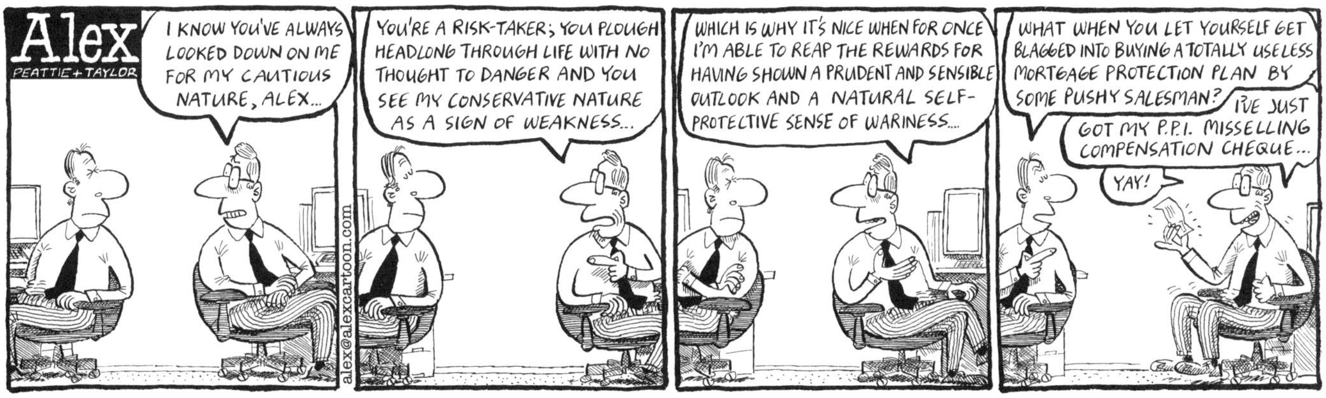
Alex
PEATTIE + TAYLOR
I KNOW YOU'VE ALWAYS LOOKED DOWN ON ME FOR MY CAUTIOUS NATURE, ALEX...
alex@alexcartoon.com
YOU'RE A RISK-TAKER; YOU PLOUGH HEADLONG THROUGH LIFE WITH NO THOUGHT TO DANGER AND YOU SEE MY CONSERVATIVE NATURE AS A SIGN OF WEAKNESS...
WHICH IS WHY IT'S NICE WHEN FOR ONCE I'M ABLE TO REAP THE REWARDS FOR HAVING SHOWN A PRUDENT AND SENSIBLE OUTLOOK AND A NATURAL SELF-PROTECTIVE SENSE OF WARINESS...
WHAT WHEN YOU LET YOURSELF GET BLAGGED INTO BUYING A TOTALLY USELESS MORTGAGE PROTECTION PLAN BY SOME PUSHY SALESMAN?
I'VE JUST GOT MY P.P.I. MISSELLING COMPENSATION CHEQUE...
YAY!

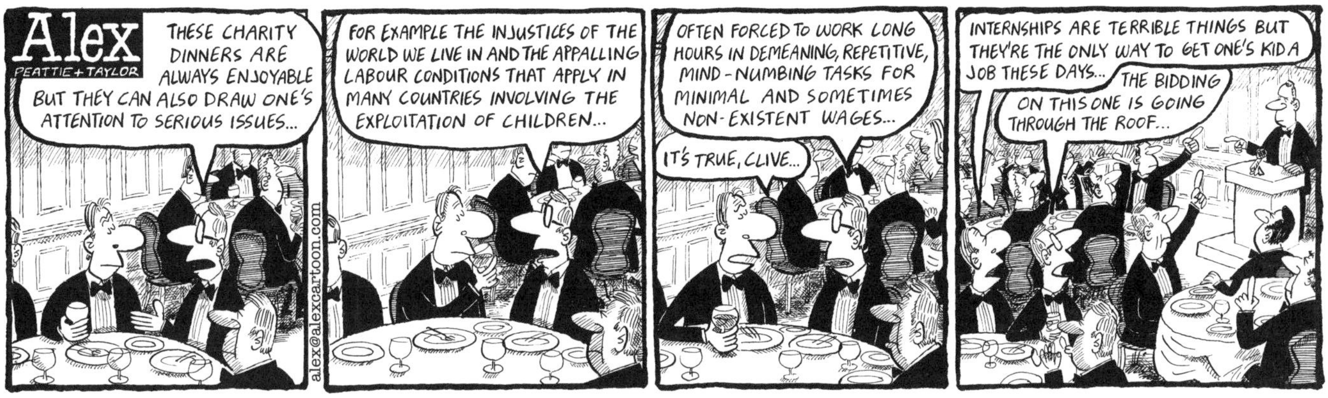
Alex
PEATTIE + TAYLOR
THESE CHARITY DINNERS ARE ALWAYS ENJOYABLE BUT THEY CAN ALSO DRAW ONE'S ATTENTION TO SERIOUS ISSUES...
alex@alexcartoon.com
FOR EXAMPLE THE INJUSTICES OF THE WORLD WE LIVE IN AND THE APPALLING LABOUR CONDITIONS THAT APPLY IN MANY COUNTRIES INVOLVING THE EXPLOITATION OF CHILDREN...
OFTEN FORCED TO WORK LONG HOURS IN DEMEANING, REPETITIVE, MIND-NUMBING TASKS FOR MINIMAL AND SOMETIMES NON-EXISTENT WAGES...
IT'S TRUE, CLIVE...
INTERNSHIPS ARE TERRIBLE THINGS BUT THEY'RE THE ONLY WAY TO GET ONE'S KID A JOB THESE DAYS...
THE BIDDING ON THIS ONE IS GOING THROUGH THE ROOF...

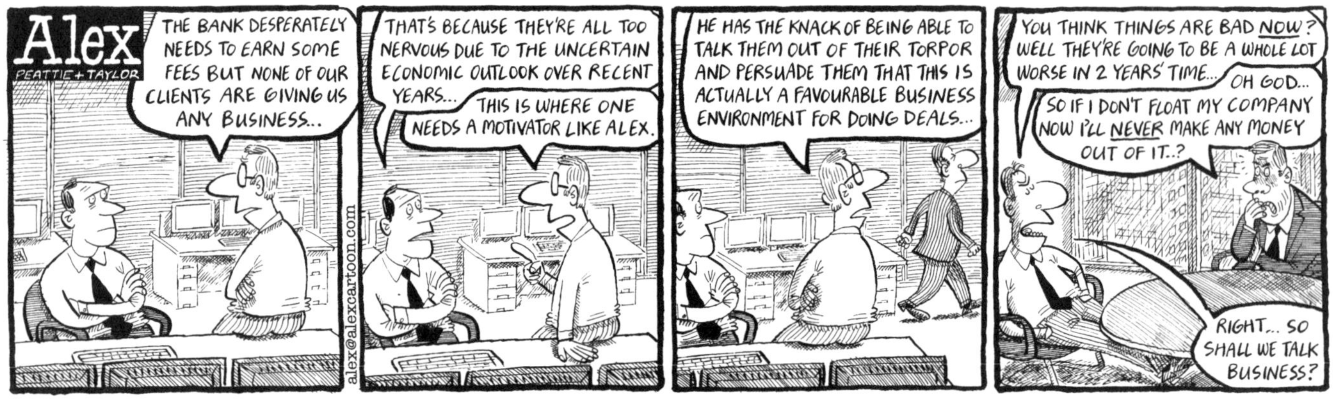
Alex
PEATTIE + TAYLOR
THE BANK DESPERATELY NEEDS TO EARN SOME FEES BUT NONE OF OUR CLIENTS ARE GIVING US ANY BUSINESS...
THAT'S BECAUSE THEY'RE ALL TOO NERVOUS DUE TO THE UNCERTAIN ECONOMIC OUTLOOK OVER RECENT YEARS...
THIS IS WHERE ONE NEEDS A MOTIVATOR LIKE ALEX.
alex@alexcartoon.com
HE HAS THE KNACK OF BEING ABLE TO TALK THEM OUT OF THEIR TORPOR AND PERSUADE THEM THAT THIS IS ACTUALLY A FAVOURABLE BUSINESS ENVIRONMENT FOR DOING DEALS...
YOU THINK THINGS ARE BAD NOW? WELL THEY'RE GOING TO BE A WHOLE LOT WORSE IN 2 YEARS' TIME...
OH GOD...
SO IF I DON'T FLOAT MY COMPANY NOW I'LL NEVER MAKE ANY MONEY OUT OF IT..?
RIGHT... SO SHALL WE TALK BUSINESS?

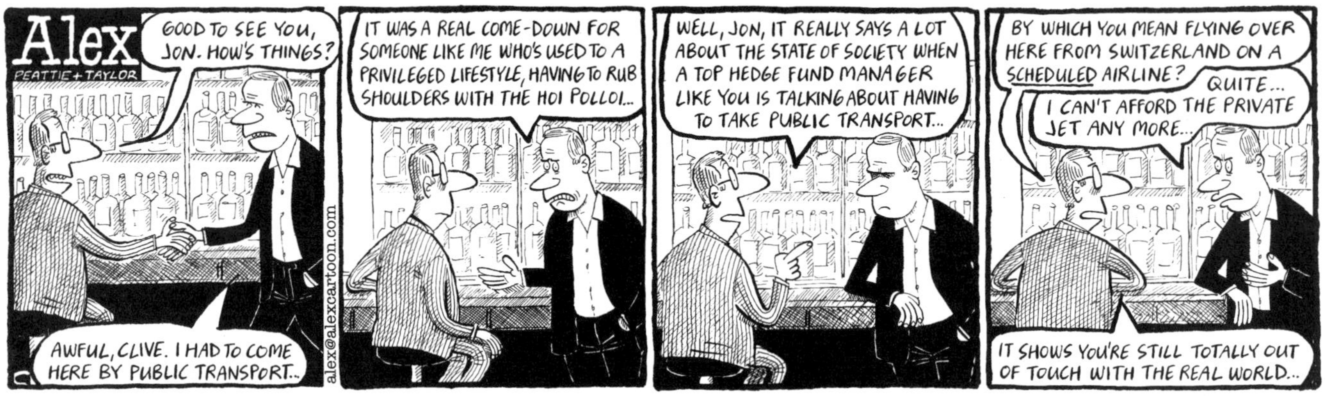
Alex
PEATTIE + TAYLOR
GOOD TO SEE YOU, JON. HOW'S THINGS?
AWFUL, CLIVE. I HAD TO COME HERE BY PUBLIC TRANSPORT...
alex@alexcartoon.com
IT WAS A REAL COME-DOWN FOR SOMEONE LIKE ME WHO'S USED TO A PRIVILEGED LIFESTYLE, HAVING TO RUB SHOULDERS WITH THE HOI POLLOI...
WELL, JON, IT REALLY SAYS A LOT ABOUT THE STATE OF SOCIETY WHEN A TOP HEDGE FUND MANAGER LIKE YOU IS TALKING ABOUT HAVING TO TAKE PUBLIC TRANSPORT...
BY WHICH YOU MEAN FLYING OVER HERE FROM SWITZERLAND ON A SCHEDULED AIRLINE?
QUITE... I CAN'T AFFORD THE PRIVATE JET ANY MORE...
IT SHOWS YOU'RE STILL TOTALLY OUT OF TOUCH WITH THE REAL WORLD...

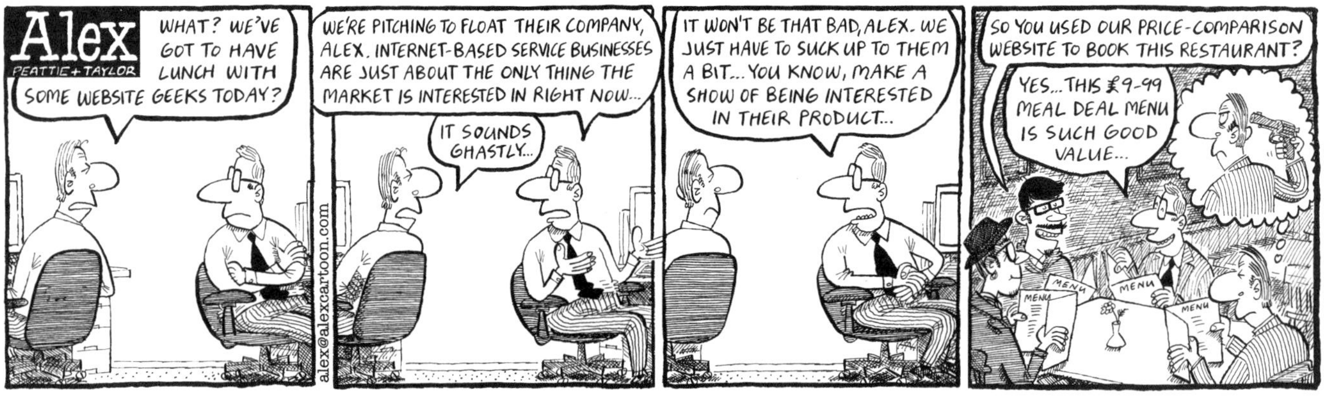
Alex
PEATTIE + TAYLOR
WHAT? WE'VE GOT TO HAVE LUNCH WITH SOME WEBSITE GEEKS TODAY?
WE'RE PITCHING TO FLOAT THEIR COMPANY, ALEX. INTERNET-BASED SERVICE BUSINESSES ARE JUST ABOUT THE ONLY THING THE MARKET IS INTERESTED IN RIGHT NOW...
IT SOUNDS GHASTLY...
alex@alexcartoon.com
IT WON'T BE THAT BAD, ALEX. WE JUST HAVE TO SUCK UP TO THEM A BIT... YOU KNOW, MAKE A SHOW OF BEING INTERESTED IN THEIR PRODUCT...
SO YOU USED OUR PRICE-COMPARISON WEBSITE TO BOOK THIS RESTAURANT?
YES... THIS £9-99 MEAL DEAL MENU IS SUCH GOOD VALUE...
MENU
MENU
MENU

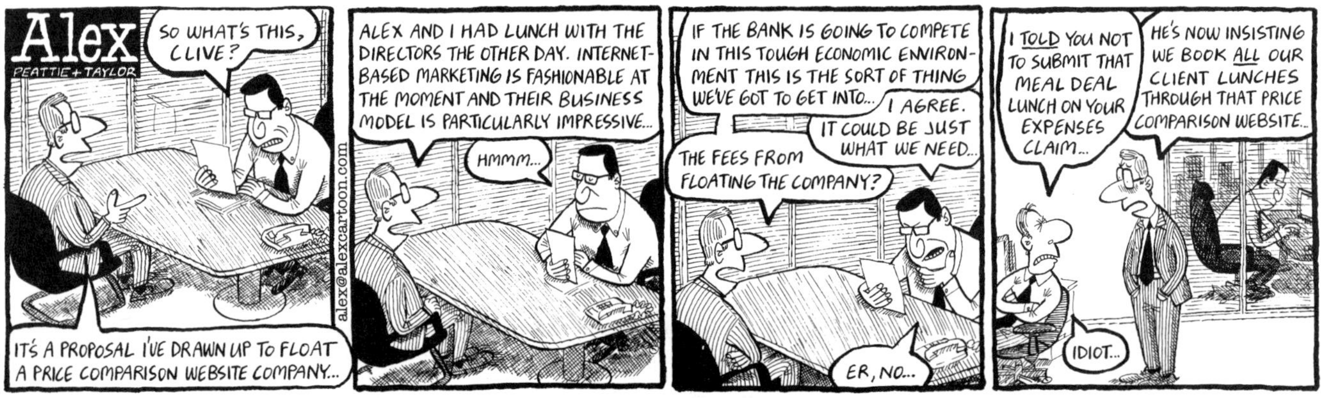
Alex
PEATTIE + TAYLOR
SO WHAT'S THIS, CLIVE?
IT'S A PROPOSAL I'VE DRAWN UP TO FLOAT A PRICE COMPARISON WEBSITE COMPANY...
alex@alexcartoon.com
ALEX AND I HAD LUNCH WITH THE DIRECTORS THE OTHER DAY. INTERNET-BASED MARKETING IS FASHIONABLE AT THE MOMENT AND THEIR BUSINESS MODEL IS PARTICULARLY IMPRESSIVE...
HMMM...
IF THE BANK IS GOING TO COMPETE IN THIS TOUGH ECONOMIC ENVIRONMENT THIS IS THE SORT OF THING WE'VE GOT TO GET INTO...
I AGREE. IT COULD BE JUST WHAT WE NEED...
THE FEES FROM FLOATING THE COMPANY?
ER, NO...
I TOLD YOU NOT TO SUBMIT THAT MEAL DEAL LUNCH ON YOUR EXPENSES CLAIM...
HE'S NOW INSISTING WE BOOK ALL OUR CLIENT LUNCHES THROUGH THAT PRICE COMPARISON WEBSITE...
IDIOT...

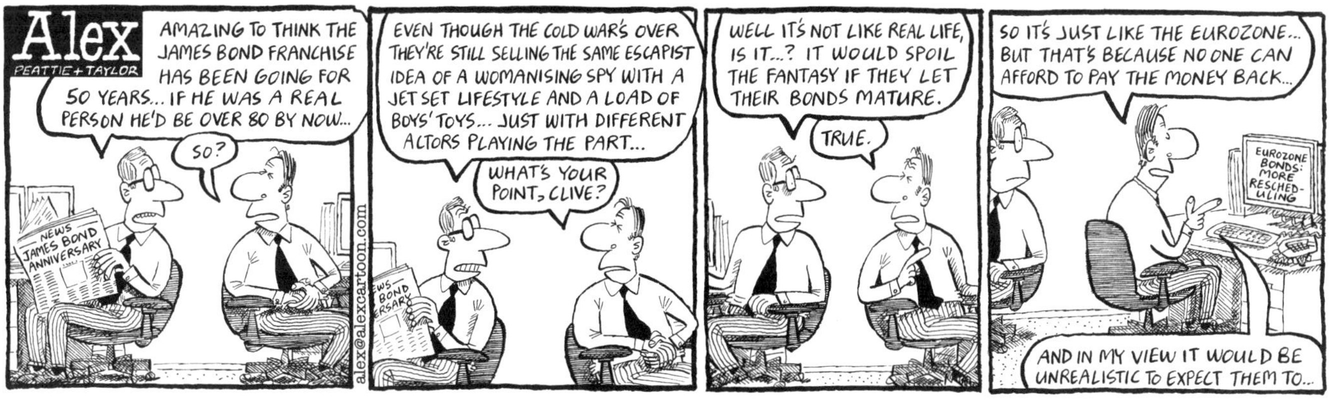
Alex
PEATTIE+TAYLOR
AMAZING TO THINK THE JAMES BOND FRANCHISE HAS BEEN GOING FOR 50 YEARS... IF HE WAS A REAL PERSON HE'D BE OVER 80 BY NOW...
SO?
NEWS JAMES BOND ANNIVERSARY
EVEN THOUGH THE COLD WAR'S OVER THEY'RE STILL SELLING THE SAME ESCAPIST IDEA OF A WOMANISING SPY WITH A JET SET LIFESTYLE AND A LOAD OF BOYS' TOYS... JUST WITH DIFFERENT ACTORS PLAYING THE PART...
WHAT'S YOUR POINT, CLIVE?
alex@alexcartoon.com
WELL IT'S NOT LIKE REAL LIFE, IS IT...? IT WOULD SPOIL THE FANTASY IF THEY LET THEIR BONDS MATURE.
TRUE.
SO IT'S JUST LIKE THE EUROZONE... BUT THAT'S BECAUSE NO ONE CAN AFFORD TO PAY THE MONEY BACK...
EUROZONE BONDS: MORE RESCHED-ULING
AND IN MY VIEW IT WOULD BE UNREALISTIC TO EXPECT THEM TO...

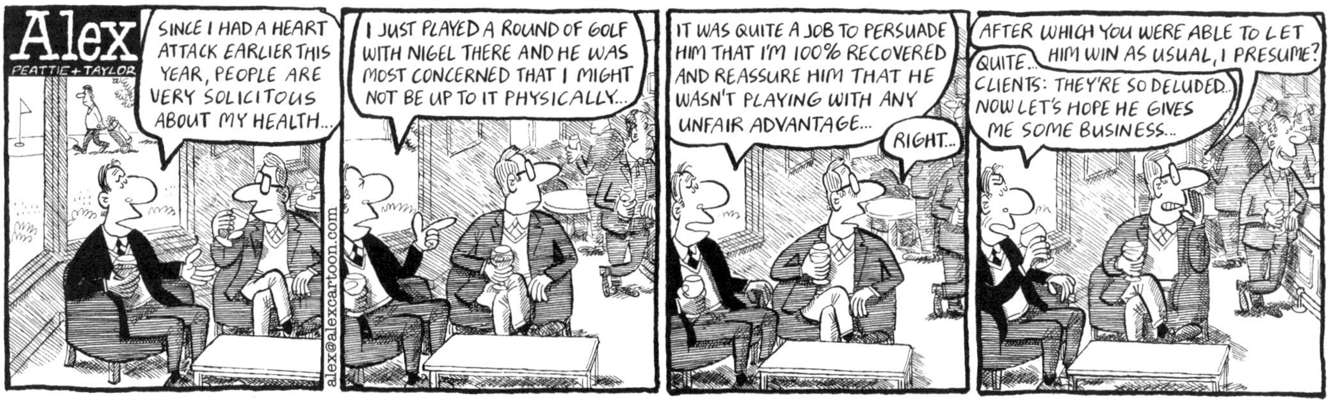
Alex
PEATTIE+TAYLOR
SINCE I HAD A HEART ATTACK EARLIER THIS YEAR, PEOPLE ARE VERY SOLICITOUS ABOUT MY HEALTH...
I JUST PLAYED A ROUND OF GOLF WITH NIGEL THERE AND HE WAS MOST CONCERNED THAT I MIGHT NOT BE UP TO IT PHYSICALLY...
alex@alexcartoon.com
IT WAS QUITE A JOB TO PERSUADE HIM THAT I'M 100% RECOVERED AND REASSURE HIM THAT HE WASN'T PLAYING WITH ANY UNFAIR ADVANTAGE...
RIGHT...
AFTER WHICH YOU WERE ABLE TO LET HIM WIN AS USUAL, I PRESUME?
QUITE... CLIENTS: THEY'RE SO DELUDED... NOW LET'S HOPE HE GIVES ME SOME BUSINESS...

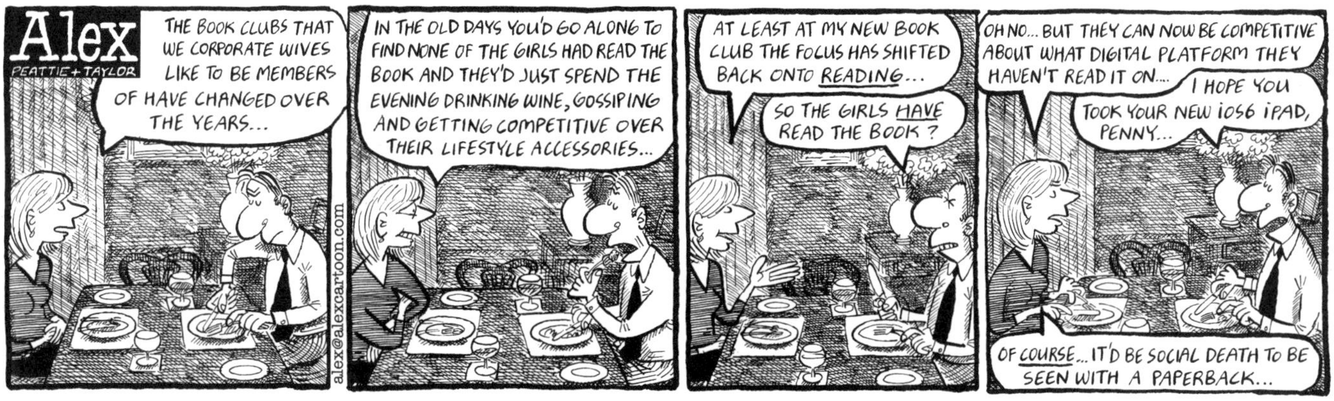
Alex
PEATTIE+TAYLOR
THE BOOK CLUBS THAT WE CORPORATE WIVES LIKE TO BE MEMBERS OF HAVE CHANGED OVER THE YEARS...
IN THE OLD DAYS YOU'D GO ALONG TO FIND NONE OF THE GIRLS HAD READ THE BOOK AND THEY'D JUST SPEND THE EVENING DRINKING WINE, GOSSIPING AND GETTING COMPETITIVE OVER THEIR LIFESTYLE ACCESSORIES...
alex@alexcartoon.com
AT LEAST AT MY NEW BOOK CLUB THE FOCUS HAS SHIFTED BACK ONTO READING...
SO THE GIRLS HAVE READ THE BOOK?
OH NO... BUT THEY CAN NOW BE COMPETITIVE ABOUT WHAT DIGITAL PLATFORM THEY HAVEN'T READ IT ON....
I HOPE YOU TOOK YOUR NEW IOS6 IPAD, PENNY...
OF COURSE... IT'D BE SOCIAL DEATH TO BE SEEN WITH A PAPERBACK...

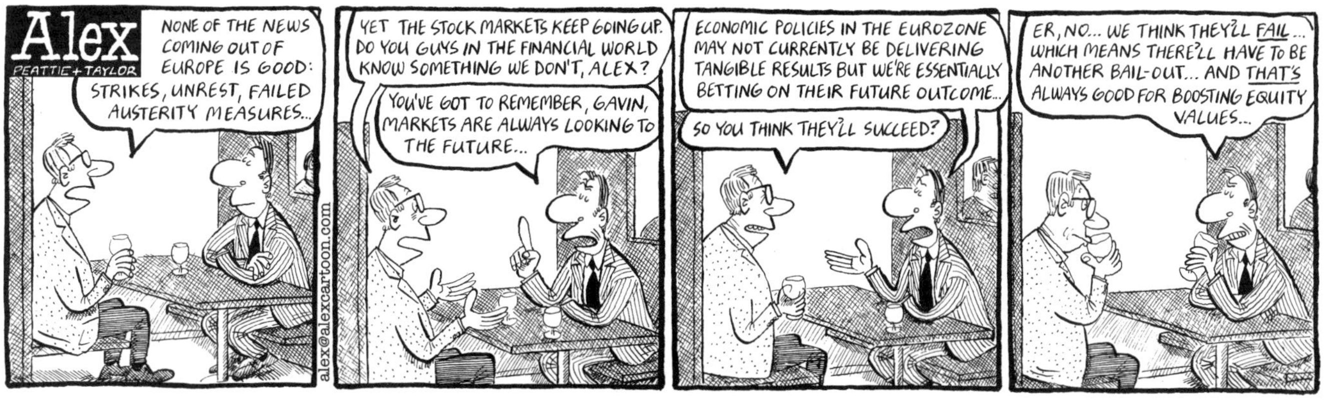
Alex
PEATTIE+TAYLOR
NONE OF THE NEWS COMING OUT OF EUROPE IS GOOD: STRIKES, UNREST, FAILED AUSTERITY MEASURES...
YET THE STOCK MARKETS KEEP GOING UP. DO YOU GUYS IN THE FINANCIAL WORLD KNOW SOMETHING WE DON'T, ALEX?
YOU'VE GOT TO REMEMBER, GAVIN, MARKETS ARE ALWAYS LOOKING TO THE FUTURE...
alex@alexcartoon.com
ECONOMIC POLICIES IN THE EUROZONE MAY NOT CURRENTLY BE DELIVERING TANGIBLE RESULTS BUT WE'RE ESSENTIALLY BETTING ON THEIR FUTURE OUTCOME...
SO YOU THINK THEY'LL SUCCEED?
ER, NO... WE THINK THEY'LL FAIL... WHICH MEANS THERE'LL HAVE TO BE ANOTHER BAIL-OUT... AND THAT'S ALWAYS GOOD FOR BOOSTING EQUITY VALUES...

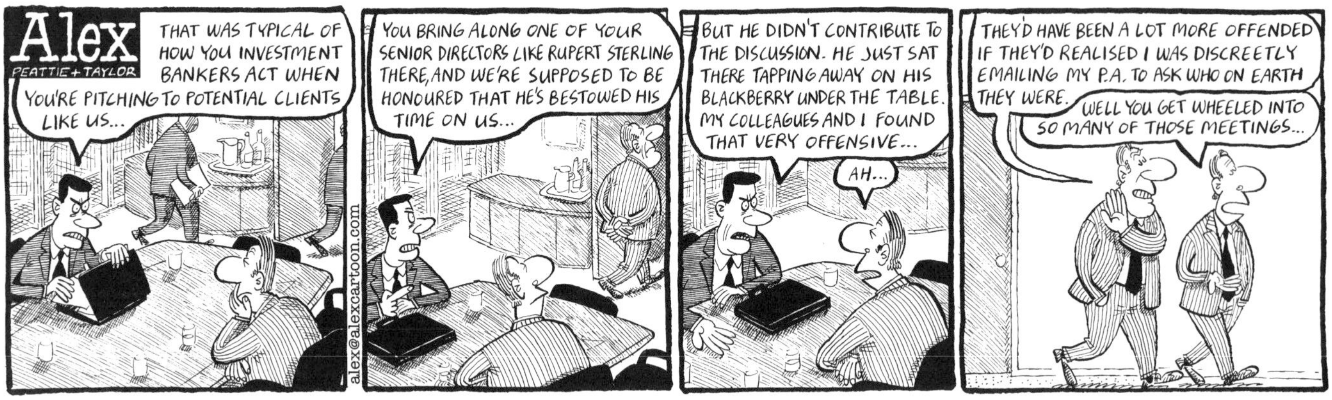
Alex
PEATTIE+TAYLOR
THAT WAS TYPICAL OF HOW YOU INVESTMENT BANKERS ACT WHEN YOU'RE PITCHING TO POTENTIAL CLIENTS LIKE US...
YOU BRING ALONG ONE OF YOUR SENIOR DIRECTORS LIKE RUPERT STERLING THERE, AND WE'RE SUPPOSED TO BE HONOURED THAT HE'S BESTOWED HIS TIME ON US...
alex@alexcartoon.com
BUT HE DIDN'T CONTRIBUTE TO THE DISCUSSION. HE JUST SAT THERE TAPPING AWAY ON HIS BLACKBERRY UNDER THE TABLE. MY COLLEAGUES AND I FOUND THAT VERY OFFENSIVE...
AH...
THEY'D HAVE BEEN A LOT MORE OFFENDED IF THEY'D REALISED I WAS DISCREETLY EMAILING MY P.A. TO ASK WHO ON EARTH THEY WERE.
WELL YOU GET WHEELED INTO SO MANY OF THOSE MEETINGS...

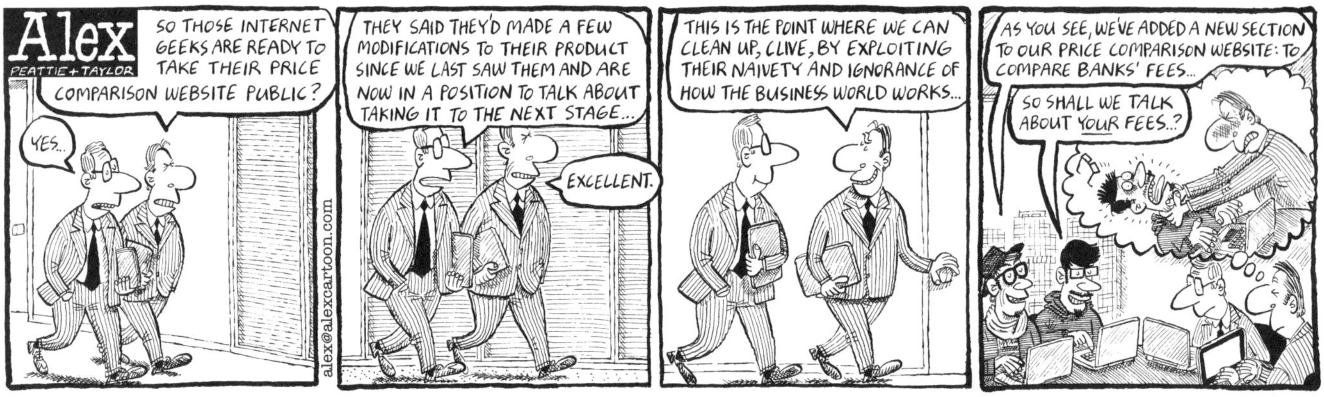
Alex
PEATTIE+TAYLOR
SO THOSE INTERNET GEEKS ARE READY TO TAKE THEIR PRICE COMPARISON WEBSITE PUBLIC?
YES...
THEY SAID THEY'D MADE A FEW MODIFICATIONS TO THEIR PRODUCT SINCE WE LAST SAW THEM AND ARE NOW IN A POSITION TO TALK ABOUT TAKING IT TO THE NEXT STAGE...
EXCELLENT.
alex@alexcartoon.com
THIS IS THE POINT WHERE WE CAN CLEAN UP, CLIVE, BY EXPLOITING THEIR NAIVETY AND IGNORANCE OF HOW THE BUSINESS WORLD WORKS...
AS YOU SEE, WE'VE ADDED A NEW SECTION TO OUR PRICE COMPARISON WEBSITE: TO COMPARE BANKS' FEES...
SO SHALL WE TALK ABOUT YOUR FEES..?

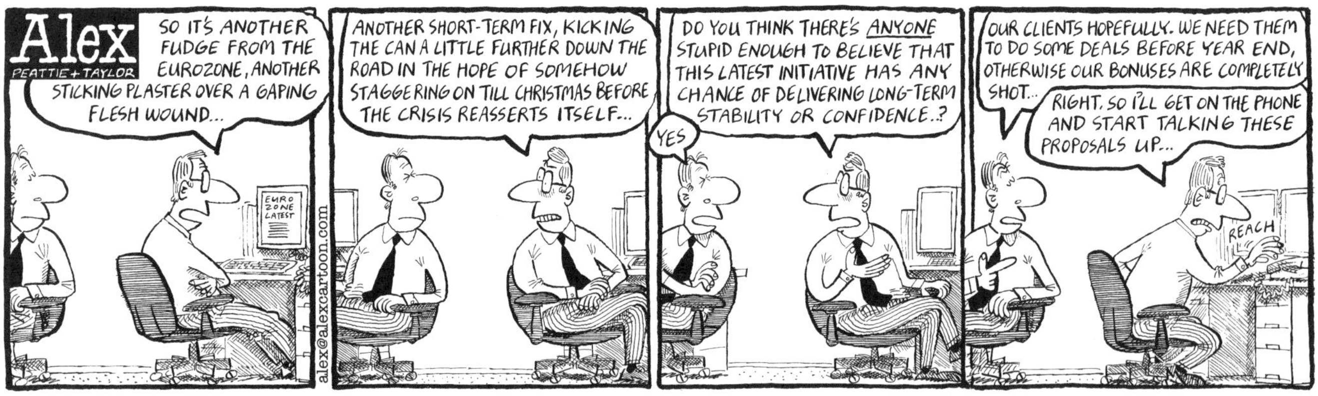
Alex
PEATTIE+TAYLOR
SO IT'S ANOTHER FUDGE FROM THE EUROZONE, ANOTHER STICKING PLASTER OVER A GAPING FLESH WOUND...
EURO ZONE LATEST
alex@alexcartoon.com
ANOTHER SHORT-TERM FIX, KICKING THE CAN A LITTLE FURTHER DOWN THE ROAD IN THE HOPE OF SOMEHOW STAGGERING ON TILL CHRISTMAS BEFORE THE CRISIS REASSERTS ITSELF...
DO YOU THINK THERE'S ANYONE STUPID ENOUGH TO BELIEVE THAT THIS LATEST INITIATIVE HAS ANY CHANCE OF DELIVERING LONG-TERM STABILITY OR CONFIDENCE..?
YES
OUR CLIENTS HOPEFULLY. WE NEED THEM TO DO SOME DEALS BEFORE YEAR END, OTHERWISE OUR BONUSES ARE COMPLETELY SHOT...
RIGHT. SO I'LL GET ON THE PHONE AND START TALKING THESE PROPOSALS UP...
REACH

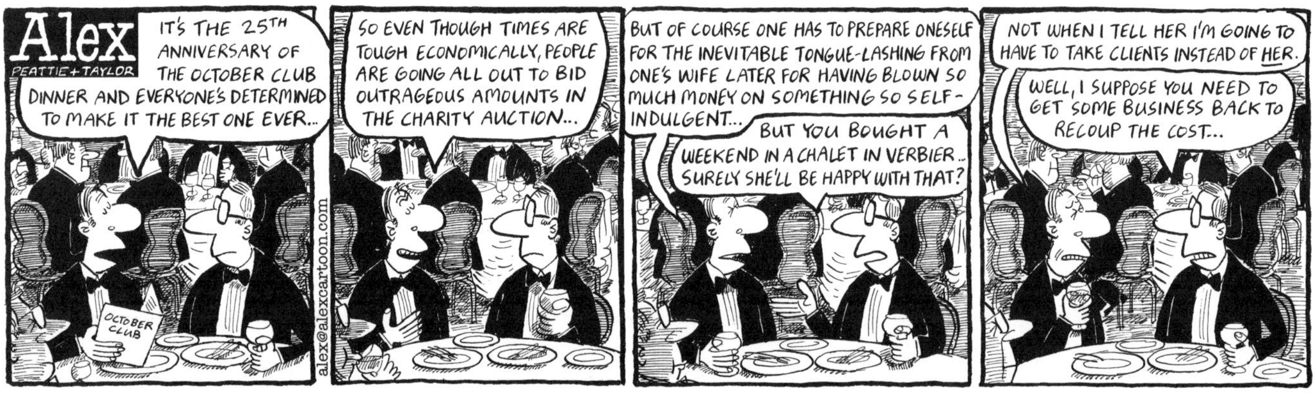
Alex
PEATTIE+TAYLOR
IT'S THE 25TH ANNIVERSARY OF THE OCTOBER CLUB DINNER AND EVERYONE'S DETERMINED TO MAKE IT THE BEST ONE EVER...
OCTOBER CLUB
alex@alexcartoon.com
SO EVEN THOUGH TIMES ARE TOUGH ECONOMICALLY, PEOPLE ARE GOING ALL OUT TO BID OUTRAGEOUS AMOUNTS IN THE CHARITY AUCTION...
BUT OF COURSE ONE HAS TO PREPARE ONESELF FOR THE INEVITABLE TONGUE-LASHING FROM ONE'S WIFE LATER FOR HAVING BLOWN SO MUCH MONEY ON SOMETHING SO SELF-INDULGENT...
BUT YOU BOUGHT A WEEKEND IN A CHALET IN VERBIER... SURELY SHE'LL BE HAPPY WITH THAT?
NOT WHEN I TELL HER I'M GOING TO HAVE TO TAKE CLIENTS INSTEAD OF HER.
WELL, I SUPPOSE YOU NEED TO GET SOME BUSINESS BACK TO RECOUP THE COST...

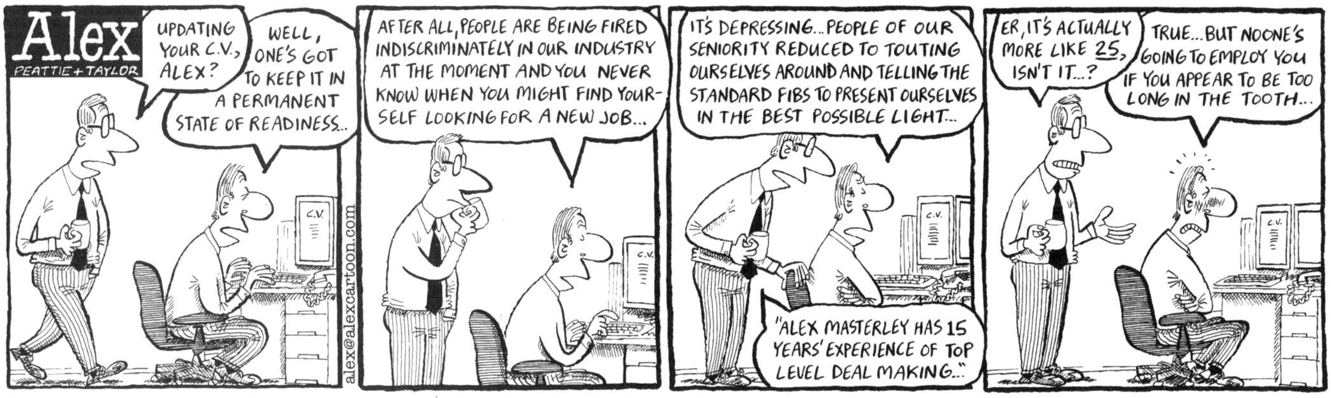
Alex
PEATTIE + TAYLOR
UPDATING YOUR C.V., ALEX?
WELL, ONE'S GOT TO KEEP IT IN A PERMANENT STATE OF READINESS...
AFTER ALL, PEOPLE ARE BEING FIRED INDISCRIMINATELY IN OUR INDUSTRY AT THE MOMENT AND YOU NEVER KNOW WHEN YOU MIGHT FIND YOURSELF LOOKING FOR A NEW JOB...
IT'S DEPRESSING... PEOPLE OF OUR SENIORITY REDUCED TO TOUTING OURSELVES AROUND AND TELLING THE STANDARD FIBS TO PRESENT OURSELVES IN THE BEST POSSIBLE LIGHT...
"ALEX MASTERLEY HAS 15 YEARS' EXPERIENCE OF TOP LEVEL DEAL MAKING..."
ER, IT'S ACTUALLY MORE LIKE 25, ISN'T IT...?
TRUE... BUT NOONE'S GOING TO EMPLOY YOU IF YOU APPEAR TO BE TOO LONG IN THE TOOTH...
alex@alexcartoon.com

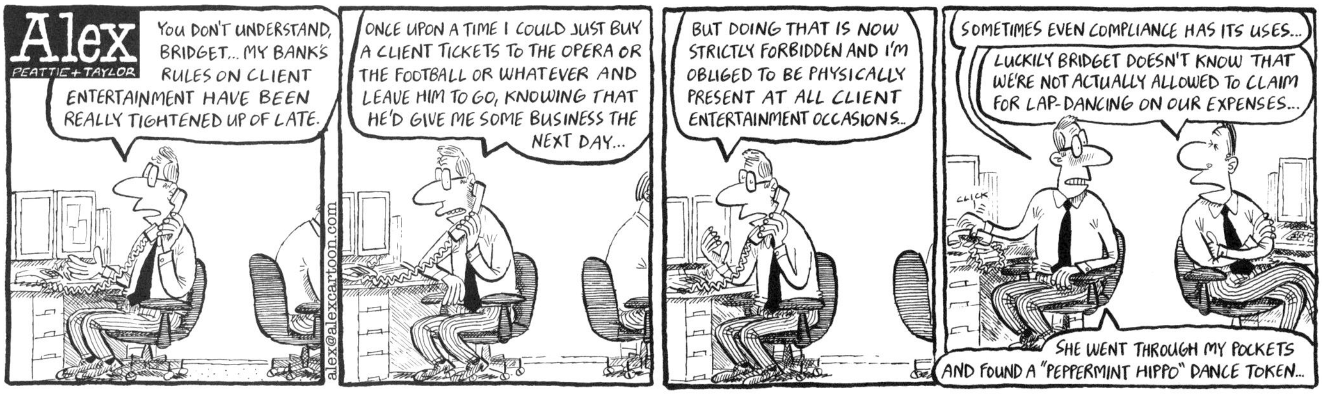
Alex
PEATTIE + TAYLOR
YOU DON'T UNDERSTAND, BRIDGET... MY BANK'S RULES ON CLIENT ENTERTAINMENT HAVE BEEN REALLY TIGHTENED UP OF LATE.
ONCE UPON A TIME I COULD JUST BUY A CLIENT TICKETS TO THE OPERA OR THE FOOTBALL OR WHATEVER AND LEAVE HIM TO GO, KNOWING THAT HE'D GIVE ME SOME BUSINESS THE NEXT DAY...
BUT DOING THAT IS NOW STRICTLY FORBIDDEN AND I'M OBLIGED TO BE PHYSICALLY PRESENT AT ALL CLIENT ENTERTAINMENT OCCASIONS...
SOMETIMES EVEN COMPLIANCE HAS ITS USES...
LUCKILY BRIDGET DOESN'T KNOW THAT WE'RE NOT ACTUALLY ALLOWED TO CLAIM FOR LAP-DANCING ON OUR EXPENSES...
CLICK
SHE WENT THROUGH MY POCKETS AND FOUND A "PEPPERMINT HIPPO" DANCE TOKEN...
alex@alexcartoon.com

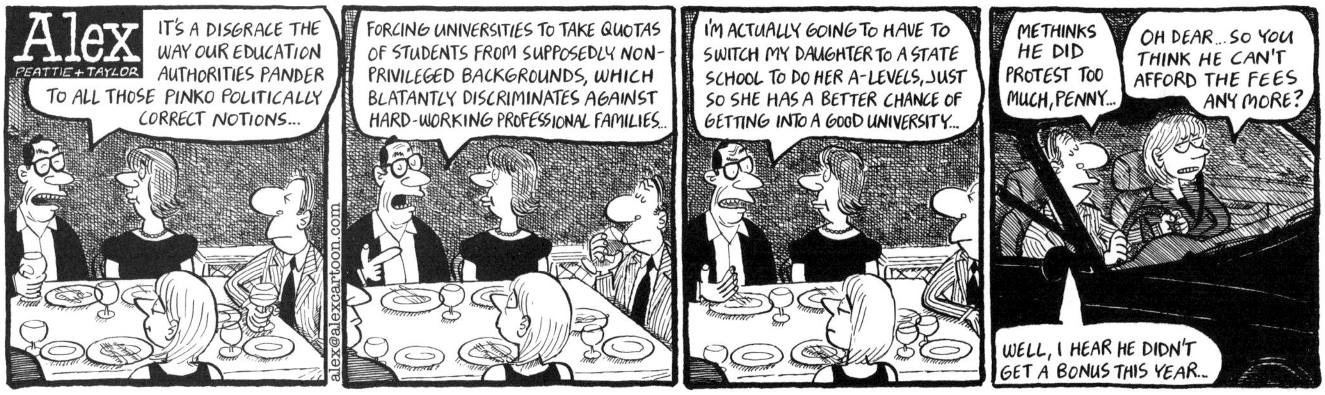
Alex
PEATTIE + TAYLOR
IT'S A DISGRACE THE WAY OUR EDUCATION AUTHORITIES PANDER TO ALL THOSE PINKO POLITICALLY CORRECT NOTIONS...
FORCING UNIVERSITIES TO TAKE QUOTAS OF STUDENTS FROM SUPPOSEDLY NON-PRIVILEGED BACKGROUNDS, WHICH BLATANTLY DISCRIMINATES AGAINST HARD-WORKING PROFESSIONAL FAMILIES...
I'M ACTUALLY GOING TO HAVE TO SWITCH MY DAUGHTER TO A STATE SCHOOL TO DO HER A-LEVELS, JUST SO SHE HAS A BETTER CHANCE OF GETTING INTO A GOOD UNIVERSITY...
METHINKS HE DID PROTEST TOO MUCH, PENNY...
OH DEAR... SO YOU THINK HE CAN'T AFFORD THE FEES ANY MORE?
WELL, I HEAR HE DIDN'T GET A BONUS THIS YEAR...
alex@alexcartoon.com

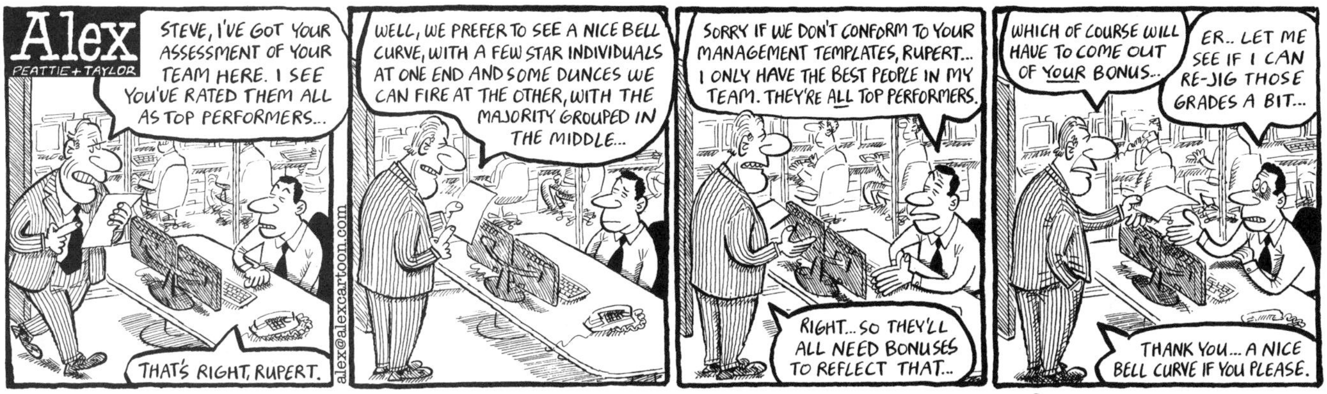
Alex
PEATTIE + TAYLOR
STEVE, I'VE GOT YOUR ASSESSMENT OF YOUR TEAM HERE. I SEE YOU'VE RATED THEM ALL AS TOP PERFORMERS...
THAT'S RIGHT, RUPERT.
WELL, WE PREFER TO SEE A NICE BELL CURVE, WITH A FEW STAR INDIVIDUALS AT ONE END AND SOME DUNCES WE CAN FIRE AT THE OTHER, WITH THE MAJORITY GROUPED IN THE MIDDLE...
SORRY IF WE DON'T CONFORM TO YOUR MANAGEMENT TEMPLATES, RUPERT... I ONLY HAVE THE BEST PEOPLE IN MY TEAM. THEY'RE ALL TOP PERFORMERS.
RIGHT... SO THEY'LL ALL NEED BONUSES TO REFLECT THAT...
WHICH OF COURSE WILL HAVE TO COME OUT OF YOUR BONUS...
ER... LET ME SEE IF I CAN RE-JIG THOSE GRADES A BIT...
THANK YOU... A NICE BELL CURVE IF YOU PLEASE.
alex@alexcartoon.com

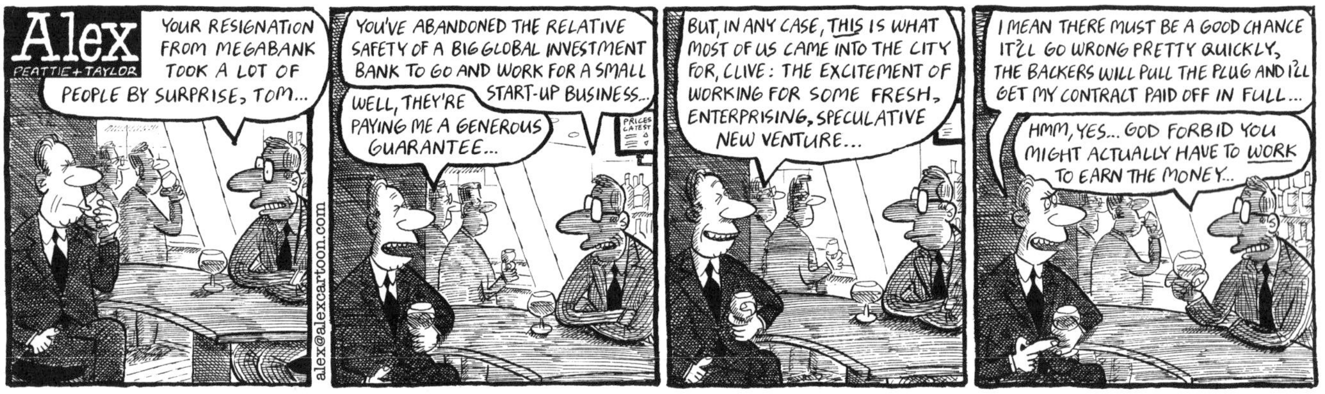
Alex
PEATTIE + TAYLOR
YOUR RESIGNATION FROM MEGABANK TOOK A LOT OF PEOPLE BY SURPRISE, TOM...
YOU'VE ABANDONED THE RELATIVE SAFETY OF A BIG GLOBAL INVESTMENT BANK TO GO AND WORK FOR A SMALL START-UP BUSINESS...
WELL, THEY'RE PAYING ME A GENEROUS GUARANTEE...
alex@alexcartoon.com
BUT, IN ANY CASE, THIS IS WHAT MOST OF US CAME INTO THE CITY FOR, CLIVE: THE EXCITEMENT OF WORKING FOR SOME FRESH, ENTERPRISING, SPECULATIVE NEW VENTURE...
I MEAN THERE MUST BE A GOOD CHANCE IT'LL GO WRONG PRETTY QUICKLY, THE BACKERS WILL PULL THE PLUG AND I'LL GET MY CONTRACT PAID OFF IN FULL...
HMM, YES... GOD FORBID YOU MIGHT ACTUALLY HAVE TO WORK TO EARN THE MONEY...

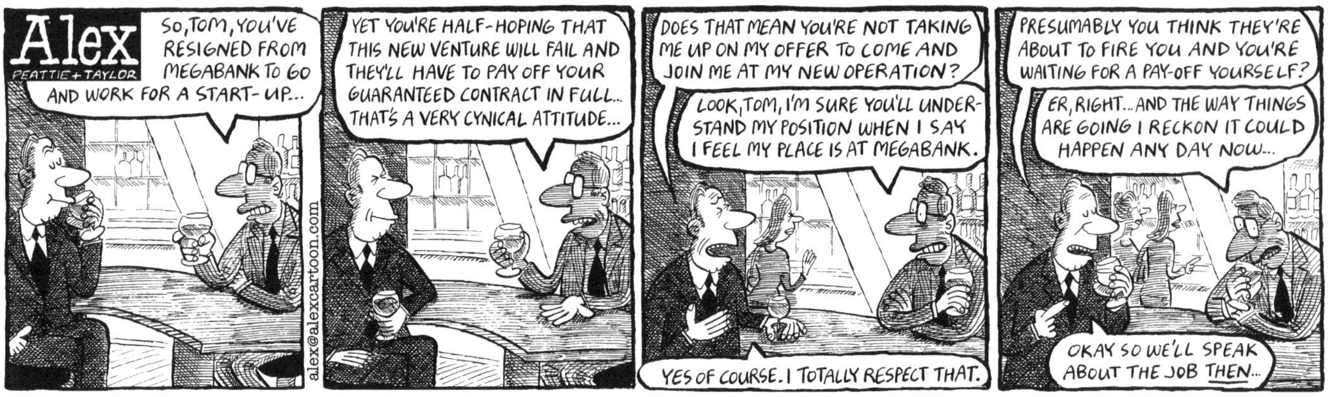
Alex
PEATTIE + TAYLOR
SO, TOM, YOU'VE RESIGNED FROM MEGABANK TO GO AND WORK FOR A START-UP...
YET YOU'RE HALF-HOPING THAT THIS NEW VENTURE WILL FAIL AND THEY'LL HAVE TO PAY OFF YOUR GUARANTEED CONTRACT IN FULL... THAT'S A VERY CYNICAL ATTITUDE...
alex@alexcartoon.com
DOES THAT MEAN YOU'RE NOT TAKING ME UP ON MY OFFER TO COME AND JOIN ME AT MY NEW OPERATION?
LOOK, TOM, I'M SURE YOU'LL UNDERSTAND MY POSITION WHEN I SAY I FEEL MY PLACE IS AT MEGABANK.
YES OF COURSE. I TOTALLY RESPECT THAT.
PRESUMABLY YOU THINK THEY'RE ABOUT TO FIRE YOU AND YOU'RE WAITING FOR A PAY-OFF YOURSELF?
ER, RIGHT... AND THE WAY THINGS ARE GOING I RECKON IT COULD HAPPEN ANY DAY NOW...
OKAY SO WE'LL SPEAK ABOUT THE JOB THEN...

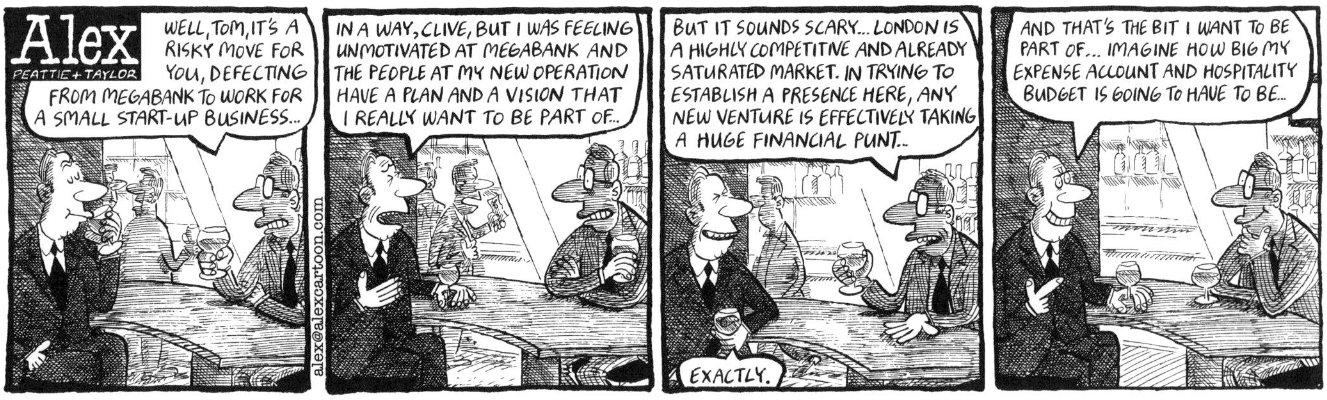
Alex
PEATTIE + TAYLOR
WELL, TOM, IT'S A RISKY MOVE FOR YOU, DEFECTING FROM MEGABANK TO WORK FOR A SMALL START-UP BUSINESS...
IN A WAY, CLIVE, BUT I WAS FEELING UNMOTIVATED AT MEGABANK AND THE PEOPLE AT MY NEW OPERATION HAVE A PLAN AND A VISION THAT I REALLY WANT TO BE PART OF...
alex@alexcartoon.com
BUT IT SOUNDS SCARY... LONDON IS A HIGHLY COMPETITIVE AND ALREADY SATURATED MARKET. IN TRYING TO ESTABLISH A PRESENCE HERE, ANY NEW VENTURE IS EFFECTIVELY TAKING A HUGE FINANCIAL PUNT...
EXACTLY.
AND THAT'S THE BIT I WANT TO BE PART OF... IMAGINE HOW BIG MY EXPENSE ACCOUNT AND HOSPITALITY BUDGET IS GOING TO HAVE TO BE...

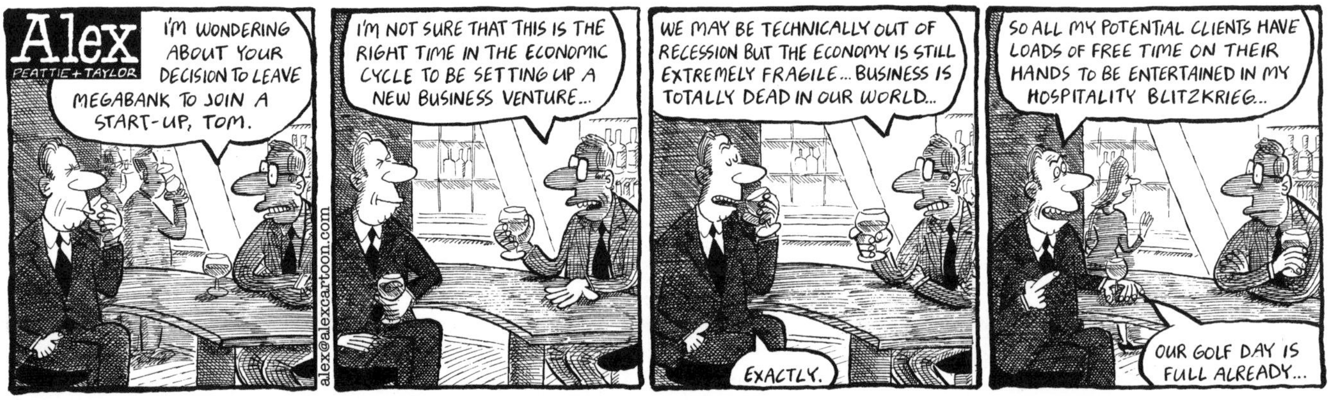
Alex
PEATTIE + TAYLOR
I'M WONDERING ABOUT YOUR DECISION TO LEAVE MEGABANK TO JOIN A START-UP, TOM.
I'M NOT SURE THAT THIS IS THE RIGHT TIME IN THE ECONOMIC CYCLE TO BE SETTING UP A NEW BUSINESS VENTURE...
alex@alexcartoon.com
WE MAY BE TECHNICALLY OUT OF RECESSION BUT THE ECONOMY IS STILL EXTREMELY FRAGILE... BUSINESS IS TOTALLY DEAD IN OUR WORLD...
EXACTLY.
SO ALL MY POTENTIAL CLIENTS HAVE LOADS OF FREE TIME ON THEIR HANDS TO BE ENTERTAINED IN MY HOSPITALITY BLITZKRIEG...
OUR GOLF DAY IS FULL ALREADY...

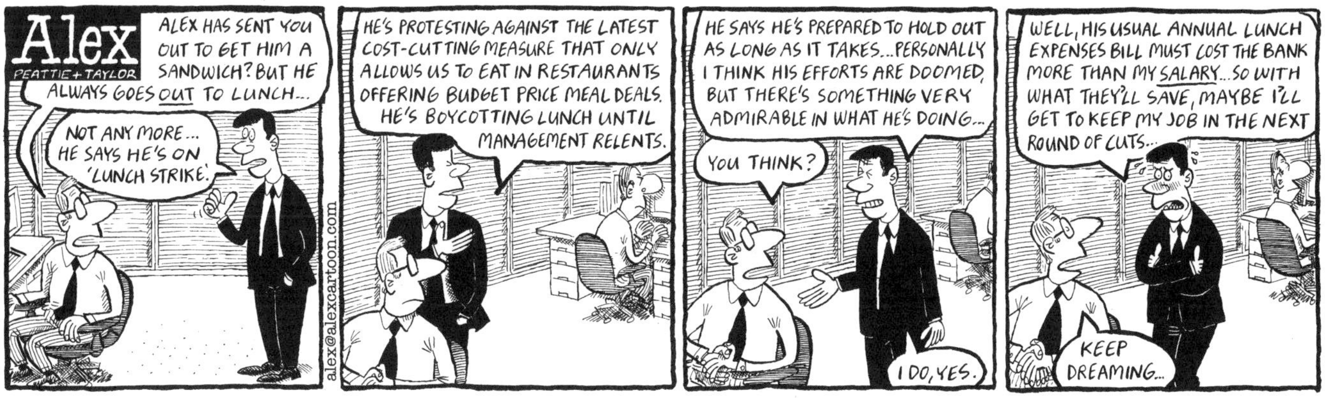
Alex
PEATTIE+TAYLOR
ALEX HAS SENT YOU OUT TO GET HIM A SANDWICH? BUT HE ALWAYS GOES OUT TO LUNCH...
NOT ANY MORE... HE SAYS HE'S ON 'LUNCH STRIKE'.
HE'S PROTESTING AGAINST THE LATEST COST-CUTTING MEASURE THAT ONLY ALLOWS US TO EAT IN RESTAURANTS OFFERING BUDGET PRICE MEAL DEALS. HE'S BOYCOTTING LUNCH UNTIL MANAGEMENT RELENTS.
alex@alexcartoon.com
HE SAYS HE'S PREPARED TO HOLD OUT AS LONG AS IT TAKES...PERSONALLY I THINK HIS EFFORTS ARE DOOMED, BUT THERE'S SOMETHING VERY ADMIRABLE IN WHAT HE'S DOING...
YOU THINK?
I DO, YES.
WELL, HIS USUAL ANNUAL LUNCH EXPENSES BILL MUST COST THE BANK MORE THAN MY SALARY...SO WITH WHAT THEY'LL SAVE, MAYBE I'LL GET TO KEEP MY JOB IN THE NEXT ROUND OF CUTS...
KEEP DREAMING...

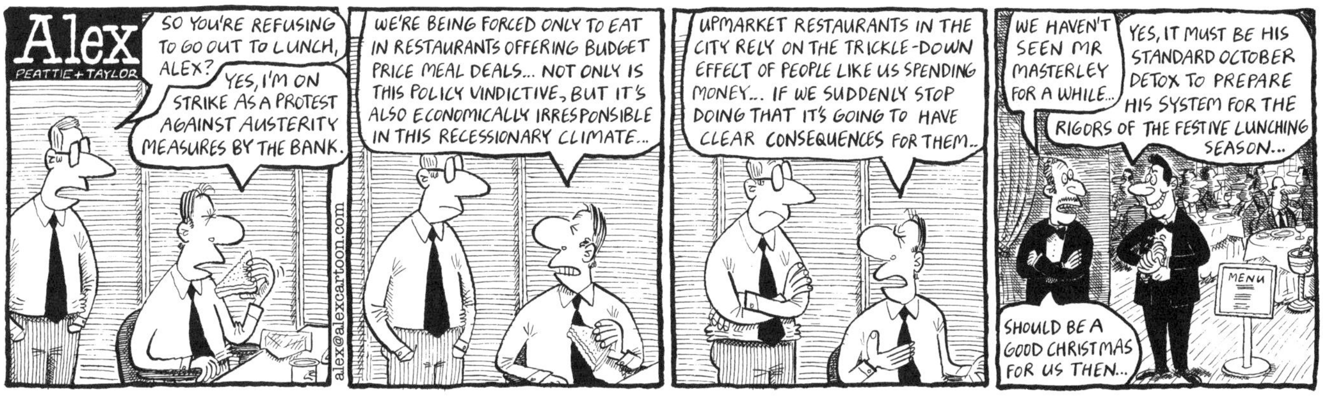
Alex
PEATTIE+TAYLOR
SO YOU'RE REFUSING TO GO OUT TO LUNCH, ALEX?
YES, I'M ON STRIKE AS A PROTEST AGAINST AUSTERITY MEASURES BY THE BANK.
WE'RE BEING FORCED ONLY TO EAT IN RESTAURANTS OFFERING BUDGET PRICE MEAL DEALS... NOT ONLY IS THIS POLICY VINDICTIVE, BUT IT'S ALSO ECONOMICALLY IRRESPONSIBLE IN THIS RECESSIONARY CLIMATE...
alex@alexcartoon.com
UPMARKET RESTAURANTS IN THE CITY RELY ON THE TRICKLE-DOWN EFFECT OF PEOPLE LIKE US SPENDING MONEY... IF WE SUDDENLY STOP DOING THAT IT'S GOING TO HAVE CLEAR CONSEQUENCES FOR THEM...
WE HAVEN'T SEEN MR MASTERLEY FOR A WHILE...
YES, IT MUST BE HIS STANDARD OCTOBER DETOX TO PREPARE HIS SYSTEM FOR THE RIGORS OF THE FESTIVE LUNCHING SEASON...
MENU
SHOULD BE A GOOD CHRISTMAS FOR US THEN...

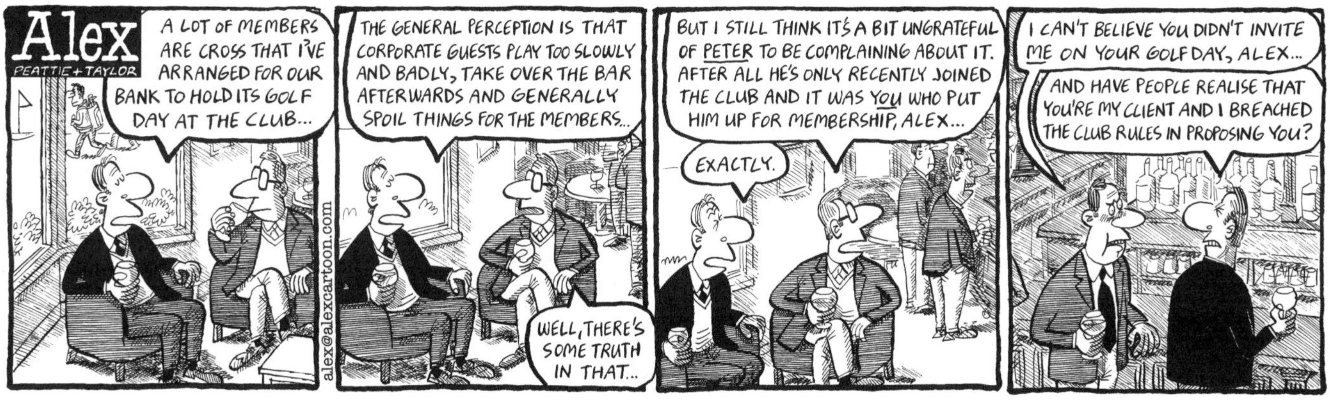
Alex
PEATTIE+TAYLOR
A LOT OF MEMBERS ARE CROSS THAT I'VE ARRANGED FOR OUR BANK TO HOLD ITS GOLF DAY AT THE CLUB...
THE GENERAL PERCEPTION IS THAT CORPORATE GUESTS PLAY TOO SLOWLY AND BADLY, TAKE OVER THE BAR AFTERWARDS AND GENERALLY SPOIL THINGS FOR THE MEMBERS...
WELL, THERE'S SOME TRUTH IN THAT...
alex@alexcartoon.com
BUT I STILL THINK IT'S A BIT UNGRATEFUL OF PETER TO BE COMPLAINING ABOUT IT. AFTER ALL HE'S ONLY RECENTLY JOINED THE CLUB AND IT WAS YOU WHO PUT HIM UP FOR MEMBERSHIP, ALEX...
EXACTLY.
I CAN'T BELIEVE YOU DIDN'T INVITE ME ON YOUR GOLF DAY, ALEX...
AND HAVE PEOPLE REALISE THAT YOU'RE MY CLIENT AND I BREACHED THE CLUB RULES IN PROPOSING YOU?

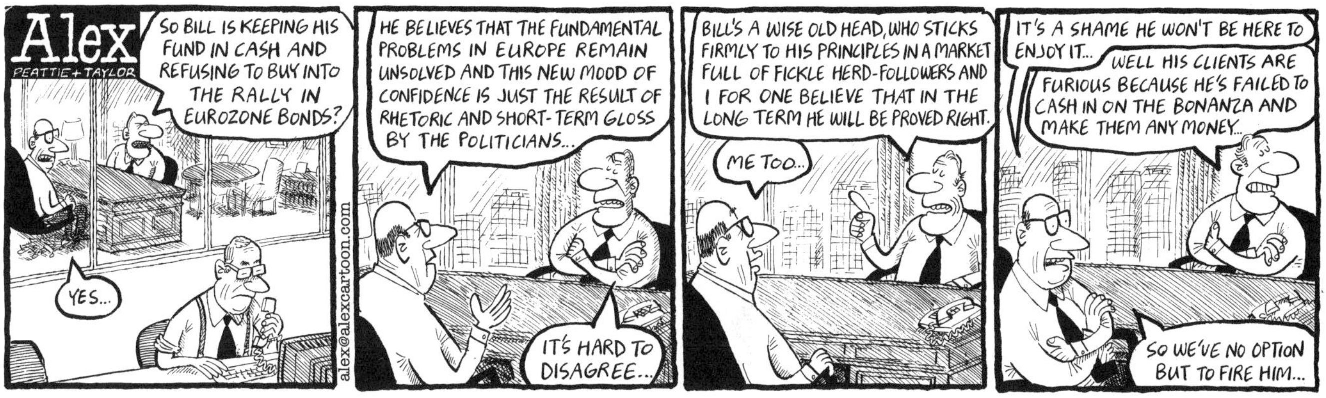
Alex
PEATTIE+TAYLOR
SO BILL IS KEEPING HIS FUND IN CASH AND REFUSING TO BUY INTO THE RALLY IN EUROZONE BONDS?
YES...
alex@alexcartoon.com
HE BELIEVES THAT THE FUNDAMENTAL PROBLEMS IN EUROPE REMAIN UNSOLVED AND THIS NEW MOOD OF CONFIDENCE IS JUST THE RESULT OF RHETORIC AND SHORT-TERM GLOSS BY THE POLITICIANS...
IT'S HARD TO DISAGREE...
BILL'S A WISE OLD HEAD, WHO STICKS FIRMLY TO HIS PRINCIPLES IN A MARKET FULL OF FICKLE HERD-FOLLOWERS AND I FOR ONE BELIEVE THAT IN THE LONG TERM HE WILL BE PROVED RIGHT.
ME TOO...
IT'S A SHAME HE WON'T BE HERE TO ENJOY IT...
WELL HIS CLIENTS ARE FURIOUS BECAUSE HE'S FAILED TO CASH IN ON THE BONANZA AND MAKE THEM ANY MONEY...
SO WE'VE NO OPTION BUT TO FIRE HIM...

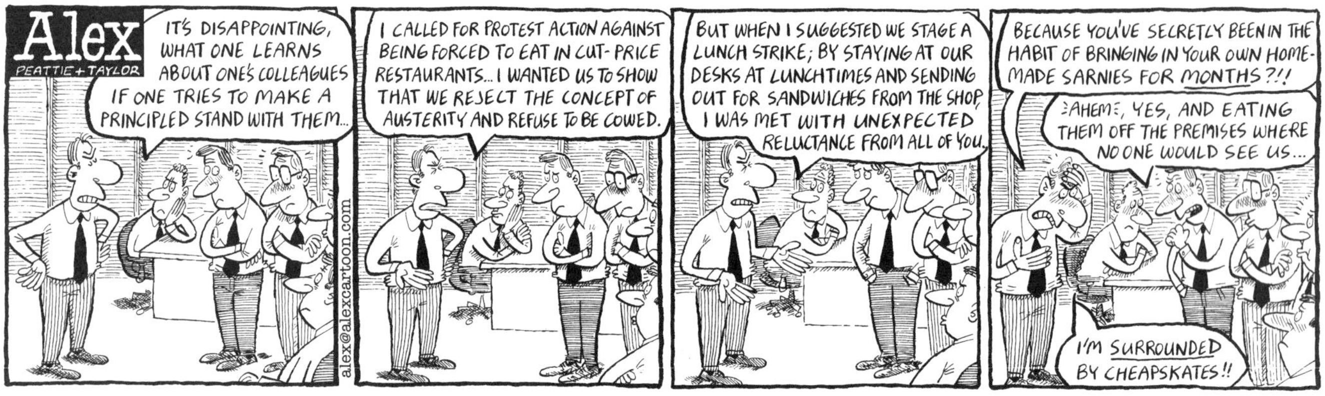
Alex
PEATTIE+TAYLOR
IT'S DISAPPOINTING, WHAT ONE LEARNS ABOUT ONE'S COLLEAGUES IF ONE TRIES TO MAKE A PRINCIPLED STAND WITH THEM...
alex@alexcartoon.com
I CALLED FOR PROTEST ACTION AGAINST BEING FORCED TO EAT IN CUT-PRICE RESTAURANTS... I WANTED US TO SHOW THAT WE REJECT THE CONCEPT OF AUSTERITY AND REFUSE TO BE COWED.
BUT WHEN I SUGGESTED WE STAGE A LUNCH STRIKE; BY STAYING AT OUR DESKS AT LUNCHTIMES AND SENDING OUT FOR SANDWICHES FROM THE SHOP, I WAS MET WITH UNEXPECTED RELUCTANCE FROM ALL OF YOU.
BECAUSE YOU'VE SECRETLY BEEN IN THE HABIT OF BRINGING IN YOUR OWN HOME-MADE SARNIES FOR MONTHS?!!
AHEM, YES, AND EATING THEM OFF THE PREMISES WHERE NO ONE WOULD SEE US...
I'M SURROUNDED BY CHEAPSKATES!!

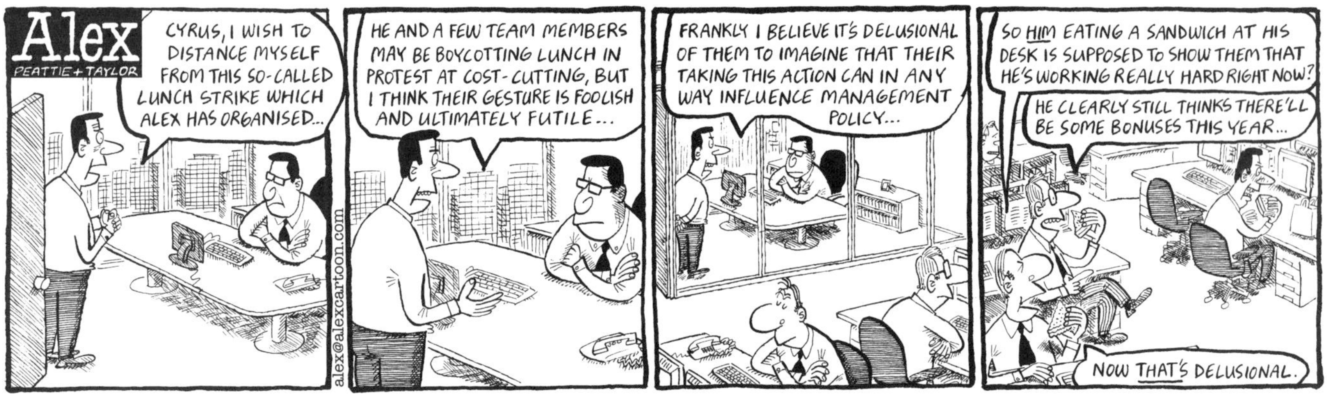
Alex
PEATTIE+TAYLOR
CYRUS, I WISH TO DISTANCE MYSELF FROM THIS SO-CALLED LUNCH STRIKE WHICH ALEX HAS ORGANISED...
alex@alexcartoon.com
HE AND A FEW TEAM MEMBERS MAY BE BOYCOTTING LUNCH IN PROTEST AT COST-CUTTING, BUT I THINK THEIR GESTURE IS FOOLISH AND ULTIMATELY FUTILE...
FRANKLY I BELIEVE IT'S DELUSIONAL OF THEM TO IMAGINE THAT THEIR TAKING THIS ACTION CAN IN ANY WAY INFLUENCE MANAGEMENT POLICY...
SO HIM EATING A SANDWICH AT HIS DESK IS SUPPOSED TO SHOW THEM THAT HE'S WORKING REALLY HARD RIGHT NOW?
HE CLEARLY STILL THINKS THERE'LL BE SOME BONUSES THIS YEAR...
NOW THAT'S DELUSIONAL.

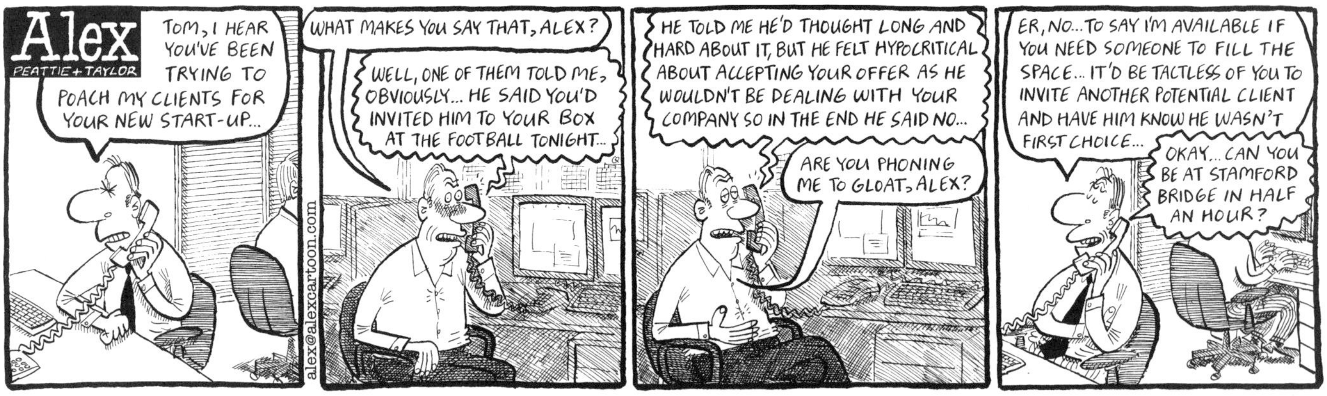
Alex
PEATTIE+TAYLOR
TOM, I HEAR YOU'VE BEEN TRYING TO POACH MY CLIENTS FOR YOUR NEW START-UP...
alex@alexcartoon.com
WHAT MAKES YOU SAY THAT, ALEX?
WELL, ONE OF THEM TOLD ME, OBVIOUSLY... HE SAID YOU'D INVITED HIM TO YOUR BOX AT THE FOOTBALL TONIGHT...
HE TOLD ME HE'D THOUGHT LONG AND HARD ABOUT IT, BUT HE FELT HYPOCRITICAL ABOUT ACCEPTING YOUR OFFER AS HE WOULDN'T BE DEALING WITH YOUR COMPANY SO IN THE END HE SAID NO...
ARE YOU PHONING ME TO GLOAT, ALEX?
ER, NO... TO SAY I'M AVAILABLE IF YOU NEED SOMEONE TO FILL THE SPACE... IT'D BE TACTLESS OF YOU TO INVITE ANOTHER POTENTIAL CLIENT AND HAVE HIM KNOW HE WASN'T FIRST CHOICE...
OKAY... CAN YOU BE AT STAMFORD BRIDGE IN HALF AN HOUR?

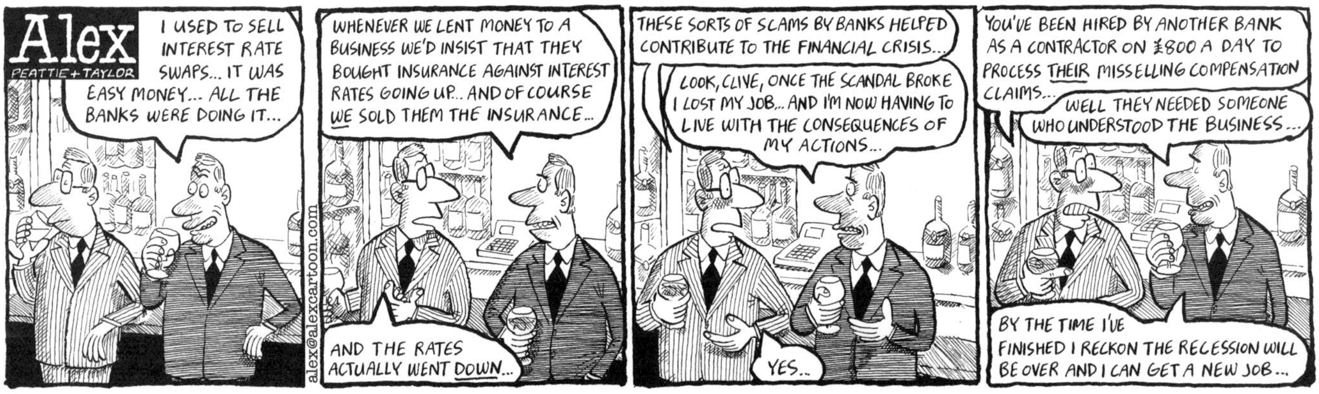
Alex
PEATTIE+TAYLOR
I USED TO SELL INTEREST RATE SWAPS... IT WAS EASY MONEY... ALL THE BANKS WERE DOING IT...
alex@alexcartoon.com
WHENEVER WE LENT MONEY TO A BUSINESS WE'D INSIST THAT THEY BOUGHT INSURANCE AGAINST INTEREST RATES GOING UP... AND OF COURSE WE SOLD THEM THE INSURANCE...
AND THE RATES ACTUALLY WENT DOWN...
THESE SORTS OF SCAMS BY BANKS HELPED CONTRIBUTE TO THE FINANCIAL CRISIS...
LOOK, CLIVE, ONCE THE SCANDAL BROKE I LOST MY JOB... AND I'M NOW HAVING TO LIVE WITH THE CONSEQUENCES OF MY ACTIONS...
YES...
YOU'VE BEEN HIRED BY ANOTHER BANK AS A CONTRACTOR ON £800 A DAY TO PROCESS THEIR MISSELLING COMPENSATION CLAIMS...
WELL THEY NEEDED SOMEONE WHO UNDERSTOOD THE BUSINESS...
BY THE TIME I'VE FINISHED I RECKON THE RECESSION WILL BE OVER AND I CAN GET A NEW JOB...

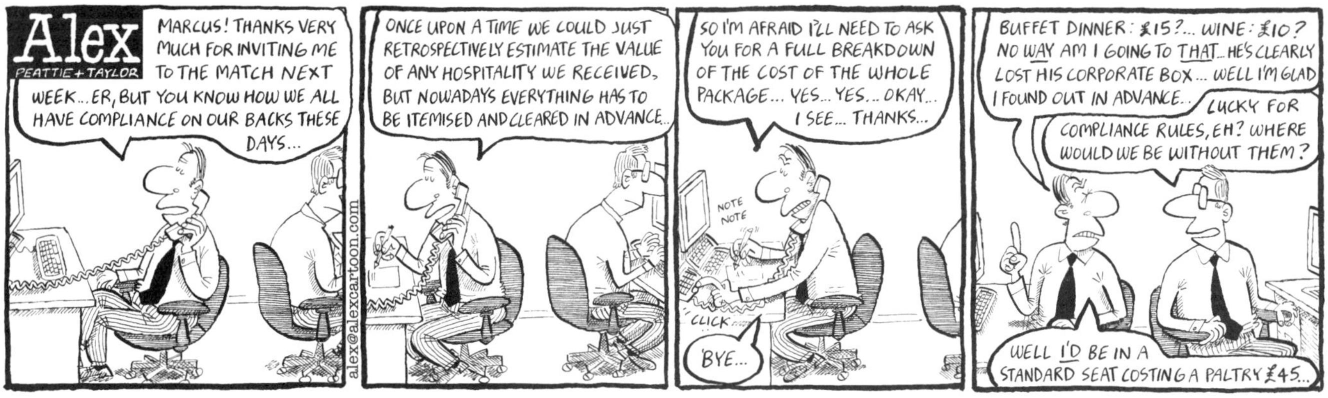
Alex
PEATTIE + TAYLOR
MARCUS! THANKS VERY MUCH FOR INVITING ME TO THE MATCH NEXT WEEK... ER, BUT YOU KNOW HOW WE ALL HAVE COMPLIANCE ON OUR BACKS THESE DAYS...
alex@alexcartoon.com
ONCE UPON A TIME WE COULD JUST RETROSPECTIVELY ESTIMATE THE VALUE OF ANY HOSPITALITY WE RECEIVED, BUT NOWADAYS EVERYTHING HAS TO BE ITEMISED AND CLEARED IN ADVANCE...
SO I'M AFRAID I'LL NEED TO ASK YOU FOR A FULL BREAKDOWN OF THE COST OF THE WHOLE PACKAGE... YES... YES... OKAY... I SEE... THANKS...
NOTE NOTE
CLICK
'BYE...
BUFFET DINNER: £15?... WINE: £10? NO WAY AM I GOING TO THAT... HE'S CLEARLY LOST HIS CORPORATE BOX... WELL I'M GLAD I FOUND OUT IN ADVANCE...
LUCKY FOR COMPLIANCE RULES, EH? WHERE WOULD WE BE WITHOUT THEM?
WELL I'D BE IN A STANDARD SEAT COSTING A PALTRY £45...

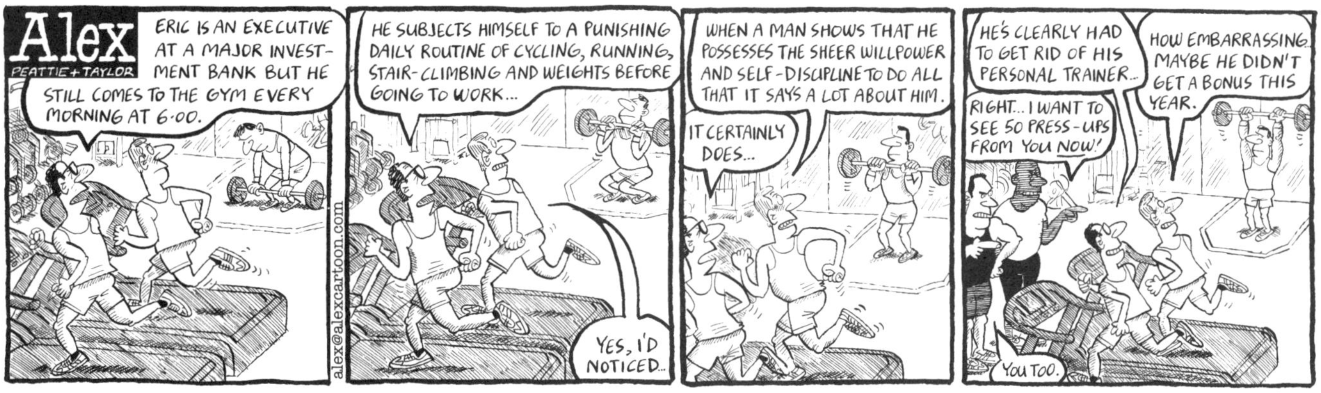
Alex
PEATTIE + TAYLOR
ERIC IS AN EXECUTIVE AT A MAJOR INVESTMENT BANK BUT HE STILL COMES TO THE GYM EVERY MORNING AT 6.00.
alex@alexcartoon.com
HE SUBJECTS HIMSELF TO A PUNISHING DAILY ROUTINE OF CYCLING, RUNNING, STAIR-CLIMBING AND WEIGHTS BEFORE GOING TO WORK...
YES, I'D NOTICED...
WHEN A MAN SHOWS THAT HE POSSESSES THE SHEER WILLPOWER AND SELF-DISCIPLINE TO DO ALL THAT IT SAYS A LOT ABOUT HIM.
IT CERTAINLY DOES...
HE'S CLEARLY HAD TO GET RID OF HIS PERSONAL TRAINER...
HOW EMBARRASSING. MAYBE HE DIDN'T GET A BONUS THIS YEAR.
RIGHT... I WANT TO SEE 50 PRESS-UPS FROM YOU NOW!
YOU TOO.

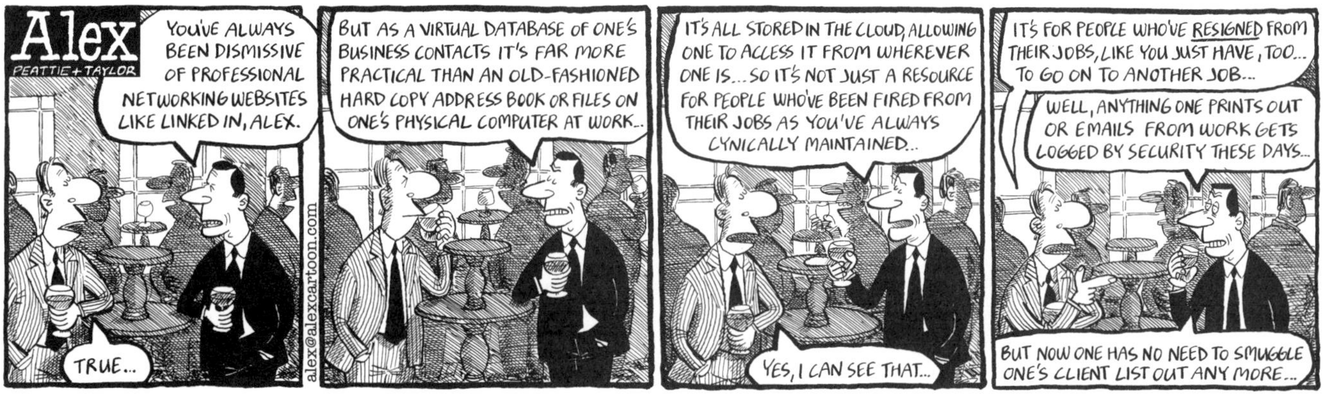
Alex
PEATTIE + TAYLOR
YOU'VE ALWAYS BEEN DISMISSIVE OF PROFESSIONAL NETWORKING WEBSITES LIKE LINKED IN, ALEX.
TRUE...
alex@alexcartoon.com
BUT AS A VIRTUAL DATABASE OF ONE'S BUSINESS CONTACTS IT'S FAR MORE PRACTICAL THAN AN OLD-FASHIONED HARD COPY ADDRESS BOOK OR FILES ON ONE'S PHYSICAL COMPUTER AT WORK...
IT'S ALL STORED IN THE CLOUD, ALLOWING ONE TO ACCESS IT FROM WHEREVER ONE IS... SO IT'S NOT JUST A RESOURCE FOR PEOPLE WHO'VE BEEN FIRED FROM THEIR JOBS AS YOU'VE ALWAYS CYNICALLY MAINTAINED...
YES, I CAN SEE THAT...
IT'S FOR PEOPLE WHO'VE RESIGNED FROM THEIR JOBS, LIKE YOU JUST HAVE, TOO... TO GO ON TO ANOTHER JOB...
WELL, ANYTHING ONE PRINTS OUT OR EMAILS FROM WORK GETS LOGGED BY SECURITY THESE DAYS...
BUT NOW ONE HAS NO NEED TO SMUGGLE ONE'S CLIENT LIST OUT ANY MORE...

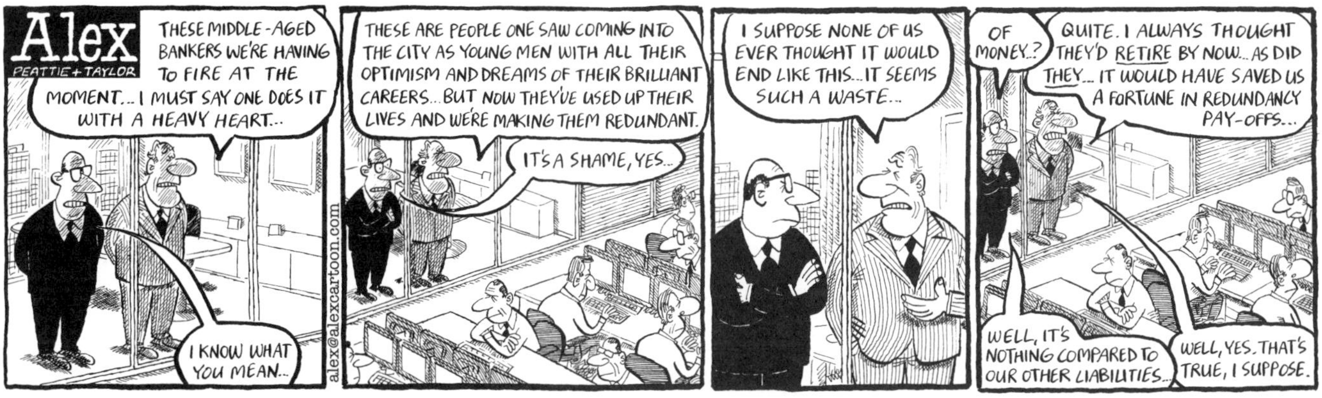
Alex
PEATTIE + TAYLOR
THESE MIDDLE-AGED BANKERS WE'RE HAVING TO FIRE AT THE MOMENT... I MUST SAY ONE DOES IT WITH A HEAVY HEART...
I KNOW WHAT YOU MEAN...
alex@alexcartoon.com
THESE ARE PEOPLE ONE SAW COMING INTO THE CITY AS YOUNG MEN WITH ALL THEIR OPTIMISM AND DREAMS OF THEIR BRILLIANT CAREERS... BUT NOW THEY'VE USED UP THEIR LIVES AND WE'RE MAKING THEM REDUNDANT.
IT'S A SHAME, YES...
I SUPPOSE NONE OF US EVER THOUGHT IT WOULD END LIKE THIS... IT SEEMS SUCH A WASTE...
OF MONEY..?
QUITE. I ALWAYS THOUGHT THEY'D RETIRE BY NOW... AS DID THEY... IT WOULD HAVE SAVED US A FORTUNE IN REDUNDANCY PAY-OFFS...
WELL, IT'S NOTHING COMPARED TO OUR OTHER LIABILITIES...
WELL, YES. THAT'S TRUE, I SUPPOSE.

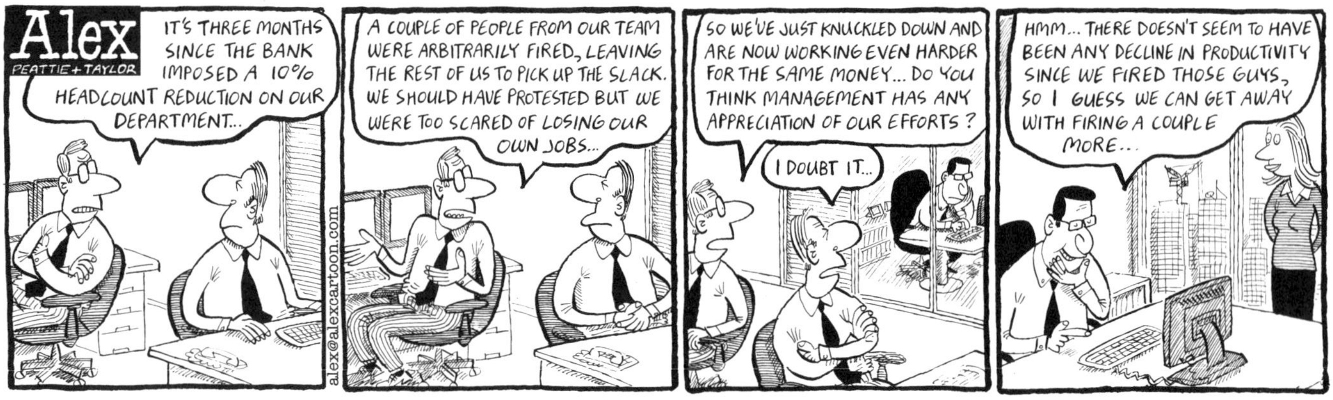
Alex
PEATTIE + TAYLOR
IT'S THREE MONTHS SINCE THE BANK IMPOSED A 10% HEADCOUNT REDUCTION ON OUR DEPARTMENT...
A COUPLE OF PEOPLE FROM OUR TEAM WERE ARBITRARILY FIRED, LEAVING THE REST OF US TO PICK UP THE SLACK. WE SHOULD HAVE PROTESTED BUT WE WERE TOO SCARED OF LOSING OUR OWN JOBS...
alex@alexcartoon.com
SO WE'VE JUST KNUCKLED DOWN AND ARE NOW WORKING EVEN HARDER FOR THE SAME MONEY... DO YOU THINK MANAGEMENT HAS ANY APPRECIATION OF OUR EFFORTS?
I DOUBT IT...
HMM... THERE DOESN'T SEEM TO HAVE BEEN ANY DECLINE IN PRODUCTIVITY SINCE WE FIRED THOSE GUYS, SO I GUESS WE CAN GET AWAY WITH FIRING A COUPLE MORE...

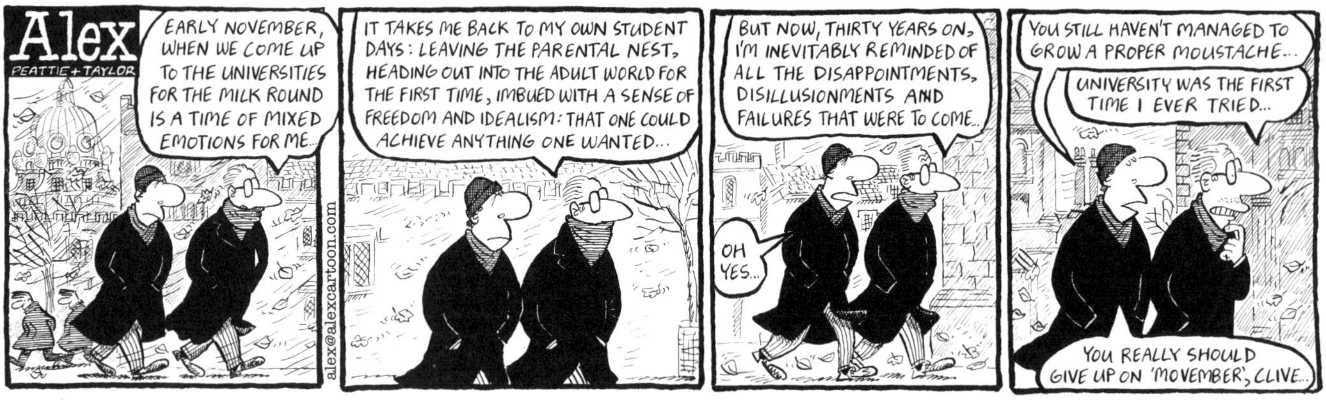
Alex
PEATTIE + TAYLOR
EARLY NOVEMBER, WHEN WE COME UP TO THE UNIVERSITIES FOR THE MILK ROUND IS A TIME OF MIXED EMOTIONS FOR ME...
IT TAKES ME BACK TO MY OWN STUDENT DAYS: LEAVING THE PARENTAL NEST, HEADING OUT INTO THE ADULT WORLD FOR THE FIRST TIME, IMBUED WITH A SENSE OF FREEDOM AND IDEALISM: THAT ONE COULD ACHIEVE ANYTHING ONE WANTED...
alex@alexcartoon.com
BUT NOW, THIRTY YEARS ON, I'M INEVITABLY REMINDED OF ALL THE DISAPPOINTMENTS, DISILLUSIONMENTS AND FAILURES THAT WERE TO COME...
OH YES...
YOU STILL HAVEN'T MANAGED TO GROW A PROPER MOUSTACHE...
UNIVERSITY WAS THE FIRST TIME I EVER TRIED...
YOU REALLY SHOULD GIVE UP ON 'MOVEMBER', CLIVE...

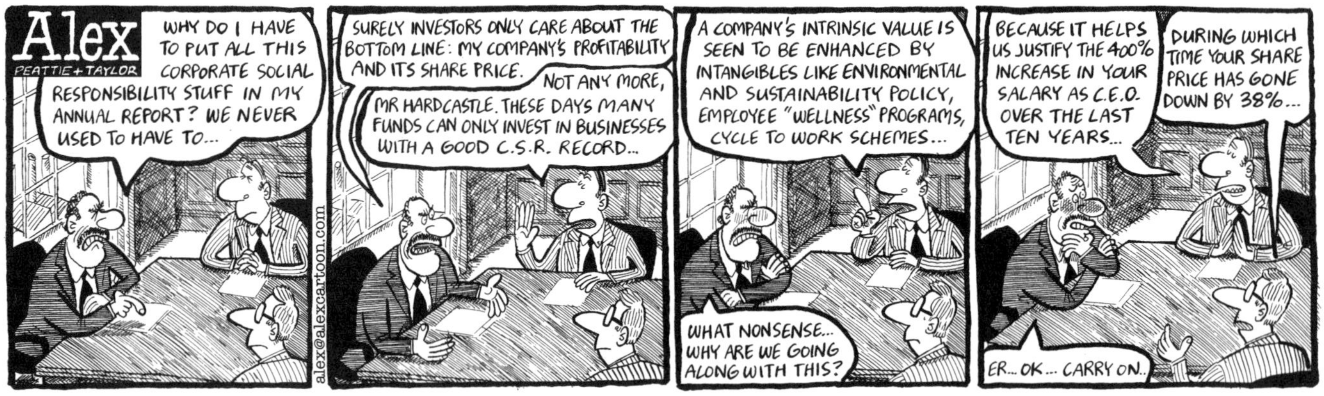
Alex
PEATTIE + TAYLOR
WHY DO I HAVE TO PUT ALL THIS CORPORATE SOCIAL RESPONSIBILITY STUFF IN MY ANNUAL REPORT? WE NEVER USED TO HAVE TO...
SURELY INVESTORS ONLY CARE ABOUT THE BOTTOM LINE: MY COMPANY'S PROFITABILITY AND ITS SHARE PRICE.
NOT ANY MORE, MR HARDCASTLE. THESE DAYS MANY FUNDS CAN ONLY INVEST IN BUSINESSES WITH A GOOD C.S.R. RECORD...
alex@alexcartoon.com
A COMPANY'S INTRINSIC VALUE IS SEEN TO BE ENHANCED BY INTANGIBLES LIKE ENVIRONMENTAL AND SUSTAINABILITY POLICY, EMPLOYEE "WELLNESS" PROGRAMS, CYCLE TO WORK SCHEMES...
WHAT NONSENSE... WHY ARE WE GOING ALONG WITH THIS?
BECAUSE IT HELPS US JUSTIFY THE 400% INCREASE IN YOUR SALARY AS C.E.O. OVER THE LAST TEN YEARS...
DURING WHICH TIME YOUR SHARE PRICE HAS GONE DOWN BY 38%...
ER... OK... CARRY ON...

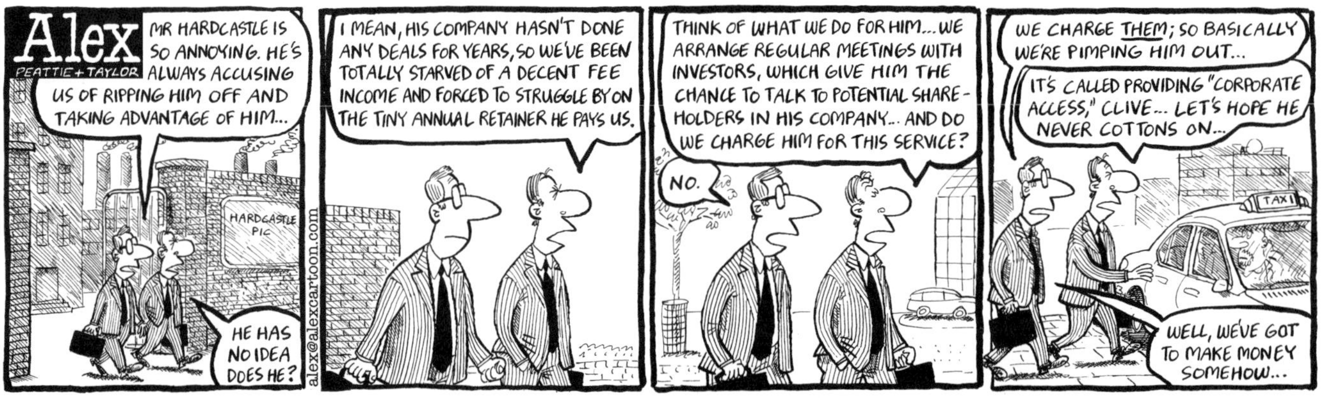
Alex
PEATTIE + TAYLOR
MR HARDCASTLE IS SO ANNOYING. HE'S ALWAYS ACCUSING US OF RIPPING HIM OFF AND TAKING ADVANTAGE OF HIM...
HARDCASTLE plc
HE HAS NO IDEA DOES HE?
alex@alexcartoon.com
I MEAN, HIS COMPANY HASN'T DONE ANY DEALS FOR YEARS, SO WE'VE BEEN TOTALLY STARVED OF A DECENT FEE INCOME AND FORCED TO STRUGGLE BY ON THE TINY ANNUAL RETAINER HE PAYS US.
THINK OF WHAT WE DO FOR HIM... WE ARRANGE REGULAR MEETINGS WITH INVESTORS, WHICH GIVE HIM THE CHANCE TO TALK TO POTENTIAL SHARE-HOLDERS IN HIS COMPANY... AND DO WE CHARGE HIM FOR THIS SERVICE?
NO.
WE CHARGE THEM; SO BASICALLY WE'RE PIMPING HIM OUT...
IT'S CALLED PROVIDING "CORPORATE ACCESS," CLIVE... LET'S HOPE HE NEVER COTTONS ON...
TAXI
WELL, WE'VE GOT TO MAKE MONEY SOMEHOW...

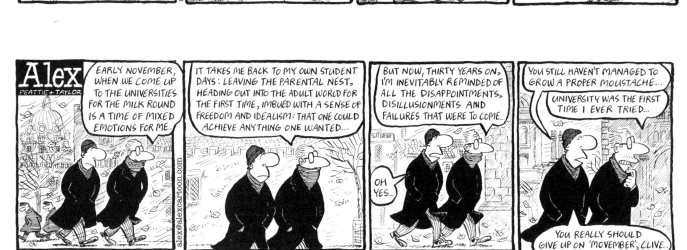

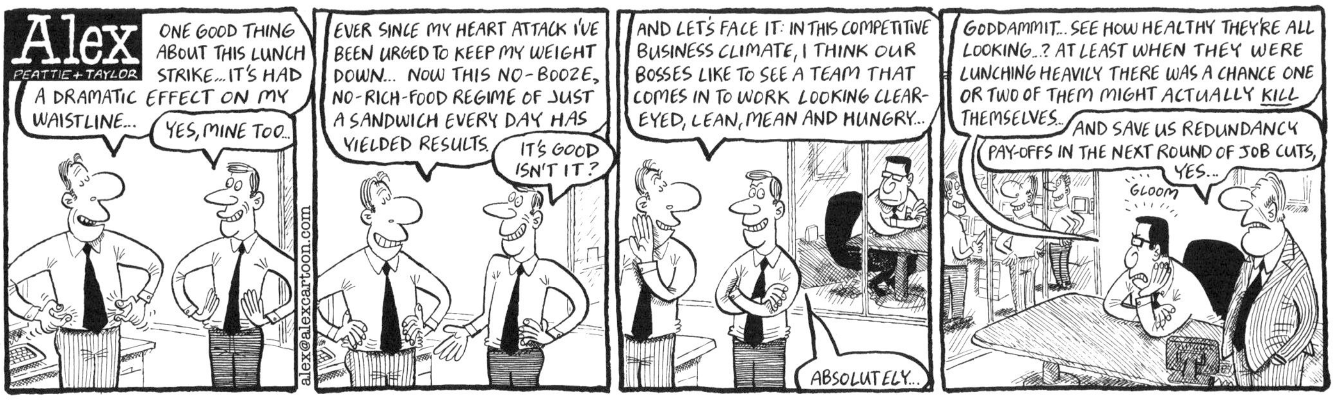
Alex
PEATTIE + TAYLOR
ONE GOOD THING ABOUT THIS LUNCH STRIKE... IT'S HAD A DRAMATIC EFFECT ON MY WAISTLINE...
YES, MINE TOO...
alex@alexcartoon.com
EVER SINCE MY HEART ATTACK I'VE BEEN URGED TO KEEP MY WEIGHT DOWN... NOW THIS NO-BOOZE, NO-RICH-FOOD REGIME OF JUST A SANDWICH EVERY DAY HAS YIELDED RESULTS.
IT'S GOOD ISN'T IT?
AND LET'S FACE IT: IN THIS COMPETITIVE BUSINESS CLIMATE, I THINK OUR BOSSES LIKE TO SEE A TEAM THAT COMES IN TO WORK LOOKING CLEAR-EYED, LEAN, MEAN AND HUNGRY...
ABSOLUTELY...
GODDAMMIT... SEE HOW HEALTHY THEY'RE ALL LOOKING..? AT LEAST WHEN THEY WERE LUNCHING HEAVILY THERE WAS A CHANCE ONE OR TWO OF THEM MIGHT ACTUALLY KILL THEMSELVES...
AND SAVE US REDUNDANCY PAY-OFFS IN THE NEXT ROUND OF JOB CUTS, YES...
GLOOM

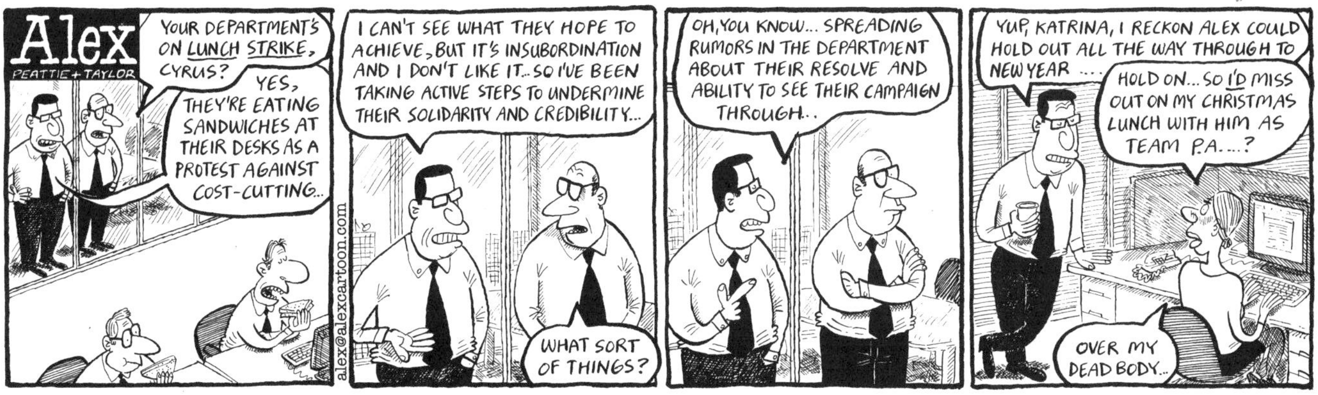
Alex
PEATTIE + TAYLOR
YOUR DEPARTMENT'S ON LUNCH STRIKE, CYRUS?
YES, THEY'RE EATING SANDWICHES AT THEIR DESKS AS A PROTEST AGAINST COST-CUTTING...
alex@alexcartoon.com
I CAN'T SEE WHAT THEY HOPE TO ACHIEVE, BUT IT'S INSUBORDINATION AND I DON'T LIKE IT... SO I'VE BEEN TAKING ACTIVE STEPS TO UNDERMINE THEIR SOLIDARITY AND CREDIBILITY...
WHAT SORT OF THINGS?
OH, YOU KNOW... SPREADING RUMORS IN THE DEPARTMENT ABOUT THEIR RESOLVE AND ABILITY TO SEE THEIR CAMPAIGN THROUGH...
YUP, KATRINA, I RECKON ALEX COULD HOLD OUT ALL THE WAY THROUGH TO NEW YEAR ....
HOLD ON... SO I'D MISS OUT ON MY CHRISTMAS LUNCH WITH HIM AS TEAM P.A. ...?
OVER MY DEAD BODY...

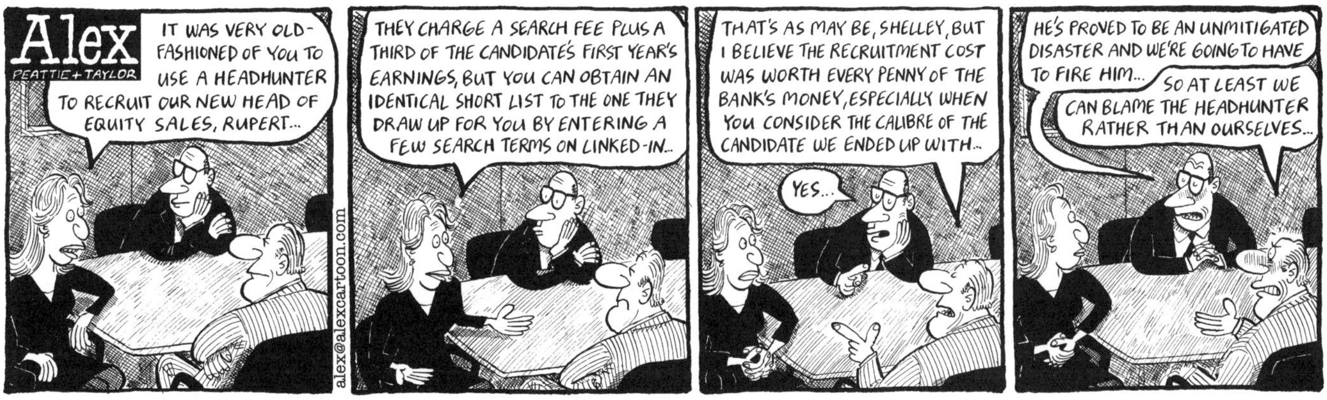
Alex
PEATTIE + TAYLOR
IT WAS VERY OLD-FASHIONED OF YOU TO USE A HEADHUNTER TO RECRUIT OUR NEW HEAD OF EQUITY SALES, RUPERT...
alex@alexcartoon.com
THEY CHARGE A SEARCH FEE PLUS A THIRD OF THE CANDIDATE'S FIRST YEAR'S EARNINGS, BUT YOU CAN OBTAIN AN IDENTICAL SHORT LIST TO THE ONE THEY DRAW UP FOR YOU BY ENTERING A FEW SEARCH TERMS ON LINKED-IN...
THAT'S AS MAY BE, SHELLEY, BUT I BELIEVE THE RECRUITMENT COST WAS WORTH EVERY PENNY OF THE BANK'S MONEY, ESPECIALLY WHEN YOU CONSIDER THE CALIBRE OF THE CANDIDATE WE ENDED UP WITH...
YES...
HE'S PROVED TO BE AN UNMITIGATED DISASTER AND WE'RE GOING TO HAVE TO FIRE HIM...
SO AT LEAST WE CAN BLAME THE HEADHUNTER RATHER THAN OURSELVES...

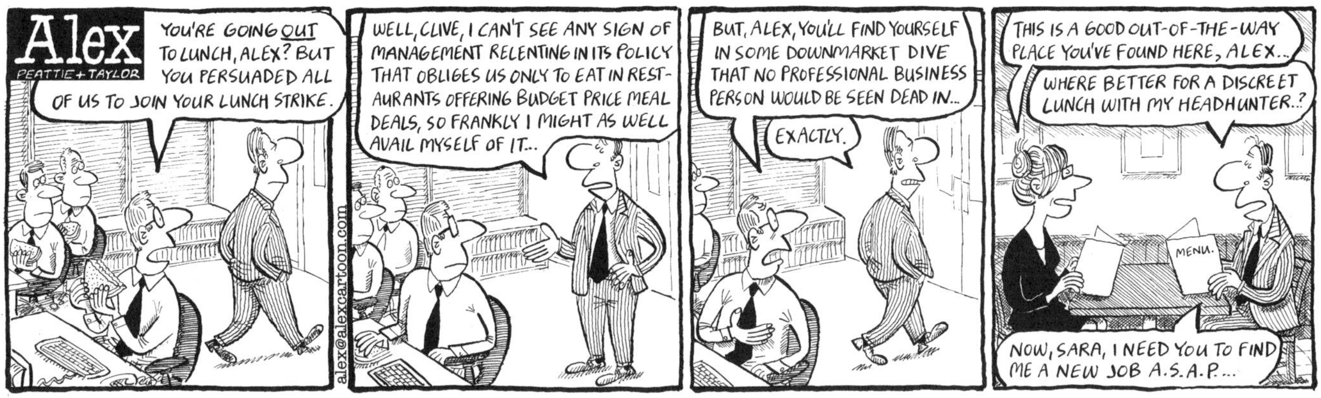
Alex
PEATTIE + TAYLOR
YOU'RE GOING OUT TO LUNCH, ALEX? BUT YOU PERSUADED ALL OF US TO JOIN YOUR LUNCH STRIKE.
alex@alexcartoon.com
WELL, CLIVE, I CAN'T SEE ANY SIGN OF MANAGEMENT RELENTING IN ITS POLICY THAT OBLIGES US ONLY TO EAT IN RESTAURANTS OFFERING BUDGET PRICE MEAL DEALS, SO FRANKLY I MIGHT AS WELL AVAIL MYSELF OF IT...
BUT, ALEX, YOU'LL FIND YOURSELF IN SOME DOWNMARKET DIVE THAT NO PROFESSIONAL BUSINESS PERSON WOULD BE SEEN DEAD IN...
EXACTLY.
THIS IS A GOOD OUT-OF-THE-WAY PLACE YOU'VE FOUND HERE, ALEX...
WHERE BETTER FOR A DISCREET LUNCH WITH MY HEADHUNTER..?
MENU.
NOW, SARA, I NEED YOU TO FIND ME A NEW JOB A.S.A.P...

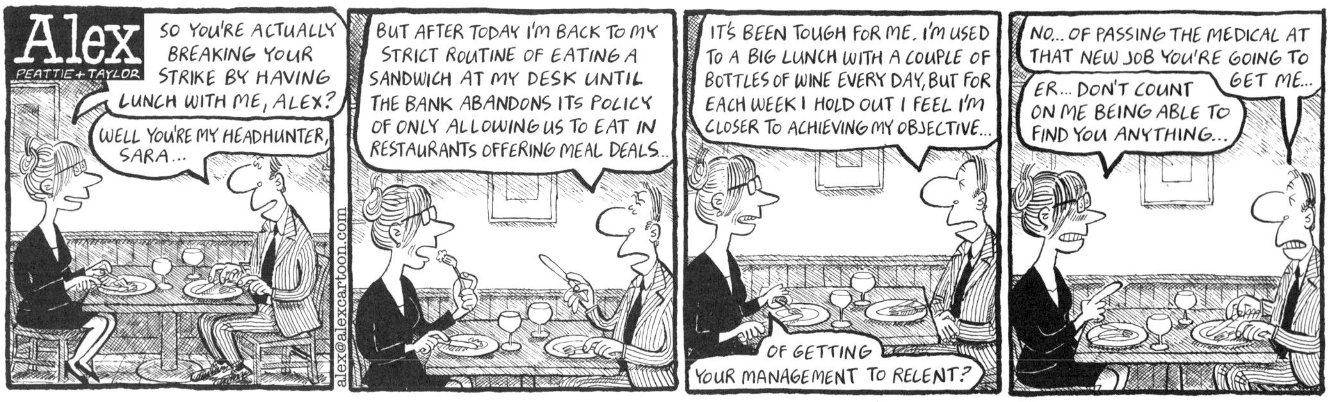
Alex
PEATTIE + TAYLOR
SO YOU'RE ACTUALLY BREAKING YOUR STRIKE BY HAVING LUNCH WITH ME, ALEX?
WELL YOU'RE MY HEADHUNTER, SARA...
BUT AFTER TODAY I'M BACK TO MY STRICT ROUTINE OF EATING A SANDWICH AT MY DESK UNTIL THE BANK ABANDONS ITS POLICY OF ONLY ALLOWING US TO EAT IN RESTAURANTS OFFERING MEAL DEALS...
alex@alexcartoon.com
IT'S BEEN TOUGH FOR ME. I'M USED TO A BIG LUNCH WITH A COUPLE OF BOTTLES OF WINE EVERY DAY, BUT FOR EACH WEEK I HOLD OUT I FEEL I'M CLOSER TO ACHIEVING MY OBJECTIVE...
OF GETTING YOUR MANAGEMENT TO RELENT?
NO... OF PASSING THE MEDICAL AT THAT NEW JOB YOU'RE GOING TO GET ME...
ER... DON'T COUNT ON ME BEING ABLE TO FIND YOU ANYTHING...

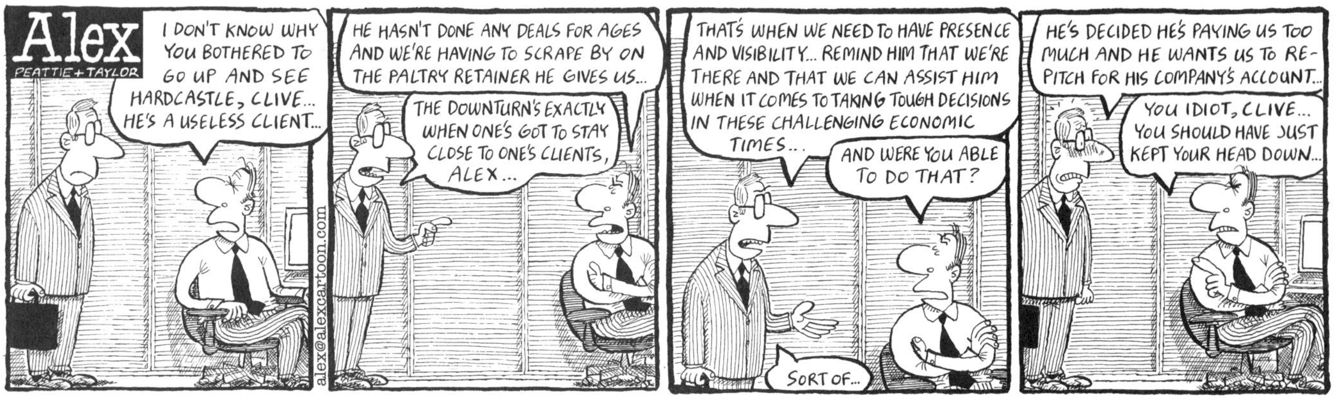
Alex
PEATTIE + TAYLOR
I DON'T KNOW WHY YOU BOTHERED TO GO UP AND SEE HARDCASTLE, CLIVE... HE'S A USELESS CLIENT...
HE HASN'T DONE ANY DEALS FOR AGES AND WE'RE HAVING TO SCRAPE BY ON THE PALTRY RETAINER HE GIVES US...
THE DOWNTURN'S EXACTLY WHEN ONE'S GOT TO STAY CLOSE TO ONE'S CLIENTS, ALEX...
alex@alexcartoon.com
THAT'S WHEN WE NEED TO HAVE PRESENCE AND VISIBILITY... REMIND HIM THAT WE'RE THERE AND THAT WE CAN ASSIST HIM WHEN IT COMES TO TAKING TOUGH DECISIONS IN THESE CHALLENGING ECONOMIC TIMES...
AND WERE YOU ABLE TO DO THAT?
SORT OF...
HE'S DECIDED HE'S PAYING US TOO MUCH AND HE WANTS US TO RE-PITCH FOR HIS COMPANY'S ACCOUNT...
YOU IDIOT, CLIVE... YOU SHOULD HAVE JUST KEPT YOUR HEAD DOWN...

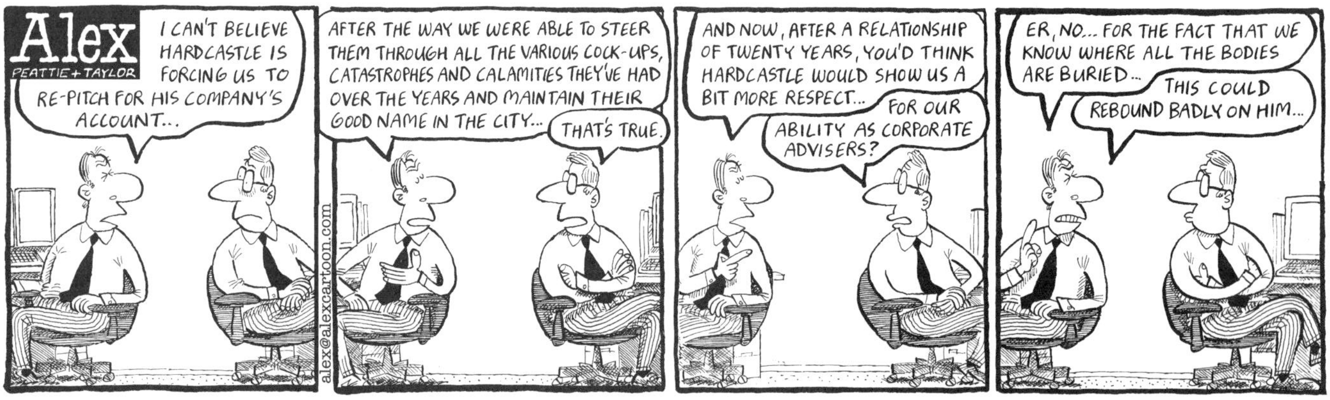
Alex
PEATTIE + TAYLOR
I CAN'T BELIEVE HARDCASTLE IS FORCING US TO RE-PITCH FOR HIS COMPANY'S ACCOUNT...
AFTER THE WAY WE WERE ABLE TO STEER THEM THROUGH ALL THE VARIOUS COCK-UPS, CATASTROPHES AND CALAMITIES THEY'VE HAD OVER THE YEARS AND MAINTAIN THEIR GOOD NAME IN THE CITY...
THAT'S TRUE.
alex@alexcartoon.com
AND NOW, AFTER A RELATIONSHIP OF TWENTY YEARS, YOU'D THINK HARDCASTLE WOULD SHOW US A BIT MORE RESPECT...
FOR OUR ABILITY AS CORPORATE ADVISERS?
ER, NO... FOR THE FACT THAT WE KNOW WHERE ALL THE BODIES ARE BURIED...
THIS COULD REBOUND BADLY ON HIM...

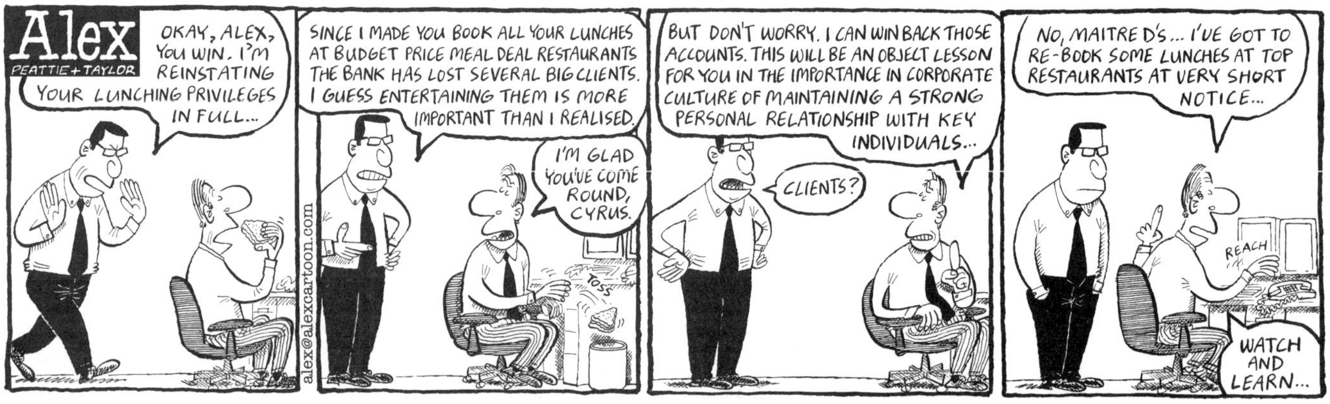
Alex
PEATTIE + TAYLOR
OKAY, ALEX, YOU WIN. I'M REINSTATING YOUR LUNCHING PRIVILEGES IN FULL...
SINCE I MADE YOU BOOK ALL YOUR LUNCHES AT BUDGET PRICE MEAL DEAL RESTAURANTS THE BANK HAS LOST SEVERAL BIG CLIENTS. I GUESS ENTERTAINING THEM IS MORE IMPORTANT THAN I REALISED.
I'M GLAD YOU'VE COME ROUND, CYRUS.
TOSS
alex@alexcartoon.com
BUT DON'T WORRY. I CAN WIN BACK THOSE ACCOUNTS. THIS WILL BE AN OBJECT LESSON FOR YOU IN THE IMPORTANCE IN CORPORATE CULTURE OF MAINTAINING A STRONG PERSONAL RELATIONSHIP WITH KEY INDIVIDUALS...
CLIENTS?
NO, MAITRE D'S... I'VE GOT TO RE-BOOK SOME LUNCHES AT TOP RESTAURANTS AT VERY SHORT NOTICE...
REACH
WATCH AND LEARN...

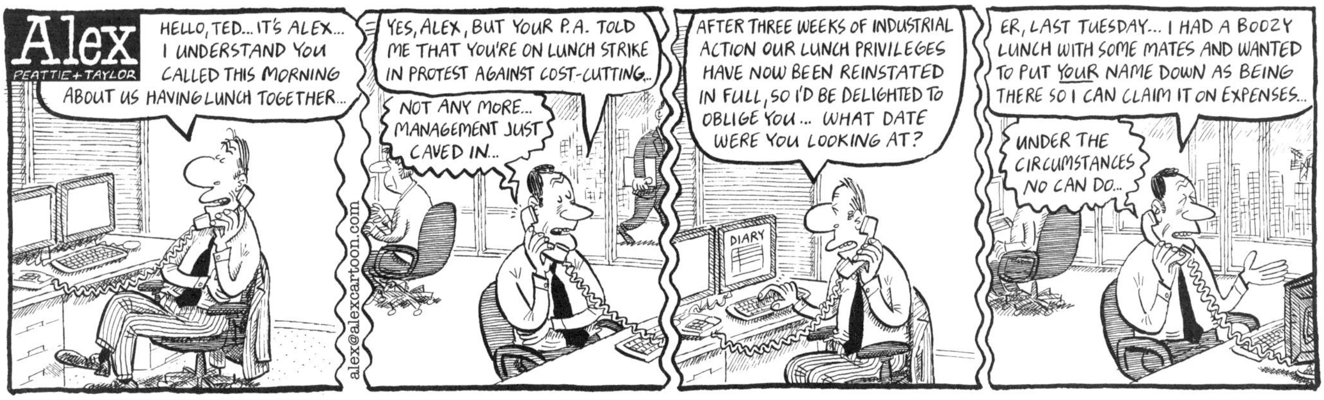
Alex
PEATTIE+TAYLOR
HELLO, TED... IT'S ALEX... I UNDERSTAND YOU CALLED THIS MORNING ABOUT US HAVING LUNCH TOGETHER...
YES, ALEX, BUT YOUR P.A. TOLD ME THAT YOU'RE ON LUNCH STRIKE IN PROTEST AGAINST COST-CUTTING...
NOT ANY MORE... MANAGEMENT JUST CAVED IN...
alex@alexcartoon.com
AFTER THREE WEEKS OF INDUSTRIAL ACTION OUR LUNCH PRIVILEGES HAVE NOW BEEN REINSTATED IN FULL, SO I'D BE DELIGHTED TO OBLIGE YOU... WHAT DATE WERE YOU LOOKING AT?
DIARY
ER, LAST TUESDAY... I HAD A BOOZY LUNCH WITH SOME MATES AND WANTED TO PUT YOUR NAME DOWN AS BEING THERE SO I CAN CLAIM IT ON EXPENSES...
UNDER THE CIRCUMSTANCES NO CAN DO...

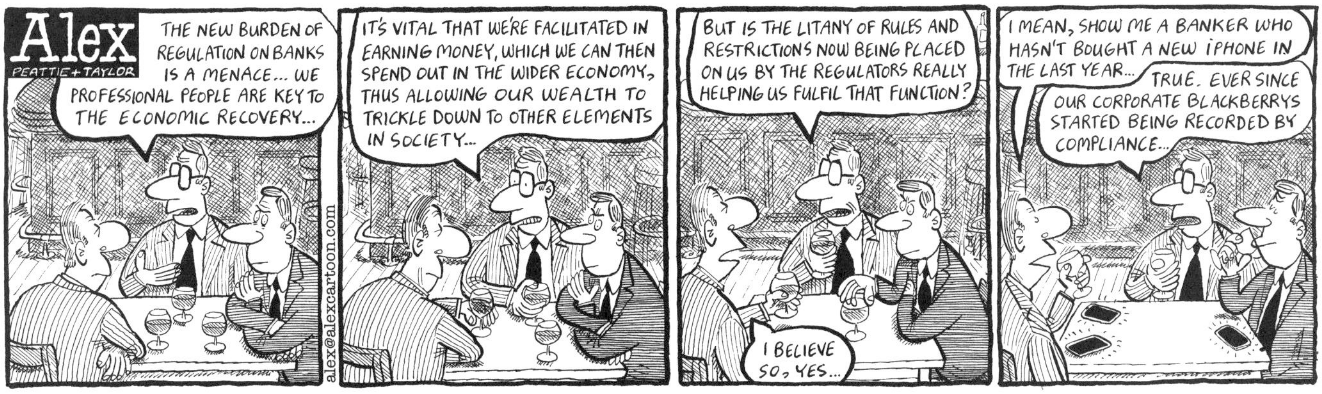
Alex
PEATTIE+TAYLOR
THE NEW BURDEN OF REGULATION ON BANKS IS A MENACE... WE PROFESSIONAL PEOPLE ARE KEY TO THE ECONOMIC RECOVERY...
IT'S VITAL THAT WE'RE FACILITATED IN EARNING MONEY, WHICH WE CAN THEN SPEND OUT IN THE WIDER ECONOMY, THUS ALLOWING OUR WEALTH TO TRICKLE DOWN TO OTHER ELEMENTS IN SOCIETY...
alex@alexcartoon.com
BUT IS THE LITANY OF RULES AND RESTRICTIONS NOW BEING PLACED ON US BY THE REGULATORS REALLY HELPING US FULFIL THAT FUNCTION?
I BELIEVE SO, YES...
I MEAN, SHOW ME A BANKER WHO HASN'T BOUGHT A NEW iPHONE IN THE LAST YEAR...
TRUE. EVER SINCE OUR CORPORATE BLACKBERRYS STARTED BEING RECORDED BY COMPLIANCE...

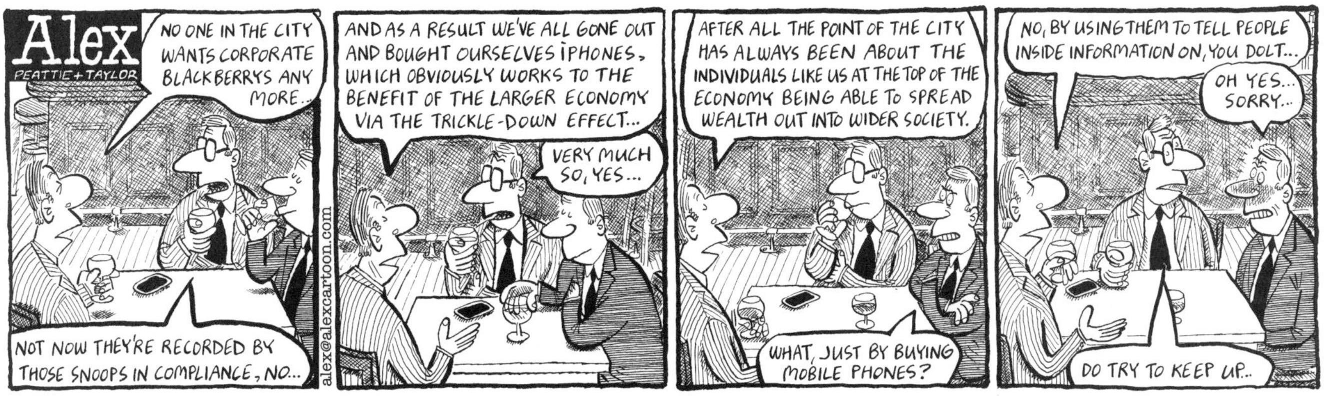
Alex
PEATTIE+TAYLOR
NO ONE IN THE CITY WANTS CORPORATE BLACKBERRYS ANY MORE...
NOT NOW THEY'RE RECORDED BY THOSE SNOOPS IN COMPLIANCE, NO...
alex@alexcartoon.com
AND AS A RESULT WE'VE ALL GONE OUT AND BOUGHT OURSELVES iPHONES, WHICH OBVIOUSLY WORKS TO THE BENEFIT OF THE LARGER ECONOMY VIA THE TRICKLE-DOWN EFFECT...
VERY MUCH SO, YES...
AFTER ALL THE POINT OF THE CITY HAS ALWAYS BEEN ABOUT THE INDIVIDUALS LIKE US AT THE TOP OF THE ECONOMY BEING ABLE TO SPREAD WEALTH OUT INTO WIDER SOCIETY.
WHAT, JUST BY BUYING MOBILE PHONES?
NO, BY USING THEM TO TELL PEOPLE INSIDE INFORMATION ON, YOU DOLT...
OH YES... SORRY...
DO TRY TO KEEP UP...

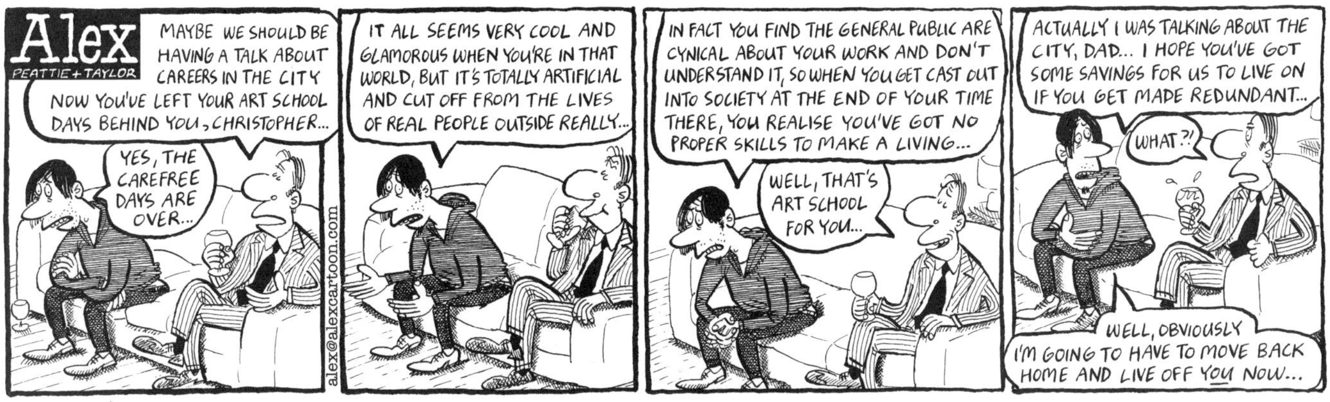
Alex
PEATTIE+TAYLOR
MAYBE WE SHOULD BE HAVING A TALK ABOUT CAREERS IN THE CITY NOW YOU'VE LEFT YOUR ART SCHOOL DAYS BEHIND YOU, CHRISTOPHER...
YES, THE CAREFREE DAYS ARE OVER...
alex@alexcartoon.com
IT ALL SEEMS VERY COOL AND GLAMOROUS WHEN YOU'RE IN THAT WORLD, BUT IT'S TOTALLY ARTIFICIAL AND CUT OFF FROM THE LIVES OF REAL PEOPLE OUTSIDE REALLY...
IN FACT YOU FIND THE GENERAL PUBLIC ARE CYNICAL ABOUT YOUR WORK AND DON'T UNDERSTAND IT, SO WHEN YOU GET CAST OUT INTO SOCIETY AT THE END OF YOUR TIME THERE, YOU REALISE YOU'VE GOT NO PROPER SKILLS TO MAKE A LIVING...
WELL, THAT'S ART SCHOOL FOR YOU...
ACTUALLY I WAS TALKING ABOUT THE CITY, DAD... I HOPE YOU'VE GOT SOME SAVINGS FOR US TO LIVE ON IF YOU GET MADE REDUNDANT...
WHAT?!
WELL, OBVIOUSLY I'M GOING TO HAVE TO MOVE BACK HOME AND LIVE OFF YOU NOW...

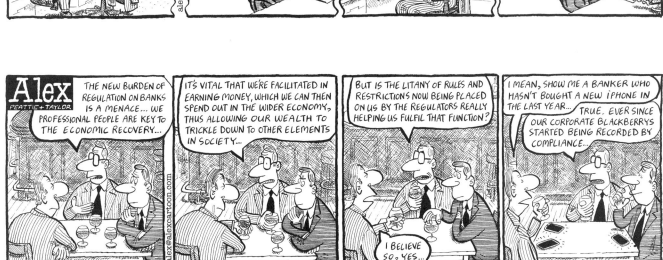

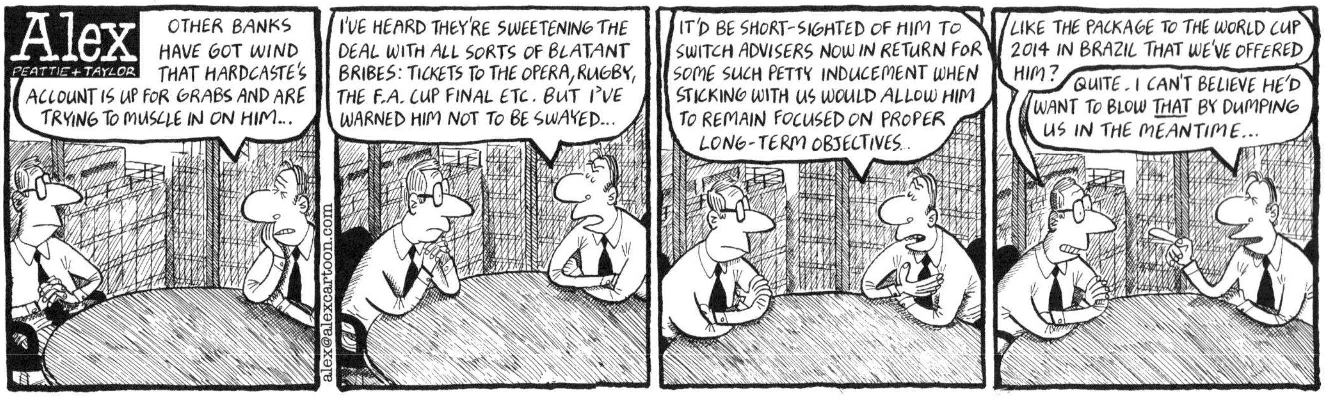
Alex
PEATTIE + TAYLOR
OTHER BANKS HAVE GOT WIND THAT HARDCASTE'S ACCOUNT IS UP FOR GRABS AND ARE TRYING TO MUSCLE IN ON HIM...
I'VE HEARD THEY'RE SWEETENING THE DEAL WITH ALL SORTS OF BLATANT BRIBES: TICKETS TO THE OPERA, RUGBY, THE F.A. CUP FINAL ETC. BUT I'VE WARNED HIM NOT TO BE SWAYED...
alex@alexcartoon.com
IT'D BE SHORT-SIGHTED OF HIM TO SWITCH ADVISERS NOW IN RETURN FOR SOME SUCH PETTY INDUCEMENT WHEN STICKING WITH US WOULD ALLOW HIM TO REMAIN FOCUSED ON PROPER LONG-TERM OBJECTIVES...
LIKE THE PACKAGE TO THE WORLD CUP 2014 IN BRAZIL THAT WE'VE OFFERED HIM?
QUITE. I CAN'T BELIEVE HE'D WANT TO BLOW THAT BY DUMPING US IN THE MEANTIME...

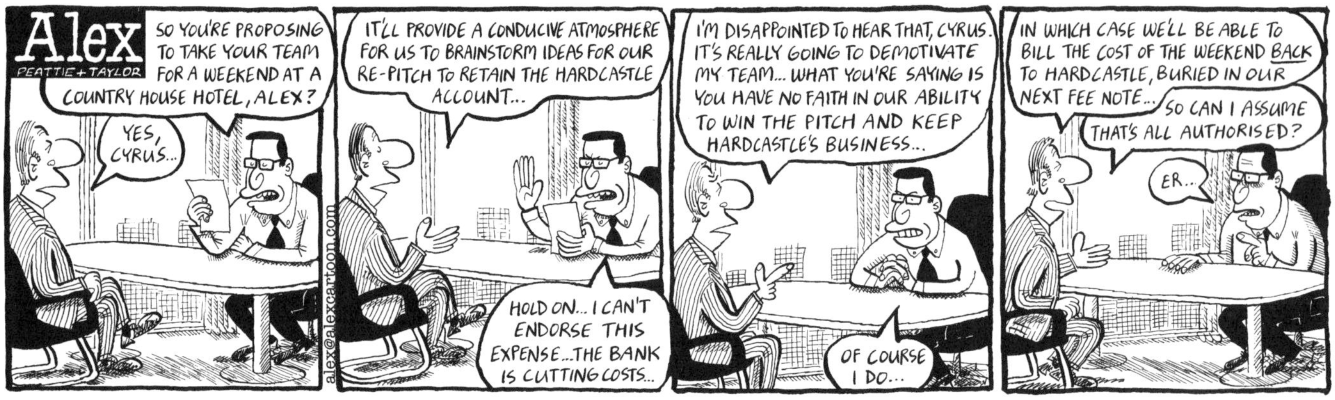
Alex
PEATTIE + TAYLOR
SO YOU'RE PROPOSING TO TAKE YOUR TEAM FOR A WEEKEND AT A COUNTRY HOUSE HOTEL, ALEX?
YES, CYRUS...
IT'LL PROVIDE A CONDUCIVE ATMOSPHERE FOR US TO BRAINSTORM IDEAS FOR OUR RE-PITCH TO RETAIN THE HARDCASTLE ACCOUNT...
HOLD ON... I CAN'T ENDORSE THIS EXPENSE...THE BANK IS CUTTING COSTS...
alex@alexcartoon.com
I'M DISAPPOINTED TO HEAR THAT, CYRUS. IT'S REALLY GOING TO DEMOTIVATE MY TEAM... WHAT YOU'RE SAYING IS YOU HAVE NO FAITH IN OUR ABILITY TO WIN THE PITCH AND KEEP HARDCASTLE'S BUSINESS...
OF COURSE I DO...
IN WHICH CASE WE'LL BE ABLE TO BILL THE COST OF THE WEEKEND BACK TO HARDCASTLE, BURIED IN OUR NEXT FEE NOTE...
SO CAN I ASSUME THAT'S ALL AUTHORISED?
ER...

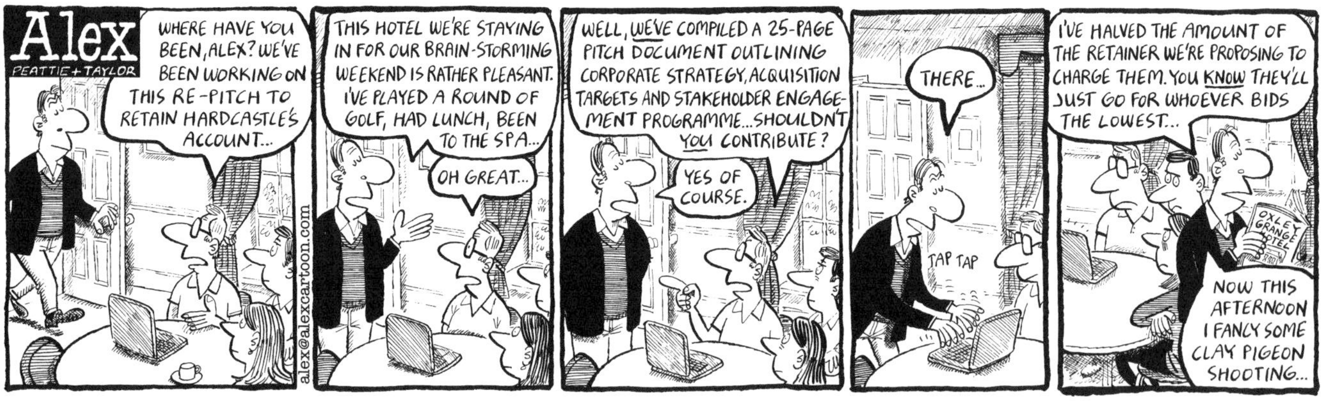
Alex
PEATTIE + TAYLOR
WHERE HAVE YOU BEEN, ALEX? WE'VE BEEN WORKING ON THIS RE-PITCH TO RETAIN HARDCASTLE'S ACCOUNT...
alex@alexcartoon.com
THIS HOTEL WE'RE STAYING IN FOR OUR BRAIN-STORMING WEEKEND IS RATHER PLEASANT. I'VE PLAYED A ROUND OF GOLF, HAD LUNCH, BEEN TO THE SPA...
OH GREAT...
WELL, WE'VE COMPILED A 25-PAGE PITCH DOCUMENT OUTLINING CORPORATE STRATEGY, ACQUISITION TARGETS AND STAKEHOLDER ENGAGEMENT PROGRAMME...SHOULDN'T YOU CONTRIBUTE?
YES OF COURSE.
THERE...
TAP TAP
I'VE HALVED THE AMOUNT OF THE RETAINER WE'RE PROPOSING TO CHARGE THEM. YOU KNOW THEY'LL JUST GO FOR WHOEVER BIDS THE LOWEST...
OXLEY GRANGE
NOW THIS AFTERNOON I FANCY SOME CLAY PIGEON SHOOTING...

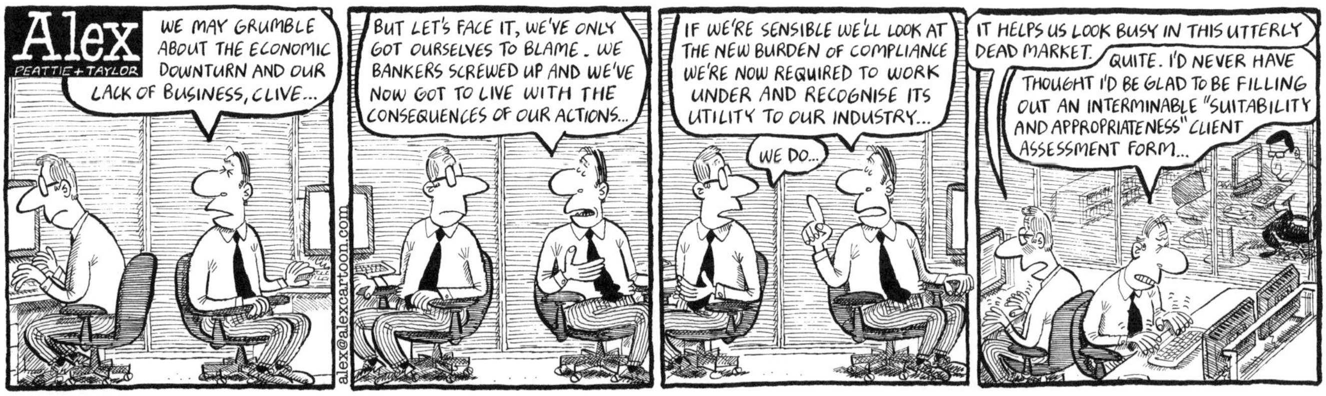
Alex
PEATTIE + TAYLOR
WE MAY GRUMBLE ABOUT THE ECONOMIC DOWNTURN AND OUR LACK OF BUSINESS, CLIVE...
alex@alexcartoon.com
BUT LET'S FACE IT, WE'VE ONLY GOT OURSELVES TO BLAME. WE BANKERS SCREWED UP AND WE'VE NOW GOT TO LIVE WITH THE CONSEQUENCES OF OUR ACTIONS...
IF WE'RE SENSIBLE WE'LL LOOK AT THE NEW BURDEN OF COMPLIANCE WE'RE NOW REQUIRED TO WORK UNDER AND RECOGNISE ITS UTILITY TO OUR INDUSTRY...
WE DO...
IT HELPS US LOOK BUSY IN THIS UTTERLY DEAD MARKET.
QUITE. I'D NEVER HAVE THOUGHT I'D BE GLAD TO BE FILLING OUT AN INTERMINABLE "SUITABILITY AND APPROPRIATENESS" CLIENT ASSESSMENT FORM...

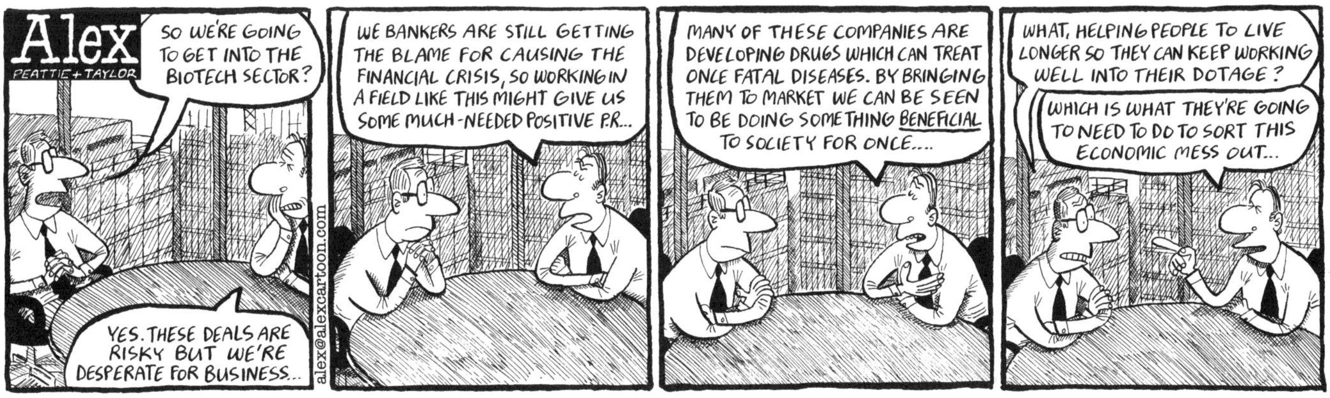
Alex
PEATTIE + TAYLOR
SO WE'RE GOING TO GET INTO THE BIOTECH SECTOR?
YES. THESE DEALS ARE RISKY BUT WE'RE DESPERATE FOR BUSINESS...
alex@alexcartoon.com
WE BANKERS ARE STILL GETTING THE BLAME FOR CAUSING THE FINANCIAL CRISIS, SO WORKING IN A FIELD LIKE THIS MIGHT GIVE US SOME MUCH-NEEDED POSITIVE P.R...
MANY OF THESE COMPANIES ARE DEVELOPING DRUGS WHICH CAN TREAT ONCE FATAL DISEASES. BY BRINGING THEM TO MARKET WE CAN BE SEEN TO BE DOING SOMETHING BENEFICIAL TO SOCIETY FOR ONCE....
WHAT, HELPING PEOPLE TO LIVE LONGER SO THEY CAN KEEP WORKING WELL INTO THEIR DOTAGE?
WHICH IS WHAT THEY'RE GOING TO NEED TO DO TO SORT THIS ECONOMIC MESS OUT...

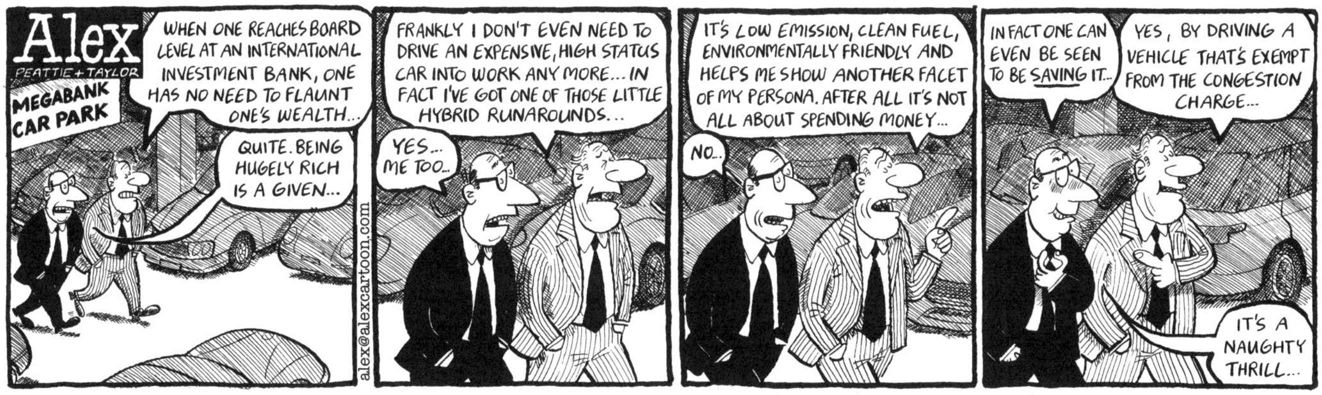
Alex
PEATTIE + TAYLOR
MEGABANK CAR PARK
WHEN ONE REACHES BOARD LEVEL AT AN INTERNATIONAL INVESTMENT BANK, ONE HAS NO NEED TO FLAUNT ONE'S WEALTH...
QUITE. BEING HUGELY RICH IS A GIVEN...
alex@alexcartoon.com
FRANKLY I DON'T EVEN NEED TO DRIVE AN EXPENSIVE, HIGH STATUS CAR INTO WORK ANY MORE... IN FACT I'VE GOT ONE OF THOSE LITTLE HYBRID RUNAROUNDS...
YES... ME TOO...
IT'S LOW EMISSION, CLEAN FUEL, ENVIRONMENTALLY FRIENDLY AND HELPS ME SHOW ANOTHER FACET OF MY PERSONA. AFTER ALL IT'S NOT ALL ABOUT SPENDING MONEY...
NO...
IN FACT ONE CAN EVEN BE SEEN TO BE SAVING IT...
YES, BY DRIVING A VEHICLE THAT'S EXEMPT FROM THE CONGESTION CHARGE...
IT'S A NAUGHTY THRILL...

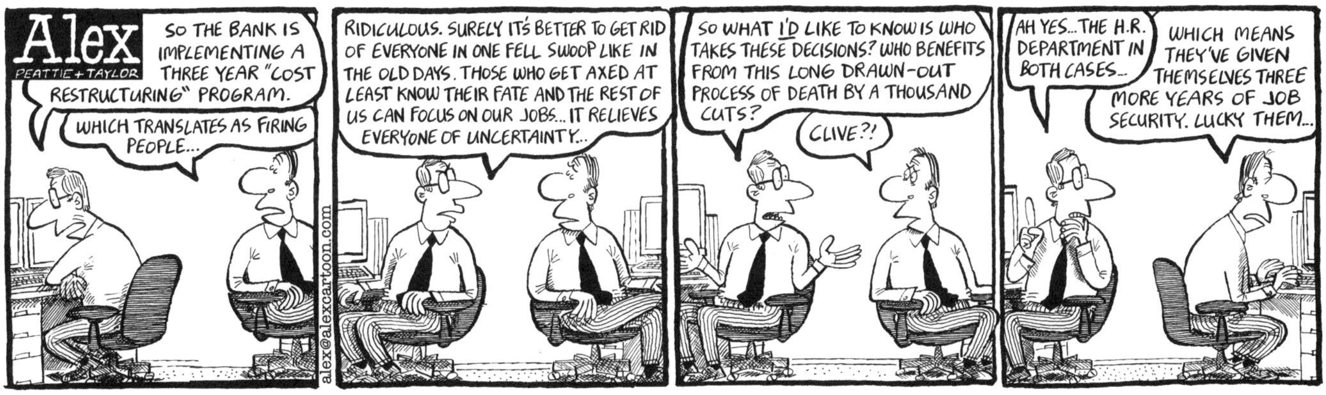
Alex
PEATTIE + TAYLOR
SO THE BANK IS IMPLEMENTING A THREE YEAR "COST RESTRUCTURING" PROGRAM.
WHICH TRANSLATES AS FIRING PEOPLE...
alex@alexcartoon.com
RIDICULOUS. SURELY IT'S BETTER TO GET RID OF EVERYONE IN ONE FELL SWOOP LIKE IN THE OLD DAYS. THOSE WHO GET AXED AT LEAST KNOW THEIR FATE AND THE REST OF US CAN FOCUS ON OUR JOBS... IT RELIEVES EVERYONE OF UNCERTAINTY...
SO WHAT I'D LIKE TO KNOW IS WHO TAKES THESE DECISIONS? WHO BENEFITS FROM THIS LONG DRAWN-OUT PROCESS OF DEATH BY A THOUSAND CUTS?
CLIVE?!
AH YES... THE H.R. DEPARTMENT IN BOTH CASES...
WHICH MEANS THEY'VE GIVEN THEMSELVES THREE MORE YEARS OF JOB SECURITY. LUCKY THEM...

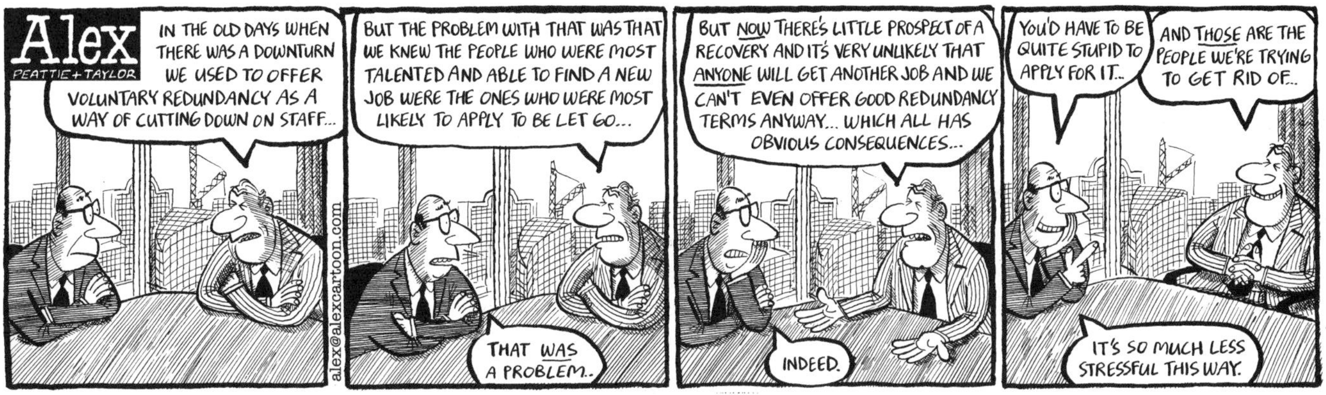
Alex
PEATTIE + TAYLOR
IN THE OLD DAYS WHEN THERE WAS A DOWNTURN WE USED TO OFFER VOLUNTARY REDUNDANCY AS A WAY OF CUTTING DOWN ON STAFF...
alex@alexcartoon.com
BUT THE PROBLEM WITH THAT WAS THAT WE KNEW THE PEOPLE WHO WERE MOST TALENTED AND ABLE TO FIND A NEW JOB WERE THE ONES WHO WERE MOST LIKELY TO APPLY TO BE LET GO...
THAT WAS A PROBLEM..
BUT NOW THERE'S LITTLE PROSPECT OF A RECOVERY AND IT'S VERY UNLIKELY THAT ANYONE WILL GET ANOTHER JOB AND WE CAN'T EVEN OFFER GOOD REDUNDANCY TERMS ANYWAY... WHICH ALL HAS OBVIOUS CONSEQUENCES...
INDEED.
YOU'D HAVE TO BE QUITE STUPID TO APPLY FOR IT...
AND THOSE ARE THE PEOPLE WE'RE TRYING TO GET RID OF...
IT'S SO MUCH LESS STRESSFUL THIS WAY.

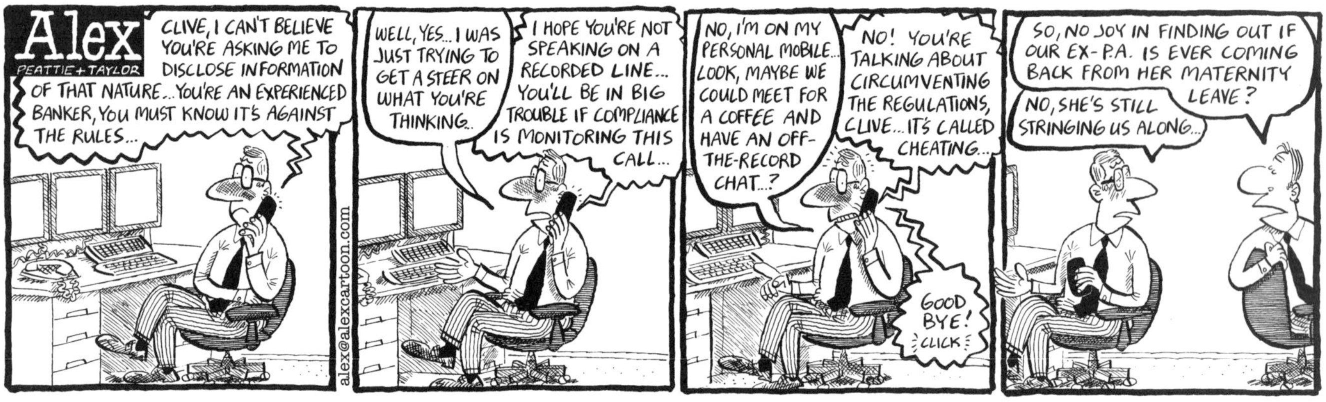
Alex
PEATTIE+TAYLOR
CLIVE, I CAN'T BELIEVE YOU'RE ASKING ME TO DISCLOSE INFORMATION OF THAT NATURE... YOU'RE AN EXPERIENCED BANKER, YOU MUST KNOW IT'S AGAINST THE RULES...
alex@alexcartoon.com
WELL, YES... I WAS JUST TRYING TO GET A STEER ON WHAT YOU'RE THINKING...
I HOPE YOU'RE NOT SPEAKING ON A RECORDED LINE... YOU'LL BE IN BIG TROUBLE IF COMPLIANCE IS MONITORING THIS CALL...
NO, I'M ON MY PERSONAL MOBILE... LOOK, MAYBE WE COULD MEET FOR A COFFEE AND HAVE AN OFF-THE-RECORD CHAT...?
NO! YOU'RE TALKING ABOUT CIRCUMVENTING THE REGULATIONS, CLIVE... IT'S CALLED CHEATING...
GOOD BYE!
CLICK
SO, NO JOY IN FINDING OUT IF OUR EX-P.A. IS EVER COMING BACK FROM HER MATERNITY LEAVE?
NO, SHE'S STILL STRINGING US ALONG...

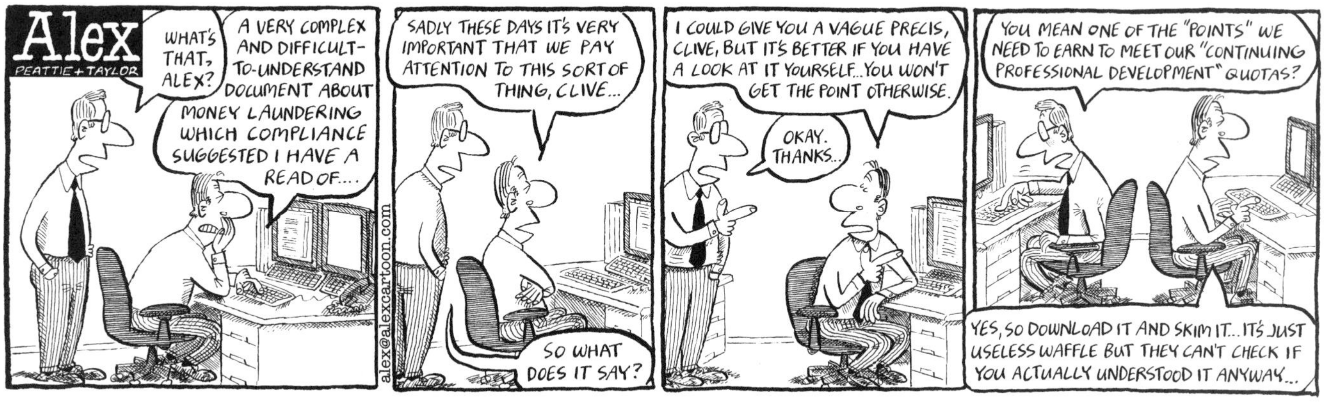
Alex
PEATTIE+TAYLOR
WHAT'S THAT, ALEX?
A VERY COMPLEX AND DIFFICULT-TO-UNDERSTAND DOCUMENT ABOUT MONEY LAUNDERING WHICH COMPLIANCE SUGGESTED I HAVE A READ OF....
alex@alexcartoon.com
SADLY THESE DAYS IT'S VERY IMPORTANT THAT WE PAY ATTENTION TO THIS SORT OF THING, CLIVE...
SO WHAT DOES IT SAY?
I COULD GIVE YOU A VAGUE PRECIS, CLIVE, BUT IT'S BETTER IF YOU HAVE A LOOK AT IT YOURSELF... YOU WON'T GET THE POINT OTHERWISE.
OKAY. THANKS...
YOU MEAN ONE OF THE "POINTS" WE NEED TO EARN TO MEET OUR "CONTINUING PROFESSIONAL DEVELOPMENT" QUOTAS?
YES, SO DOWNLOAD IT AND SKIM IT... IT'S JUST USELESS WAFFLE BUT THEY CAN'T CHECK IF YOU ACTUALLY UNDERSTOOD IT ANYWAY...

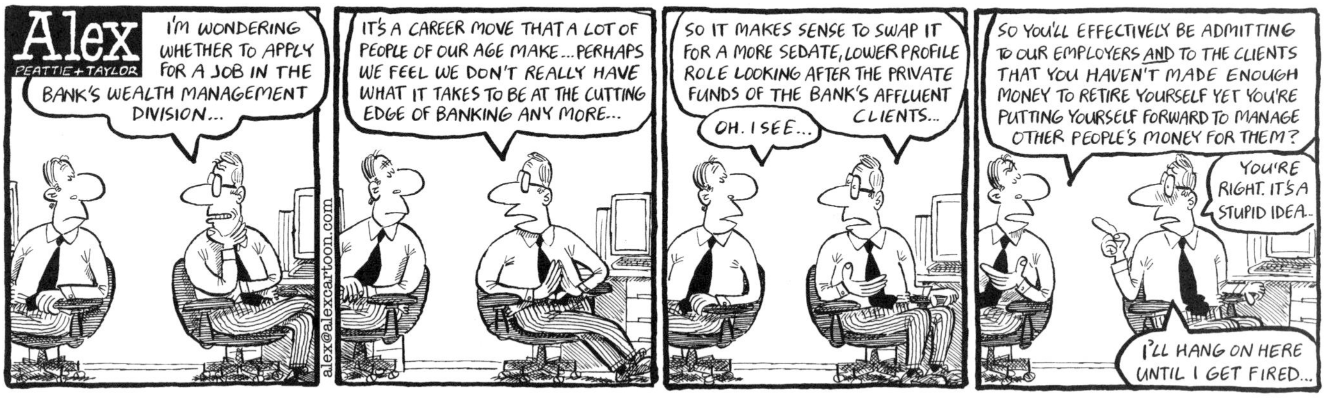
Alex
PEATTIE+TAYLOR
I'M WONDERING WHETHER TO APPLY FOR A JOB IN THE BANK'S WEALTH MANAGEMENT DIVISION...
alex@alexcartoon.com
IT'S A CAREER MOVE THAT A LOT OF PEOPLE OF OUR AGE MAKE... PERHAPS WE FEEL WE DON'T REALLY HAVE WHAT IT TAKES TO BE AT THE CUTTING EDGE OF BANKING ANY MORE...
SO IT MAKES SENSE TO SWAP IT FOR A MORE SEDATE, LOWER PROFILE ROLE LOOKING AFTER THE PRIVATE FUNDS OF THE BANK'S AFFLUENT CLIENTS...
OH. I SEE...
SO YOU'LL EFFECTIVELY BE ADMITTING TO OUR EMPLOYERS AND TO THE CLIENTS THAT YOU HAVEN'T MADE ENOUGH MONEY TO RETIRE YOURSELF YET YOU'RE PUTTING YOURSELF FORWARD TO MANAGE OTHER PEOPLE'S MONEY FOR THEM?
YOU'RE RIGHT. IT'S A STUPID IDEA...
I'LL HANG ON HERE UNTIL I GET FIRED...

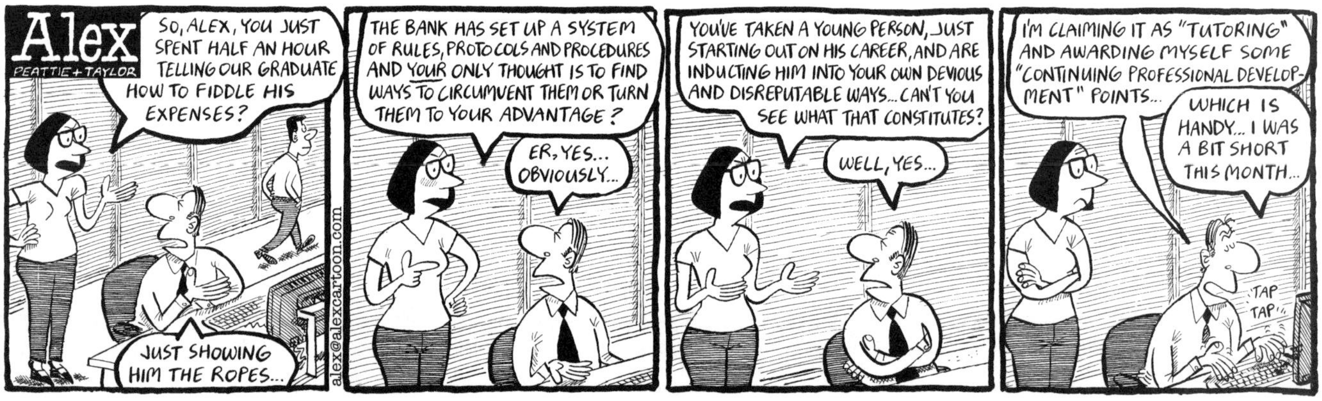
Alex
PEATTIE+TAYLOR
SO, ALEX, YOU JUST SPENT HALF AN HOUR TELLING OUR GRADUATE HOW TO FIDDLE HIS EXPENSES?
JUST SHOWING HIM THE ROPES...
alex@alexcartoon.com
THE BANK HAS SET UP A SYSTEM OF RULES, PROTOCOLS AND PROCEDURES AND YOUR ONLY THOUGHT IS TO FIND WAYS TO CIRCUMVENT THEM OR TURN THEM TO YOUR ADVANTAGE?
ER, YES... OBVIOUSLY...
YOU'VE TAKEN A YOUNG PERSON, JUST STARTING OUT ON HIS CAREER, AND ARE INDUCTING HIM INTO YOUR OWN DEVIOUS AND DISREPUTABLE WAYS... CAN'T YOU SEE WHAT THAT CONSTITUTES?
WELL, YES...
I'M CLAIMING IT AS "TUTORING" AND AWARDING MYSELF SOME "CONTINUING PROFESSIONAL DEVELOPMENT" POINTS...
WHICH IS HANDY... I WAS A BIT SHORT THIS MONTH...
TAP TAP

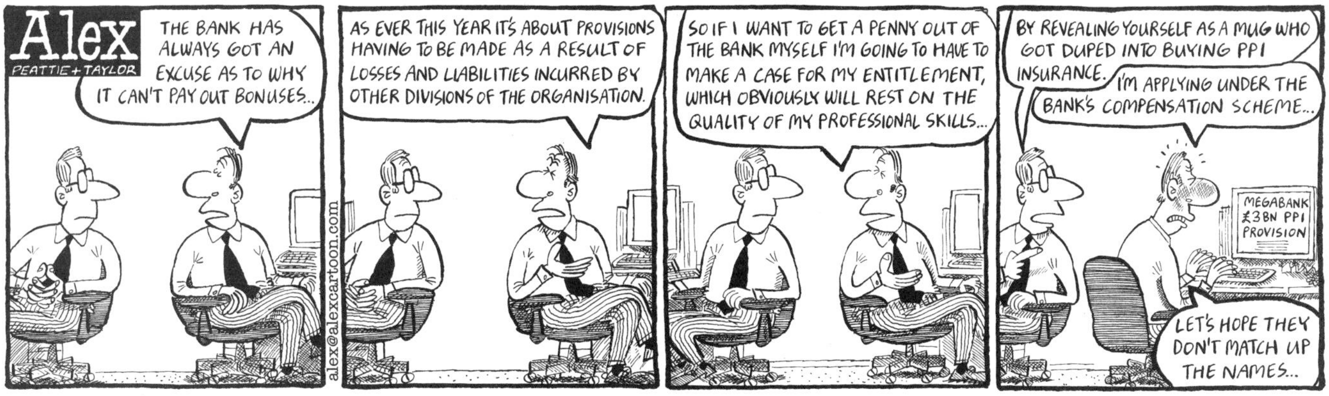
Alex
PEATTIE + TAYLOR
THE BANK HAS ALWAYS GOT AN EXCUSE AS TO WHY IT CAN'T PAY OUT BONUSES...
alex@alexcartoon.com
AS EVER THIS YEAR IT'S ABOUT PROVISIONS HAVING TO BE MADE AS A RESULT OF LOSSES AND LIABILITIES INCURRED BY OTHER DIVISIONS OF THE ORGANISATION.
SO IF I WANT TO GET A PENNY OUT OF THE BANK MYSELF I'M GOING TO HAVE TO MAKE A CASE FOR MY ENTITLEMENT, WHICH OBVIOUSLY WILL REST ON THE QUALITY OF MY PROFESSIONAL SKILLS...
BY REVEALING YOURSELF AS A MUG WHO GOT DUPED INTO BUYING PPI INSURANCE.
I'M APPLYING UNDER THE BANK'S COMPENSATION SCHEME...
MEGABANK £3BN PPI PROVISION
LET'S HOPE THEY DON'T MATCH UP THE NAMES...

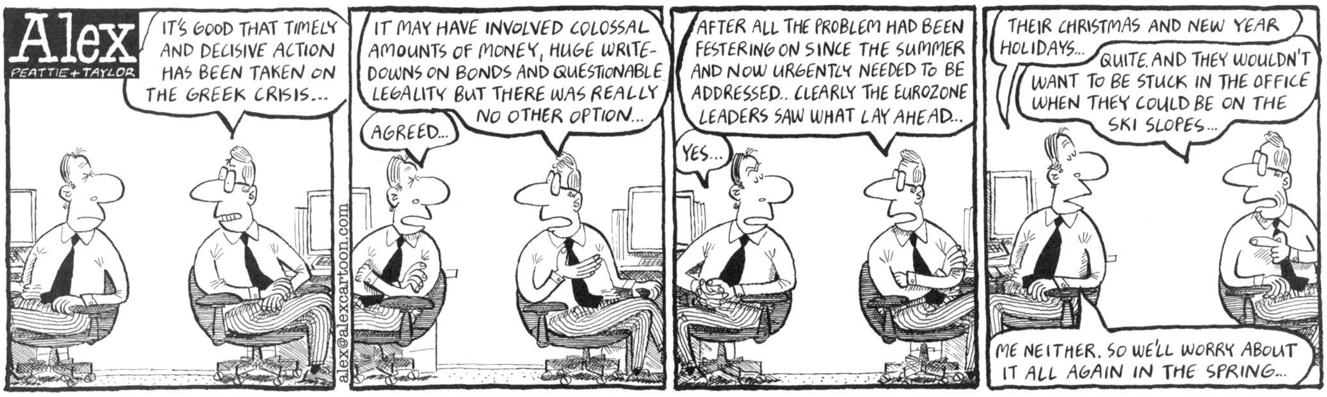
Alex
PEATTIE + TAYLOR
IT'S GOOD THAT TIMELY AND DECISIVE ACTION HAS BEEN TAKEN ON THE GREEK CRISIS...
alex@alexcartoon.com
IT MAY HAVE INVOLVED COLOSSAL AMOUNTS OF MONEY, HUGE WRITE-DOWNS ON BONDS AND QUESTIONABLE LEGALITY BUT THERE WAS REALLY NO OTHER OPTION...
AGREED...
AFTER ALL THE PROBLEM HAD BEEN FESTERING ON SINCE THE SUMMER AND NOW URGENTLY NEEDED TO BE ADDRESSED.. CLEARLY THE EUROZONE LEADERS SAW WHAT LAY AHEAD...
YES...
THEIR CHRISTMAS AND NEW YEAR HOLIDAYS...
QUITE. AND THEY WOULDN'T WANT TO BE STUCK IN THE OFFICE WHEN THEY COULD BE ON THE SKI SLOPES...
ME NEITHER. SO WE'LL WORRY ABOUT IT ALL AGAIN IN THE SPRING...

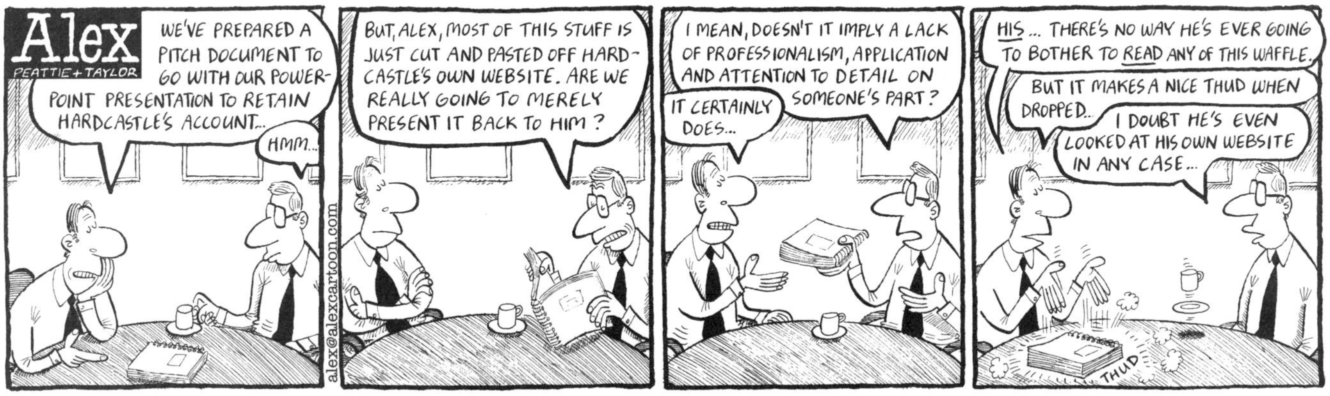
Alex
PEATTIE + TAYLOR
WE'VE PREPARED A PITCH DOCUMENT TO GO WITH OUR POWER-POINT PRESENTATION TO RETAIN HARDCASTLE'S ACCOUNT...
HMM...
alex@alexcartoon.com
BUT, ALEX, MOST OF THIS STUFF IS JUST CUT AND PASTED OFF HARD-CASTLE'S OWN WEBSITE. ARE WE REALLY GOING TO MERELY PRESENT IT BACK TO HIM?
I MEAN, DOESN'T IT IMPLY A LACK OF PROFESSIONALISM, APPLICATION AND ATTENTION TO DETAIL ON SOMEONE'S PART?
IT CERTAINLY DOES...
HIS ... THERE'S NO WAY HE'S EVER GOING TO BOTHER TO READ ANY OF THIS WAFFLE.
BUT IT MAKES A NICE THUD WHEN DROPPED..
I DOUBT HE'S EVEN LOOKED AT HIS OWN WEBSITE IN ANY CASE...
THUD

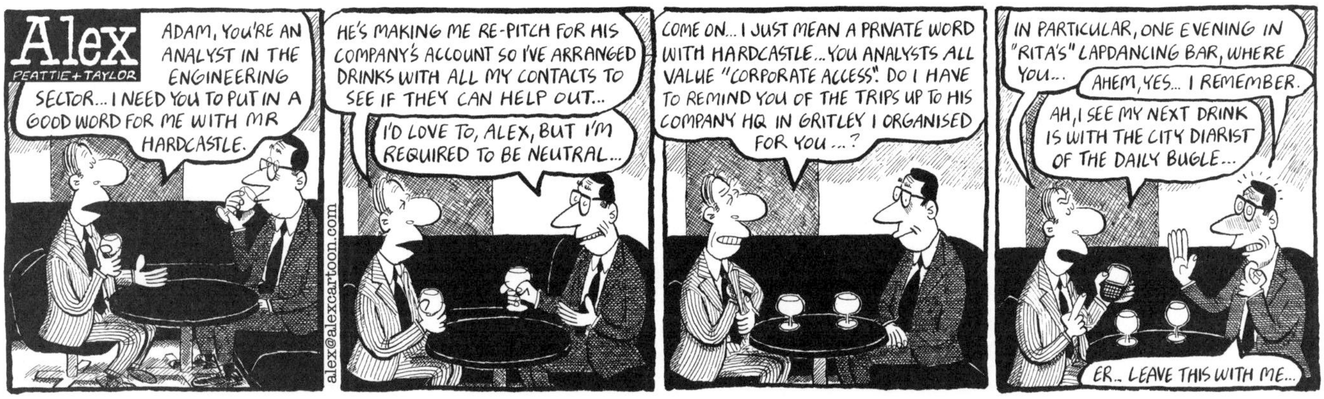
Alex
PEATTIE + TAYLOR
ADAM, YOU'RE AN ANALYST IN THE ENGINEERING SECTOR... I NEED YOU TO PUT IN A GOOD WORD FOR ME WITH MR HARDCASTLE.
alex@alexcartoon.com
HE'S MAKING ME RE-PITCH FOR HIS COMPANY'S ACCOUNT SO I'VE ARRANGED DRINKS WITH ALL MY CONTACTS TO SEE IF THEY CAN HELP OUT...
I'D LOVE TO, ALEX, BUT I'M REQUIRED TO BE NEUTRAL...
COME ON... I JUST MEAN A PRIVATE WORD WITH HARDCASTLE... YOU ANALYSTS ALL VALUE "CORPORATE ACCESS". DO I HAVE TO REMIND YOU OF THE TRIPS UP TO HIS COMPANY HQ IN GRITLEY I ORGANISED FOR YOU...?
IN PARTICULAR, ONE EVENING IN "RITA'S" LAPDANCING BAR, WHERE YOU...
AHEM, YES... I REMEMBER.
AH, I SEE MY NEXT DRINK IS WITH THE CITY DIARIST OF THE DAILY BUGLE...
ER.. LEAVE THIS WITH ME...

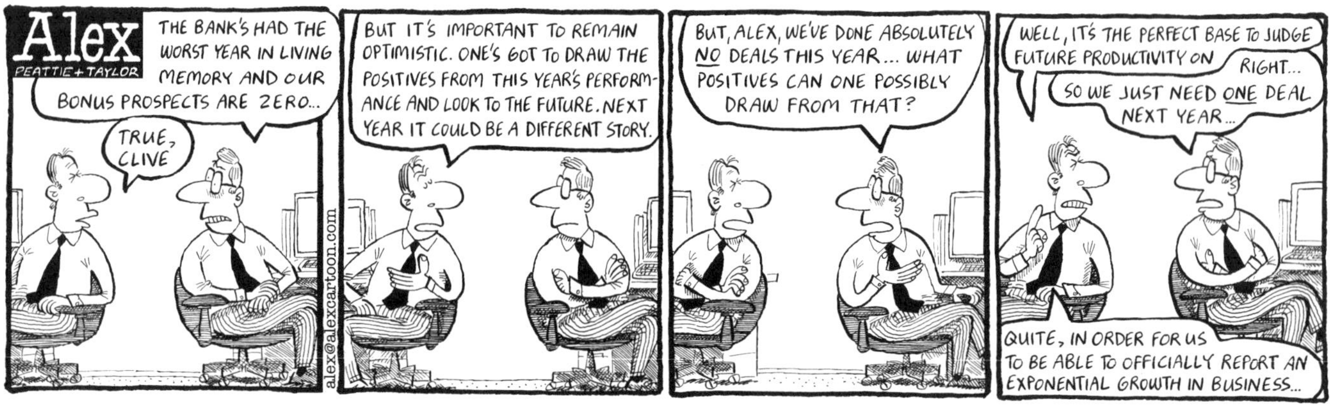
Alex
PEATTIE + TAYLOR
THE BANK'S HAD THE WORST YEAR IN LIVING MEMORY AND OUR BONUS PROSPECTS ARE ZERO...
TRUE, CLIVE
alex@alexcartoon.com
BUT IT'S IMPORTANT TO REMAIN OPTIMISTIC. ONE'S GOT TO DRAW THE POSITIVES FROM THIS YEAR'S PERFORMANCE AND LOOK TO THE FUTURE. NEXT YEAR IT COULD BE A DIFFERENT STORY.
BUT, ALEX, WE'VE DONE ABSOLUTELY NO DEALS THIS YEAR... WHAT POSITIVES CAN ONE POSSIBLY DRAW FROM THAT?
WELL, IT'S THE PERFECT BASE TO JUDGE FUTURE PRODUCTIVITY ON
RIGHT... SO WE JUST NEED ONE DEAL NEXT YEAR...
QUITE, IN ORDER FOR US TO BE ABLE TO OFFICIALLY REPORT AN EXPONENTIAL GROWTH IN BUSINESS...

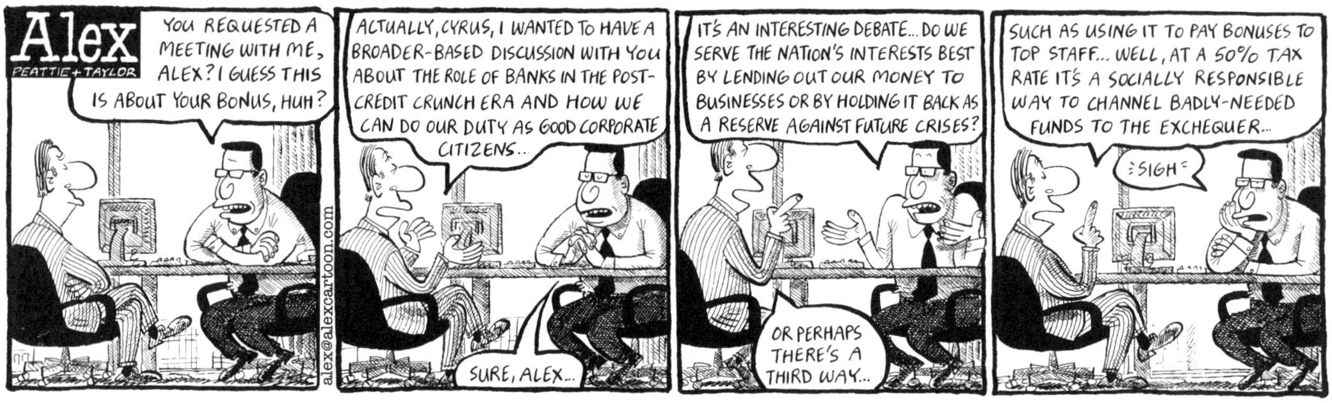
Alex
PEATTIE + TAYLOR
YOU REQUESTED A MEETING WITH ME, ALEX? I GUESS THIS IS ABOUT YOUR BONUS, HUH?
alex@alexcartoon.com
ACTUALLY, CYRUS, I WANTED TO HAVE A BROADER-BASED DISCUSSION WITH YOU ABOUT THE ROLE OF BANKS IN THE POST-CREDIT CRUNCH ERA AND HOW WE CAN DO OUR DUTY AS GOOD CORPORATE CITIZENS...
SURE, ALEX...
IT'S AN INTERESTING DEBATE... DO WE SERVE THE NATION'S INTERESTS BEST BY LENDING OUT OUR MONEY TO BUSINESSES OR BY HOLDING IT BACK AS A RESERVE AGAINST FUTURE CRISES?
OR PERHAPS THERE'S A THIRD WAY...
SUCH AS USING IT TO PAY BONUSES TO TOP STAFF... WELL, AT A 50% TAX RATE IT'S A SOCIALLY RESPONSIBLE WAY TO CHANNEL BADLY-NEEDED FUNDS TO THE EXCHEQUER...
SIGH

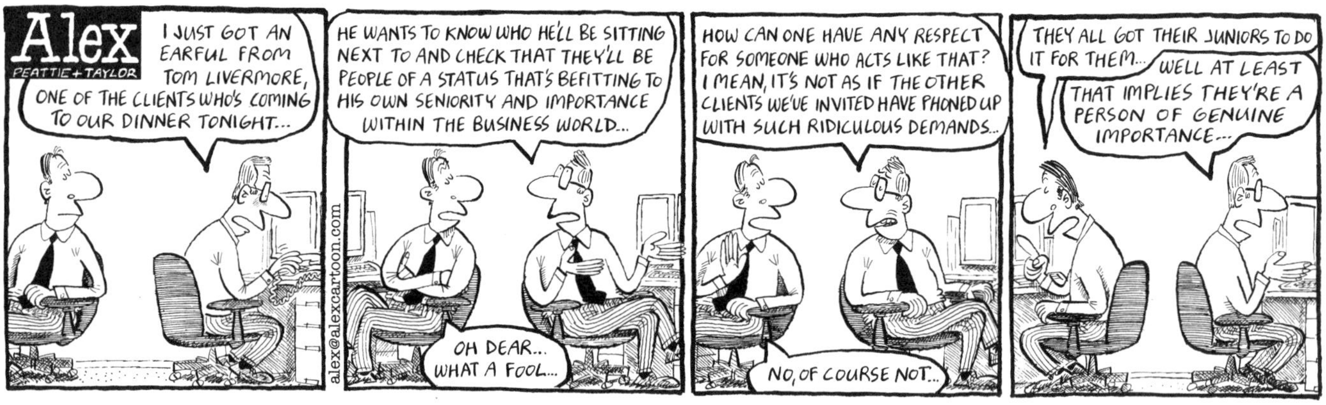
Alex
PEATTIE + TAYLOR
I JUST GOT AN EARFUL FROM TOM LIVERMORE, ONE OF THE CLIENTS WHO'S COMING TO OUR DINNER TONIGHT...
alex@alexcartoon.com
HE WANTS TO KNOW WHO HE'LL BE SITTING NEXT TO AND CHECK THAT THEY'LL BE PEOPLE OF A STATUS THAT'S BEFITTING TO HIS OWN SENIORITY AND IMPORTANCE WITHIN THE BUSINESS WORLD...
OH DEAR... WHAT A FOOL...
HOW CAN ONE HAVE ANY RESPECT FOR SOMEONE WHO ACTS LIKE THAT? I MEAN, IT'S NOT AS IF THE OTHER CLIENTS WE'VE INVITED HAVE PHONED UP WITH SUCH RIDICULOUS DEMANDS...
NO, OF COURSE NOT...
THEY ALL GOT THEIR JUNIORS TO DO IT FOR THEM...
WELL AT LEAST THAT IMPLIES THEY'RE A PERSON OF GENUINE IMPORTANCE...

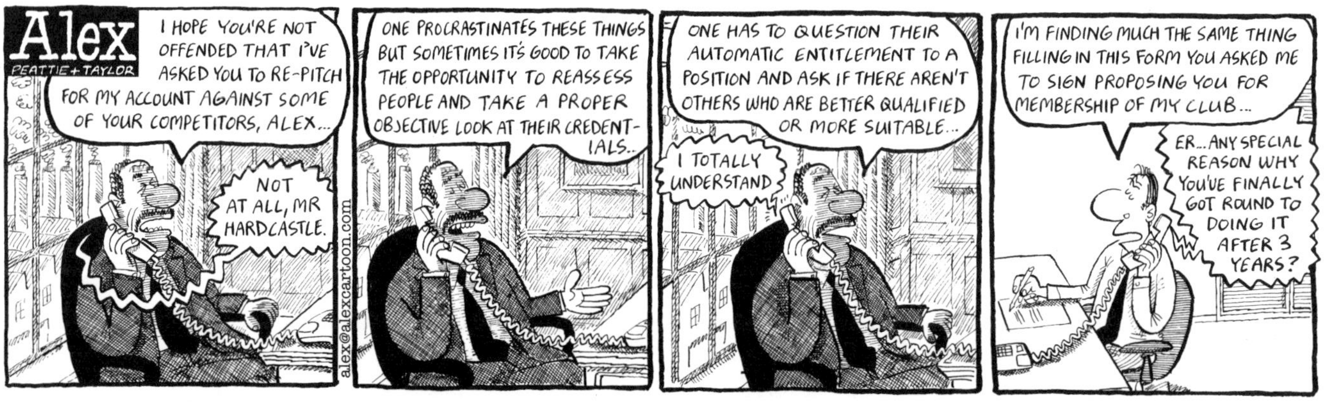
Alex
PEATTIE + TAYLOR
I HOPE YOU'RE NOT OFFENDED THAT I'VE ASKED YOU TO RE-PITCH FOR MY ACCOUNT AGAINST SOME OF YOUR COMPETITORS, ALEX...
NOT AT ALL, MR HARDCASTLE.
alex@alexcartoon.com
ONE PROCRASTINATES THESE THINGS BUT SOMETIMES IT'S GOOD TO TAKE THE OPPORTUNITY TO REASSESS PEOPLE AND TAKE A PROPER OBJECTIVE LOOK AT THEIR CREDENTIALS...
ONE HAS TO QUESTION THEIR AUTOMATIC ENTITLEMENT TO A POSITION AND ASK IF THERE AREN'T OTHERS WHO ARE BETTER QUALIFIED OR MORE SUITABLE...
I TOTALLY UNDERSTAND
I'M FINDING MUCH THE SAME THING FILLING IN THIS FORM YOU ASKED ME TO SIGN PROPOSING YOU FOR MEMBERSHIP OF MY CLUB...
ER... ANY SPECIAL REASON WHY YOU'VE FINALLY GOT ROUND TO DOING IT AFTER 3 YEARS?

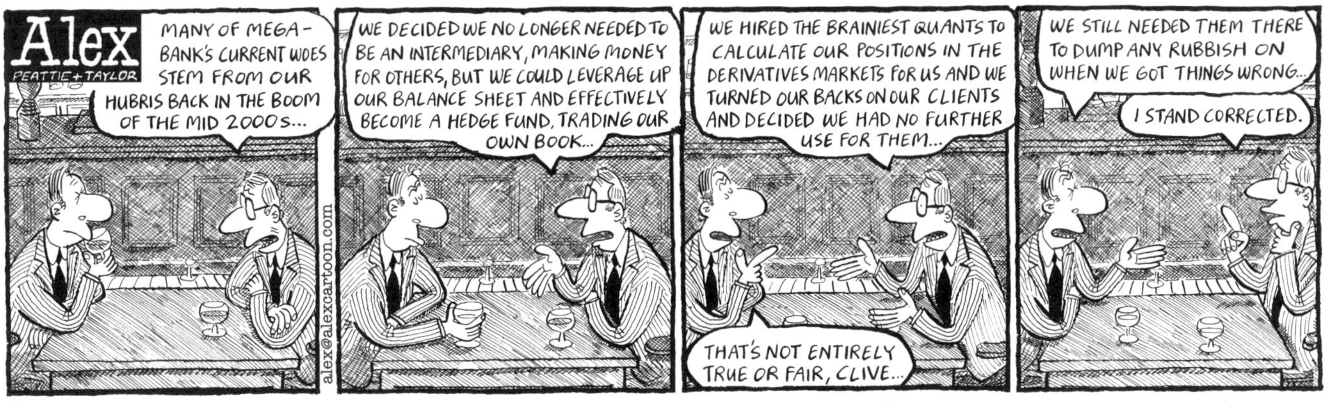
Alex
PEATTIE+TAYLOR
MANY OF MEGA-BANK'S CURRENT WOES STEM FROM OUR HUBRIS BACK IN THE BOOM OF THE MID 2000S...
alex@alexcartoon.com
WE DECIDED WE NO LONGER NEEDED TO BE AN INTERMEDIARY, MAKING MONEY FOR OTHERS, BUT WE COULD LEVERAGE UP OUR BALANCE SHEET AND EFFECTIVELY BECOME A HEDGE FUND, TRADING OUR OWN BOOK...
WE HIRED THE BRAINIEST QUANTS TO CALCULATE OUR POSITIONS IN THE DERIVATIVES MARKETS FOR US AND WE TURNED OUR BACKS ON OUR CLIENTS AND DECIDED WE HAD NO FURTHER USE FOR THEM...
THAT'S NOT ENTIRELY TRUE OR FAIR, CLIVE...
WE STILL NEEDED THEM THERE TO DUMP ANY RUBBISH ON WHEN WE GOT THINGS WRONG...
I STAND CORRECTED.

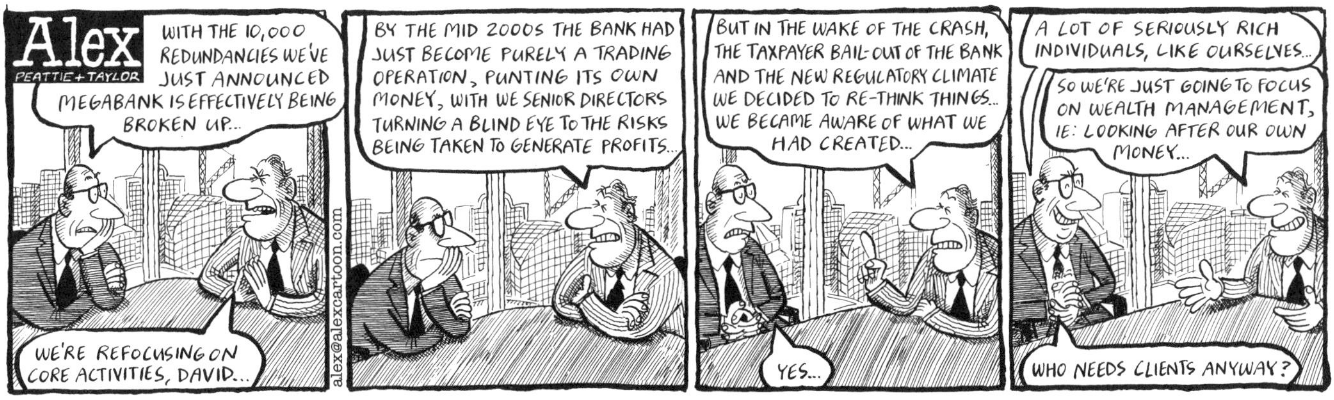
Alex
PEATTIE+TAYLOR
WITH THE 10,000 REDUNDANCIES WE'VE JUST ANNOUNCED MEGABANK IS EFFECTIVELY BEING BROKEN UP...
WE'RE REFOCUSING ON CORE ACTIVITIES, DAVID...
alex@alexcartoon.com
BY THE MID 2000S THE BANK HAD JUST BECOME PURELY A TRADING OPERATION, PUNTING ITS OWN MONEY, WITH WE SENIOR DIRECTORS TURNING A BLIND EYE TO THE RISKS BEING TAKEN TO GENERATE PROFITS...
BUT IN THE WAKE OF THE CRASH, THE TAXPAYER BAIL-OUT OF THE BANK AND THE NEW REGULATORY CLIMATE WE DECIDED TO RE-THINK THINGS... WE BECAME AWARE OF WHAT WE HAD CREATED...
YES...
A LOT OF SERIOUSLY RICH INDIVIDUALS, LIKE OURSELVES...
SO WE'RE JUST GOING TO FOCUS ON WEALTH MANAGEMENT, IE: LOOKING AFTER OUR OWN MONEY...
WHO NEEDS CLIENTS ANYWAY?

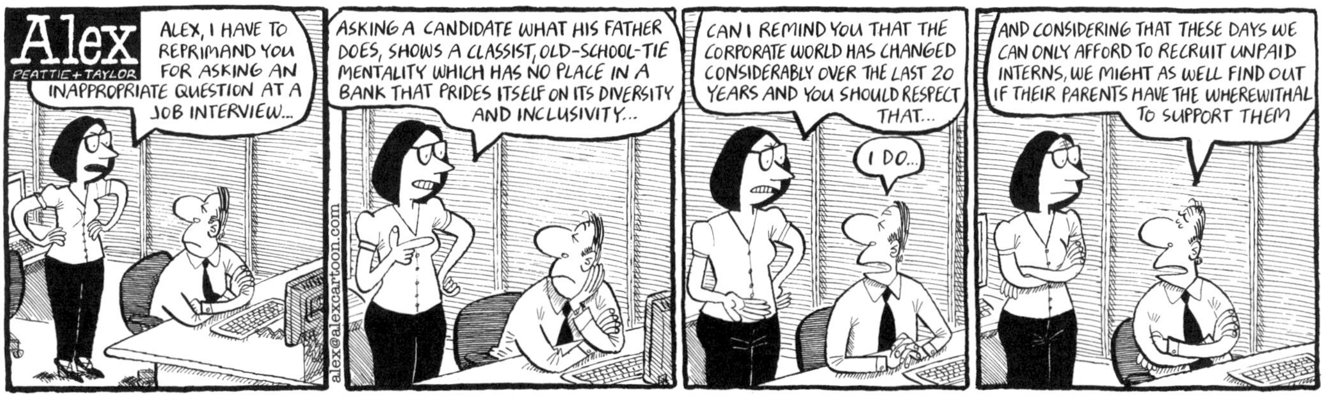
Alex
PEATTIE+TAYLOR
ALEX, I HAVE TO REPRIMAND YOU FOR ASKING AN INAPPROPRIATE QUESTION AT A JOB INTERVIEW...
alex@alexcartoon.com
ASKING A CANDIDATE WHAT HIS FATHER DOES, SHOWS A CLASSIST, OLD-SCHOOL-TIE MENTALITY WHICH HAS NO PLACE IN A BANK THAT PRIDES ITSELF ON ITS DIVERSITY AND INCLUSIVITY...
CAN I REMIND YOU THAT THE CORPORATE WORLD HAS CHANGED CONSIDERABLY OVER THE LAST 20 YEARS AND YOU SHOULD RESPECT THAT...
I DO...
AND CONSIDERING THAT THESE DAYS WE CAN ONLY AFFORD TO RECRUIT UNPAID INTERNS, WE MIGHT AS WELL FIND OUT IF THEIR PARENTS HAVE THE WHEREWITHAL TO SUPPORT THEM

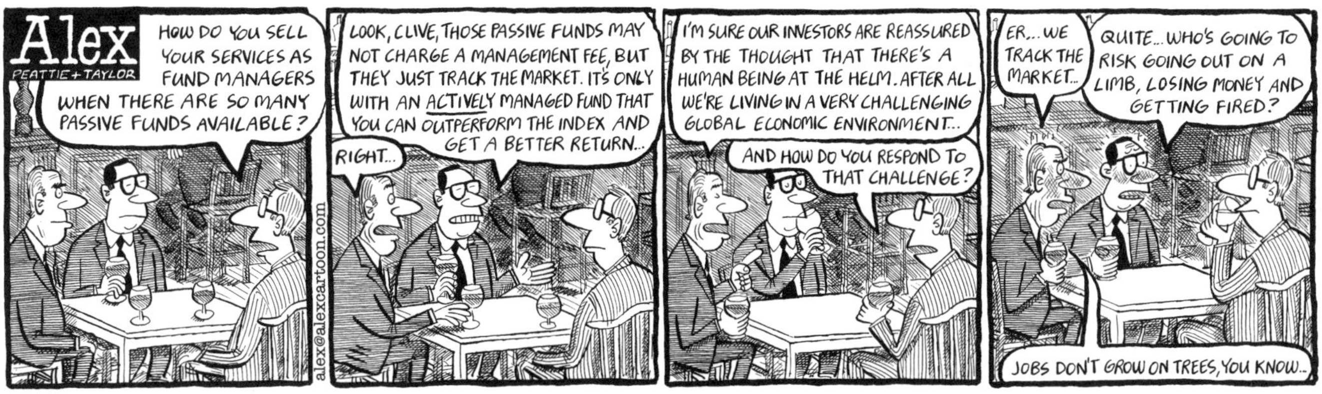
Alex
PEATTIE+TAYLOR
HOW DO YOU SELL YOUR SERVICES AS FUND MANAGERS WHEN THERE ARE SO MANY PASSIVE FUNDS AVAILABLE?
alex@alexcartoon.com
LOOK, CLIVE, THOSE PASSIVE FUNDS MAY NOT CHARGE A MANAGEMENT FEE, BUT THEY JUST TRACK THE MARKET. IT'S ONLY WITH AN ACTIVELY MANAGED FUND THAT YOU CAN OUTPERFORM THE INDEX AND GET A BETTER RETURN...
RIGHT...
I'M SURE OUR INVESTORS ARE REASSURED BY THE THOUGHT THAT THERE'S A HUMAN BEING AT THE HELM. AFTER ALL WE'RE LIVING IN A VERY CHALLENGING GLOBAL ECONOMIC ENVIRONMENT...
AND HOW DO YOU RESPOND TO THAT CHALLENGE?
ER... WE TRACK THE MARKET...
QUITE... WHO'S GOING TO RISK GOING OUT ON A LIMB, LOSING MONEY AND GETTING FIRED?
JOBS DON'T GROW ON TREES, YOU KNOW...

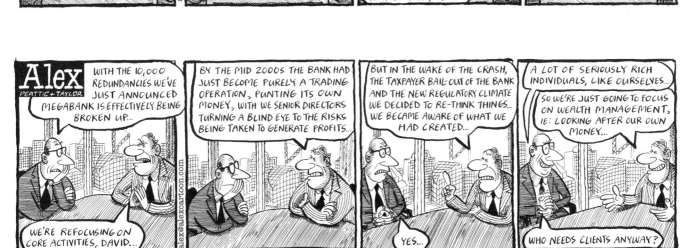

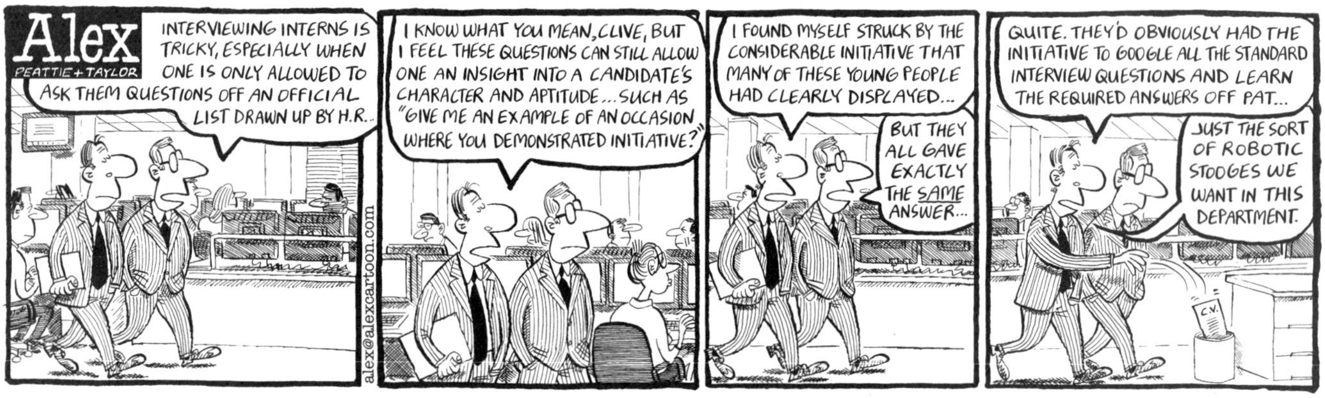
Alex
PEATTIE+TAYLOR
INTERVIEWING INTERNS IS TRICKY, ESPECIALLY WHEN ONE IS ONLY ALLOWED TO ASK THEM QUESTIONS OFF AN OFFICIAL LIST DRAWN UP BY H.R...
I KNOW WHAT YOU MEAN, CLIVE, BUT I FEEL THESE QUESTIONS CAN STILL ALLOW ONE AN INSIGHT INTO A CANDIDATE'S CHARACTER AND APTITUDE... SUCH AS "GIVE ME AN EXAMPLE OF AN OCCASION WHERE YOU DEMONSTRATED INITIATIVE?"
alex@alexcartoon.com
I FOUND MYSELF STRUCK BY THE CONSIDERABLE INITIATIVE THAT MANY OF THESE YOUNG PEOPLE HAD CLEARLY DISPLAYED...
BUT THEY ALL GAVE EXACTLY THE SAME ANSWER...
QUITE. THEY'D OBVIOUSLY HAD THE INITIATIVE TO GOOGLE ALL THE STANDARD INTERVIEW QUESTIONS AND LEARN THE REQUIRED ANSWERS OFF PAT...
JUST THE SORT OF ROBOTIC STOOGES WE WANT IN THIS DEPARTMENT.
C.V.

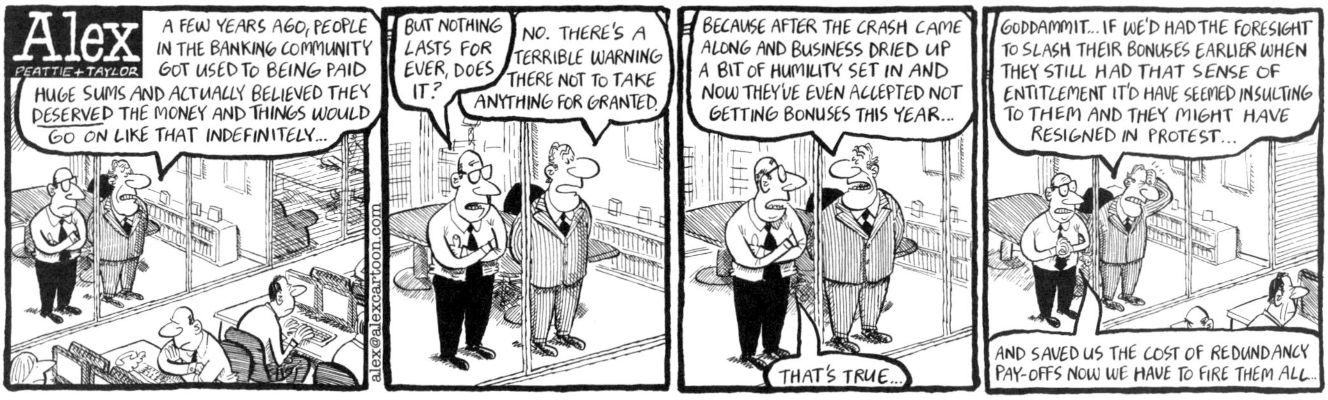
Alex
PEATTIE+TAYLOR
A FEW YEARS AGO, PEOPLE IN THE BANKING COMMUNITY GOT USED TO BEING PAID HUGE SUMS AND ACTUALLY BELIEVED THEY DESERVED THE MONEY AND THINGS WOULD GO ON LIKE THAT INDEFINITELY...
alex@alexcartoon.com
BUT NOTHING LASTS FOR EVER, DOES IT?
NO. THERE'S A TERRIBLE WARNING THERE NOT TO TAKE ANYTHING FOR GRANTED.
BECAUSE AFTER THE CRASH CAME ALONG AND BUSINESS DRIED UP A BIT OF HUMILITY SET IN AND NOW THEY'VE EVEN ACCEPTED NOT GETTING BONUSES THIS YEAR...
THAT'S TRUE...
GODDAMMIT... IF WE'D HAD THE FORESIGHT TO SLASH THEIR BONUSES EARLIER WHEN THEY STILL HAD THAT SENSE OF ENTITLEMENT IT'D HAVE SEEMED INSULTING TO THEM AND THEY MIGHT HAVE RESIGNED IN PROTEST...
AND SAVED US THE COST OF REDUNDANCY PAY-OFFS NOW WE HAVE TO FIRE THEM ALL...

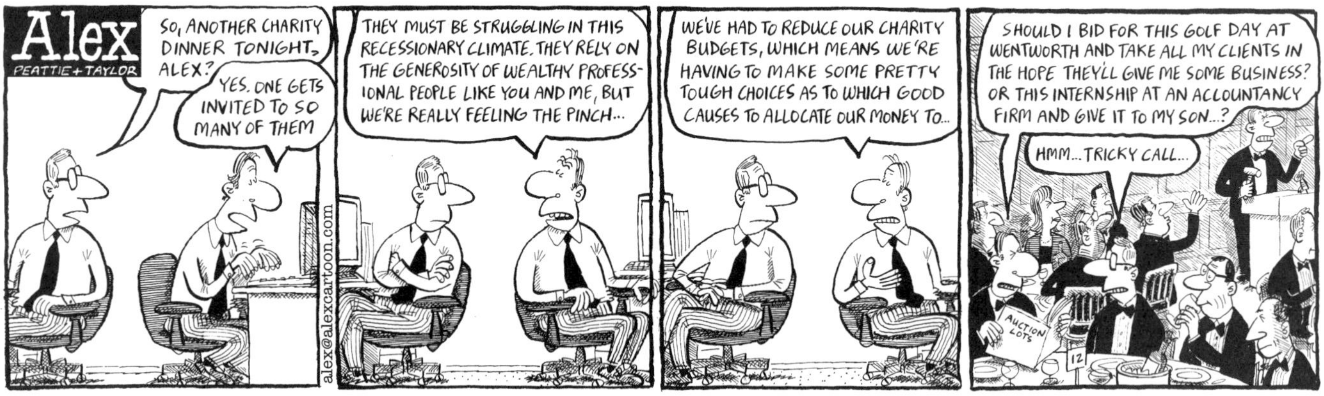
Alex
PEATTIE+TAYLOR
SO, ANOTHER CHARITY DINNER TONIGHT, ALEX?
YES. ONE GETS INVITED TO SO MANY OF THEM
alex@alexcartoon.com
THEY MUST BE STRUGGLING IN THIS RECESSIONARY CLIMATE. THEY RELY ON THE GENEROSITY OF WEALTHY PROFESSIONAL PEOPLE LIKE YOU AND ME, BUT WE'RE REALLY FEELING THE PINCH...
WE'VE HAD TO REDUCE OUR CHARITY BUDGETS, WHICH MEANS WE'RE HAVING TO MAKE SOME PRETTY TOUGH CHOICES AS TO WHICH GOOD CAUSES TO ALLOCATE OUR MONEY TO...
SHOULD I BID FOR THIS GOLF DAY AT WENTWORTH AND TAKE ALL MY CLIENTS IN THE HOPE THEY'LL GIVE ME SOME BUSINESS? OR THIS INTERNSHIP AT AN ACCOUNTANCY FIRM AND GIVE IT TO MY SON...?
HMM... TRICKY CALL...
AUCTION LOTS
12

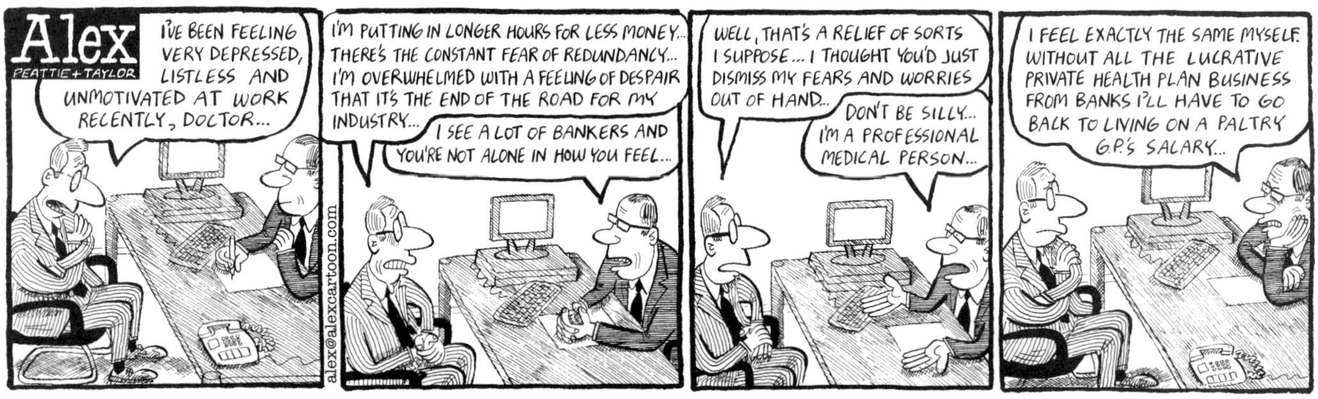
Alex
PEATTIE+TAYLOR
I'VE BEEN FEELING VERY DEPRESSED, LISTLESS AND UNMOTIVATED AT WORK RECENTLY, DOCTOR...
alex@alexcartoon.com
I'M PUTTING IN LONGER HOURS FOR LESS MONEY... THERE'S THE CONSTANT FEAR OF REDUNDANCY... I'M OVERWHELMED WITH A FEELING OF DESPAIR THAT IT'S THE END OF THE ROAD FOR MY INDUSTRY...
I SEE A LOT OF BANKERS AND YOU'RE NOT ALONE IN HOW YOU FEEL...
WELL, THAT'S A RELIEF OF SORTS I SUPPOSE... I THOUGHT YOU'D JUST DISMISS MY FEARS AND WORRIES OUT OF HAND...
DON'T BE SILLY... I'M A PROFESSIONAL MEDICAL PERSON...
I FEEL EXACTLY THE SAME MYSELF. WITHOUT ALL THE LUCRATIVE PRIVATE HEALTH PLAN BUSINESS FROM BANKS I'LL HAVE TO GO BACK TO LIVING ON A PALTRY G.P.'S SALARY...

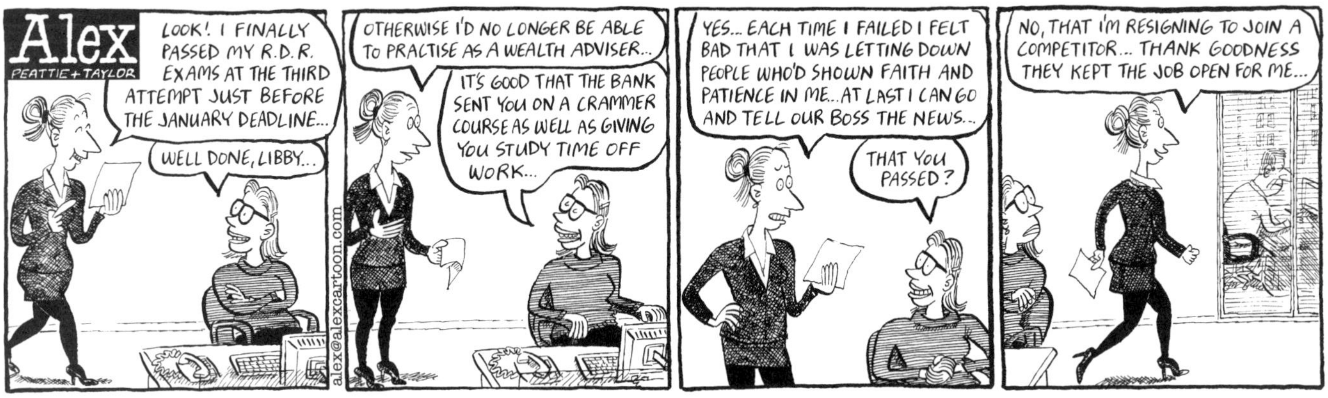
Alex
PEATTIE + TAYLOR
LOOK! I FINALLY PASSED MY R.D.R. EXAMS AT THE THIRD ATTEMPT JUST BEFORE THE JANUARY DEADLINE...
WELL DONE, LIBBY...
alex@alexcartoon.com
OTHERWISE I'D NO LONGER BE ABLE TO PRACTISE AS A WEALTH ADVISER...
IT'S GOOD THAT THE BANK SENT YOU ON A CRAMMER COURSE AS WELL AS GIVING YOU STUDY TIME OFF WORK...
YES... EACH TIME I FAILED I FELT BAD THAT I WAS LETTING DOWN PEOPLE WHO'D SHOWN FAITH AND PATIENCE IN ME... AT LAST I CAN GO AND TELL OUR BOSS THE NEWS...
THAT YOU PASSED?
NO, THAT I'M RESIGNING TO JOIN A COMPETITOR... THANK GOODNESS THEY KEPT THE JOB OPEN FOR ME...

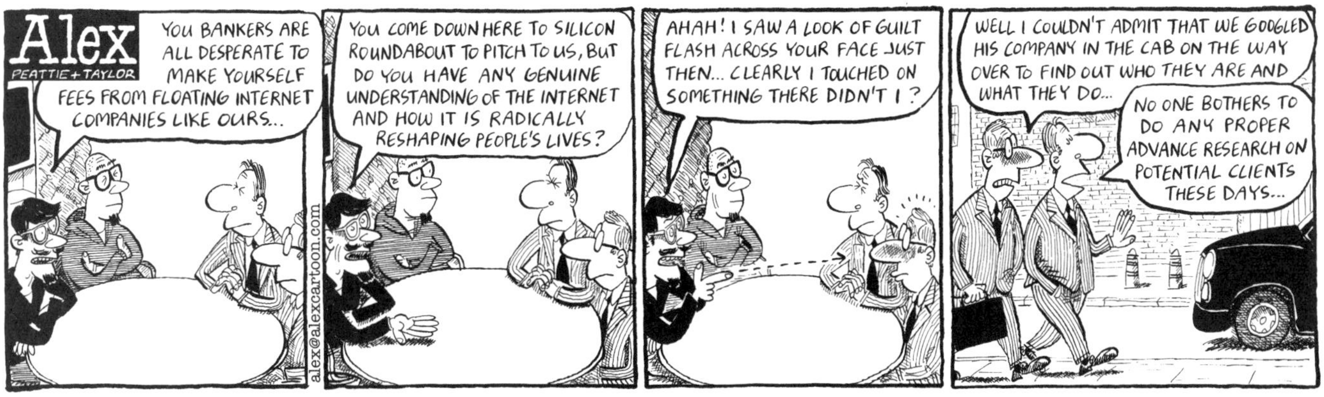
Alex
PEATTIE + TAYLOR
YOU BANKERS ARE ALL DESPERATE TO MAKE YOURSELF FEES FROM FLOATING INTERNET COMPANIES LIKE OURS...
alex@alexcartoon.com
YOU COME DOWN HERE TO SILICON ROUNDABOUT TO PITCH TO US, BUT DO YOU HAVE ANY GENUINE UNDERSTANDING OF THE INTERNET AND HOW IT IS RADICALLY RESHAPING PEOPLE'S LIVES?
AHAH! I SAW A LOOK OF GUILT FLASH ACROSS YOUR FACE JUST THEN... CLEARLY I TOUCHED ON SOMETHING THERE DIDN'T I?
WELL I COULDN'T ADMIT THAT WE GOOGLED HIS COMPANY IN THE CAB ON THE WAY OVER TO FIND OUT WHO THEY ARE AND WHAT THEY DO...
NO ONE BOTHERS TO DO ANY PROPER ADVANCE RESEARCH ON POTENTIAL CLIENTS THESE DAYS...

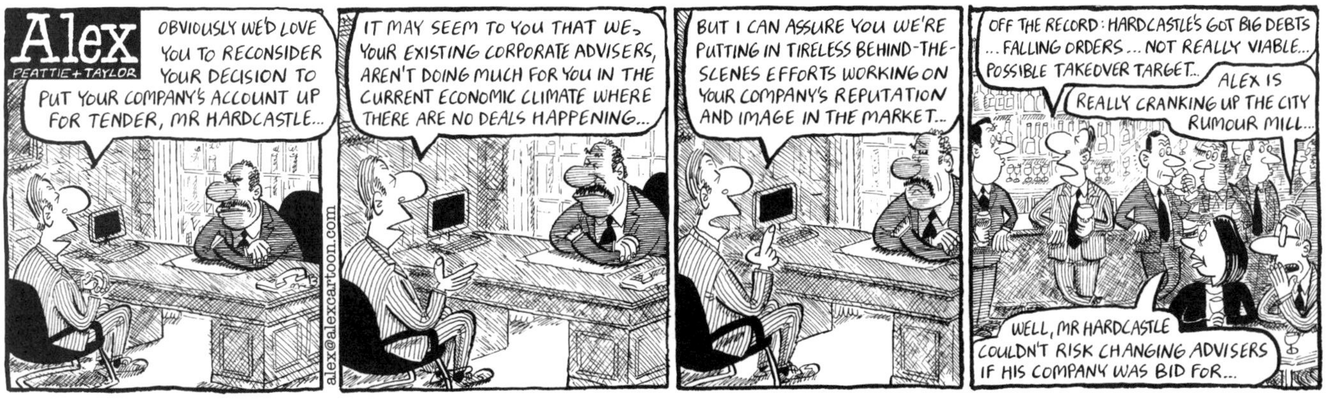
Alex
PEATTIE + TAYLOR
OBVIOUSLY WE'D LOVE YOU TO RECONSIDER YOUR DECISION TO PUT YOUR COMPANY'S ACCOUNT UP FOR TENDER, MR HARDCASTLE...
alex@alexcartoon.com
IT MAY SEEM TO YOU THAT WE, YOUR EXISTING CORPORATE ADVISERS, AREN'T DOING MUCH FOR YOU IN THE CURRENT ECONOMIC CLIMATE WHERE THERE ARE NO DEALS HAPPENING...
BUT I CAN ASSURE YOU WE'RE PUTTING IN TIRELESS BEHIND-THE-SCENES EFFORTS WORKING ON YOUR COMPANY'S REPUTATION AND IMAGE IN THE MARKET...
OFF THE RECORD: HARDCASTLE'S GOT BIG DEBTS ... FALLING ORDERS ... NOT REALLY VIABLE... POSSIBLE TAKEOVER TARGET...
ALEX IS REALLY CRANKING UP THE CITY RUMOUR MILL...
WELL, MR HARDCASTLE COULDN'T RISK CHANGING ADVISERS IF HIS COMPANY WAS BID FOR...

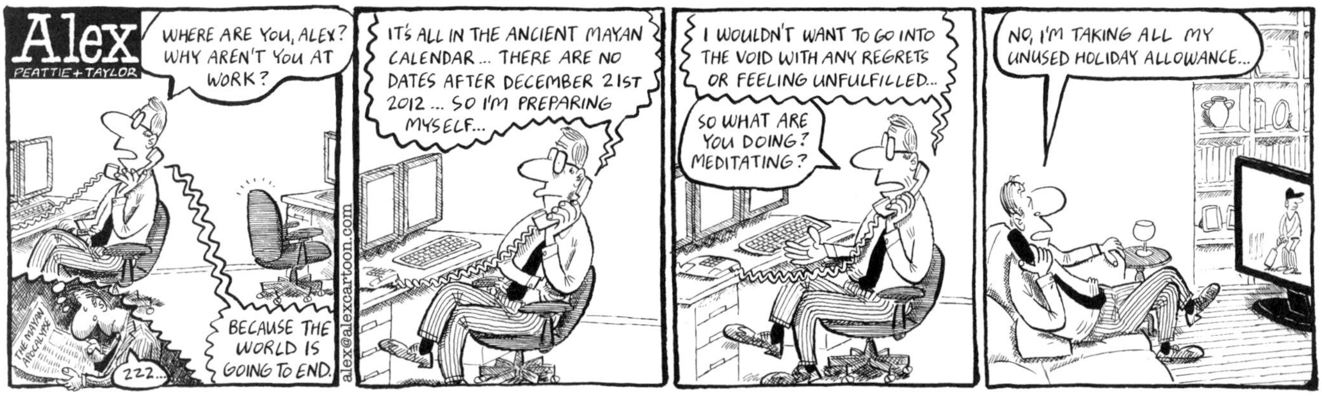
Alex
PEATTIE + TAYLOR
WHERE ARE YOU, ALEX? WHY AREN'T YOU AT WORK?
BECAUSE THE WORLD IS GOING TO END.
THE MAYAN APOCALYPSE
ZZZ...
alex@alexcartoon.com
IT'S ALL IN THE ANCIENT MAYAN CALENDAR... THERE ARE NO DATES AFTER DECEMBER 21ST 2012 ... SO I'M PREPARING MYSELF...
I WOULDN'T WANT TO GO INTO THE VOID WITH ANY REGRETS OR FEELING UNFULFILLED...
SO WHAT ARE YOU DOING? MEDITATING?
NO, I'M TAKING ALL MY UNUSED HOLIDAY ALLOWANCE...

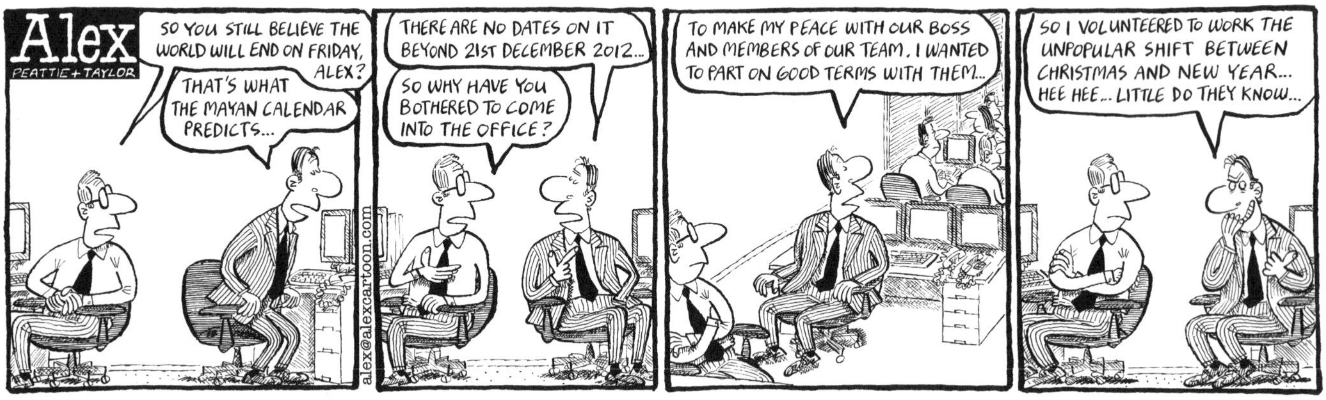
Alex
PEATTIE + TAYLOR
SO YOU STILL BELIEVE THE WORLD WILL END ON FRIDAY, ALEX?
THAT'S WHAT THE MAYAN CALENDAR PREDICTS...
THERE ARE NO DATES ON IT BEYOND 21ST DECEMBER 2012...
SO WHY HAVE YOU BOTHERED TO COME INTO THE OFFICE?
alex@alexcartoon.com
TO MAKE MY PEACE WITH OUR BOSS AND MEMBERS OF OUR TEAM. I WANTED TO PART ON GOOD TERMS WITH THEM...
SO I VOLUNTEERED TO WORK THE UNPOPULAR SHIFT BETWEEN CHRISTMAS AND NEW YEAR... HEE HEE... LITTLE DO THEY KNOW...

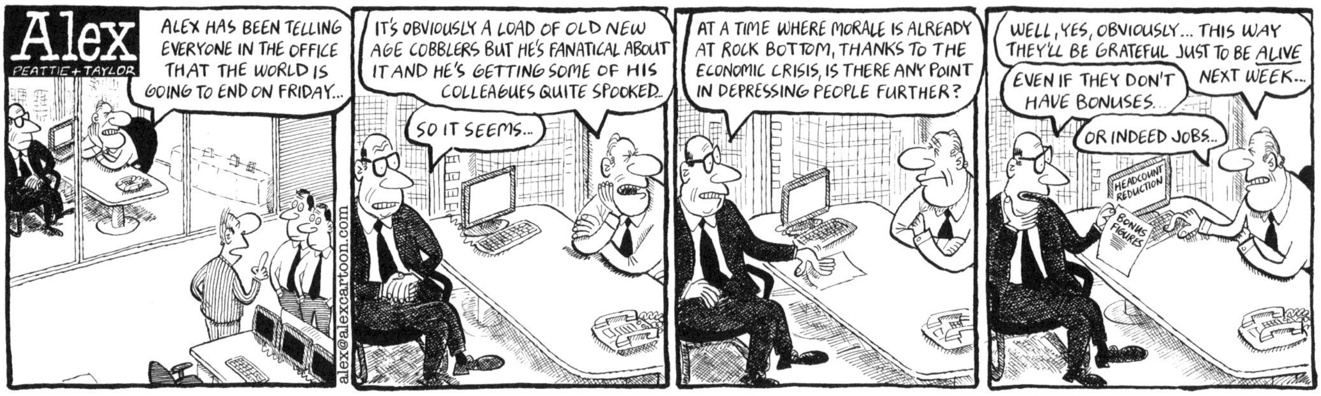
Alex
PEATTIE + TAYLOR
ALEX HAS BEEN TELLING EVERYONE IN THE OFFICE THAT THE WORLD IS GOING TO END ON FRIDAY...
alex@alexcartoon.com
IT'S OBVIOUSLY A LOAD OF OLD NEW AGE COBBLERS BUT HE'S FANATICAL ABOUT IT AND HE'S GETTING SOME OF HIS COLLEAGUES QUITE SPOOKED...
SO IT SEEMS...
AT A TIME WHERE MORALE IS ALREADY AT ROCK BOTTOM, THANKS TO THE ECONOMIC CRISIS, IS THERE ANY POINT IN DEPRESSING PEOPLE FURTHER?
WELL, YES, OBVIOUSLY... THIS WAY THEY'LL BE GRATEFUL JUST TO BE ALIVE NEXT WEEK...
EVEN IF THEY DON'T HAVE BONUSES...
OR INDEED JOBS...
HEADCOUNT REDUCTION
BONUS FIGURES

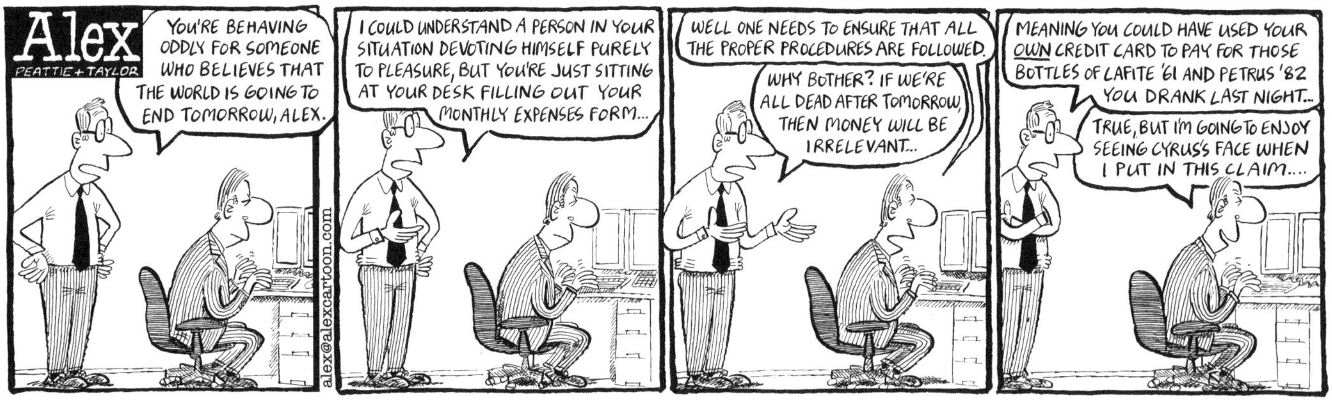
Alex
PEATTIE + TAYLOR
YOU'RE BEHAVING ODDLY FOR SOMEONE WHO BELIEVES THAT THE WORLD IS GOING TO END TOMORROW, ALEX.
alex@alexcartoon.com
I COULD UNDERSTAND A PERSON IN YOUR SITUATION DEVOTING HIMSELF PURELY TO PLEASURE, BUT YOU'RE JUST SITTING AT YOUR DESK FILLING OUT YOUR MONTHLY EXPENSES FORM...
WELL ONE NEEDS TO ENSURE THAT ALL THE PROPER PROCEDURES ARE FOLLOWED.
WHY BOTHER? IF WE'RE ALL DEAD AFTER TOMORROW, THEN MONEY WILL BE IRRELEVANT...
MEANING YOU COULD HAVE USED YOUR OWN CREDIT CARD TO PAY FOR THOSE BOTTLES OF LAFITE '61 AND PETRUS '82 YOU DRANK LAST NIGHT...
TRUE, BUT I'M GOING TO ENJOY SEEING CYRUS'S FACE WHEN I PUT IN THIS CLAIM....

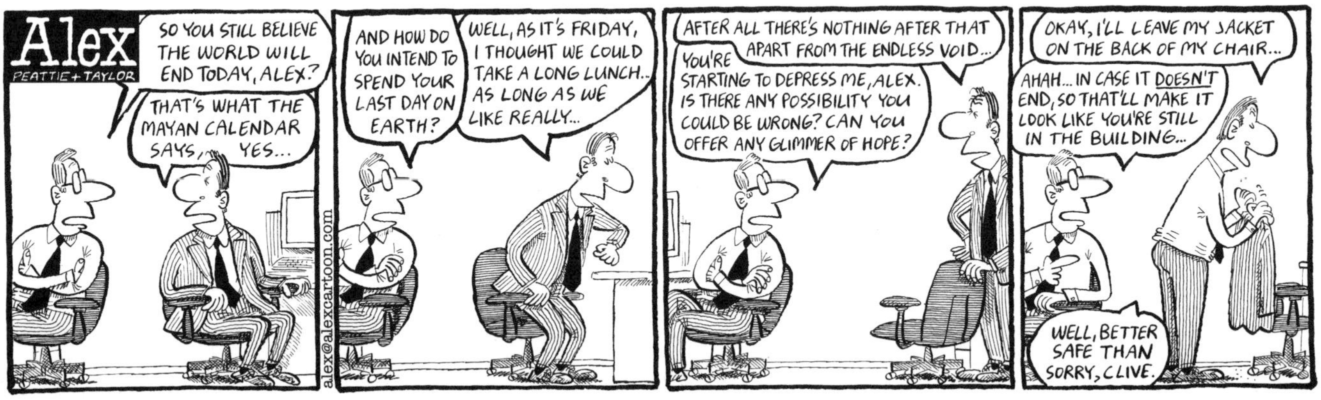
Alex
PEATTIE + TAYLOR
SO YOU STILL BELIEVE THE WORLD WILL END TODAY, ALEX?
THAT'S WHAT THE MAYAN CALENDAR SAYS,... YES...
alex@alexcartoon.com
AND HOW DO YOU INTEND TO SPEND YOUR LAST DAY ON EARTH?
WELL, AS IT'S FRIDAY, I THOUGHT WE COULD TAKE A LONG LUNCH... AS LONG AS WE LIKE REALLY...
AFTER ALL THERE'S NOTHING AFTER THAT APART FROM THE ENDLESS VOID...
YOU'RE STARTING TO DEPRESS ME, ALEX. IS THERE ANY POSSIBILITY YOU COULD BE WRONG? CAN YOU OFFER ANY GLIMMER OF HOPE?
OKAY, I'LL LEAVE MY JACKET ON THE BACK OF MY CHAIR...
AHAH... IN CASE IT DOESN'T END, SO THAT'LL MAKE IT LOOK LIKE YOU'RE STILL IN THE BUILDING...
WELL, BETTER SAFE THAN SORRY, CLIVE.

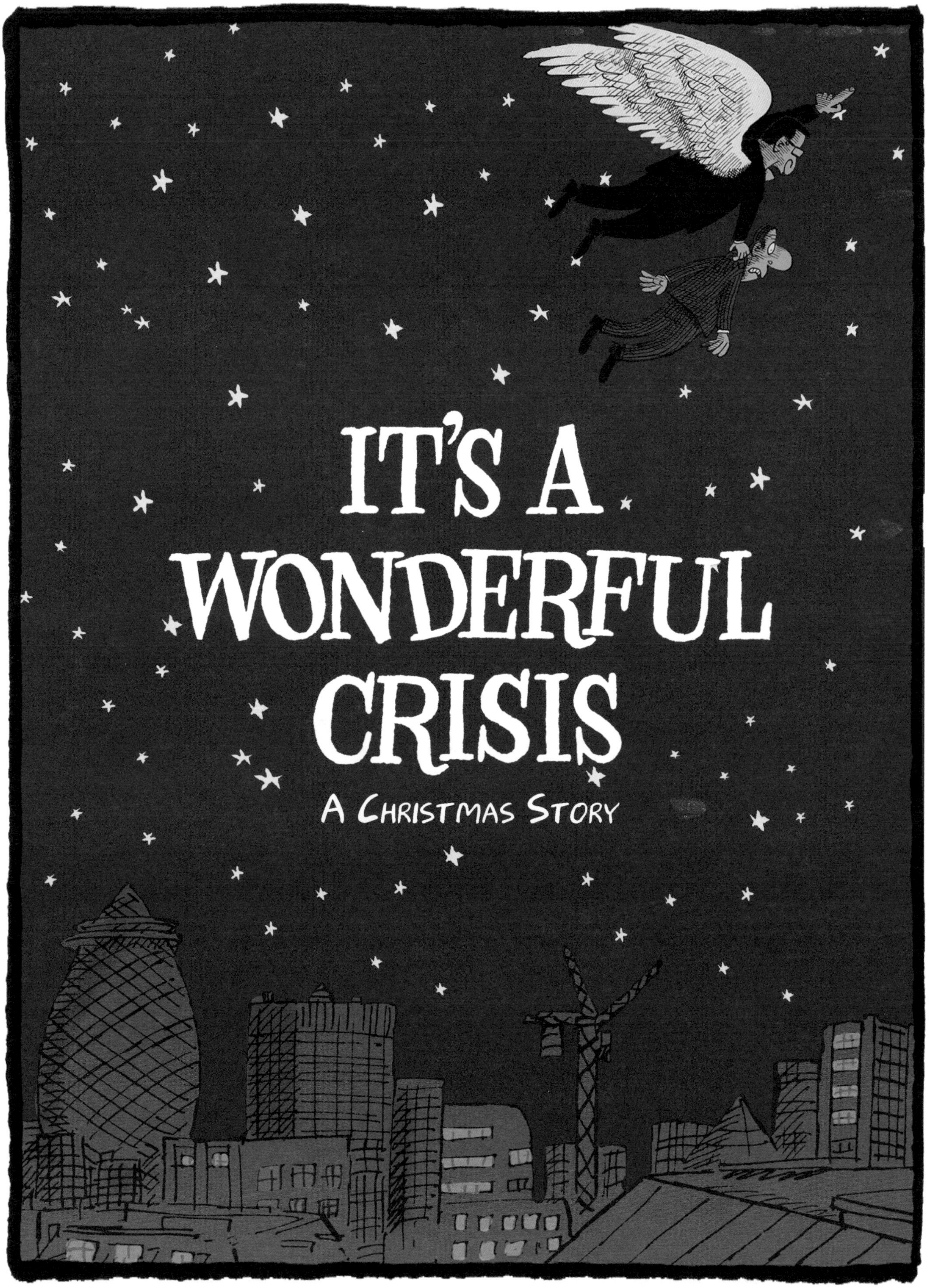
IT'S A
WONDERFUL
CRISIS
A CHRISTMAS STORY

THE CITY OF LONDON... DECEMBER... NOT TOO FAR IN THE FUTURE...

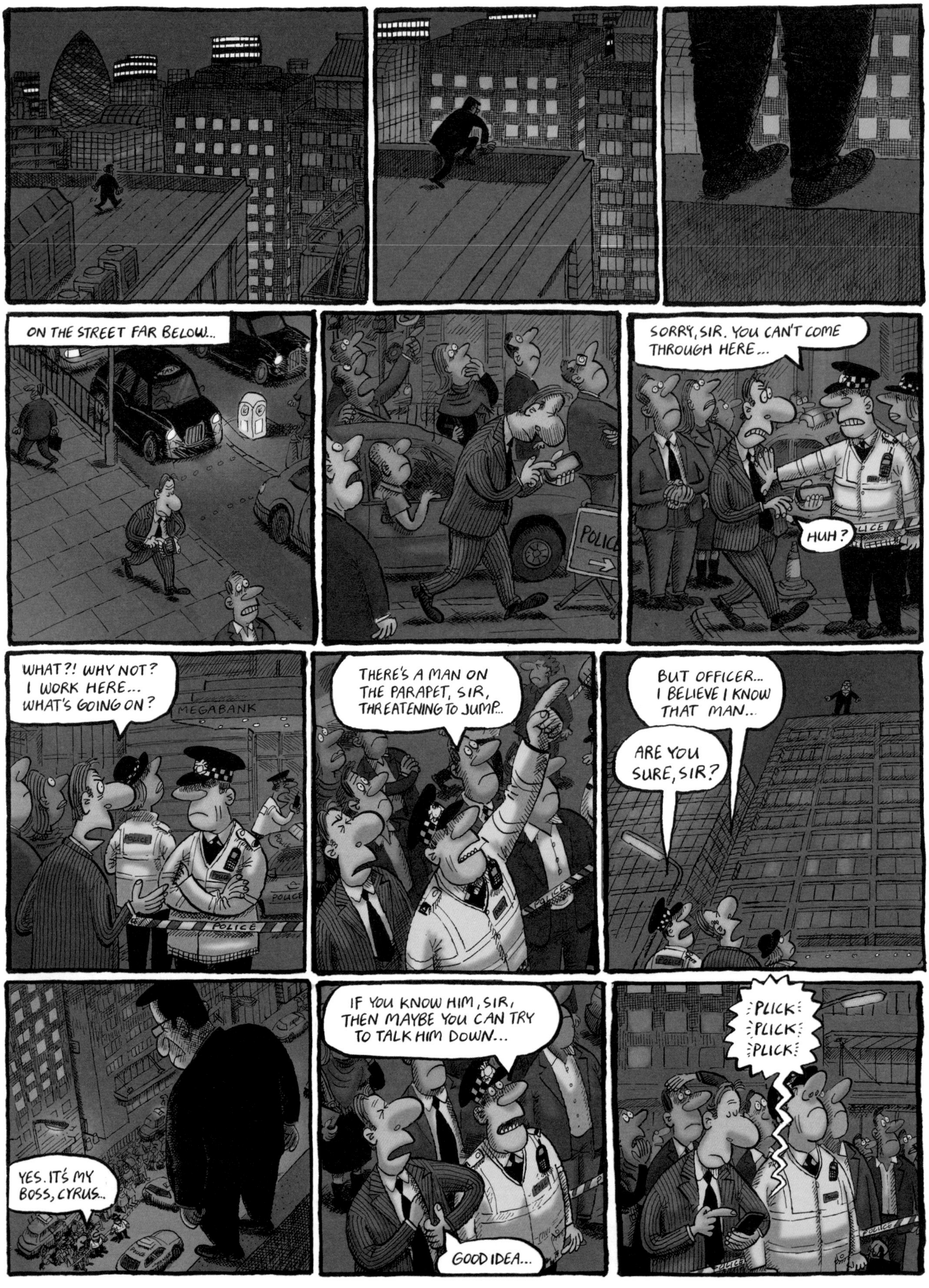
ON THE STREET FAR BELOW...
SORRY, SIR. YOU CAN'T COME THROUGH HERE...
HUH?
POLICE
WHAT?! WHY NOT? I WORK HERE... WHAT'S GOING ON?
MEGABANK
POLICE
THERE'S A MAN ON THE PARAPET, SIR, THREATENING TO JUMP...
BUT OFFICER... I BELIEVE I KNOW THAT MAN...
ARE YOU SURE, SIR?
YES. IT'S MY BOSS, CYRUS...
IF YOU KNOW HIM, SIR, THEN MAYBE YOU CAN TRY TO TALK HIM DOWN...
GOOD IDEA...
PLICK
PLICK
PLICK

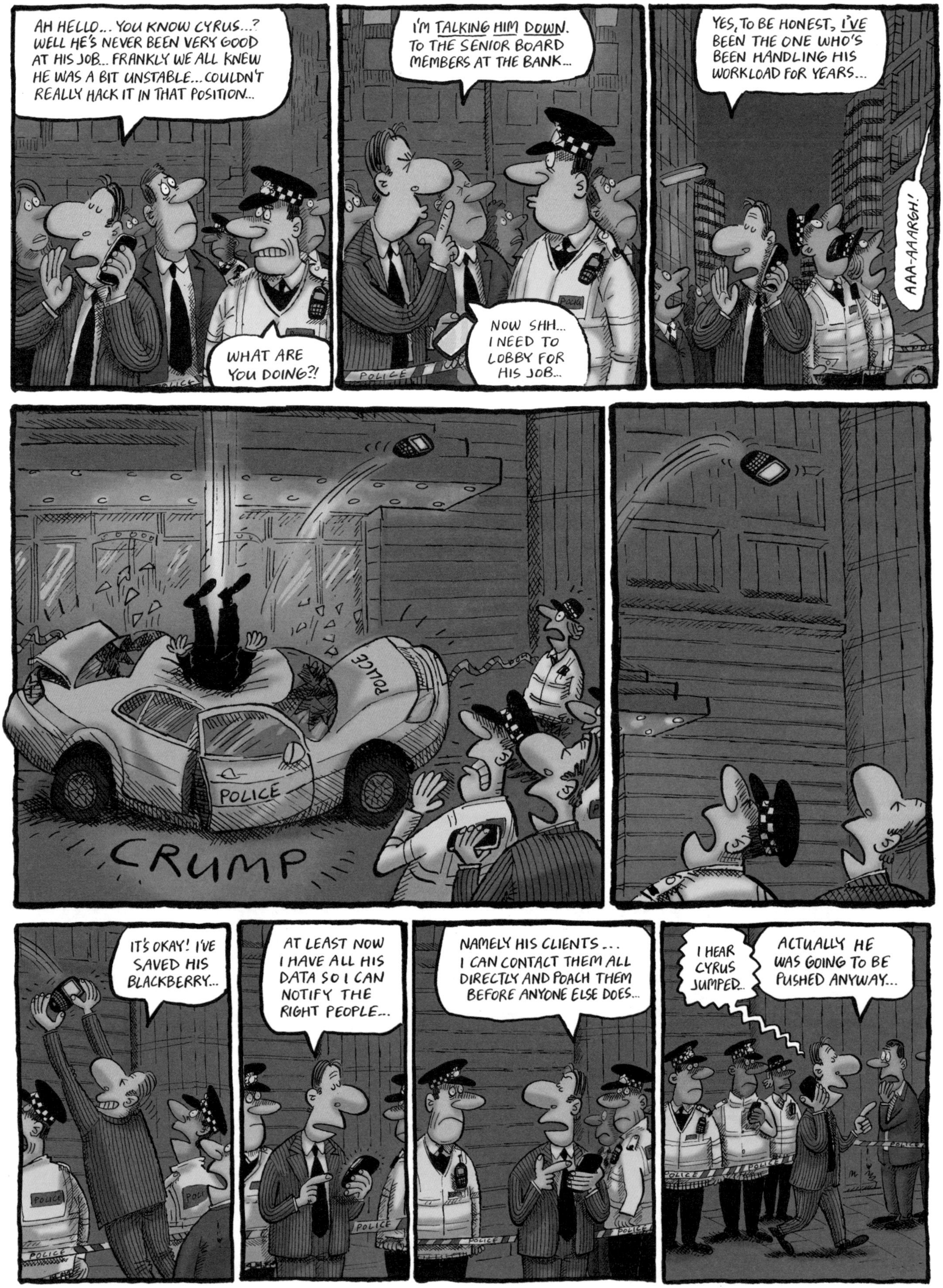
AH HELLO... YOU KNOW CYRUS...? WELL HE'S NEVER BEEN VERY GOOD AT HIS JOB... FRANKLY WE ALL KNEW HE WAS A BIT UNSTABLE... COULDN'T REALLY HACK IT IN THAT POSITION...
WHAT ARE YOU DOING?!
I'M TALKING HIM DOWN. TO THE SENIOR BOARD MEMBERS AT THE BANK...
NOW SHH... I NEED TO LOBBY FOR HIS JOB...
YES, TO BE HONEST, I'VE BEEN THE ONE WHO'S BEEN HANDLING HIS WORKLOAD FOR YEARS...
AAA-AAARGH!
POLICE
CRUMP
IT'S OKAY! I'VE SAVED HIS BLACKBERRY...
AT LEAST NOW I HAVE ALL HIS DATA SO I CAN NOTIFY THE RIGHT PEOPLE...
NAMELY HIS CLIENTS... I CAN CONTACT THEM ALL DIRECTLY AND POACH THEM BEFORE ANYONE ELSE DOES...
I HEAR CYRUS JUMPED...
ACTUALLY HE WAS GOING TO BE PUSHED ANYWAY...

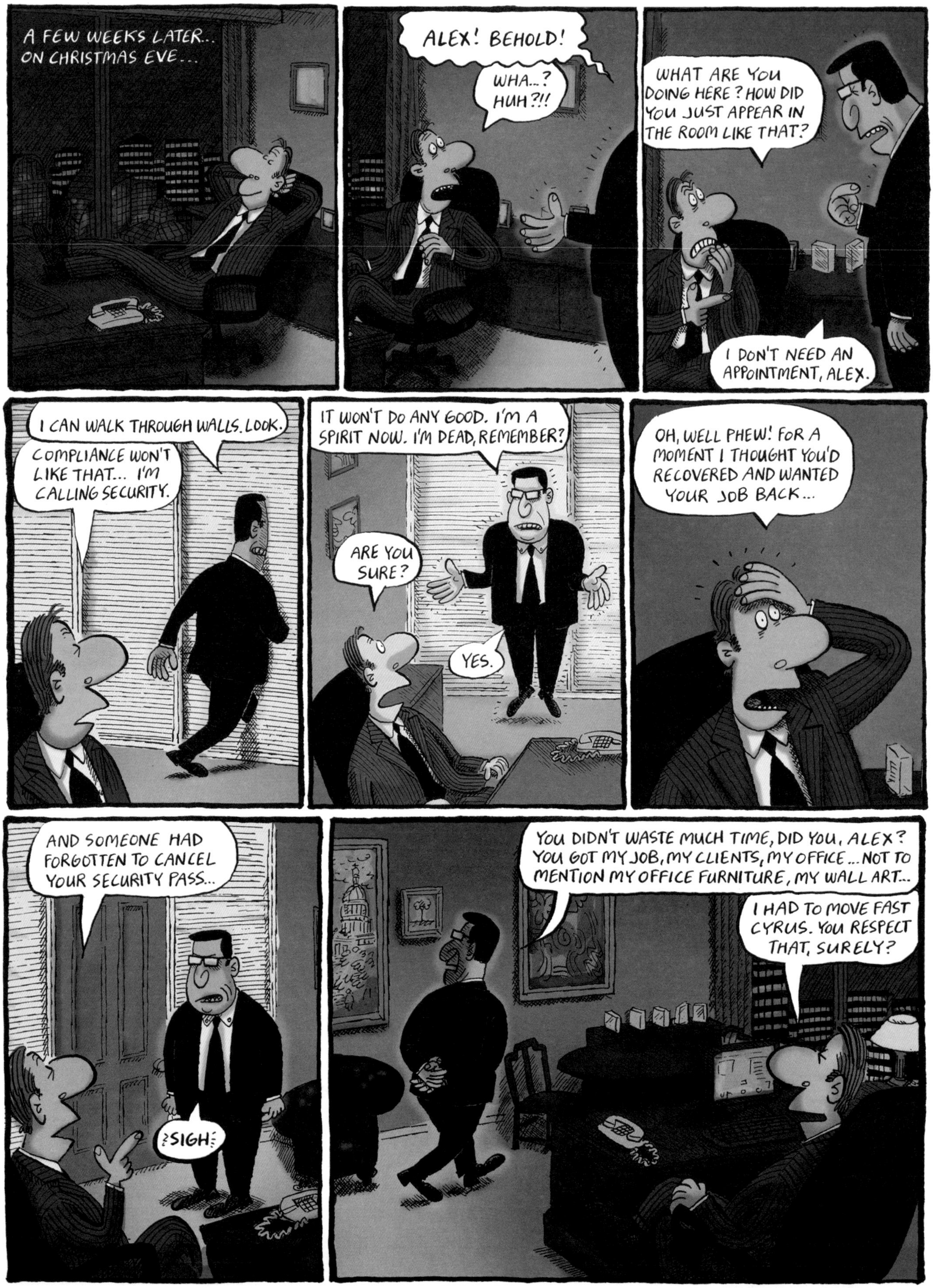
A FEW WEEKS LATER... ON CHRISTMAS EVE...
ALEX! BEHOLD!
WHA...? HUH?!!
WHAT ARE YOU DOING HERE? HOW DID YOU JUST APPEAR IN THE ROOM LIKE THAT?
I DON'T NEED AN APPOINTMENT, ALEX.
I CAN WALK THROUGH WALLS. LOOK.
COMPLIANCE WON'T LIKE THAT... I'M CALLING SECURITY.
IT WON'T DO ANY GOOD. I'M A SPIRIT NOW. I'M DEAD, REMEMBER?
ARE YOU SURE?
YES.
OH, WELL PHEW! FOR A MOMENT I THOUGHT YOU'D RECOVERED AND WANTED YOUR JOB BACK...
AND SOMEONE HAD FORGOTTEN TO CANCEL YOUR SECURITY PASS...
SIGH
YOU DIDN'T WASTE MUCH TIME, DID YOU, ALEX? YOU GOT MY JOB, MY CLIENTS, MY OFFICE... NOT TO MENTION MY OFFICE FURNITURE, MY WALL ART...
I HAD TO MOVE FAST CYRUS. YOU RESPECT THAT, SURELY?

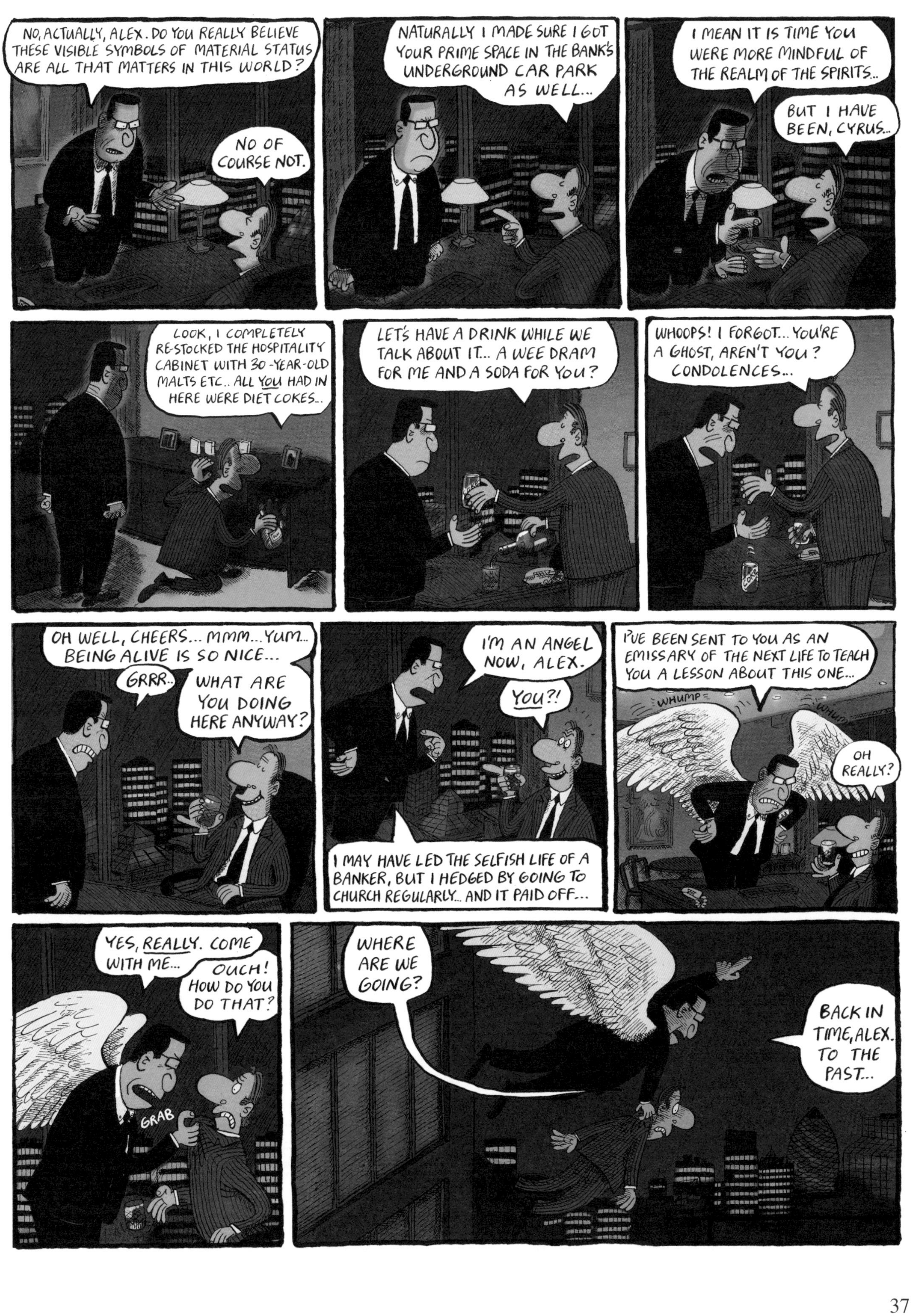
NO, ACTUALLY, ALEX. DO YOU REALLY BELIEVE THESE VISIBLE SYMBOLS OF MATERIAL STATUS ARE ALL THAT MATTERS IN THIS WORLD?
NO OF COURSE NOT.
NATURALLY I MADE SURE I GOT YOUR PRIME SPACE IN THE BANK'S UNDERGROUND CAR PARK AS WELL...
I MEAN IT IS TIME YOU WERE MORE MINDFUL OF THE REALM OF THE SPIRITS...
BUT I HAVE BEEN, CYRUS...
LOOK, I COMPLETELY RE-STOCKED THE HOSPITALITY CABINET WITH 30-YEAR-OLD MALTS ETC.. ALL YOU HAD IN HERE WERE DIET COKES...
LET'S HAVE A DRINK WHILE WE TALK ABOUT IT... A WEE DRAM FOR ME AND A SODA FOR YOU?
WHOOPS! I FORGOT... YOU'RE A GHOST, AREN'T YOU? CONDOLENCES...
OH WELL, CHEERS... MMM... YUM... BEING ALIVE IS SO NICE...
GRRR..
WHAT ARE YOU DOING HERE ANYWAY?
I'M AN ANGEL NOW, ALEX.
YOU?!
I MAY HAVE LED THE SELFISH LIFE OF A BANKER, BUT I HEDGED BY GOING TO CHURCH REGULARLY... AND IT PAID OFF...
I'VE BEEN SENT TO YOU AS AN EMISSARY OF THE NEXT LIFE TO TEACH YOU A LESSON ABOUT THIS ONE...
WHUMP
OH REALLY?
YES, REALLY. COME WITH ME...
OUCH! HOW DO YOU DO THAT?
GRAB
WHERE ARE WE GOING?
BACK IN TIME, ALEX. TO THE PAST...

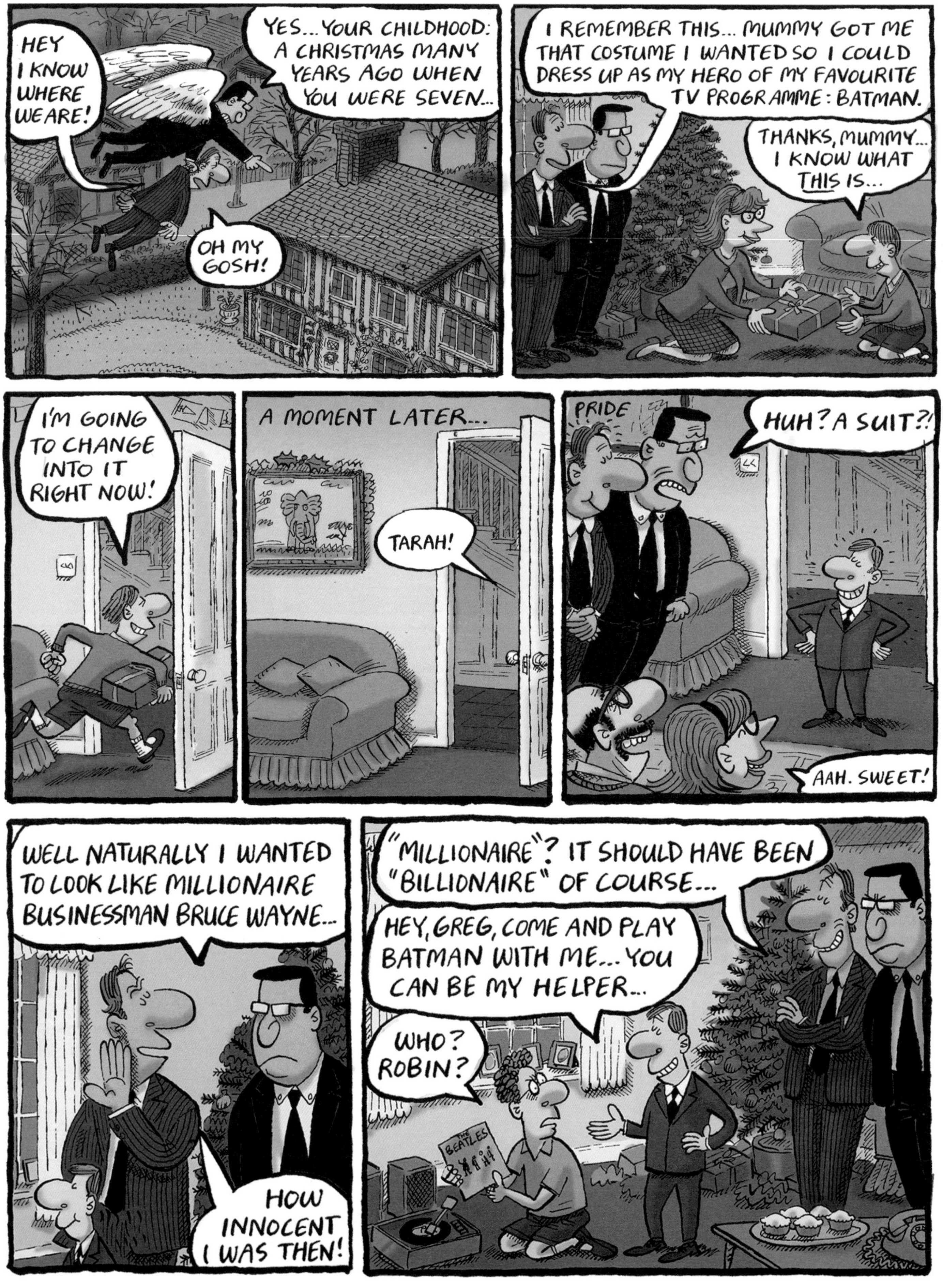
HEY I KNOW WHERE WE ARE!
YES... YOUR CHILDHOOD: A CHRISTMAS MANY YEARS AGO WHEN YOU WERE SEVEN...
OH MY GOSH!
I REMEMBER THIS... MUMMY GOT ME THAT COSTUME I WANTED SO I COULD DRESS UP AS MY HERO OF MY FAVOURITE TV PROGRAMME: BATMAN.
THANKS, MUMMY... I KNOW WHAT THIS IS...
I'M GOING TO CHANGE INTO IT RIGHT NOW!
A MOMENT LATER...
TARAH!
PRIDE
HUH? A SUIT?!
AAH. SWEET!
WELL NATURALLY I WANTED TO LOOK LIKE MILLIONAIRE BUSINESSMAN BRUCE WAYNE...
HOW INNOCENT I WAS THEN!
"MILLIONAIRE"? IT SHOULD HAVE BEEN "BILLIONAIRE" OF COURSE...
HEY, GREG, COME AND PLAY BATMAN WITH ME... YOU CAN BE MY HELPER...
WHO? ROBIN?
THE BEATLES

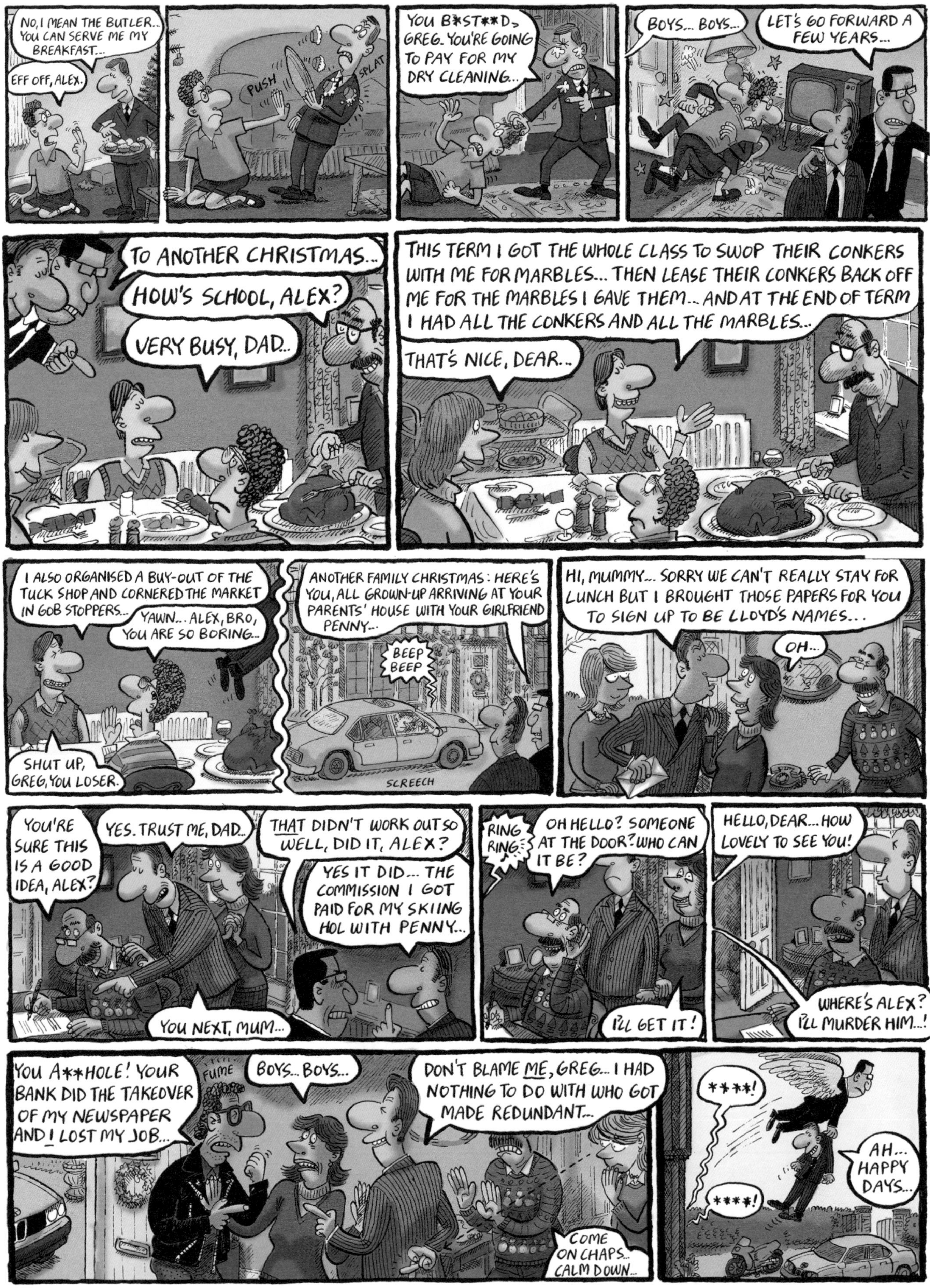
NO, I MEAN THE BUTLER... YOU CAN SERVE ME MY BREAKFAST...
EFF OFF, ALEX.
PUSH
SPLAT
YOU B*ST**D, GREG. YOU'RE GOING TO PAY FOR MY DRY CLEANING...
BOYS... BOYS...
LET'S GO FORWARD A FEW YEARS...
TO ANOTHER CHRISTMAS...
HOW'S SCHOOL, ALEX?
VERY BUSY, DAD...
THIS TERM I GOT THE WHOLE CLASS TO SWOP THEIR CONKERS WITH ME FOR MARBLES... THEN LEASE THEIR CONKERS BACK OFF ME FOR THE MARBLES I GAVE THEM... AND AT THE END OF TERM I HAD ALL THE CONKERS AND ALL THE MARBLES...
THAT'S NICE, DEAR...
I ALSO ORGANISED A BUY-OUT OF THE TUCK SHOP AND CORNERED THE MARKET IN GOB STOPPERS...
YAWN... ALEX, BRO, YOU ARE SO BORING...
SHUT UP, GREG, YOU LOSER.
ANOTHER FAMILY CHRISTMAS: HERE'S YOU, ALL GROWN-UP ARRIVING AT YOUR PARENTS' HOUSE WITH YOUR GIRLFRIEND PENNY...
BEEP BEEP
SCREECH
HI, MUMMY... SORRY WE CAN'T REALLY STAY FOR LUNCH BUT I BROUGHT THOSE PAPERS FOR YOU TO SIGN UP TO BE LLOYD'S NAMES...
OH...
YOU'RE SURE THIS IS A GOOD IDEA, ALEX?
YES. TRUST ME, DAD...
YOU NEXT, MUM...
THAT DIDN'T WORK OUT SO WELL, DID IT, ALEX?
YES IT DID... THE COMMISSION I GOT PAID FOR MY SKIING HOL WITH PENNY...
RING RING
OH HELLO? SOMEONE AT THE DOOR? WHO CAN IT BE?
I'LL GET IT!
HELLO, DEAR... HOW LOVELY TO SEE YOU!
WHERE'S ALEX? I'LL MURDER HIM...!
YOU A**HOLE! YOUR BANK DID THE TAKEOVER OF MY NEWSPAPER AND I LOST MY JOB...
FUME
BOYS... BOYS...
DON'T BLAME ME, GREG... I HAD NOTHING TO DO WITH WHO GOT MADE REDUNDANT...
COME ON CHAPS... CALM DOWN...
****!
****!
AH... HAPPY DAYS...

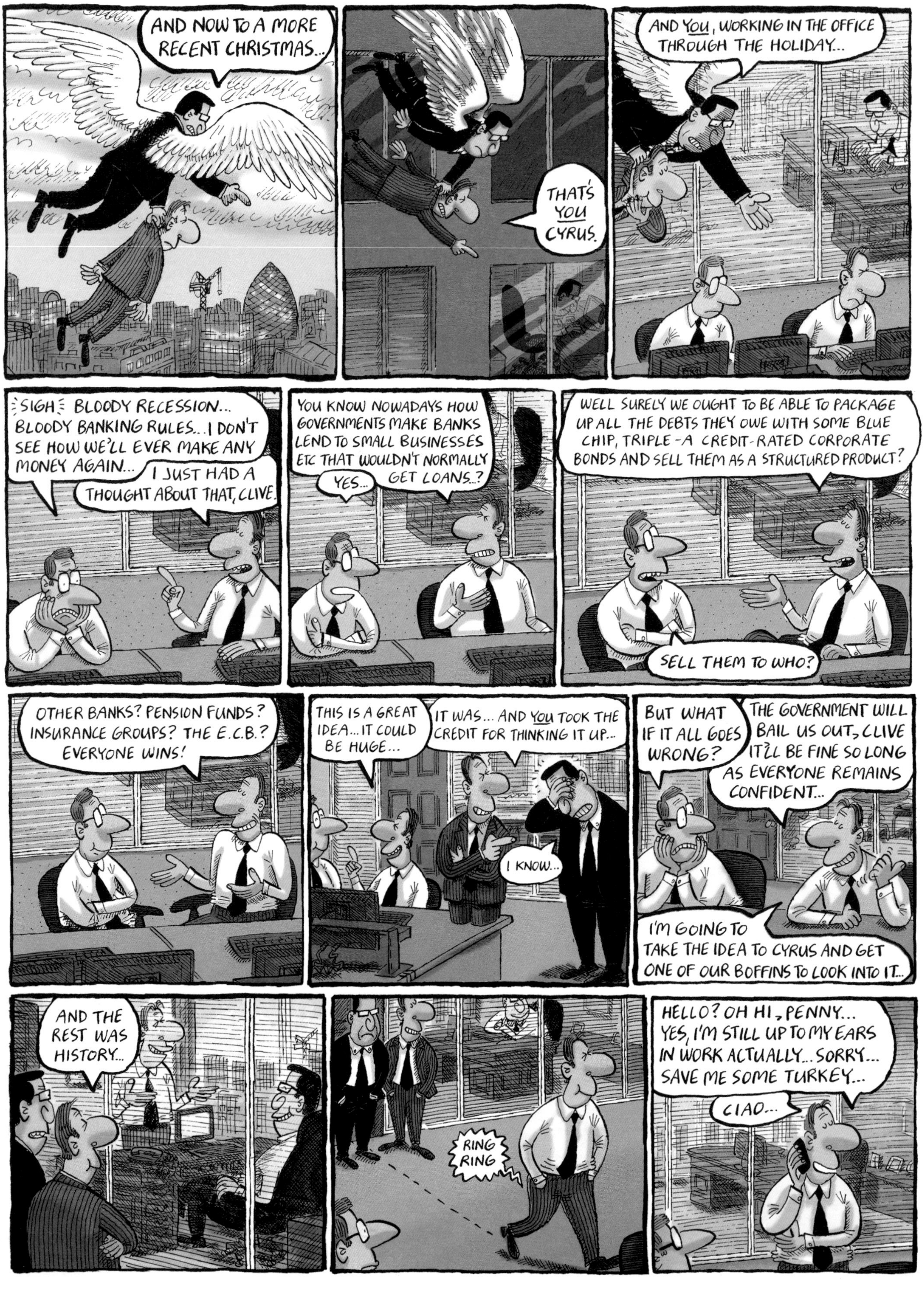
AND NOW TO A MORE RECENT CHRISTMAS...
THAT'S YOU CYRUS.
AND YOU, WORKING IN THE OFFICE THROUGH THE HOLIDAY...
SIGH BLOODY RECESSION... BLOODY BANKING RULES... I DON'T SEE HOW WE'LL EVER MAKE ANY MONEY AGAIN...
I JUST HAD A THOUGHT ABOUT THAT, CLIVE.
YOU KNOW NOWADAYS HOW GOVERNMENTS MAKE BANKS LEND TO SMALL BUSINESSES ETC THAT WOULDN'T NORMALLY GET LOANS...?
YES...
WELL SURELY WE OUGHT TO BE ABLE TO PACKAGE UP ALL THE DEBTS THEY OWE WITH SOME BLUE CHIP, TRIPLE-A CREDIT-RATED CORPORATE BONDS AND SELL THEM AS A STRUCTURED PRODUCT?
SELL THEM TO WHO?
OTHER BANKS? PENSION FUNDS? INSURANCE GROUPS? THE E.C.B.? EVERYONE WINS!
THIS IS A GREAT IDEA... IT COULD BE HUGE...
IT WAS... AND YOU TOOK THE CREDIT FOR THINKING IT UP...
I KNOW...
BUT WHAT IF IT ALL GOES WRONG?
THE GOVERNMENT WILL BAIL US OUT, CLIVE IT'LL BE FINE SO LONG AS EVERYONE REMAINS CONFIDENT...
I'M GOING TO TAKE THE IDEA TO CYRUS AND GET ONE OF OUR BOFFINS TO LOOK INTO IT...
AND THE REST WAS HISTORY...
RING RING
HELLO? OH HI, PENNY... YES, I'M STILL UP TO MY EARS IN WORK ACTUALLY... SORRY... SAVE ME SOME TURKEY...
CIAO...

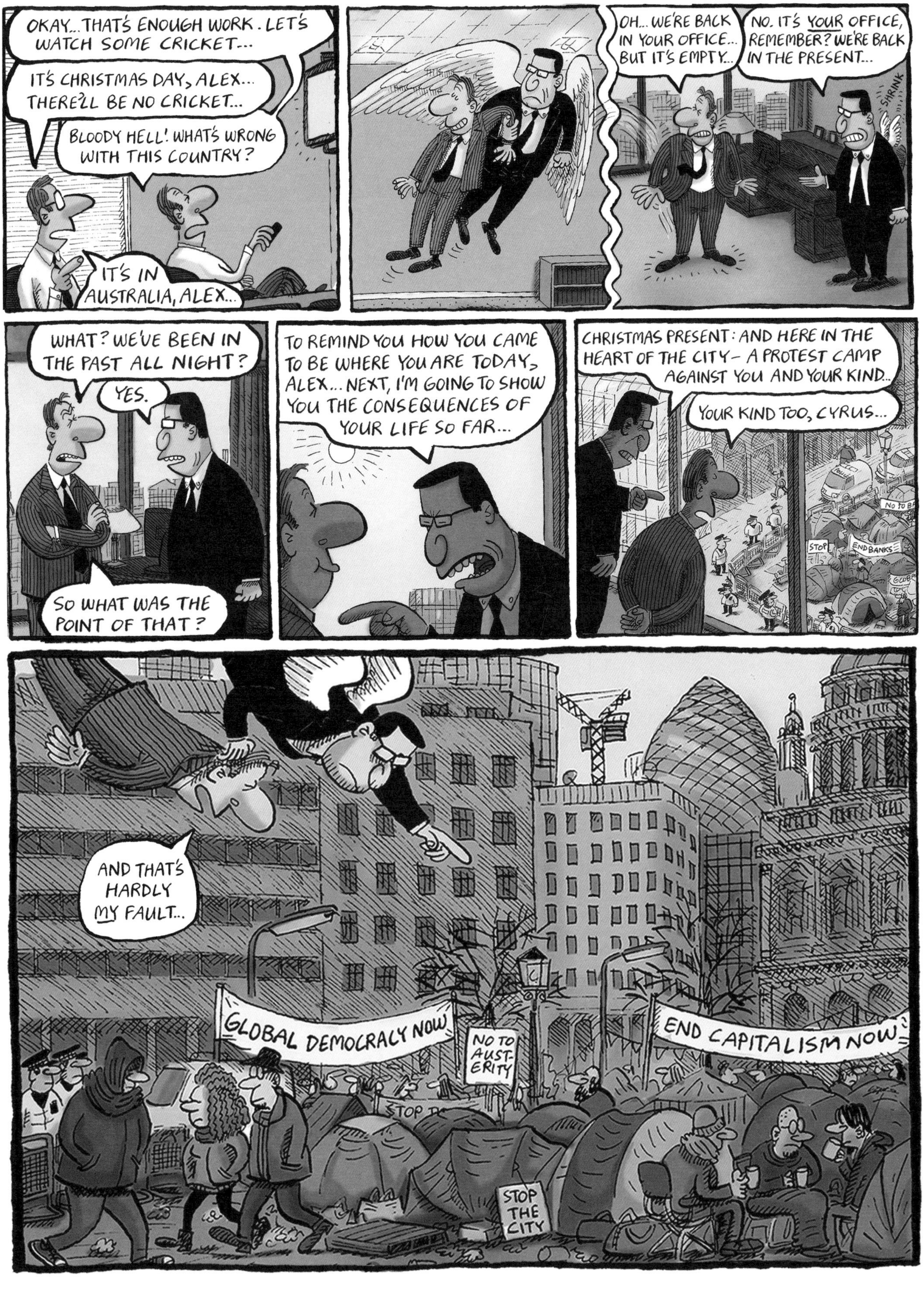
OKAY... THAT'S ENOUGH WORK. LET'S WATCH SOME CRICKET...
IT'S CHRISTMAS DAY, ALEX... THERE'LL BE NO CRICKET...
BLOODY HELL! WHAT'S WRONG WITH THIS COUNTRY?
IT'S IN AUSTRALIA, ALEX...
OH... WE'RE BACK IN YOUR OFFICE... BUT IT'S EMPTY...
NO. IT'S YOUR OFFICE, REMEMBER? WE'RE BACK IN THE PRESENT...
SHRINK
WHAT? WE'VE BEEN IN THE PAST ALL NIGHT?
YES.
SO WHAT WAS THE POINT OF THAT?
TO REMIND YOU HOW YOU CAME TO BE WHERE YOU ARE TODAY, ALEX... NEXT, I'M GOING TO SHOW YOU THE CONSEQUENCES OF YOUR LIFE SO FAR...
CHRISTMAS PRESENT: AND HERE IN THE HEART OF THE CITY – A PROTEST CAMP AGAINST YOU AND YOUR KIND...
YOUR KIND TOO, CYRUS...
STOP
END BANKS
AND THAT'S HARDLY MY FAULT...
GLOBAL DEMOCRACY NOW
NO TO AUSTERITY
END CAPITALISM NOW
STOP THE CITY

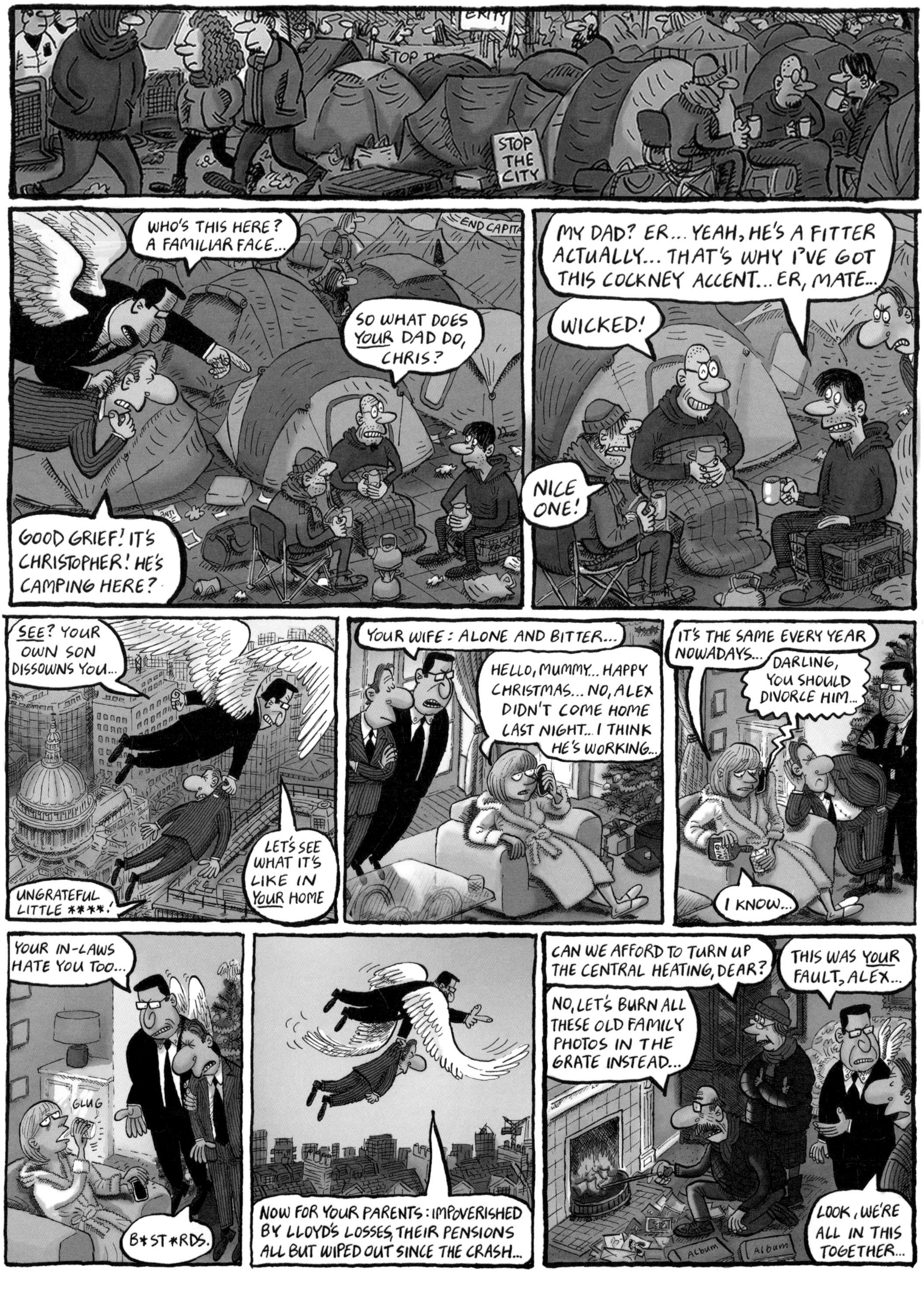
STOP THE CITY
WHO'S THIS HERE? A FAMILIAR FACE...
GOOD GRIEF! IT'S CHRISTOPHER! HE'S CAMPING HERE?
SO WHAT DOES YOUR DAD DO, CHRIS?
MY DAD? ER... YEAH, HE'S A FITTER ACTUALLY... THAT'S WHY I'VE GOT THIS COCKNEY ACCENT... ER, MATE...
WICKED!
NICE ONE!
SEE? YOUR OWN SON DISSOWNS YOU...
UNGRATEFUL LITTLE ****!
LET'S SEE WHAT IT'S LIKE IN YOUR HOME
YOUR WIFE: ALONE AND BITTER...
HELLO, MUMMY... HAPPY CHRISTMAS... NO, ALEX DIDN'T COME HOME LAST NIGHT... I THINK HE'S WORKING...
IT'S THE SAME EVERY YEAR NOWADAYS...
DARLING, YOU SHOULD DIVORCE HIM...
I KNOW...
YOUR IN-LAWS HATE YOU TOO...
GLUG
B*ST*RDS.
NOW FOR YOUR PARENTS: IMPOVERISHED BY LLOYD'S LOSSES, THEIR PENSIONS ALL BUT WIPED OUT SINCE THE CRASH...
CAN WE AFFORD TO TURN UP THE CENTRAL HEATING, DEAR?
NO, LET'S BURN ALL THESE OLD FAMILY PHOTOS IN THE GRATE INSTEAD...
THIS WAS YOUR FAULT, ALEX...
LOOK, WE'RE ALL IN THIS TOGETHER...
Album
Album

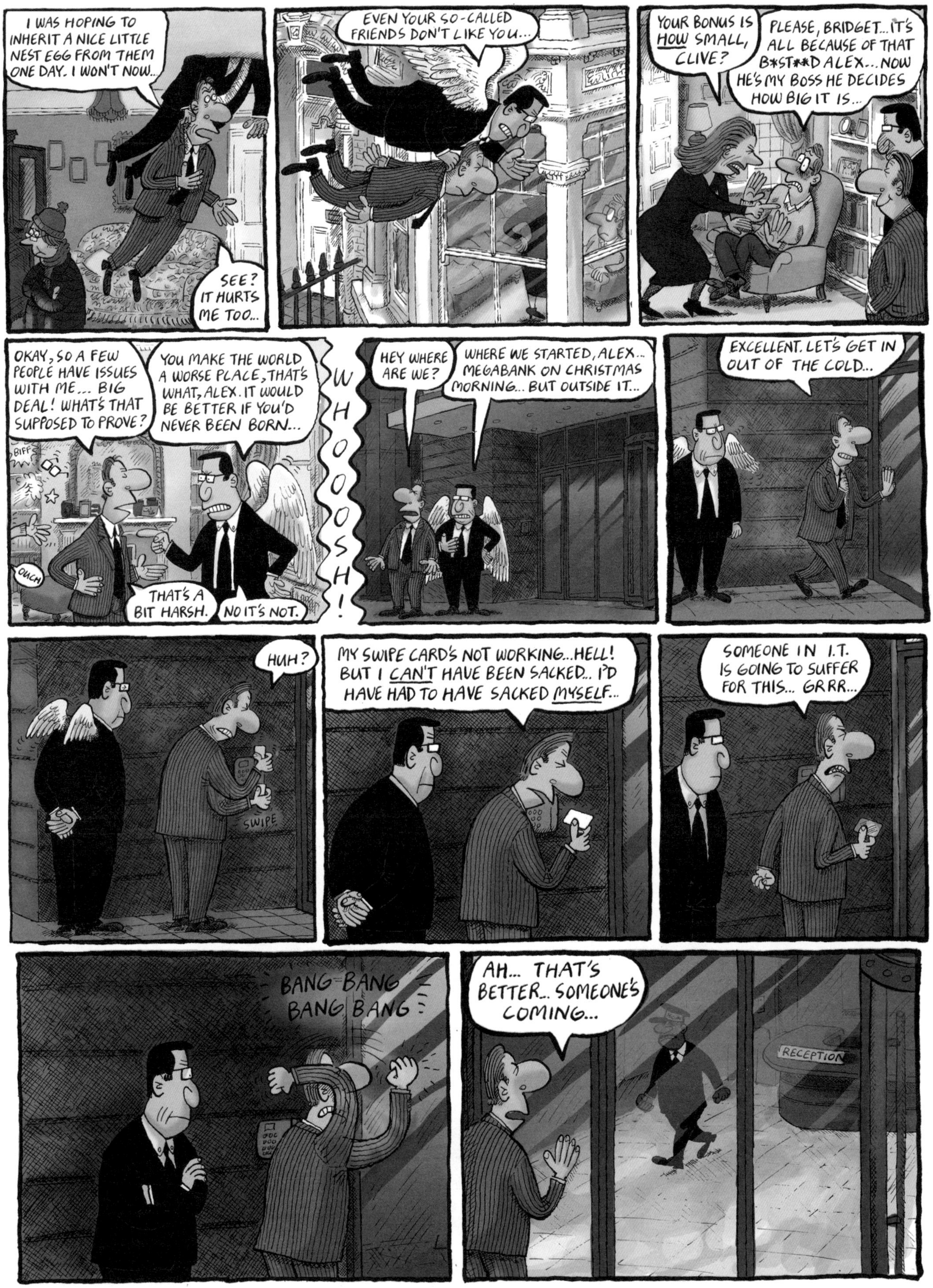
I WAS HOPING TO INHERIT A NICE LITTLE NEST EGG FROM THEM ONE DAY. I WON'T NOW...
SEE? IT HURTS ME TOO...
EVEN YOUR SO-CALLED FRIENDS DON'T LIKE YOU...
YOUR BONUS IS HOW SMALL, CLIVE?
PLEASE, BRIDGET... IT'S ALL BECAUSE OF THAT B*ST**D ALEX... NOW HE'S MY BOSS HE DECIDES HOW BIG IT IS...
OKAY, SO A FEW PEOPLE HAVE ISSUES WITH ME... BIG DEAL! WHAT'S THAT SUPPOSED TO PROVE?
YOU MAKE THE WORLD A WORSE PLACE, THAT'S WHAT, ALEX. IT WOULD BE BETTER IF YOU'D NEVER BEEN BORN...
BIFF
OUCH
THAT'S A BIT HARSH.
NO IT'S NOT.
WHOOOSH!
HEY WHERE ARE WE?
WHERE WE STARTED, ALEX... MEGABANK ON CHRISTMAS MORNING... BUT OUTSIDE IT...
EXCELLENT. LET'S GET IN OUT OF THE COLD...
HUH?
SWIPE
MY SWIPE CARD'S NOT WORKING... HELL! BUT I CAN'T HAVE BEEN SACKED... I'D HAVE HAD TO HAVE SACKED MYSELF...
SOMEONE IN I.T. IS GOING TO SUFFER FOR THIS... GRRR...
BANG BANG BANG BANG
AH... THAT'S BETTER... SOMEONE'S COMING...
RECEPTION

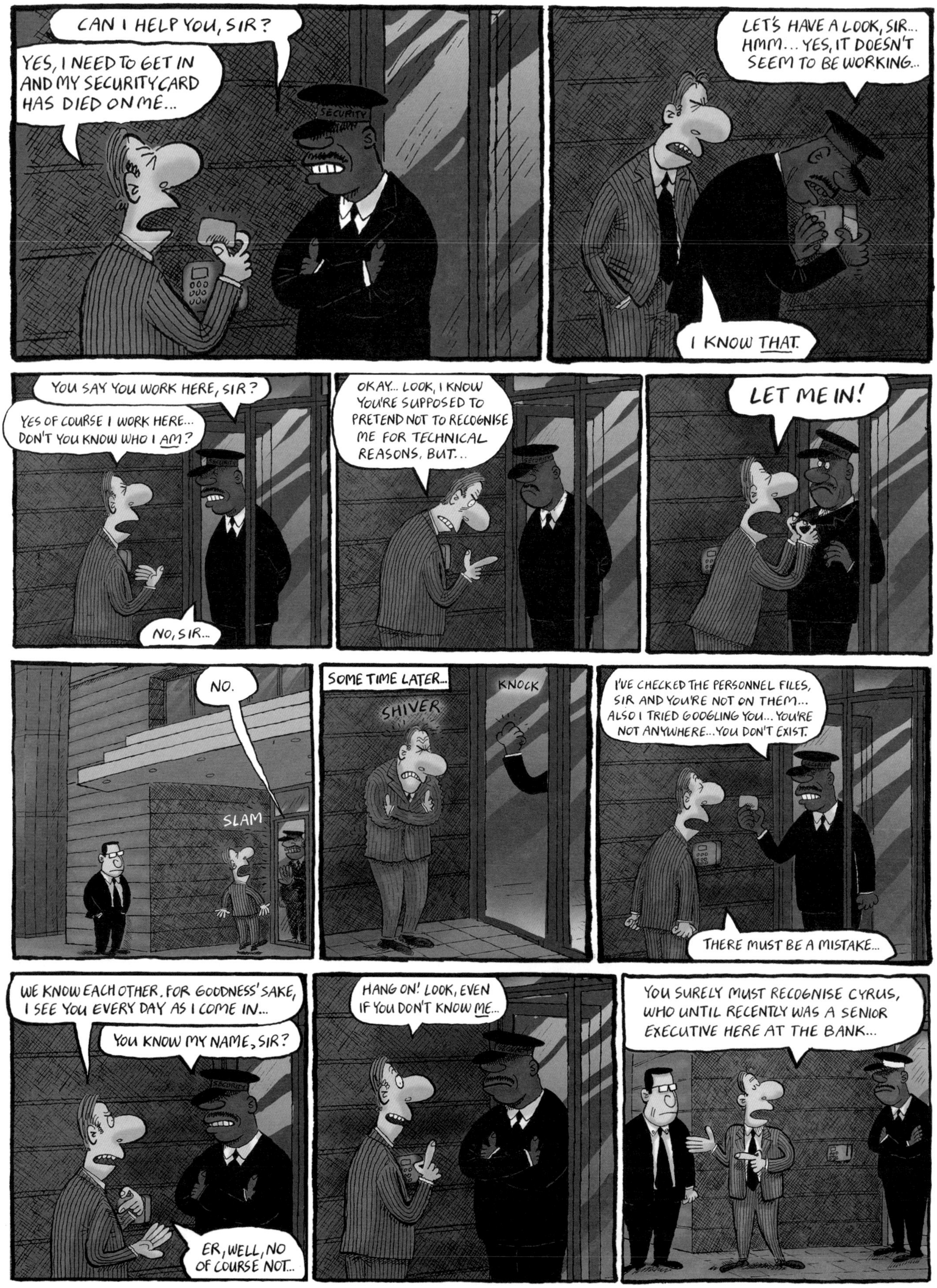
CAN I HELP YOU, SIR?
YES, I NEED TO GET IN AND MY SECURITY CARD HAS DIED ON ME...
SECURITY
LET'S HAVE A LOOK, SIR... HMM... YES, IT DOESN'T SEEM TO BE WORKING...
I KNOW THAT.
YOU SAY YOU WORK HERE, SIR?
YES OF COURSE I WORK HERE... DON'T YOU KNOW WHO I AM?
NO, SIR...
OKAY... LOOK, I KNOW YOU'RE SUPPOSED TO PRETEND NOT TO RECOGNISE ME FOR TECHNICAL REASONS, BUT...
LET ME IN!
NO.
SLAM
SOME TIME LATER...
KNOCK
SHIVER
I'VE CHECKED THE PERSONNEL FILES, SIR AND YOU'RE NOT ON THEM... ALSO I TRIED GOOGLING YOU... YOU'RE NOT ANYWHERE... YOU DON'T EXIST.
THERE MUST BE A MISTAKE...
WE KNOW EACH OTHER. FOR GOODNESS' SAKE, I SEE YOU EVERY DAY AS I COME IN...
YOU KNOW MY NAME, SIR?
ER, WELL, NO OF COURSE NOT...
HANG ON! LOOK, EVEN IF YOU DON'T KNOW ME...
YOU SURELY MUST RECOGNISE CYRUS, WHO UNTIL RECENTLY WAS A SENIOR EXECUTIVE HERE AT THE BANK...

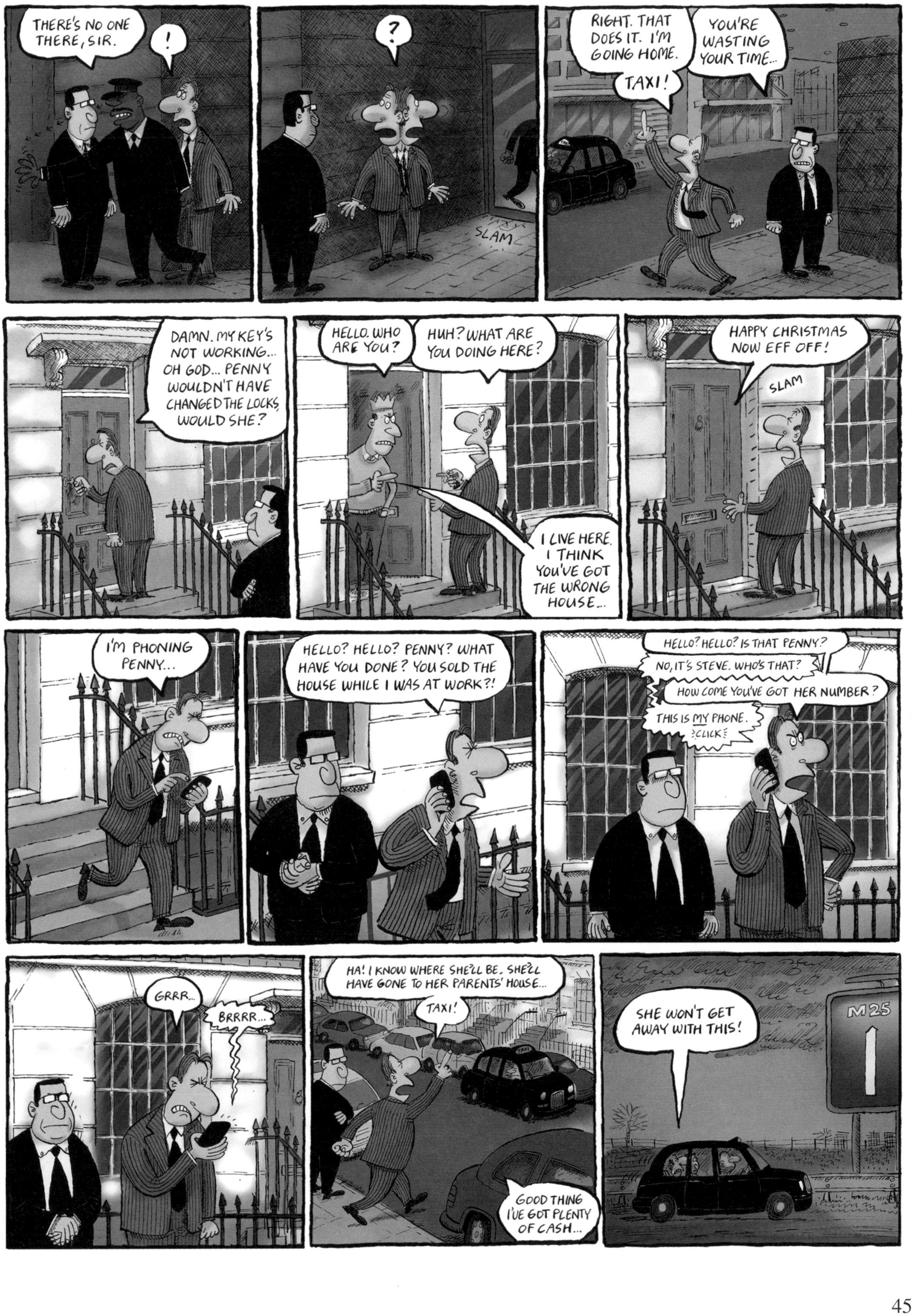
THERE'S NO ONE THERE, SIR.
!
?
SLAM
RIGHT. THAT DOES IT. I'M GOING HOME.
TAXI!
YOU'RE WASTING YOUR TIME...
DAMN. MY KEY'S NOT WORKING... OH GOD... PENNY WOULDN'T HAVE CHANGED THE LOCKS, WOULD SHE?
HELLO. WHO ARE YOU?
HUH? WHAT ARE YOU DOING HERE?
I LIVE HERE. I THINK YOU'VE GOT THE WRONG HOUSE...
HAPPY CHRISTMAS NOW EFF OFF!
SLAM
I'M PHONING PENNY...
HELLO? HELLO? PENNY? WHAT HAVE YOU DONE? YOU SOLD THE HOUSE WHILE I WAS AT WORK?!
HELLO? HELLO? IS THAT PENNY?
NO, IT'S STEVE. WHO'S THAT?
HOW COME YOU'VE GOT HER NUMBER?
THIS IS MY PHONE.
CLICK
GRRR...
BRRRR...
HA! I KNOW WHERE SHE'LL BE. SHE'LL HAVE GONE TO HER PARENTS' HOUSE...
TAXI!
GOOD THING I'VE GOT PLENTY OF CASH...
SHE WON'T GET AWAY WITH THIS!
M25

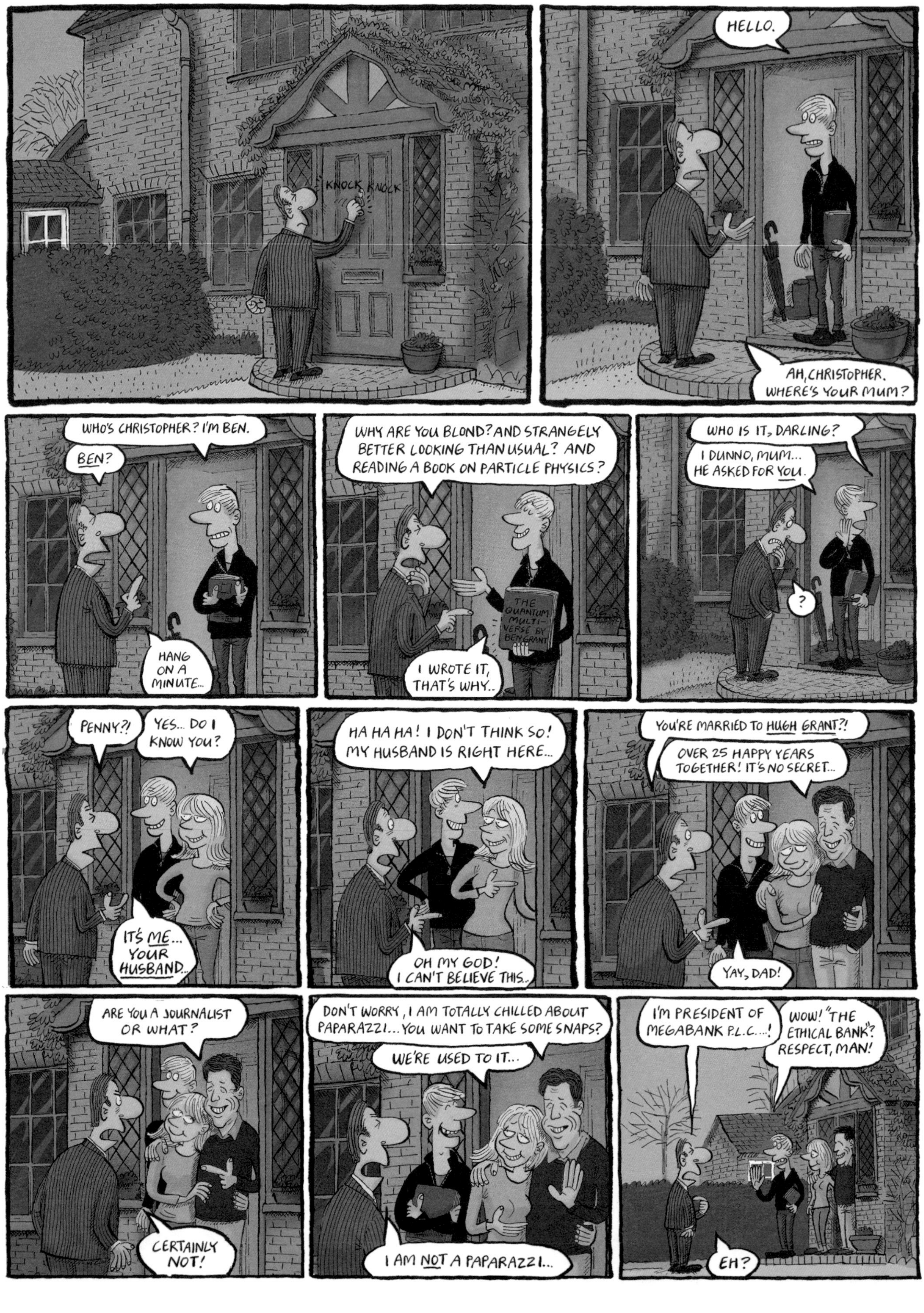
KNOCK KNOCK
HELLO.
AH, CHRISTOPHER. WHERE'S YOUR MUM?
WHO'S CHRISTOPHER? I'M BEN.
BEN?
HANG ON A MINUTE...
WHY ARE YOU BLOND? AND STRANGELY BETTER LOOKING THAN USUAL? AND READING A BOOK ON PARTICLE PHYSICS?
THE QUANTUM MULTI-VERSE BY BEN GRANT
I WROTE IT, THAT'S WHY...
WHO IS IT, DARLING?
I DUNNO, MUM... HE ASKED FOR YOU.
?
PENNY?!
YES... DO I KNOW YOU?
IT'S ME... YOUR HUSBAND...
HA HA HA! I DON'T THINK SO! MY HUSBAND IS RIGHT HERE...
OH MY GOD! I CAN'T BELIEVE THIS...
YOU'RE MARRIED TO HUGH GRANT?!
OVER 25 HAPPY YEARS TOGETHER! IT'S NO SECRET...
YAY, DAD!
ARE YOU A JOURNALIST OR WHAT?
CERTAINLY NOT!
DON'T WORRY, I AM TOTALLY CHILLED ABOUT PAPARAZZI... YOU WANT TO TAKE SOME SNAPS?
WE'RE USED TO IT...
I AM NOT A PAPARAZZI...
I'M PRESIDENT OF MEGABANK P.L.C....!
WOW! "THE ETHICAL BANK"? RESPECT, MAN!
EH?

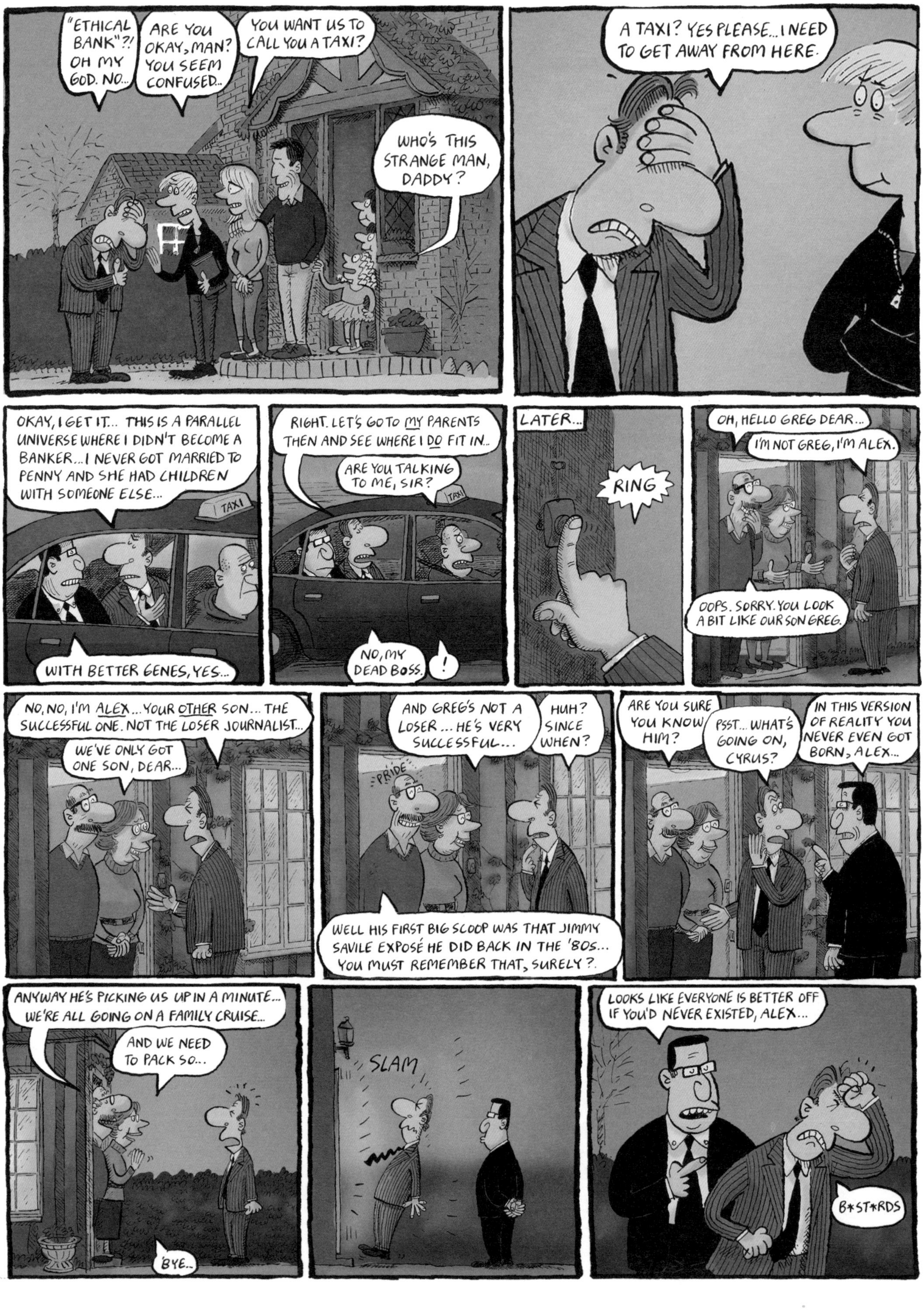
"ETHICAL BANK"?! OH MY GOD. NO...
ARE YOU OKAY, MAN? YOU SEEM CONFUSED...
YOU WANT US TO CALL YOU A TAXI?
WHO'S THIS STRANGE MAN, DADDY?
A TAXI? YES PLEASE... I NEED TO GET AWAY FROM HERE.
OKAY, I GET IT... THIS IS A PARALLEL UNIVERSE WHERE I DIDN'T BECOME A BANKER... I NEVER GOT MARRIED TO PENNY AND SHE HAD CHILDREN WITH SOMEONE ELSE...
TAXI
WITH BETTER GENES, YES...
RIGHT. LET'S GO TO MY PARENTS THEN AND SEE WHERE I DO FIT IN...
ARE YOU TALKING TO ME, SIR?
TAXI
NO, MY DEAD BOSS.
!
LATER...
RING
OH, HELLO GREG DEAR...
I'M NOT GREG, I'M ALEX.
OOPS. SORRY. YOU LOOK A BIT LIKE OUR SON GREG.
NO, NO, I'M ALEX... YOUR OTHER SON... THE SUCCESSFUL ONE. NOT THE LOSER JOURNALIST...
WE'VE ONLY GOT ONE SON, DEAR...
AND GREG'S NOT A LOSER... HE'S VERY SUCCESSFUL...
HUH? SINCE WHEN?
PRIDE
WELL HIS FIRST BIG SCOOP WAS THAT JIMMY SAVILE EXPOSÉ HE DID BACK IN THE '80S... YOU MUST REMEMBER THAT, SURELY?.
ARE YOU SURE YOU KNOW HIM?
PSST... WHAT'S GOING ON, CYRUS?
IN THIS VERSION OF REALITY YOU NEVER EVEN GOT BORN, ALEX...
ANYWAY HE'S PICKING US UP IN A MINUTE... WE'RE ALL GOING ON A FAMILY CRUISE...
AND WE NEED TO PACK SO...
BYE...
SLAM
LOOKS LIKE EVERYONE IS BETTER OFF IF YOU'D NEVER EXISTED, ALEX...
B*ST*RDS

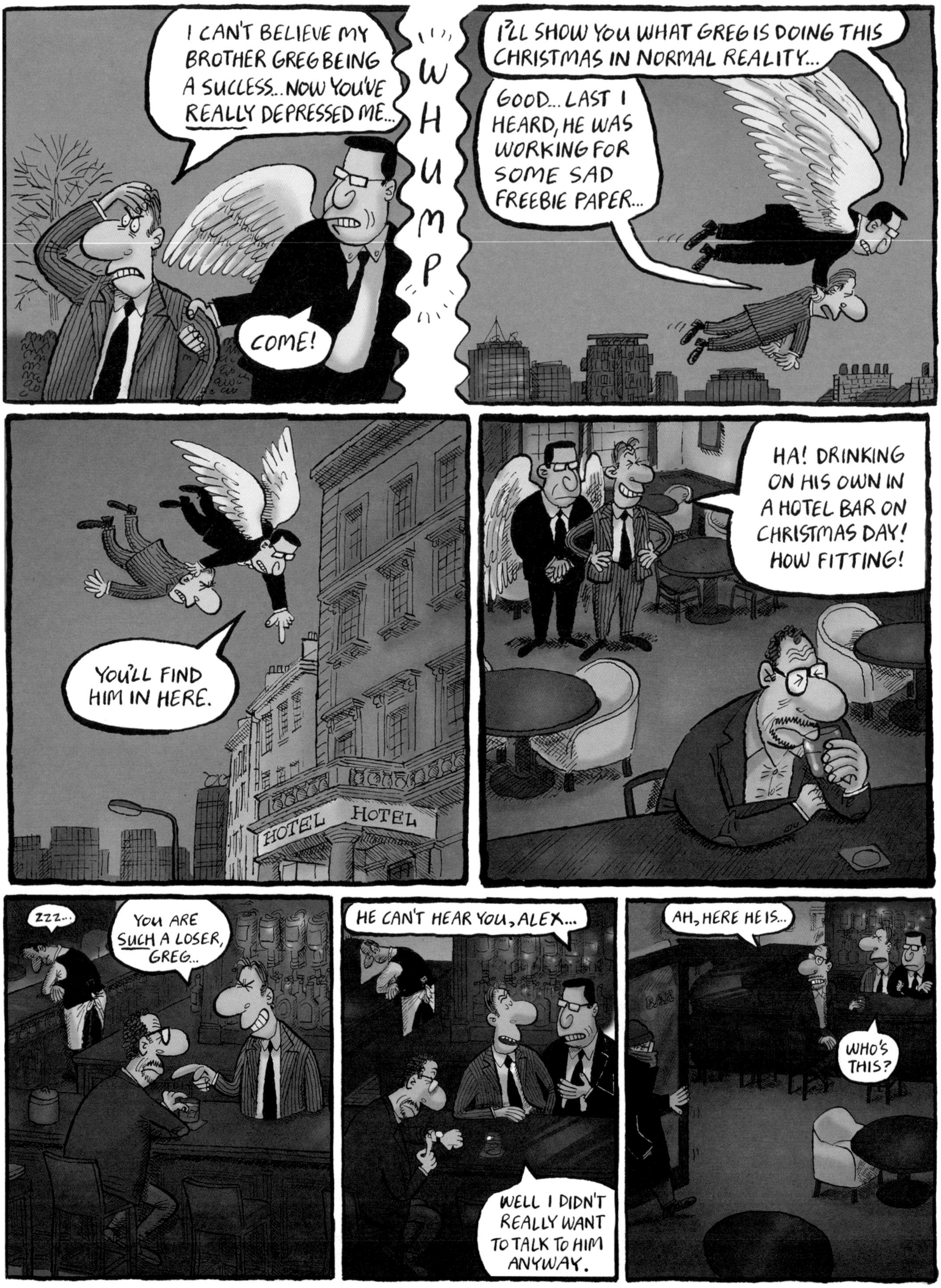
I CAN'T BELIEVE MY BROTHER GREG BEING A SUCCESS... NOW YOU'VE REALLY DEPRESSED ME...
COME!
WHUMP
I'LL SHOW YOU WHAT GREG IS DOING THIS CHRISTMAS IN NORMAL REALITY...
GOOD... LAST I HEARD, HE WAS WORKING FOR SOME SAD FREEBIE PAPER...
YOU'LL FIND HIM IN HERE.
HOTEL
HOTEL
HA! DRINKING ON HIS OWN IN A HOTEL BAR ON CHRISTMAS DAY! HOW FITTING!
ZZZ...
YOU ARE SUCH A LOSER, GREG...
HE CAN'T HEAR YOU, ALEX...
WELL I DIDN'T REALLY WANT TO TALK TO HIM ANYWAY.
AH, HERE HE IS...
WHO'S THIS?

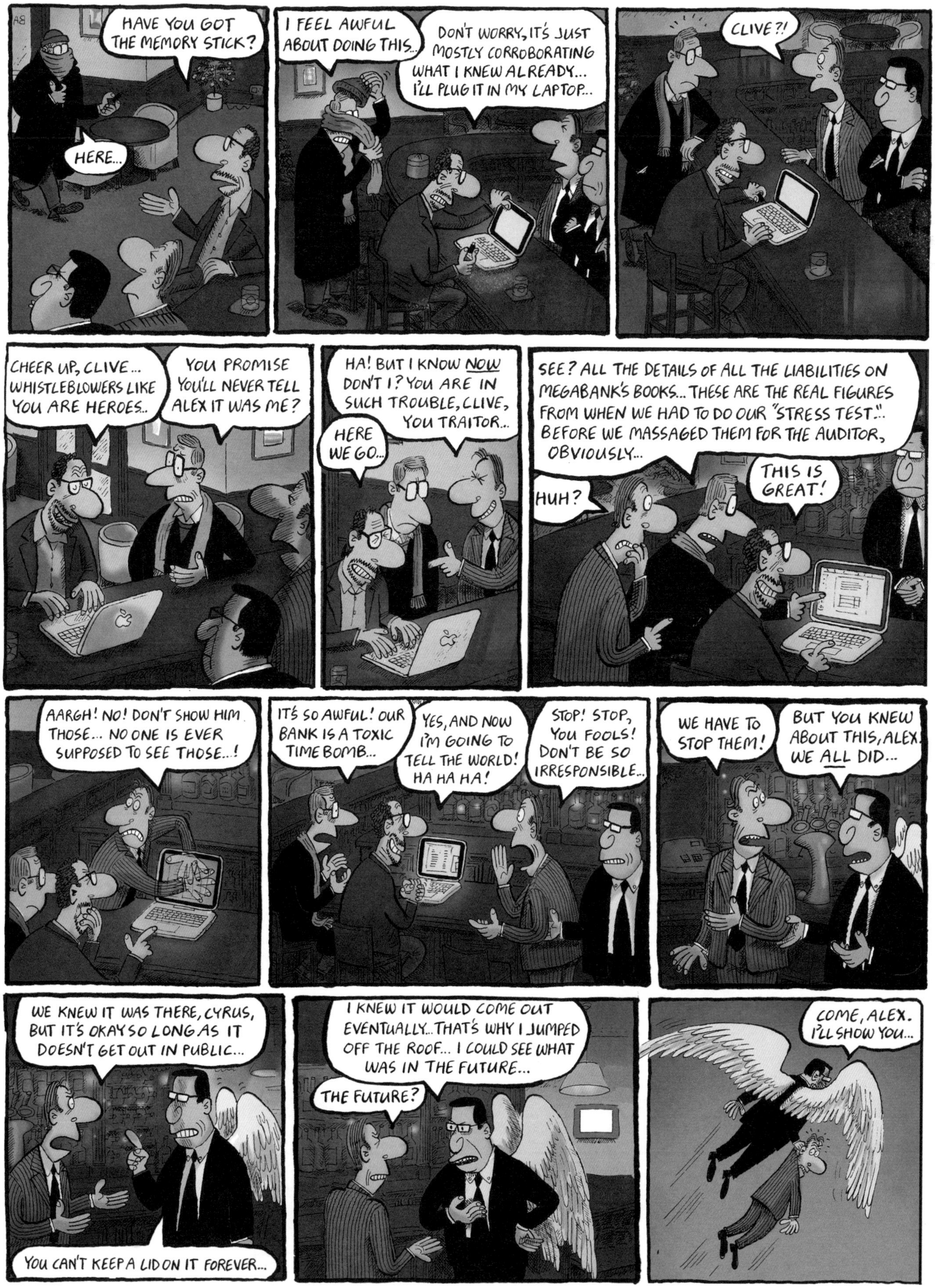
HAVE YOU GOT THE MEMORY STICK?
HERE...
I FEEL AWFUL ABOUT DOING THIS...
DON'T WORRY, IT'S JUST MOSTLY CORROBORATING WHAT I KNEW ALREADY... I'LL PLUG IT IN MY LAPTOP...
CLIVE?!
CHEER UP, CLIVE... WHISTLEBLOWERS LIKE YOU ARE HEROES..
YOU PROMISE YOU'LL NEVER TELL ALEX IT WAS ME?
HA! BUT I KNOW NOW DON'T I? YOU ARE IN SUCH TROUBLE, CLIVE, YOU TRAITOR...
HERE WE GO...
SEE? ALL THE DETAILS OF ALL THE LIABILITIES ON MEGABANK'S BOOKS... THESE ARE THE REAL FIGURES FROM WHEN WE HAD TO DO OUR "STRESS TEST."... BEFORE WE MASSAGED THEM FOR THE AUDITOR, OBVIOUSLY...
HUH?
THIS IS GREAT!
AARGH! NO! DON'T SHOW HIM THOSE... NO ONE IS EVER SUPPOSED TO SEE THOSE...!
IT'S SO AWFUL! OUR BANK IS A TOXIC TIME BOMB...
YES, AND NOW I'M GOING TO TELL THE WORLD! HA HA HA!
STOP! STOP, YOU FOOLS! DON'T BE SO IRRESPONSIBLE...
WE HAVE TO STOP THEM!
BUT YOU KNEW ABOUT THIS, ALEX. WE ALL DID...
WE KNEW IT WAS THERE, CYRUS, BUT IT'S OKAY SO LONG AS IT DOESN'T GET OUT IN PUBLIC...
YOU CAN'T KEEP A LID ON IT FOREVER...
I KNEW IT WOULD COME OUT EVENTUALLY... THAT'S WHY I JUMPED OFF THE ROOF... I COULD SEE WHAT WAS IN THE FUTURE...
THE FUTURE?
COME, ALEX. I'LL SHOW YOU...

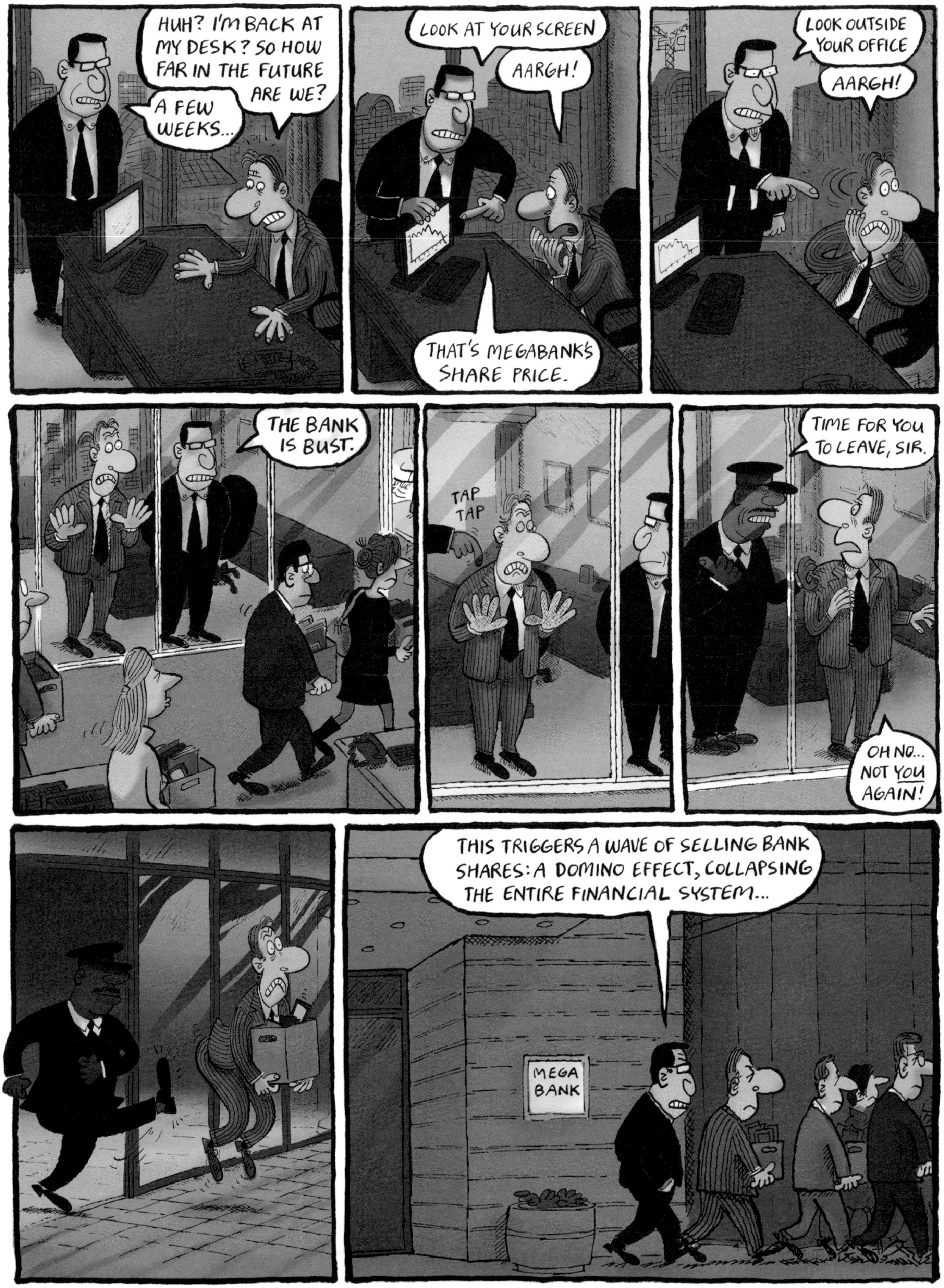
HUH? I'M BACK AT MY DESK? SO HOW FAR IN THE FUTURE ARE WE?
A FEW WEEKS...
LOOK AT YOUR SCREEN
AARGH!
THAT'S MEGABANK'S SHARE PRICE.
LOOK OUTSIDE YOUR OFFICE
AARGH!
THE BANK IS BUST.
TAP TAP
TIME FOR YOU TO LEAVE, SIR.
OH NO... NOT YOU AGAIN!
THIS TRIGGERS A WAVE OF SELLING BANK SHARES: A DOMINO EFFECT, COLLAPSING THE ENTIRE FINANCIAL SYSTEM...
MEGA BANK

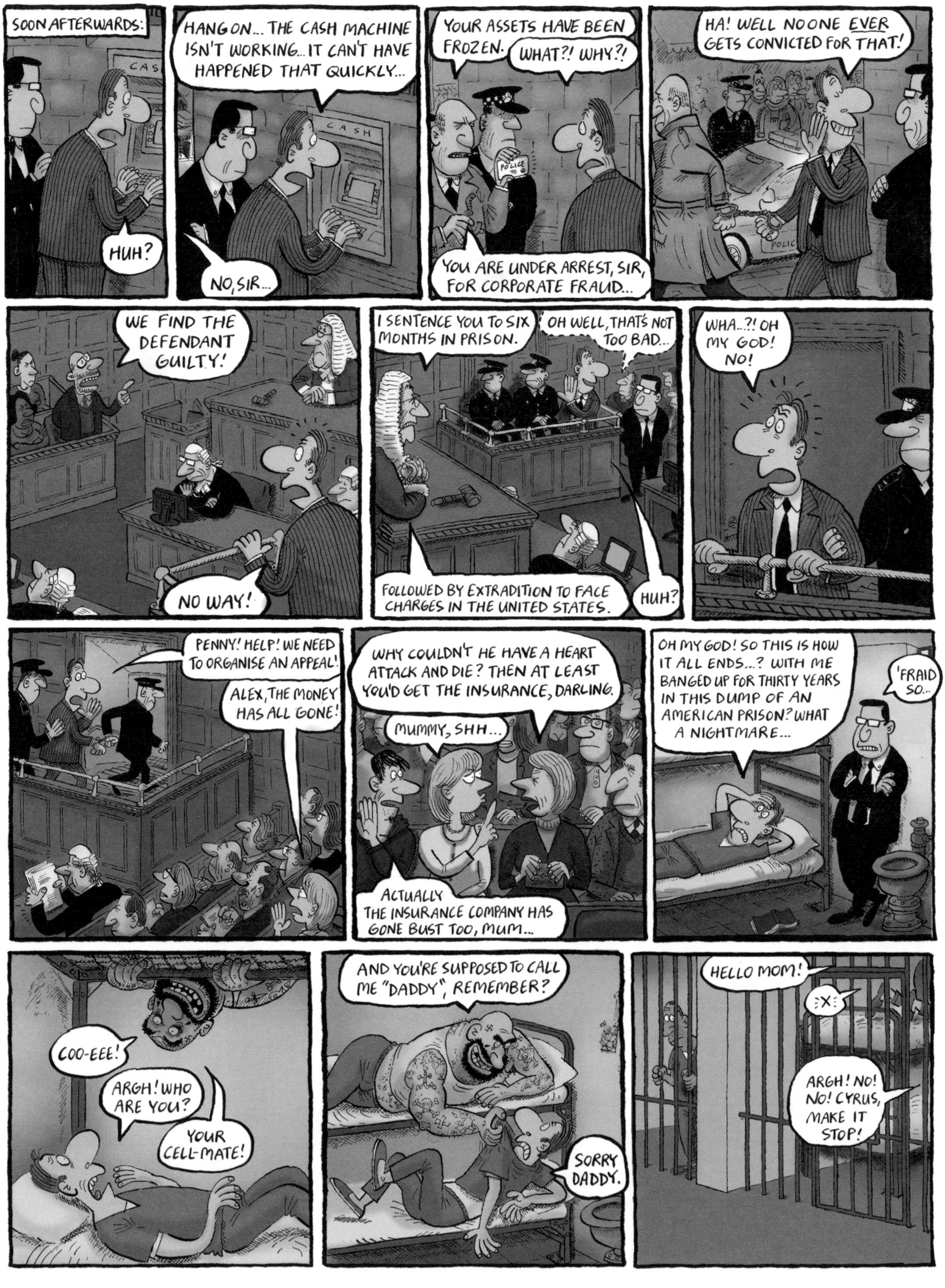
SOON AFTERWARDS:
HUH?
HANG ON... THE CASH MACHINE ISN'T WORKING... IT CAN'T HAVE HAPPENED THAT QUICKLY...
NO, SIR...
YOUR ASSETS HAVE BEEN FROZEN.
WHAT?! WHY?!
YOU ARE UNDER ARREST, SIR, FOR CORPORATE FRAUD...
HA! WELL NO ONE EVER GETS CONVICTED FOR THAT!
WE FIND THE DEFENDANT GUILTY!
NO WAY!
I SENTENCE YOU TO SIX MONTHS IN PRISON.
OH WELL, THAT'S NOT TOO BAD...
FOLLOWED BY EXTRADITION TO FACE CHARGES IN THE UNITED STATES.
HUH?
WHA...?! OH MY GOD! NO!
PENNY! HELP! WE NEED TO ORGANISE AN APPEAL!
ALEX, THE MONEY HAS ALL GONE!
WHY COULDN'T HE HAVE A HEART ATTACK AND DIE? THEN AT LEAST YOU'D GET THE INSURANCE, DARLING.
MUMMY, SHH...
ACTUALLY THE INSURANCE COMPANY HAS GONE BUST TOO, MUM...
OH MY GOD! SO THIS IS HOW IT ALL ENDS...? WITH ME BANGED UP FOR THIRTY YEARS IN THIS DUMP OF AN AMERICAN PRISON? WHAT A NIGHTMARE...
'FRAID SO...
COO-EEE!
ARGH! WHO ARE YOU?
YOUR CELL-MATE!
AND YOU'RE SUPPOSED TO CALL ME "DADDY", REMEMBER?
SORRY DADDY.
HELLO MOM!
:X:
ARGH! NO! NO! CYRUS, MAKE IT STOP!

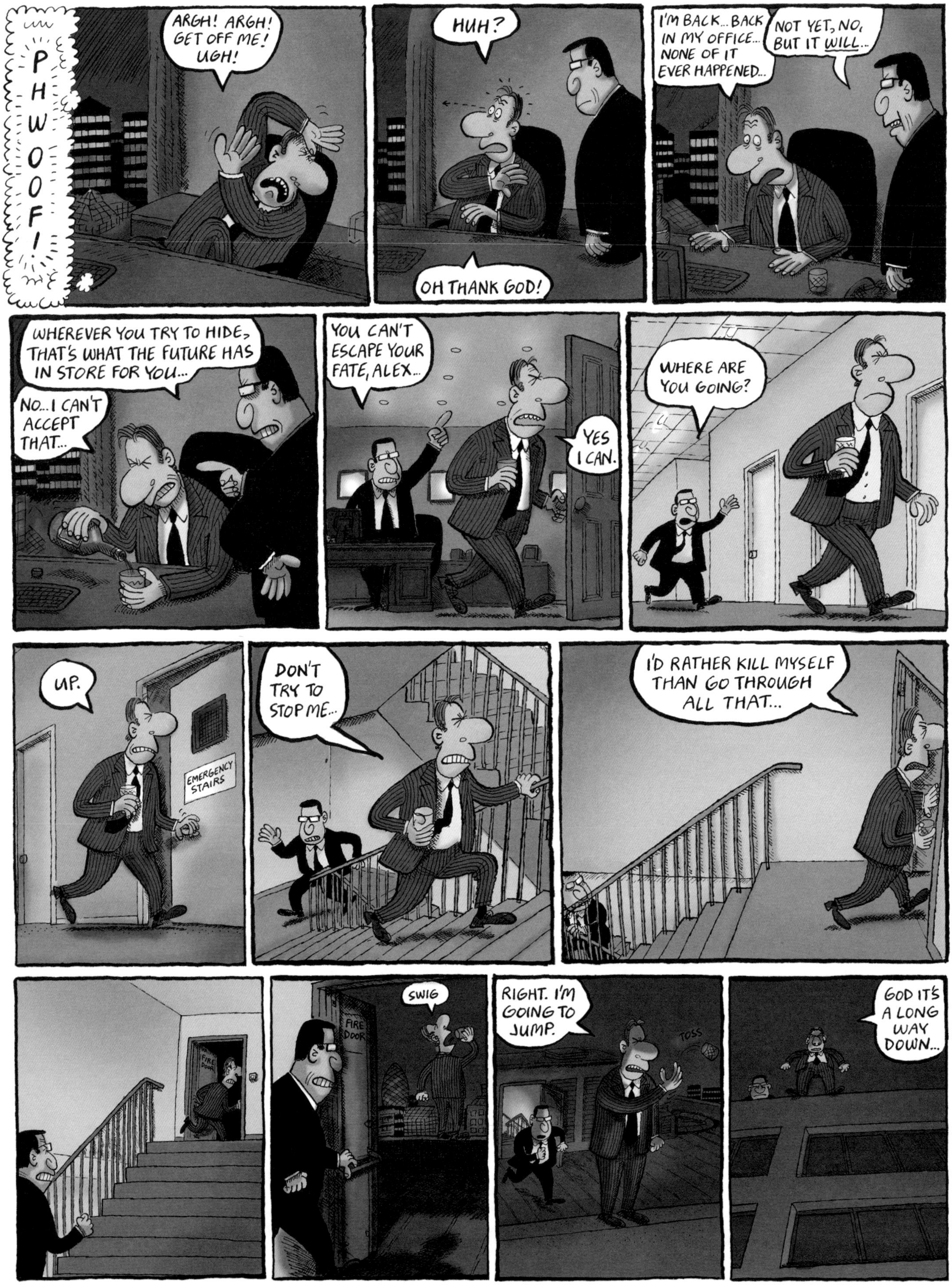
PHWOOF!
ARGH! ARGH! GET OFF ME! UGH!
HUH?
OH THANK GOD!
I'M BACK... BACK IN MY OFFICE... NONE OF IT EVER HAPPENED...
NOT YET, NO, BUT IT WILL...
WHEREVER YOU TRY TO HIDE, THAT'S WHAT THE FUTURE HAS IN STORE FOR YOU...
NO... I CAN'T ACCEPT THAT...
YOU CAN'T ESCAPE YOUR FATE, ALEX...
YES I CAN.
WHERE ARE YOU GOING?
UP.
EMERGENCY STAIRS
DON'T TRY TO STOP ME...
I'D RATHER KILL MYSELF THAN GO THROUGH ALL THAT...
FIRE DOOR
FIRE DOOR
SWIG
RIGHT. I'M GOING TO JUMP.
TOSS
GOD IT'S A LONG WAY DOWN...

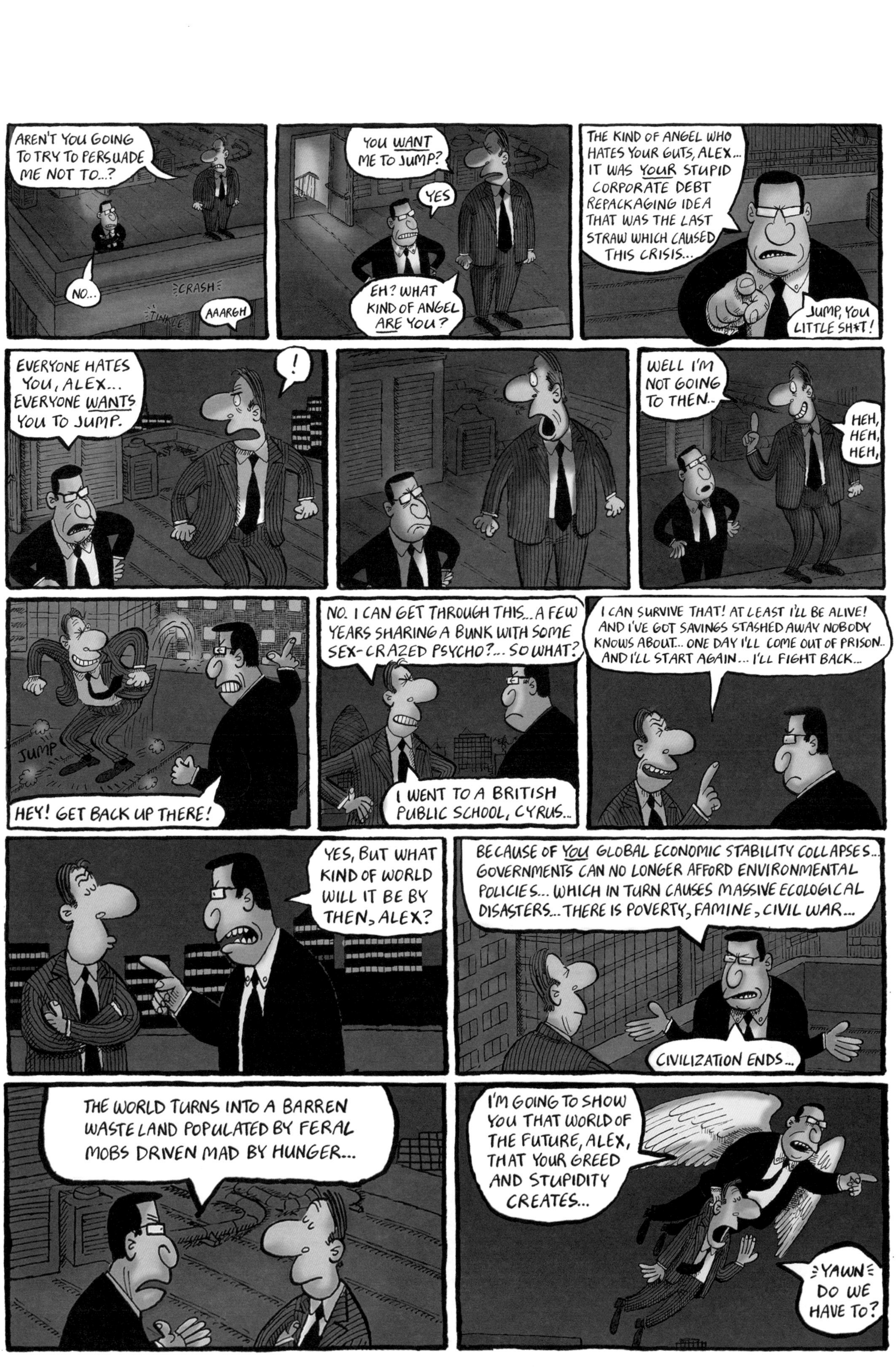
AREN'T YOU GOING TO TRY TO PERSUADE ME NOT TO...?
NO...
CRASH
TINKLE
AAARGH
YOU WANT ME TO JUMP?
YES
EH? WHAT KIND OF ANGEL ARE YOU?
THE KIND OF ANGEL WHO HATES YOUR GUTS, ALEX... IT WAS YOUR STUPID CORPORATE DEBT REPACKAGING IDEA THAT WAS THE LAST STRAW WHICH CAUSED THIS CRISIS...
JUMP, YOU LITTLE SH*T!
EVERYONE HATES YOU, ALEX... EVERYONE WANTS YOU TO JUMP.
!
WELL I'M NOT GOING TO THEN...
HEH, HEH, HEH,
JUMP
HEY! GET BACK UP THERE!
NO. I CAN GET THROUGH THIS... A FEW YEARS SHARING A BUNK WITH SOME SEX-CRAZED PSYCHO?... SO WHAT?
I WENT TO A BRITISH PUBLIC SCHOOL, CYRUS...
I CAN SURVIVE THAT! AT LEAST I'LL BE ALIVE! AND I'VE GOT SAVINGS STASHED AWAY NOBODY KNOWS ABOUT... ONE DAY I'LL COME OUT OF PRISON... AND I'LL START AGAIN... I'LL FIGHT BACK...
YES, BUT WHAT KIND OF WORLD WILL IT BE BY THEN, ALEX?
BECAUSE OF YOU GLOBAL ECONOMIC STABILITY COLLAPSES... GOVERNMENTS CAN NO LONGER AFFORD ENVIRONMENTAL POLICIES... WHICH IN TURN CAUSES MASSIVE ECOLOGICAL DISASTERS... THERE IS POVERTY, FAMINE, CIVIL WAR...
CIVILIZATION ENDS...
THE WORLD TURNS INTO A BARREN WASTELAND POPULATED BY FERAL MOBS DRIVEN MAD BY HUNGER...
I'M GOING TO SHOW YOU THAT WORLD OF THE FUTURE, ALEX, THAT YOUR GREED AND STUPIDITY CREATES...
YAWN
DO WE HAVE TO?

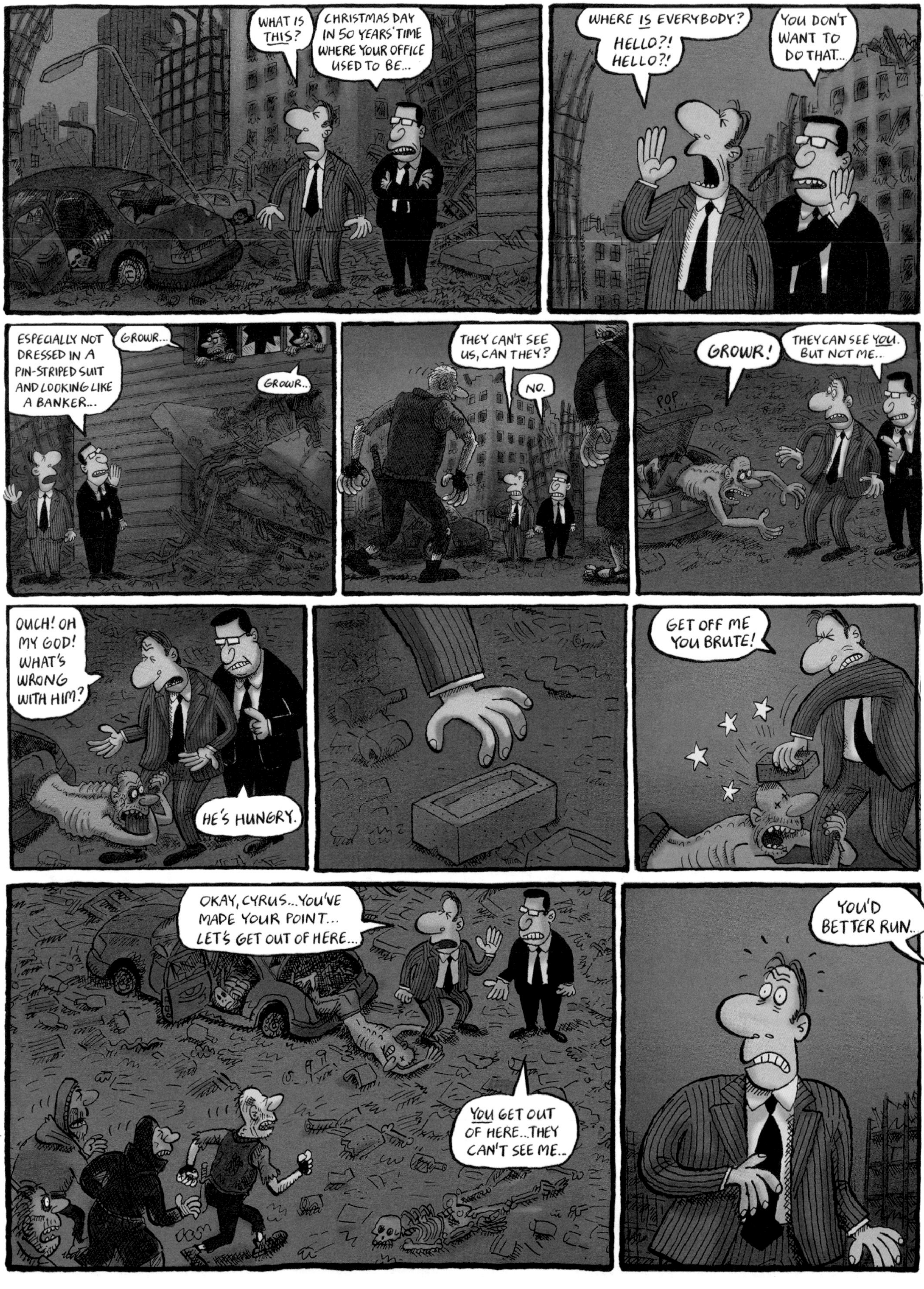
WHAT IS THIS?
CHRISTMAS DAY IN 50 YEARS' TIME WHERE YOUR OFFICE USED TO BE...
WHERE IS EVERYBODY? HELLO?! HELLO?!
YOU DON'T WANT TO DO THAT...
ESPECIALLY NOT DRESSED IN A PIN-STRIPED SUIT AND LOOKING LIKE A BANKER...
GROWR...
GROWR..
THEY CAN'T SEE US, CAN THEY?
NO.
GROWR!
THEY CAN SEE YOU. BUT NOT ME..
POP
OUCH! OH MY GOD! WHAT'S WRONG WITH HIM?
HE'S HUNGRY.
GET OFF ME YOU BRUTE!
OKAY, CYRUS...YOU'VE MADE YOUR POINT... LET'S GET OUT OF HERE...
YOU GET OUT OF HERE...THEY CAN'T SEE ME..
YOU'D BETTER RUN..

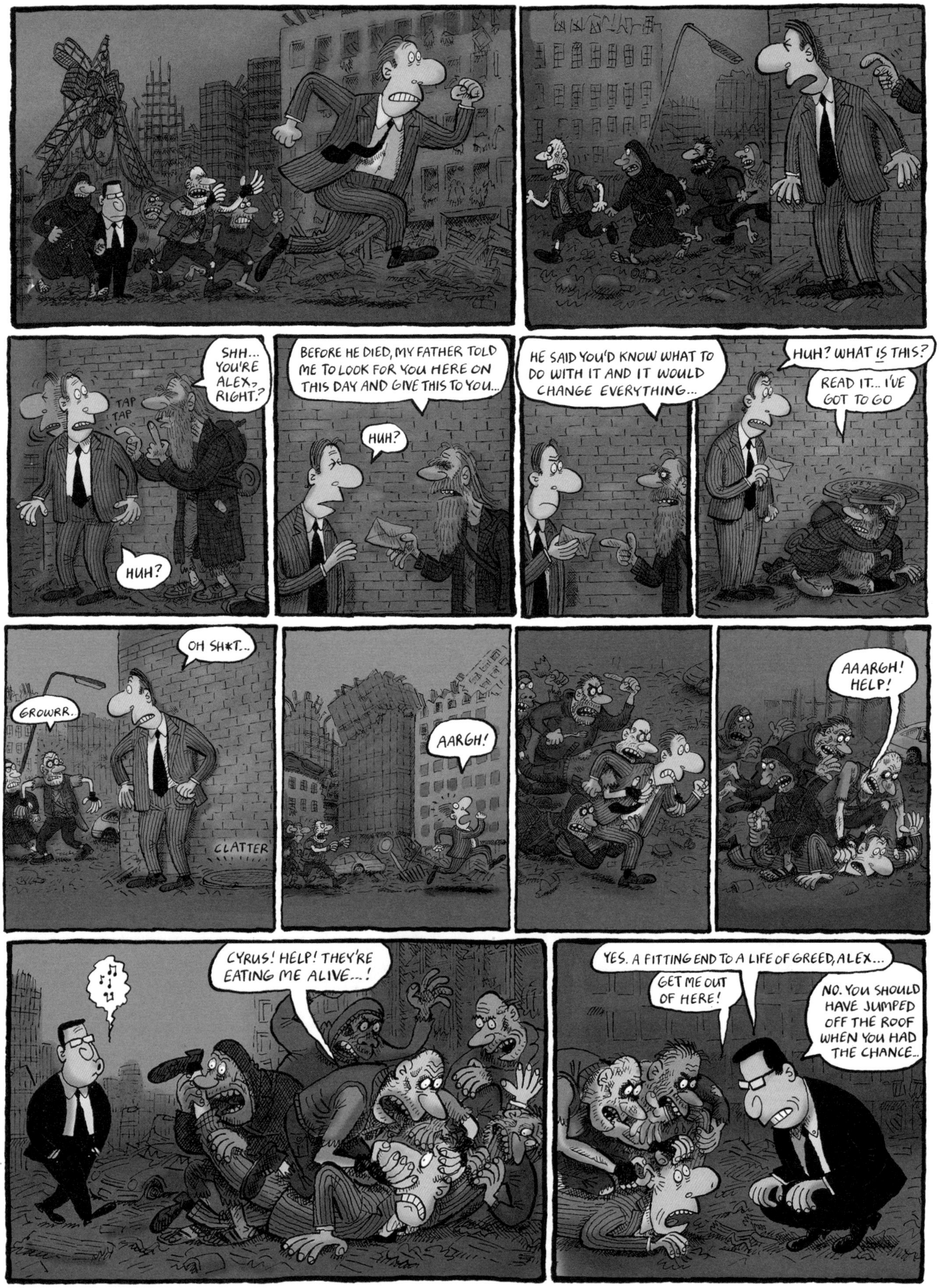
SHH... YOU'RE ALEX, RIGHT?
TAP TAP
HUH?
BEFORE HE DIED, MY FATHER TOLD ME TO LOOK FOR YOU HERE ON THIS DAY AND GIVE THIS TO YOU...
HUH?
HE SAID YOU'D KNOW WHAT TO DO WITH IT AND IT WOULD CHANGE EVERYTHING...
HUH? WHAT IS THIS?
READ IT... I'VE GOT TO GO
SEWER
OH SH*T...
GROWRR.
CLATTER
AARGH!
AAARGH! HELP!
CYRUS! HELP! THEY'RE EATING ME ALIVE...!
YES. A FITTING END TO A LIFE OF GREED, ALEX...
GET ME OUT OF HERE!
NO. YOU SHOULD HAVE JUMPED OFF THE ROOF WHEN YOU HAD THE CHANCE...

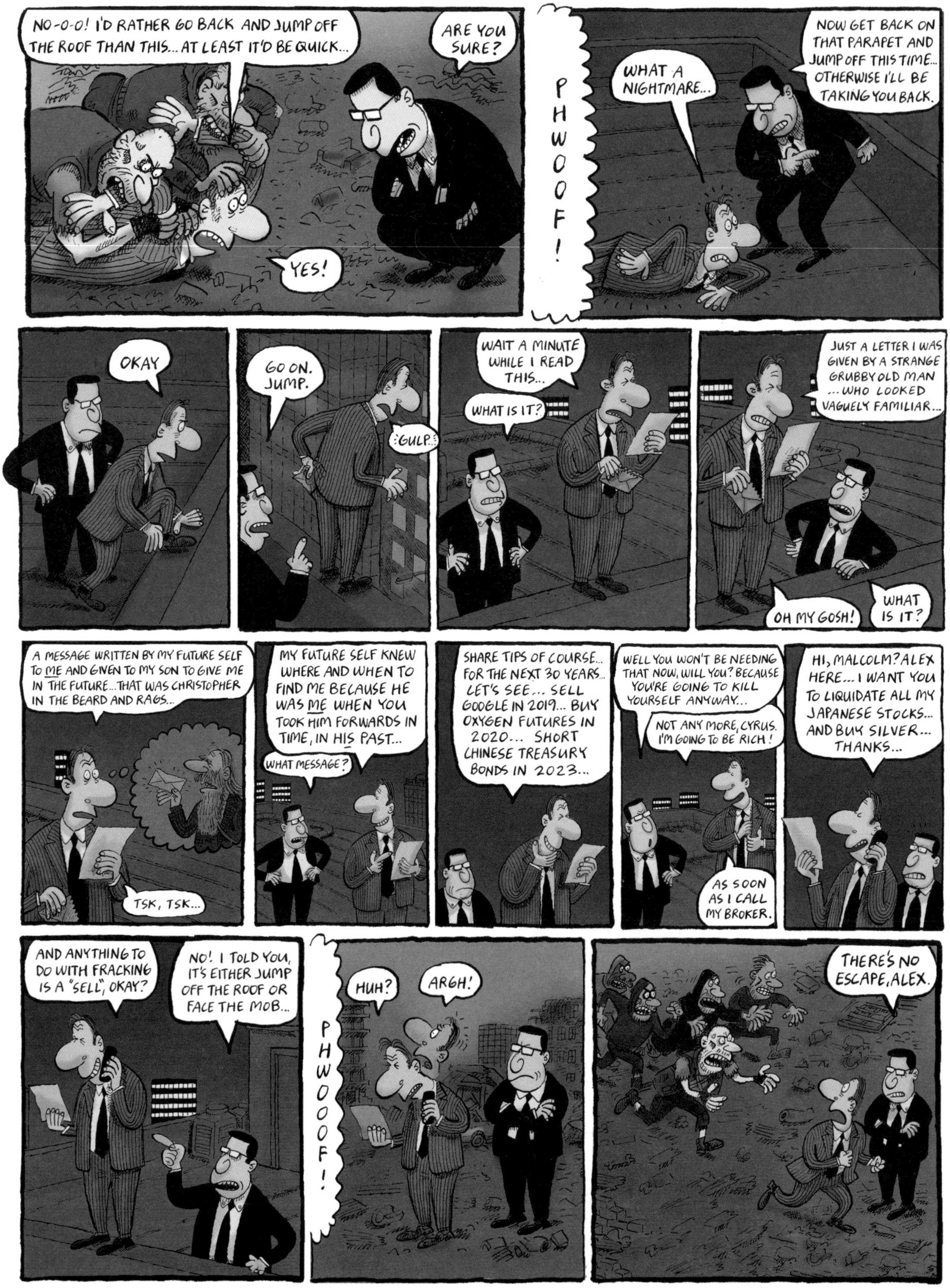
NO-O-O! I'D RATHER GO BACK AND JUMP OFF THE ROOF THAN THIS... AT LEAST IT'D BE QUICK...
ARE YOU SURE?
YES!
PHWOOF!
WHAT A NIGHTMARE...
NOW GET BACK ON THAT PARAPET AND JUMP OFF THIS TIME... OTHERWISE I'LL BE TAKING YOU BACK.
OKAY
GO ON. JUMP.
GULP
WAIT A MINUTE WHILE I READ THIS...
WHAT IS IT?
JUST A LETTER I WAS GIVEN BY A STRANGE GRUBBY OLD MAN ...WHO LOOKED VAGUELY FAMILIAR...
OH MY GOSH!
WHAT IS IT?
A MESSAGE WRITTEN BY MY FUTURE SELF TO ME AND GIVEN TO MY SON TO GIVE ME IN THE FUTURE... THAT WAS CHRISTOPHER IN THE BEARD AND RAGS...
TSK, TSK...
MY FUTURE SELF KNEW WHERE AND WHEN TO FIND ME BECAUSE HE WAS ME WHEN YOU TOOK HIM FORWARDS IN TIME, IN HIS PAST...
WHAT MESSAGE?
SHARE TIPS OF COURSE... FOR THE NEXT 30 YEARS... LET'S SEE... SELL GOOGLE IN 2019... BUY OXYGEN FUTURES IN 2020... SHORT CHINESE TREASURY BONDS IN 2023...
WELL YOU WON'T BE NEEDING THAT NOW, WILL YOU? BECAUSE YOU'RE GOING TO KILL YOURSELF ANYWAY...
NOT ANY MORE, CYRUS. I'M GOING TO BE RICH!
AS SOON AS I CALL MY BROKER.
HI, MALCOLM? ALEX HERE... I WANT YOU TO LIQUIDATE ALL MY JAPANESE STOCKS... AND BUY SILVER... THANKS...
AND ANYTHING TO DO WITH FRACKING IS A "SELL", OKAY?
NO! I TOLD YOU, IT'S EITHER JUMP OFF THE ROOF OR FACE THE MOB...
PHWOOOF!
HUH?
ARGH!
THERE'S NO ESCAPE, ALEX.

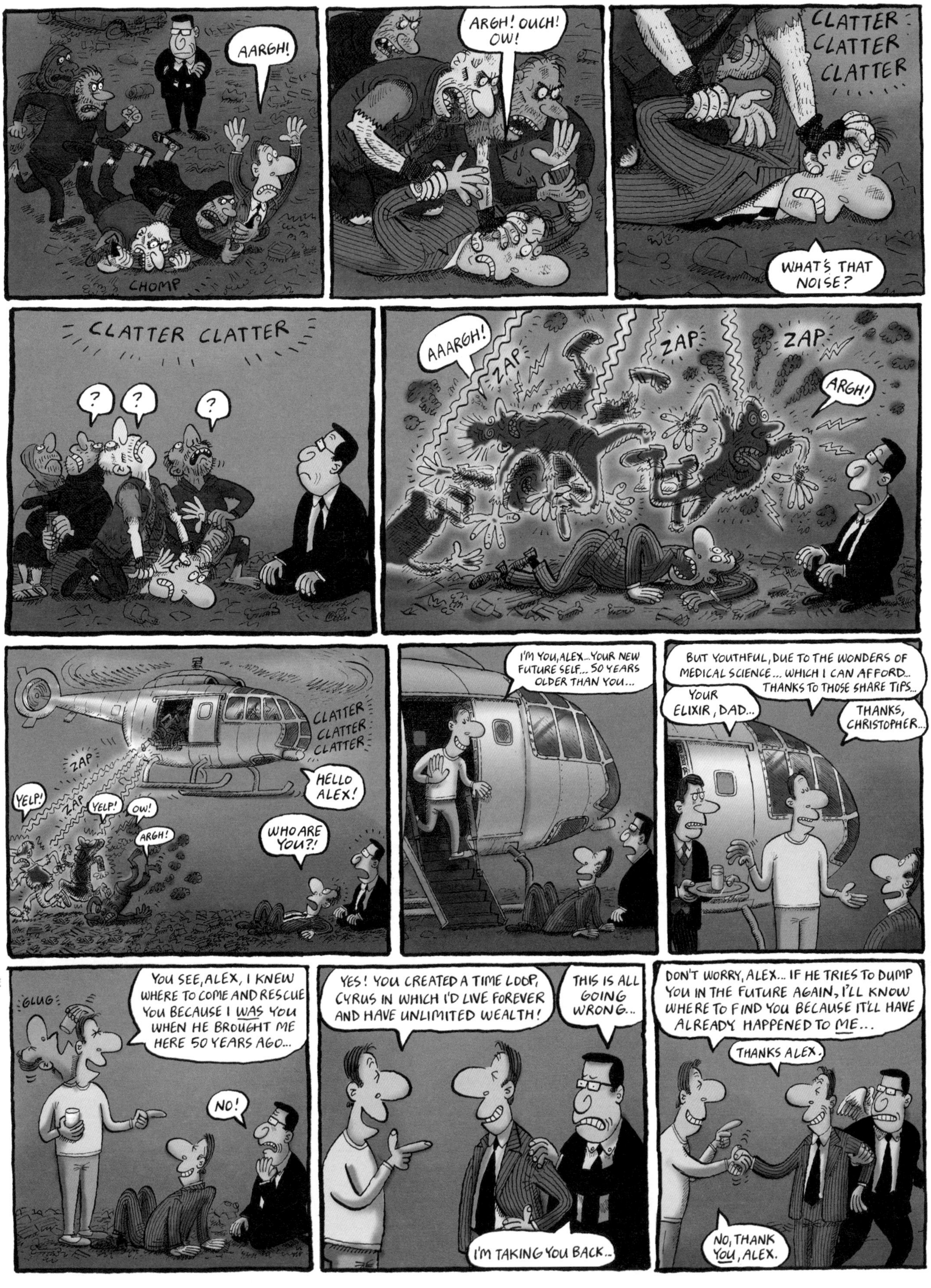
AARGH!
CHOMP
ARGH! OUCH! OW!
CLATTER CLATTER CLATTER
WHAT'S THAT NOISE?
CLATTER CLATTER
?
?
?
AAARGH!
ZAP
ZAP
ZAP
ARGH!
ZAP
CLATTER CLATTER CLATTER
HELLO ALEX!
YELP!
ZAP
YELP!
OW!
ARGH!
WHO ARE YOU?!
I'M YOU, ALEX... YOUR NEW FUTURE SELF... 50 YEARS OLDER THAN YOU...
BUT YOUTHFUL, DUE TO THE WONDERS OF MEDICAL SCIENCE... WHICH I CAN AFFORD... THANKS TO THOSE SHARE TIPS...
YOUR ELIXIR, DAD...
THANKS, CHRISTOPHER...
GLUG
YOU SEE, ALEX, I KNEW WHERE TO COME AND RESCUE YOU BECAUSE I WAS YOU WHEN HE BROUGHT ME HERE 50 YEARS AGO...
NO!
YES! YOU CREATED A TIME LOOP, CYRUS IN WHICH I'D LIVE FOREVER AND HAVE UNLIMITED WEALTH!
THIS IS ALL GOING WRONG...
I'M TAKING YOU BACK...
DON'T WORRY, ALEX... IF HE TRIES TO DUMP YOU IN THE FUTURE AGAIN, I'LL KNOW WHERE TO FIND YOU BECAUSE IT'LL HAVE ALREADY HAPPENED TO ME...
THANKS ALEX.
NO, THANK YOU, ALEX.

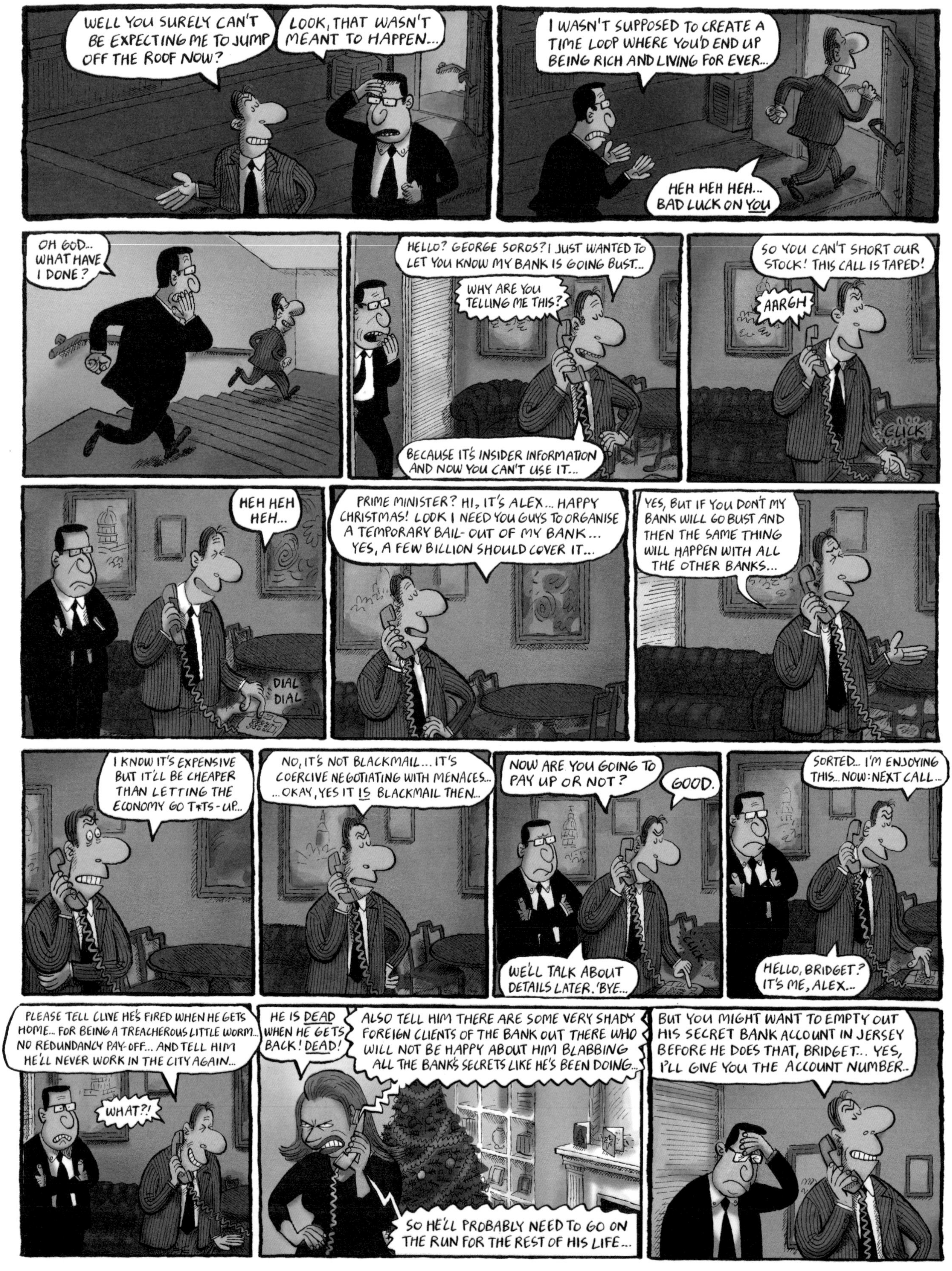
WELL YOU SURELY CAN'T BE EXPECTING ME TO JUMP OFF THE ROOF NOW?
LOOK, THAT WASN'T MEANT TO HAPPEN...
I WASN'T SUPPOSED TO CREATE A TIME LOOP WHERE YOU'D END UP BEING RICH AND LIVING FOR EVER...
HEH HEH HEH... BAD LUCK ON YOU
OH GOD.. WHAT HAVE I DONE?
HELLO? GEORGE SOROS? I JUST WANTED TO LET YOU KNOW MY BANK IS GOING BUST...
WHY ARE YOU TELLING ME THIS?
BECAUSE IT'S INSIDER INFORMATION AND NOW YOU CAN'T USE IT...
SO YOU CAN'T SHORT OUR STOCK! THIS CALL IS TAPED!
AARGH
CLICK
HEH HEH HEH...
DIAL DIAL
PRIME MINISTER? HI, IT'S ALEX... HAPPY CHRISTMAS! LOOK I NEED YOU GUYS TO ORGANISE A TEMPORARY BAIL-OUT OF MY BANK... YES, A FEW BILLION SHOULD COVER IT...
YES, BUT IF YOU DON'T MY BANK WILL GO BUST AND THEN THE SAME THING WILL HAPPEN WITH ALL THE OTHER BANKS...
I KNOW IT'S EXPENSIVE BUT IT'LL BE CHEAPER THAN LETTING THE ECONOMY GO T*TS-UP...
NO, IT'S NOT BLACKMAIL... IT'S COERCIVE NEGOTIATING WITH MENACES... ...OKAY, YES IT IS BLACKMAIL THEN...
NOW ARE YOU GOING TO PAY UP OR NOT?
GOOD.
WE'LL TALK ABOUT DETAILS LATER. 'BYE...
CLICK
SORTED... I'M ENJOYING THIS... NOW: NEXT CALL...
HELLO, BRIDGET? IT'S ME, ALEX...
PLEASE TELL CLIVE HE'S FIRED WHEN HE GETS HOME... FOR BEING A TREACHEROUS LITTLE WORM... NO REDUNDANCY PAY-OFF... AND TELL HIM HE'LL NEVER WORK IN THE CITY AGAIN...
WHAT?!
HE IS DEAD WHEN HE GETS BACK! DEAD!
ALSO TELL HIM THERE ARE SOME VERY SHADY FOREIGN CLIENTS OF THE BANK OUT THERE WHO WILL NOT BE HAPPY ABOUT HIM BLABBING ALL THE BANK'S SECRETS LIKE HE'S BEEN DOING...
SO HE'LL PROBABLY NEED TO GO ON THE RUN FOR THE REST OF HIS LIFE...
BUT YOU MIGHT WANT TO EMPTY OUT HIS SECRET BANK ACCOUNT IN JERSEY BEFORE HE DOES THAT, BRIDGET... YES, I'LL GIVE YOU THE ACCOUNT NUMBER...

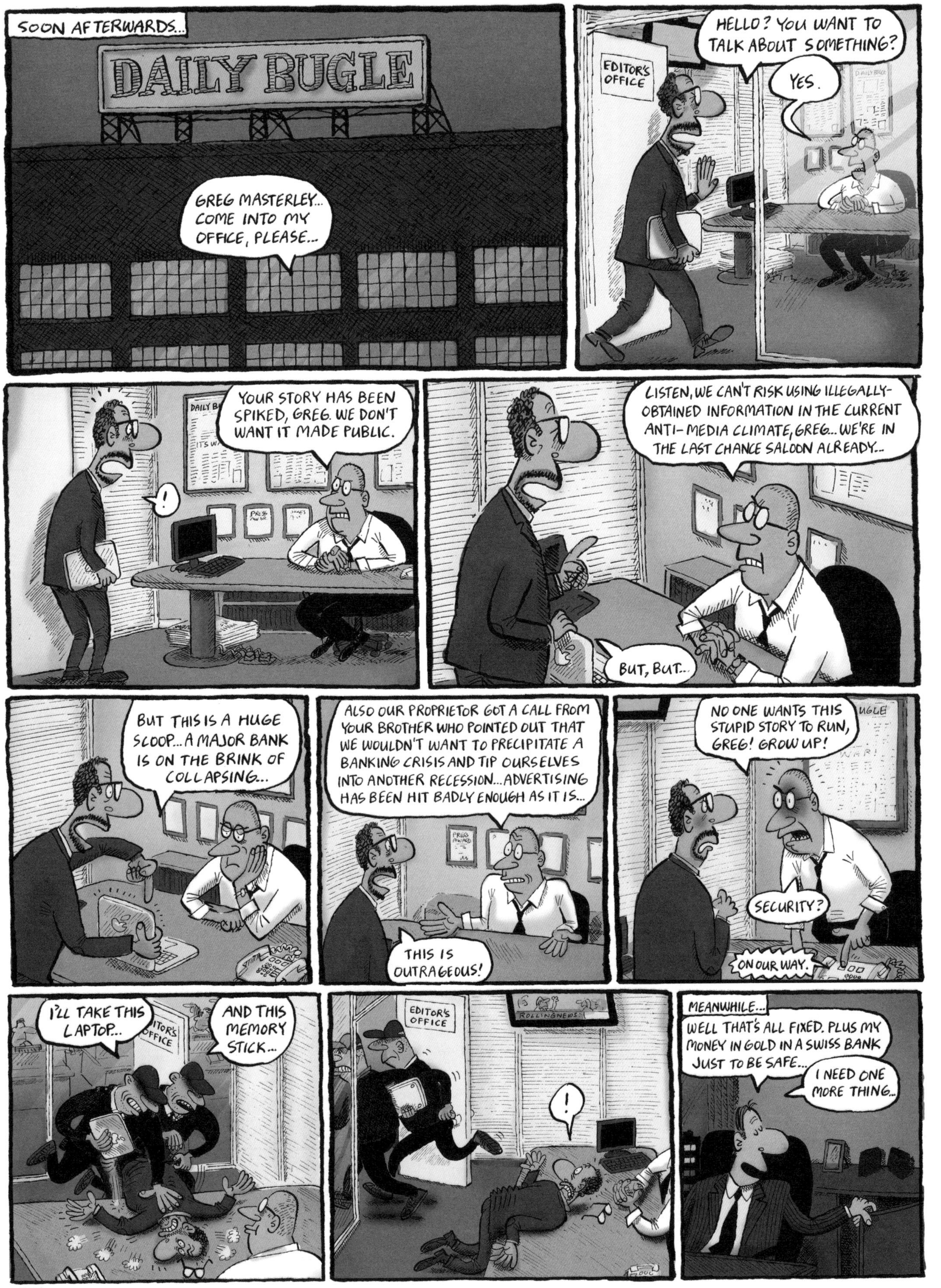

SOON AFTERWARDS...
DAILY BUGLE
GREG MASTERLEY... COME INTO MY OFFICE, PLEASE...
EDITOR'S OFFICE
HELLO? YOU WANT TO TALK ABOUT SOMETHING?
YES.
YOUR STORY HAS BEEN SPIKED, GREG. WE DON'T WANT IT MADE PUBLIC.
!
LISTEN, WE CAN'T RISK USING ILLEGALLY-OBTAINED INFORMATION IN THE CURRENT ANTI-MEDIA CLIMATE, GREG... WE'RE IN THE LAST CHANCE SALOON ALREADY...
BUT, BUT...
BUT THIS IS A HUGE SCOOP... A MAJOR BANK IS ON THE BRINK OF COLLAPSING...
ALSO OUR PROPRIETOR GOT A CALL FROM YOUR BROTHER WHO POINTED OUT THAT WE WOULDN'T WANT TO PRECIPITATE A BANKING CRISIS AND TIP OURSELVES INTO ANOTHER RECESSION... ADVERTISING HAS BEEN HIT BADLY ENOUGH AS IT IS...
THIS IS OUTRAGEOUS!
NO ONE WANTS THIS STUPID STORY TO RUN, GREG! GROW UP!
SECURITY?
ON OUR WAY.
I'LL TAKE THIS LAPTOP...
AND THIS MEMORY STICK...
EDITOR'S OFFICE
!
MEANWHILE...
WELL THAT'S ALL FIXED. PLUS MY MONEY IN GOLD IN A SWISS BANK JUST TO BE SAFE...
I NEED ONE MORE THING...

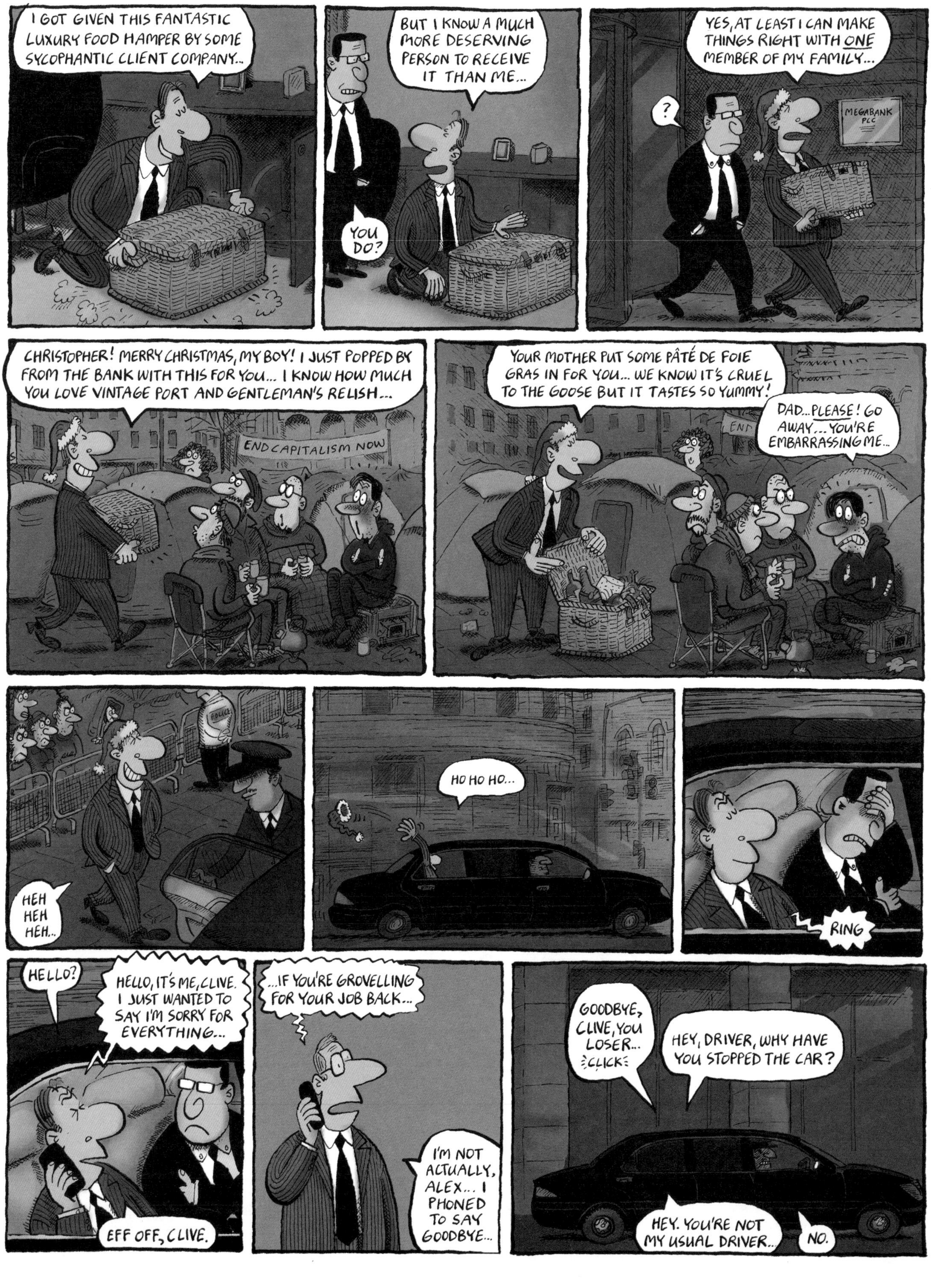
I GOT GIVEN THIS FANTASTIC LUXURY FOOD HAMPER BY SOME SYCOPHANTIC CLIENT COMPANY...
BUT I KNOW A MUCH MORE DESERVING PERSON TO RECEIVE IT THAN ME...
YOU DO?
YES, AT LEAST I CAN MAKE THINGS RIGHT WITH ONE MEMBER OF MY FAMILY...
?
MEGABANK PLC
CHRISTOPHER! MERRY CHRISTMAS, MY BOY! I JUST POPPED BY FROM THE BANK WITH THIS FOR YOU... I KNOW HOW MUCH YOU LOVE VINTAGE PORT AND GENTLEMAN'S RELISH...
END CAPITALISM NOW
YOUR MOTHER PUT SOME PÂTÉ DE FOIE GRAS IN FOR YOU... WE KNOW IT'S CRUEL TO THE GOOSE BUT IT TASTES SO YUMMY!
DAD... PLEASE! GO AWAY... YOU'RE EMBARRASSING ME...
HEH HEH HEH...
HO HO HO...
RING
HELLO?
HELLO, IT'S ME, CLIVE. I JUST WANTED TO SAY I'M SORRY FOR EVERYTHING...
EFF OFF, CLIVE.
...IF YOU'RE GROVELLING FOR YOUR JOB BACK...
I'M NOT ACTUALLY, ALEX... I PHONED TO SAY GOODBYE...
GOODBYE, CLIVE, YOU LOSER... CLICK
HEY, DRIVER, WHY HAVE YOU STOPPED THE CAR?
HEY. YOU'RE NOT MY USUAL DRIVER...
NO.

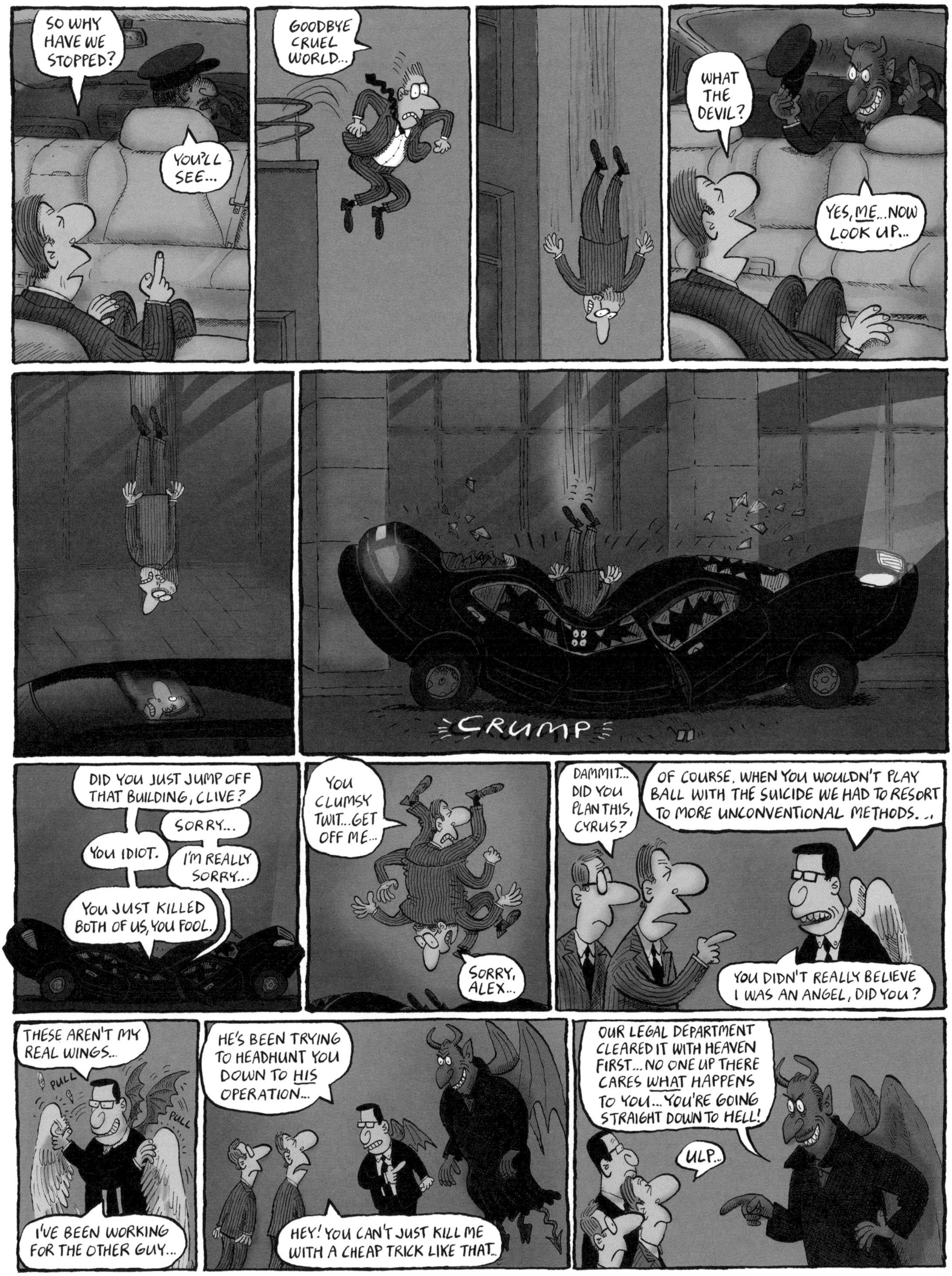
SO WHY HAVE WE STOPPED?
YOU'LL SEE...
GOODBYE CRUEL WORLD...
WHAT THE DEVIL?
YES, ME... NOW LOOK UP...
CRUMP
DID YOU JUST JUMP OFF THAT BUILDING, CLIVE?
SORRY...
YOU IDIOT.
I'M REALLY SORRY...
YOU JUST KILLED BOTH OF US, YOU FOOL.
YOU CLUMSY TWIT... GET OFF ME...
SORRY, ALEX...
DAMMIT... DID YOU PLAN THIS, CYRUS?
OF COURSE. WHEN YOU WOULDN'T PLAY BALL WITH THE SUICIDE WE HAD TO RESORT TO MORE UNCONVENTIONAL METHODS...
YOU DIDN'T REALLY BELIEVE I WAS AN ANGEL, DID YOU?
THESE AREN'T MY REAL WINGS...
PULL
PULL
I'VE BEEN WORKING FOR THE OTHER GUY...
HE'S BEEN TRYING TO HEADHUNT YOU DOWN TO HIS OPERATION...
HEY! YOU CAN'T JUST KILL ME WITH A CHEAP TRICK LIKE THAT...
OUR LEGAL DEPARTMENT CLEARED IT WITH HEAVEN FIRST... NO ONE UP THERE CARES WHAT HAPPENS TO YOU... YOU'RE GOING STRAIGHT DOWN TO HELL!
ULP...

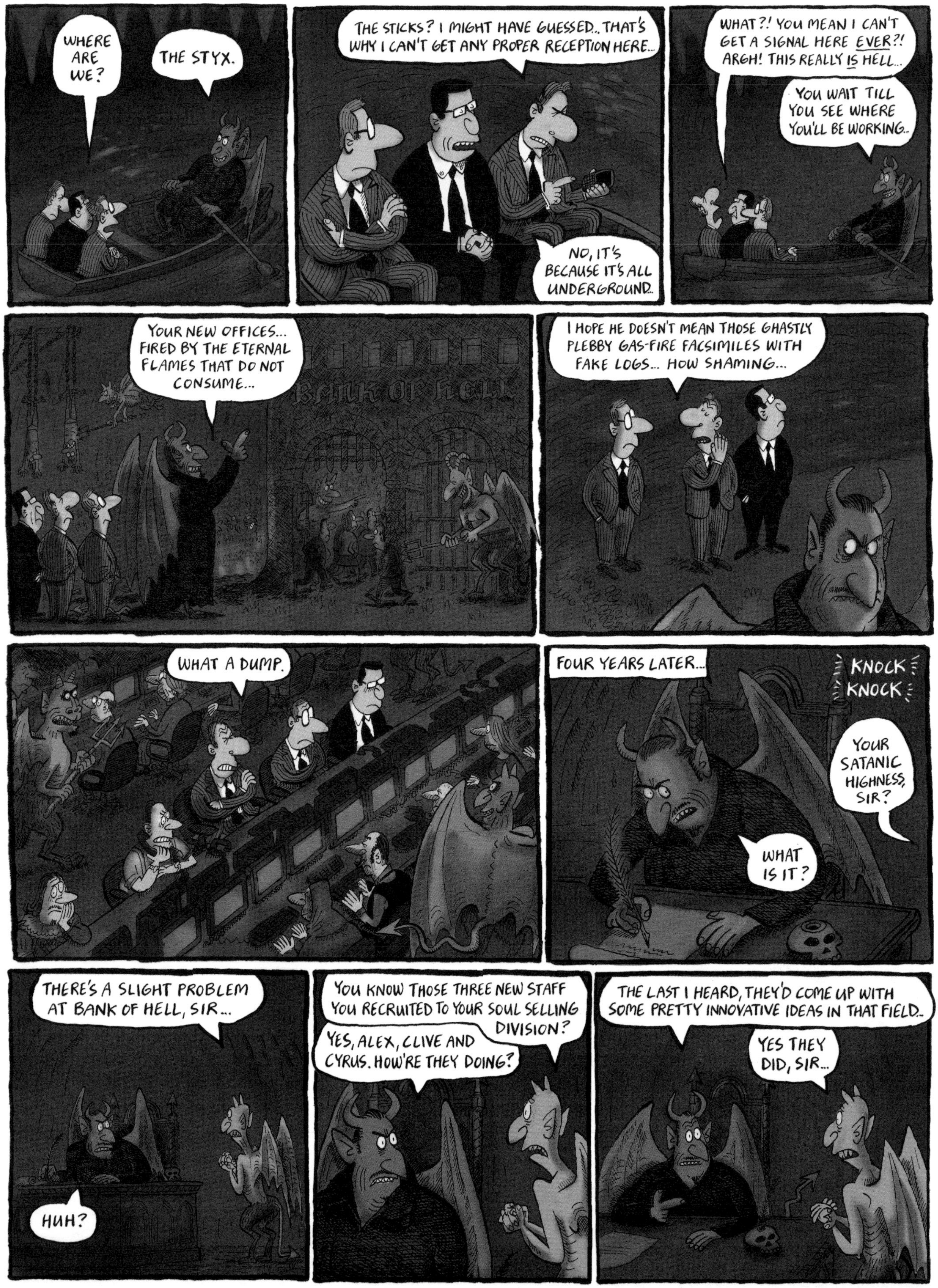
WHERE ARE WE?
THE STYX.
THE STICKS? I MIGHT HAVE GUESSED.. THAT'S WHY I CAN'T GET ANY PROPER RECEPTION HERE...
NO, IT'S BECAUSE IT'S ALL UNDERGROUND..
WHAT?! YOU MEAN I CAN'T GET A SIGNAL HERE EVER?! ARGH! THIS REALLY IS HELL...
YOU WAIT TILL YOU SEE WHERE YOU'LL BE WORKING..
YOUR NEW OFFICES... FIRED BY THE ETERNAL FLAMES THAT DO NOT CONSUME...
BANK OF HELL
I HOPE HE DOESN'T MEAN THOSE GHASTLY PLEBBY GAS-FIRE FACSIMILES WITH FAKE LOGS... HOW SHAMING...
WHAT A DUMP.
FOUR YEARS LATER...
KNOCK KNOCK
YOUR SATANIC HIGHNESS, SIR?
WHAT IS IT?
THERE'S A SLIGHT PROBLEM AT BANK OF HELL, SIR...
HUH?
YOU KNOW THOSE THREE NEW STAFF YOU RECRUITED TO YOUR SOUL SELLING DIVISION?
YES, ALEX, CLIVE AND CYRUS. HOW'RE THEY DOING?
THE LAST I HEARD, THEY'D COME UP WITH SOME PRETTY INNOVATIVE IDEAS IN THAT FIELD..
YES THEY DID, SIR...

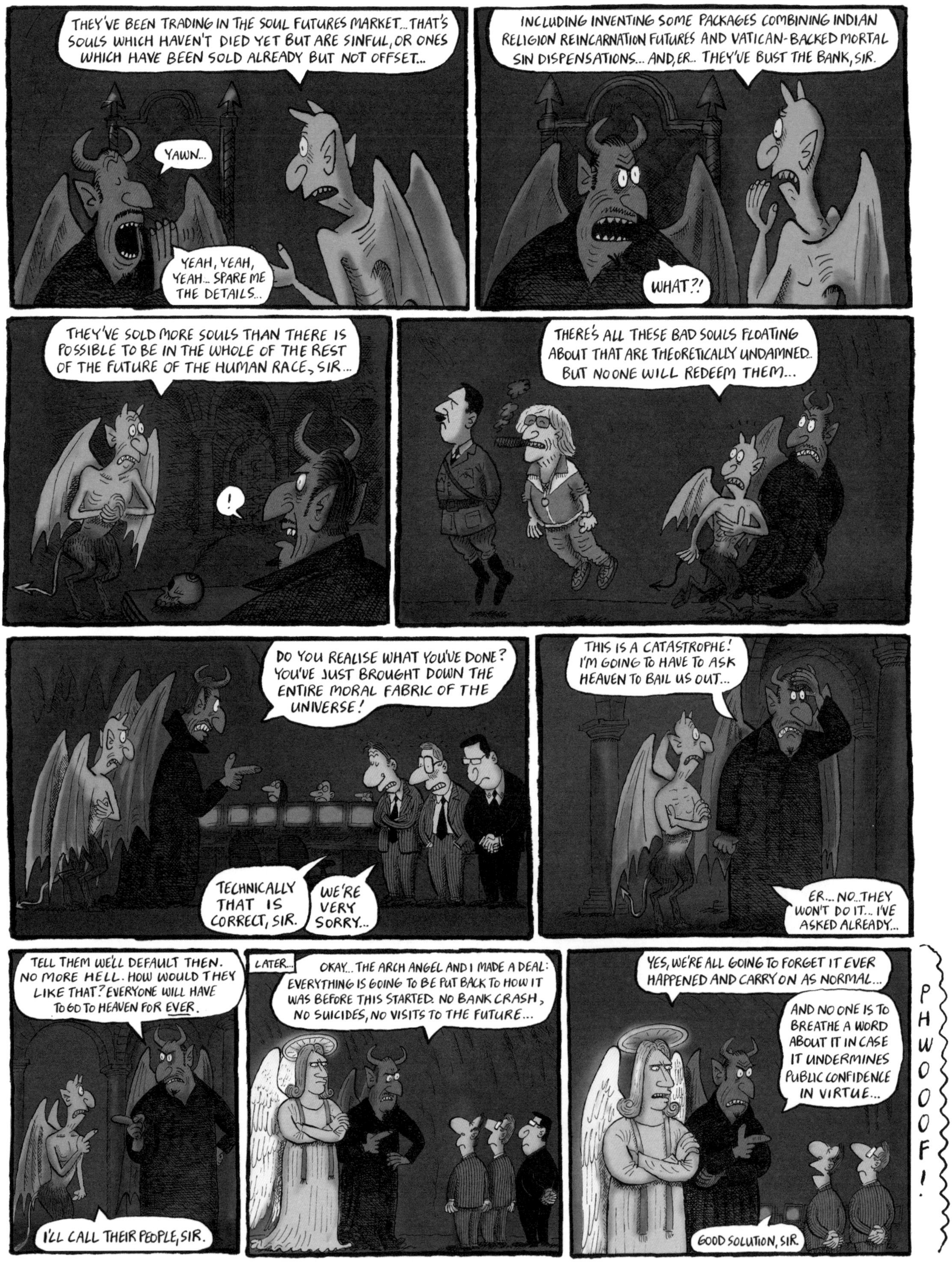
THEY'VE BEEN TRADING IN THE SOUL FUTURES MARKET... THAT'S SOULS WHICH HAVEN'T DIED YET BUT ARE SINFUL, OR ONES WHICH HAVE BEEN SOLD ALREADY BUT NOT OFFSET...
YAWN...
YEAH, YEAH, YEAH... SPARE ME THE DETAILS...
INCLUDING INVENTING SOME PACKAGES COMBINING INDIAN RELIGION REINCARNATION FUTURES AND VATICAN-BACKED MORTAL SIN DISPENSATIONS... AND, ER... THEY'VE BUST THE BANK, SIR.
WHAT?!
THEY'VE SOLD MORE SOULS THAN THERE IS POSSIBLE TO BE IN THE WHOLE OF THE REST OF THE FUTURE OF THE HUMAN RACE, SIR...
!
THERE'S ALL THESE BAD SOULS FLOATING ABOUT THAT ARE THEORETICALLY UNDAMNED... BUT NO ONE WILL REDEEM THEM...
DO YOU REALISE WHAT YOU'VE DONE? YOU'VE JUST BROUGHT DOWN THE ENTIRE MORAL FABRIC OF THE UNIVERSE!
TECHNICALLY THAT IS CORRECT, SIR.
WE'RE VERY SORRY...
THIS IS A CATASTROPHE! I'M GOING TO HAVE TO ASK HEAVEN TO BAIL US OUT...
ER... NO... THEY WON'T DO IT... I'VE ASKED ALREADY...
TELL THEM WE'LL DEFAULT THEN. NO MORE HELL. HOW WOULD THEY LIKE THAT? EVERYONE WILL HAVE TO GO TO HEAVEN FOR EVER.
I'LL CALL THEIR PEOPLE, SIR.
LATER...
OKAY... THE ARCH ANGEL AND I MADE A DEAL: EVERYTHING IS GOING TO BE PUT BACK TO HOW IT WAS BEFORE THIS STARTED. NO BANK CRASH, NO SUICIDES, NO VISITS TO THE FUTURE...
YES, WE'RE ALL GOING TO FORGET IT EVER HAPPENED AND CARRY ON AS NORMAL...
AND NO ONE IS TO BREATHE A WORD ABOUT IT IN CASE IT UNDERMINES PUBLIC CONFIDENCE IN VIRTUE...
GOOD SOLUTION, SIR.
PHWOOOF!

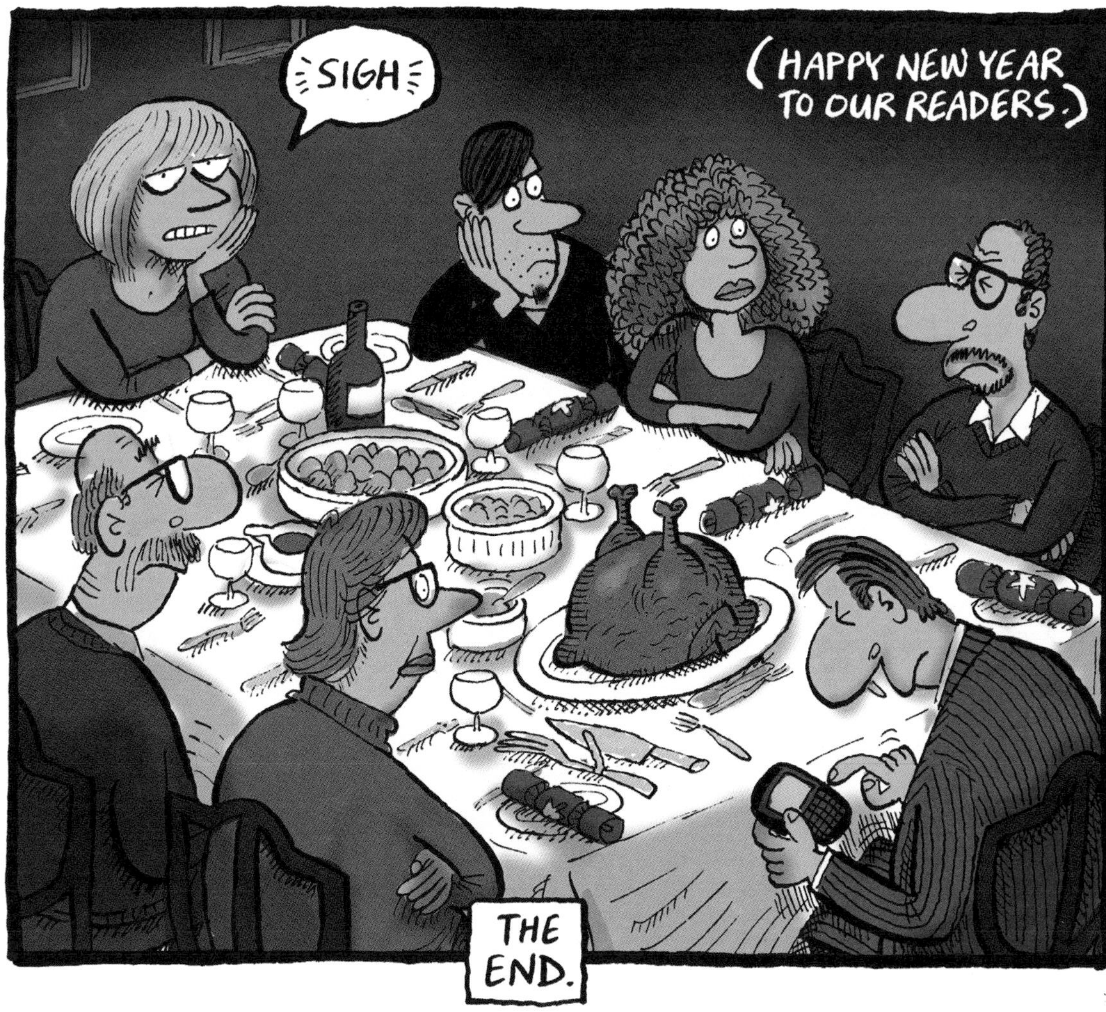
SIGH
(HAPPY NEW YEAR TO OUR READERS.)
THE END.

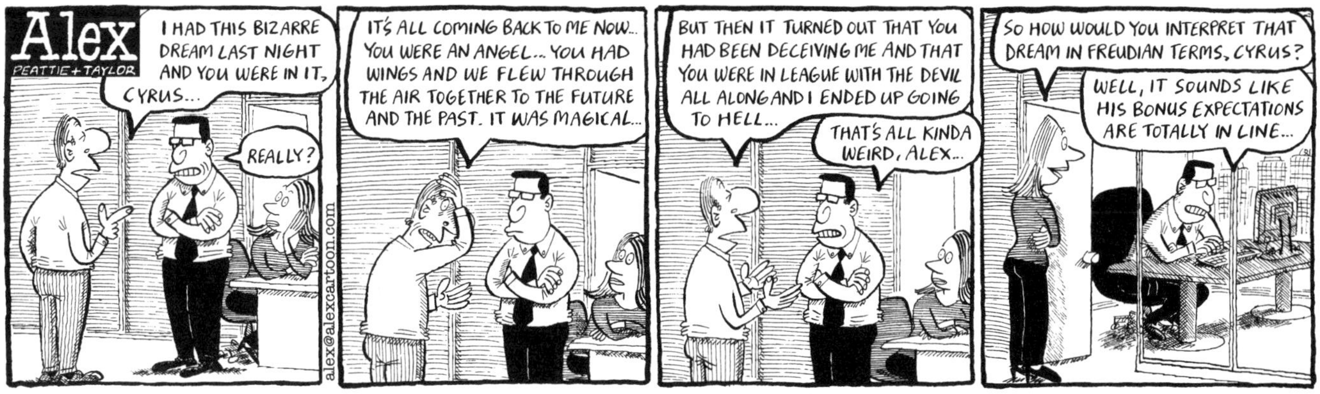
Alex
PEATTIE + TAYLOR
I HAD THIS BIZARRE DREAM LAST NIGHT AND YOU WERE IN IT, CYRUS...
REALLY?
alex@alexcartoon.com
IT'S ALL COMING BACK TO ME NOW... YOU WERE AN ANGEL... YOU HAD WINGS AND WE FLEW THROUGH THE AIR TOGETHER TO THE FUTURE AND THE PAST. IT WAS MAGICAL...
BUT THEN IT TURNED OUT THAT YOU HAD BEEN DECEIVING ME AND THAT YOU WERE IN LEAGUE WITH THE DEVIL ALL ALONG AND I ENDED UP GOING TO HELL...
THAT'S ALL KINDA WEIRD, ALEX...
SO HOW WOULD YOU INTERPRET THAT DREAM IN FREUDIAN TERMS, CYRUS?
WELL, IT SOUNDS LIKE HIS BONUS EXPECTATIONS ARE TOTALLY IN LINE...

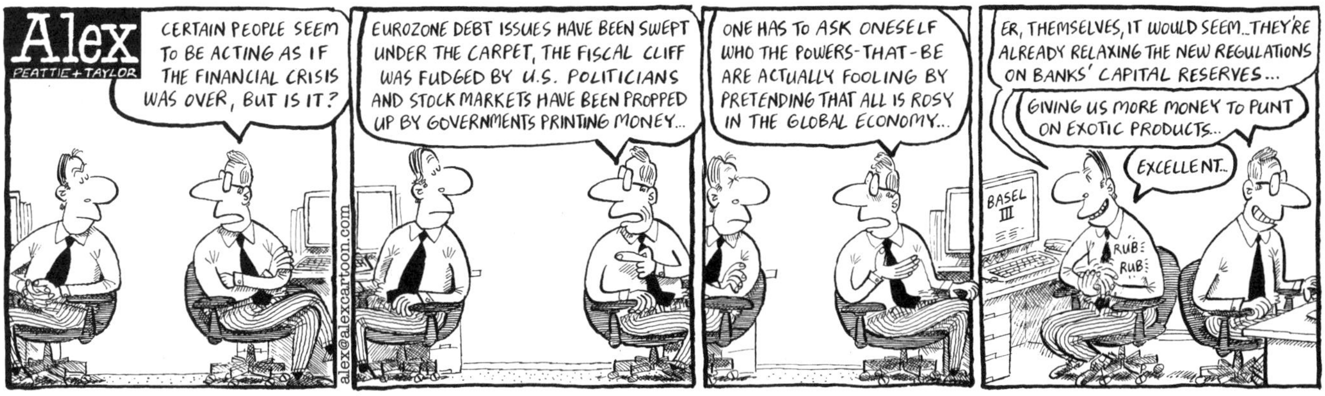
Alex
PEATTIE + TAYLOR
CERTAIN PEOPLE SEEM TO BE ACTING AS IF THE FINANCIAL CRISIS WAS OVER, BUT IS IT?
alex@alexcartoon.com
EUROZONE DEBT ISSUES HAVE BEEN SWEPT UNDER THE CARPET, THE FISCAL CLIFF WAS FUDGED BY U.S. POLITICIANS AND STOCK MARKETS HAVE BEEN PROPPED UP BY GOVERNMENTS PRINTING MONEY...
ONE HAS TO ASK ONESELF WHO THE POWERS-THAT-BE ARE ACTUALLY FOOLING BY PRETENDING THAT ALL IS ROSY IN THE GLOBAL ECONOMY...
ER, THEMSELVES, IT WOULD SEEM... THEY'RE ALREADY RELAXING THE NEW REGULATIONS ON BANKS' CAPITAL RESERVES...
GIVING US MORE MONEY TO PUNT ON EXOTIC PRODUCTS...
EXCELLENT...
BASEL III
RUB RUB

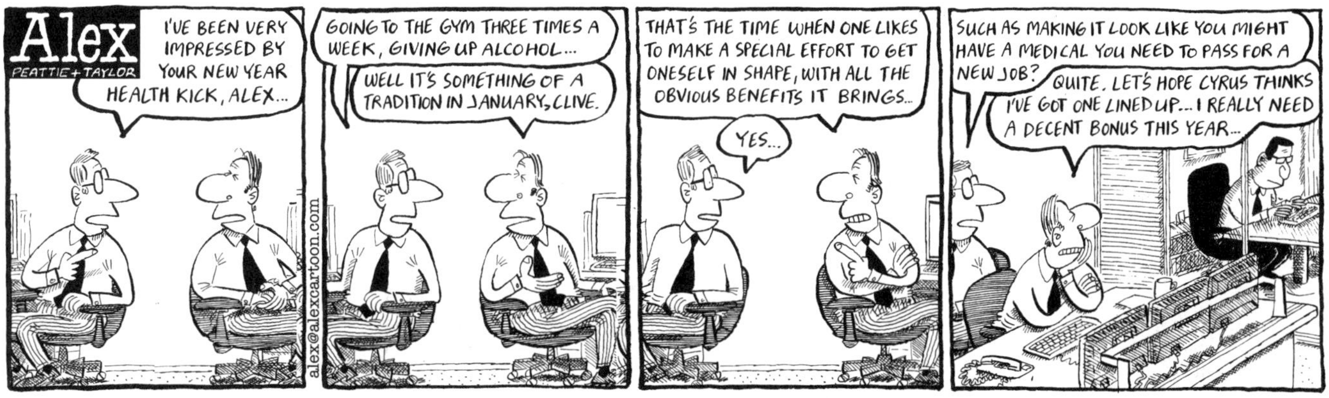
Alex
PEATTIE + TAYLOR
I'VE BEEN VERY IMPRESSED BY YOUR NEW YEAR HEALTH KICK, ALEX...
alex@alexcartoon.com
GOING TO THE GYM THREE TIMES A WEEK, GIVING UP ALCOHOL...
WELL IT'S SOMETHING OF A TRADITION IN JANUARY, CLIVE.
THAT'S THE TIME WHEN ONE LIKES TO MAKE A SPECIAL EFFORT TO GET ONESELF IN SHAPE, WITH ALL THE OBVIOUS BENEFITS IT BRINGS...
YES...
SUCH AS MAKING IT LOOK LIKE YOU MIGHT HAVE A MEDICAL YOU NEED TO PASS FOR A NEW JOB?
QUITE. LET'S HOPE CYRUS THINKS I'VE GOT ONE LINED UP... I REALLY NEED A DECENT BONUS THIS YEAR...

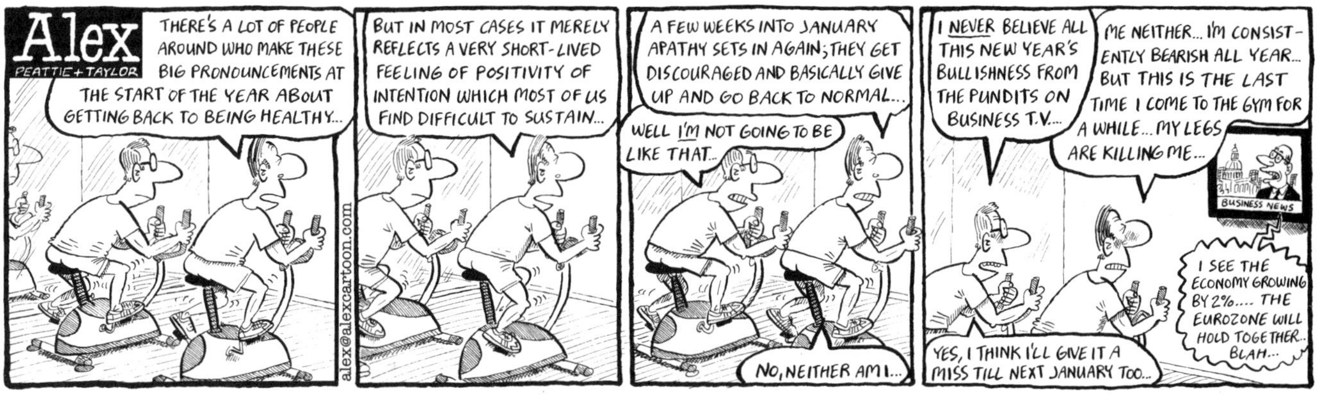
Alex
PEATTIE + TAYLOR
THERE'S A LOT OF PEOPLE AROUND WHO MAKE THESE BIG PRONOUNCEMENTS AT THE START OF THE YEAR ABOUT GETTING BACK TO BEING HEALTHY...
alex@alexcartoon.com
BUT IN MOST CASES IT MERELY REFLECTS A VERY SHORT-LIVED FEELING OF POSITIVITY OF INTENTION WHICH MOST OF US FIND DIFFICULT TO SUSTAIN...
A FEW WEEKS INTO JANUARY APATHY SETS IN AGAIN; THEY GET DISCOURAGED AND BASICALLY GIVE UP AND GO BACK TO NORMAL...
WELL I'M NOT GOING TO BE LIKE THAT...
NO, NEITHER AM I...
I NEVER BELIEVE ALL THIS NEW YEAR'S BULLISHNESS FROM THE PUNDITS ON BUSINESS T.V....
ME NEITHER... I'M CONSISTENTLY BEARISH ALL YEAR... BUT THIS IS THE LAST TIME I COME TO THE GYM FOR A WHILE... MY LEGS ARE KILLING ME...
BUSINESS NEWS
I SEE THE ECONOMY GROWING BY 2%.... THE EUROZONE WILL HOLD TOGETHER.. BLAH...
YES, I THINK I'LL GIVE IT A MISS TILL NEXT JANUARY TOO...

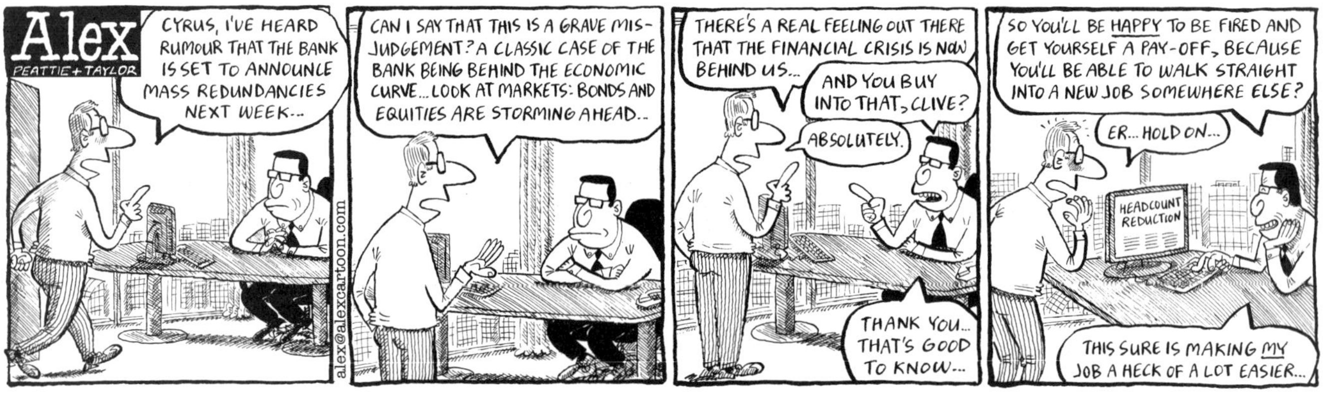
Alex
PEATTIE + TAYLOR
CYRUS, I'VE HEARD RUMOUR THAT THE BANK IS SET TO ANNOUNCE MASS REDUNDANCIES NEXT WEEK...
alex@alexcartoon.com
CAN I SAY THAT THIS IS A GRAVE MIS-JUDGEMENT? A CLASSIC CASE OF THE BANK BEING BEHIND THE ECONOMIC CURVE... LOOK AT MARKETS: BONDS AND EQUITIES ARE STORMING AHEAD..
THERE'S A REAL FEELING OUT THERE THAT THE FINANCIAL CRISIS IS NOW BEHIND US...
AND YOU BUY INTO THAT, CLIVE?
ABSOLUTELY.
THANK YOU... THAT'S GOOD TO KNOW...
SO YOU'LL BE HAPPY TO BE FIRED AND GET YOURSELF A PAY-OFF, BECAUSE YOU'LL BE ABLE TO WALK STRAIGHT INTO A NEW JOB SOMEWHERE ELSE?
ER... HOLD ON...
HEADCOUNT REDUCTION
THIS SURE IS MAKING MY JOB A HECK OF A LOT EASIER...

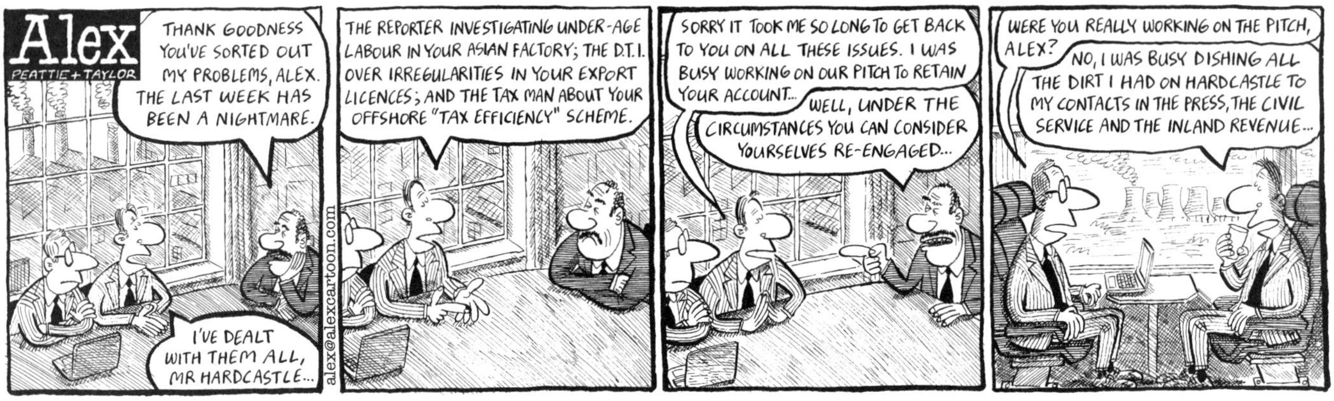
Alex
PEATTIE + TAYLOR
THANK GOODNESS YOU'VE SORTED OUT MY PROBLEMS, ALEX. THE LAST WEEK HAS BEEN A NIGHTMARE.
I'VE DEALT WITH THEM ALL, MR HARDCASTLE...
alex@alexcartoon.com
THE REPORTER INVESTIGATING UNDER-AGE LABOUR IN YOUR ASIAN FACTORY; THE D.T.I. OVER IRREGULARITIES IN YOUR EXPORT LICENCES; AND THE TAX MAN ABOUT YOUR OFFSHORE "TAX EFFICIENCY" SCHEME.
SORRY IT TOOK ME SO LONG TO GET BACK TO YOU ON ALL THESE ISSUES. I WAS BUSY WORKING ON OUR PITCH TO RETAIN YOUR ACCOUNT...
WELL, UNDER THE CIRCUMSTANCES YOU CAN CONSIDER YOURSELVES RE-ENGAGED...
WERE YOU REALLY WORKING ON THE PITCH, ALEX?
NO, I WAS BUSY DISHING ALL THE DIRT I HAD ON HARDCASTLE TO MY CONTACTS IN THE PRESS, THE CIVIL SERVICE AND THE INLAND REVENUE...

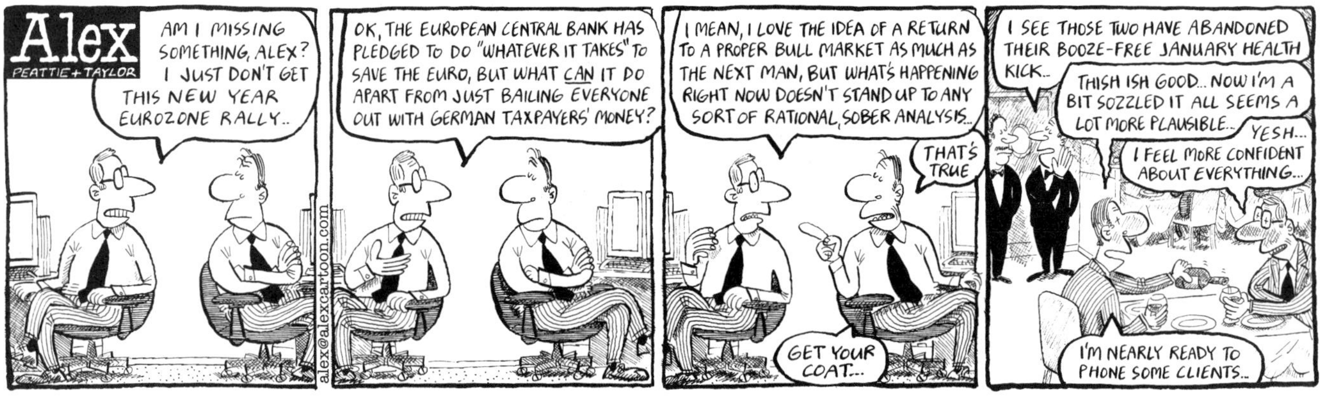
Alex
PEATTIE + TAYLOR
AM I MISSING SOMETHING, ALEX? I JUST DON'T GET THIS NEW YEAR EUROZONE RALLY..
alex@alexcartoon.com
OK, THE EUROPEAN CENTRAL BANK HAS PLEDGED TO DO "WHATEVER IT TAKES" TO SAVE THE EURO, BUT WHAT CAN IT DO APART FROM JUST BAILING EVERYONE OUT WITH GERMAN TAXPAYERS' MONEY?
I MEAN, I LOVE THE IDEA OF A RETURN TO A PROPER BULL MARKET AS MUCH AS THE NEXT MAN, BUT WHAT'S HAPPENING RIGHT NOW DOESN'T STAND UP TO ANY SORT OF RATIONAL, SOBER ANALYSIS...
THAT'S TRUE
GET YOUR COAT...
I SEE THOSE TWO HAVE ABANDONED THEIR BOOZE-FREE JANUARY HEALTH KICK..
THISH ISH GOOD... NOW I'M A BIT SOZZLED IT ALL SEEMS A LOT MORE PLAUSIBLE...
YESH...
I FEEL MORE CONFIDENT ABOUT EVERYTHING...
I'M NEARLY READY TO PHONE SOME CLIENTS...

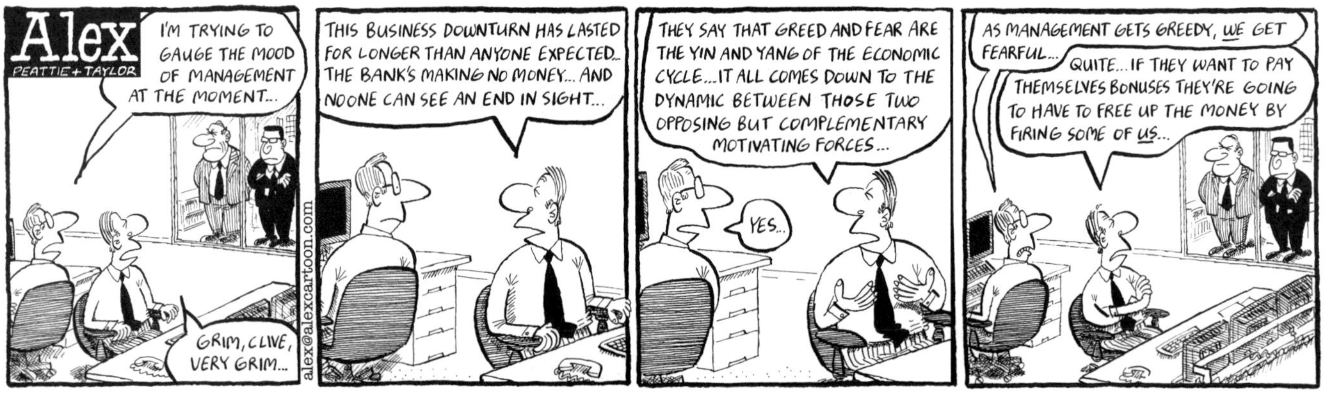
Alex
PEATTIE + TAYLOR
I'M TRYING TO GAUGE THE MOOD OF MANAGEMENT AT THE MOMENT...
GRIM, CLIVE, VERY GRIM...
alex@alexcartoon.com
THIS BUSINESS DOWNTURN HAS LASTED FOR LONGER THAN ANYONE EXPECTED... THE BANK'S MAKING NO MONEY... AND NOONE CAN SEE AN END IN SIGHT...
THEY SAY THAT GREED AND FEAR ARE THE YIN AND YANG OF THE ECONOMIC CYCLE... IT ALL COMES DOWN TO THE DYNAMIC BETWEEN THOSE TWO OPPOSING BUT COMPLEMENTARY MOTIVATING FORCES...
YES...
AS MANAGEMENT GETS GREEDY, WE GET FEARFUL...
QUITE... IF THEY WANT TO PAY THEMSELVES BONUSES THEY'RE GOING TO HAVE TO FREE UP THE MONEY BY FIRING SOME OF US...

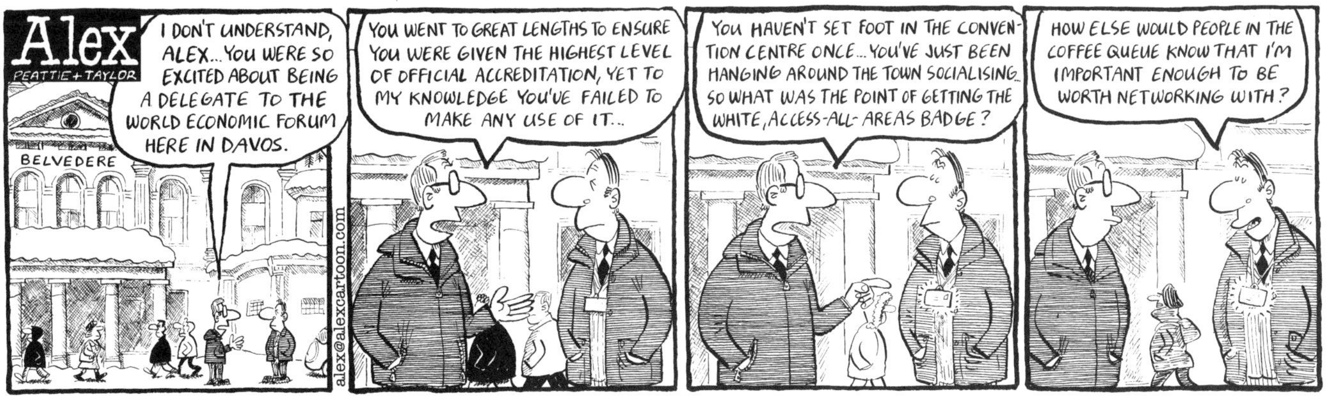
Alex
PEATTIE + TAYLOR
BELVEDERE
I DON'T UNDERSTAND, ALEX... YOU WERE SO EXCITED ABOUT BEING A DELEGATE TO THE WORLD ECONOMIC FORUM HERE IN DAVOS.
alex@alexcartoon.com
YOU WENT TO GREAT LENGTHS TO ENSURE YOU WERE GIVEN THE HIGHEST LEVEL OF OFFICIAL ACCREDITATION, YET TO MY KNOWLEDGE YOU'VE FAILED TO MAKE ANY USE OF IT...
YOU HAVEN'T SET FOOT IN THE CONVENTION CENTRE ONCE... YOU'VE JUST BEEN HANGING AROUND THE TOWN SOCIALISING, SO WHAT WAS THE POINT OF GETTING THE WHITE, ACCESS-ALL-AREAS BADGE?
HOW ELSE WOULD PEOPLE IN THE COFFEE QUEUE KNOW THAT I'M IMPORTANT ENOUGH TO BE WORTH NETWORKING WITH?

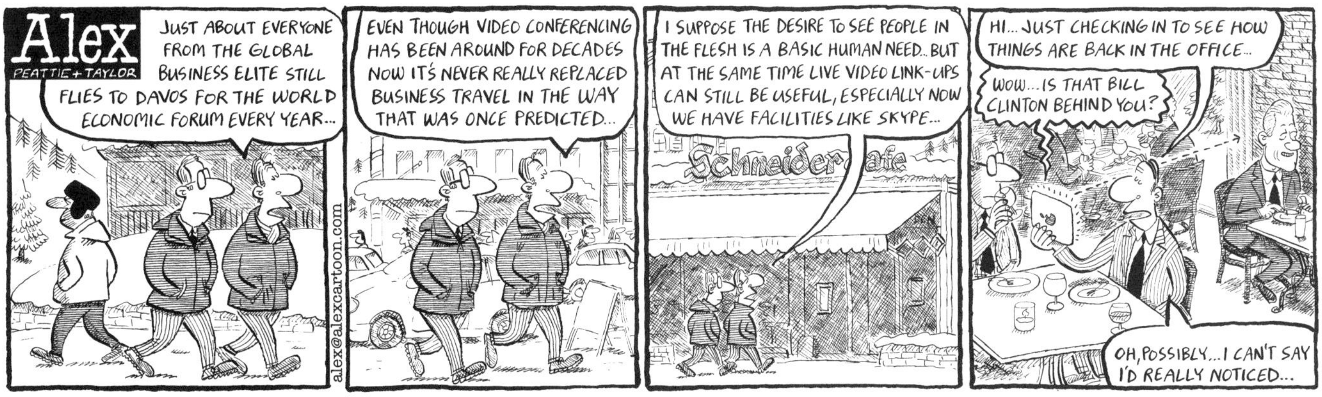
Alex
PEATTIE + TAYLOR
JUST ABOUT EVERYONE FROM THE GLOBAL BUSINESS ELITE STILL FLIES TO DAVOS FOR THE WORLD ECONOMIC FORUM EVERY YEAR...
alex@alexcartoon.com
EVEN THOUGH VIDEO CONFERENCING HAS BEEN AROUND FOR DECADES NOW IT'S NEVER REALLY REPLACED BUSINESS TRAVEL IN THE WAY THAT WAS ONCE PREDICTED...
I SUPPOSE THE DESIRE TO SEE PEOPLE IN THE FLESH IS A BASIC HUMAN NEED... BUT AT THE SAME TIME LIVE VIDEO LINK-UPS CAN STILL BE USEFUL, ESPECIALLY NOW WE HAVE FACILITIES LIKE SKYPE...
Schneider
HI... JUST CHECKING IN TO SEE HOW THINGS ARE BACK IN THE OFFICE...
WOW... IS THAT BILL CLINTON BEHIND YOU?
OH, POSSIBLY... I CAN'T SAY I'D REALLY NOTICED...

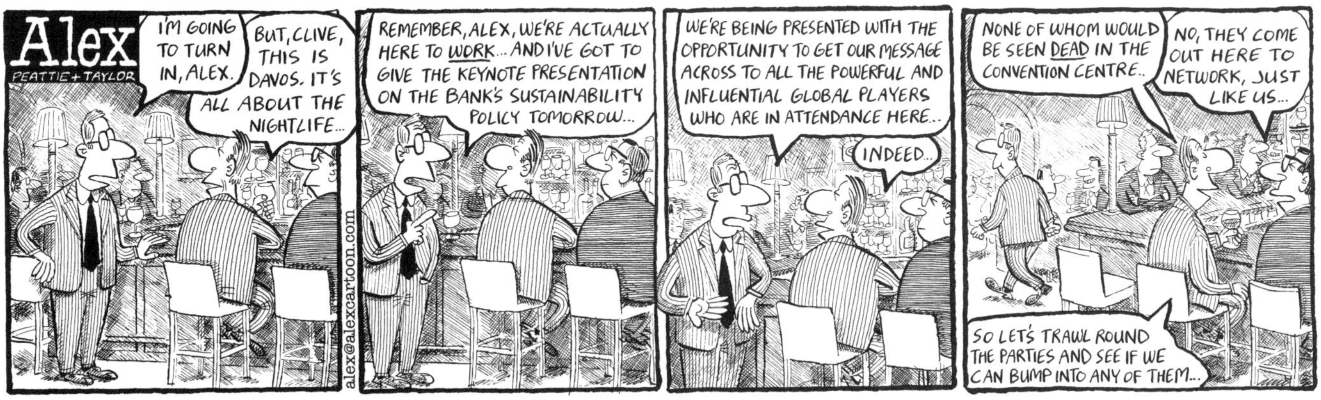
Alex
PEATTIE + TAYLOR
I'M GOING TO TURN IN, ALEX.
BUT, CLIVE, THIS IS DAVOS. IT'S ALL ABOUT THE NIGHTLIFE...
alex@alexcartoon.com
REMEMBER, ALEX, WE'RE ACTUALLY HERE TO WORK... AND I'VE GOT TO GIVE THE KEYNOTE PRESENTATION ON THE BANK'S SUSTAINABILITY POLICY TOMORROW...
WE'RE BEING PRESENTED WITH THE OPPORTUNITY TO GET OUR MESSAGE ACROSS TO ALL THE POWERFUL AND INFLUENTIAL GLOBAL PLAYERS WHO ARE IN ATTENDANCE HERE...
INDEED...
NONE OF WHOM WOULD BE SEEN DEAD IN THE CONVENTION CENTRE...
NO, THEY COME OUT HERE TO NETWORK, JUST LIKE US...
SO LET'S TRAWL ROUND THE PARTIES AND SEE IF WE CAN BUMP INTO ANY OF THEM...

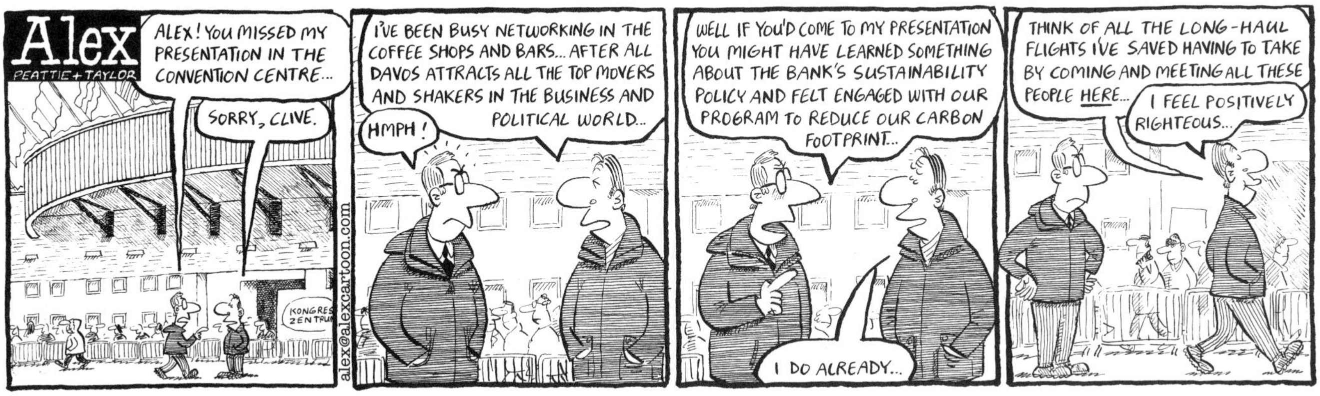
Alex
PEATTIE + TAYLOR
ALEX! YOU MISSED MY PRESENTATION IN THE CONVENTION CENTRE...
SORRY, CLIVE.
KONGRESS ZENTRUM
alex@alexcartoon.com
I'VE BEEN BUSY NETWORKING IN THE COFFEE SHOPS AND BARS... AFTER ALL DAVOS ATTRACTS ALL THE TOP MOVERS AND SHAKERS IN THE BUSINESS AND POLITICAL WORLD...
HMPH!
WELL IF YOU'D COME TO MY PRESENTATION YOU MIGHT HAVE LEARNED SOMETHING ABOUT THE BANK'S SUSTAINABILITY POLICY AND FELT ENGAGED WITH OUR PROGRAM TO REDUCE OUR CARBON FOOTPRINT...
I DO ALREADY...
THINK OF ALL THE LONG-HAUL FLIGHTS I'VE SAVED HAVING TO TAKE BY COMING AND MEETING ALL THESE PEOPLE HERE...
I FEEL POSITIVELY RIGHTEOUS...

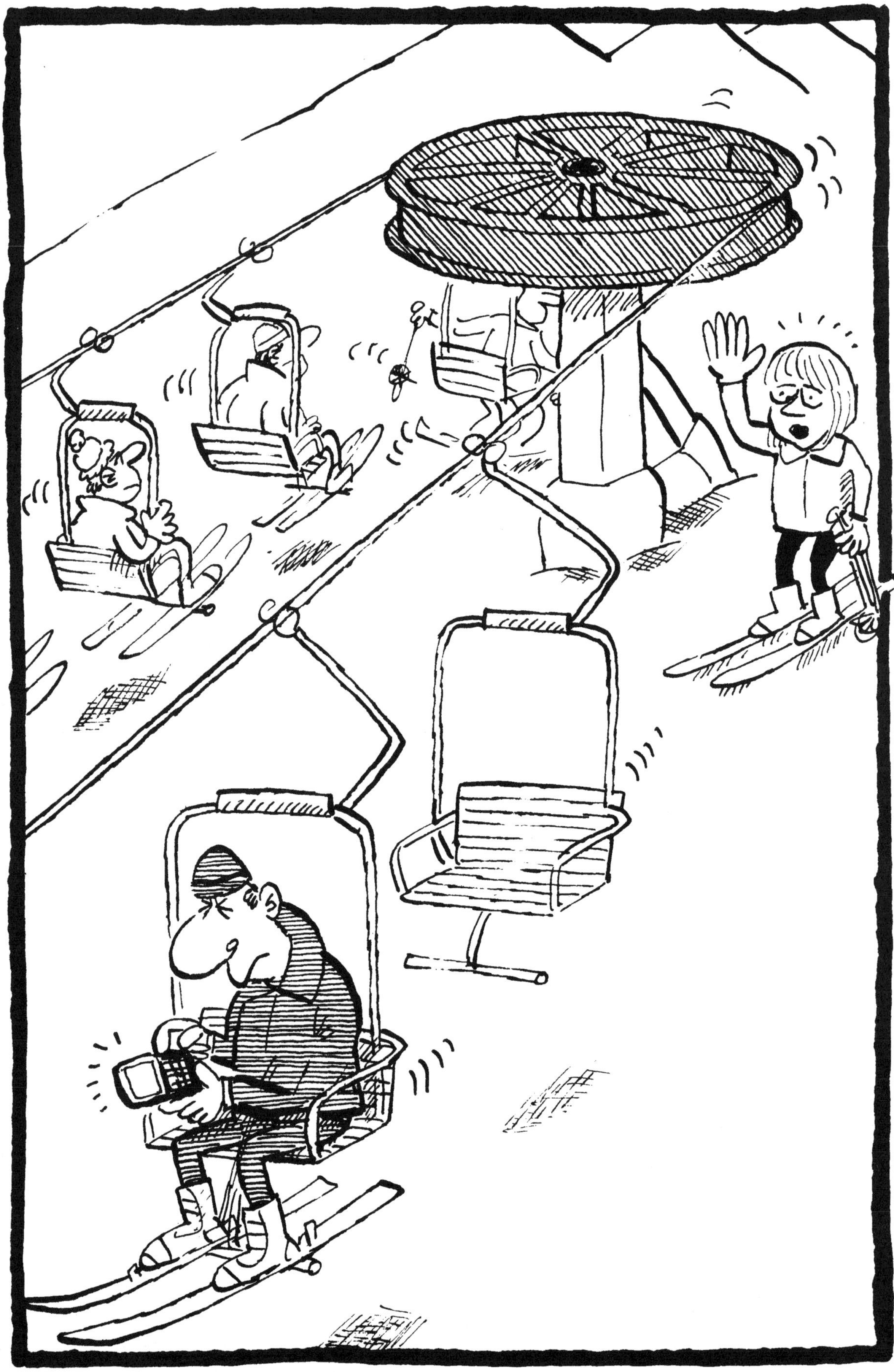

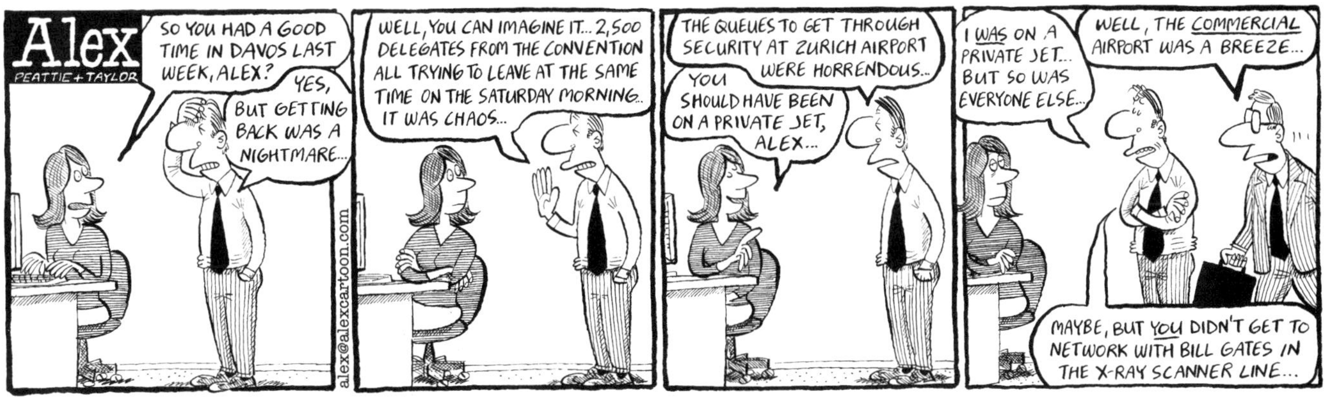
Alex
PEATTIE + TAYLOR
SO YOU HAD A GOOD TIME IN DAVOS LAST WEEK, ALEX?
YES, BUT GETTING BACK WAS A NIGHTMARE...
WELL, YOU CAN IMAGINE IT... 2,500 DELEGATES FROM THE CONVENTION ALL TRYING TO LEAVE AT THE SAME TIME ON THE SATURDAY MORNING.. IT WAS CHAOS...
alex@alexcartoon.com
THE QUEUES TO GET THROUGH SECURITY AT ZURICH AIRPORT WERE HORRENDOUS...
YOU SHOULD HAVE BEEN ON A PRIVATE JET, ALEX...
I WAS ON A PRIVATE JET... BUT SO WAS EVERYONE ELSE...
WELL, THE COMMERCIAL AIRPORT WAS A BREEZE...
MAYBE, BUT YOU DIDN'T GET TO NETWORK WITH BILL GATES IN THE X-RAY SCANNER LINE...

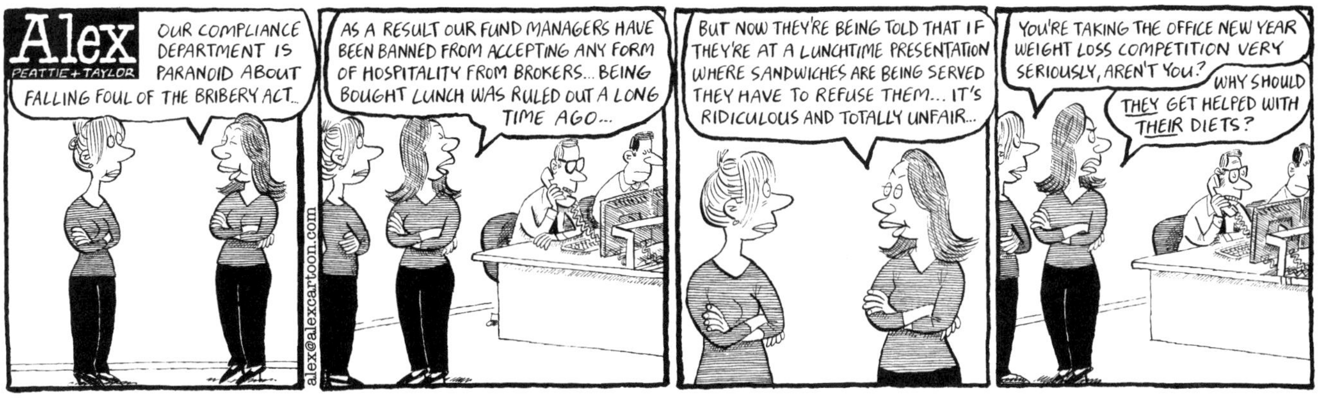
Alex
PEATTIE + TAYLOR
OUR COMPLIANCE DEPARTMENT IS PARANOID ABOUT FALLING FOUL OF THE BRIBERY ACT...
AS A RESULT OUR FUND MANAGERS HAVE BEEN BANNED FROM ACCEPTING ANY FORM OF HOSPITALITY FROM BROKERS... BEING BOUGHT LUNCH WAS RULED OUT A LONG TIME AGO...
alex@alexcartoon.com
BUT NOW THEY'RE BEING TOLD THAT IF THEY'RE AT A LUNCHTIME PRESENTATION WHERE SANDWICHES ARE BEING SERVED THEY HAVE TO REFUSE THEM... IT'S RIDICULOUS AND TOTALLY UNFAIR...
YOU'RE TAKING THE OFFICE NEW YEAR WEIGHT LOSS COMPETITION VERY SERIOUSLY, AREN'T YOU?
WHY SHOULD THEY GET HELPED WITH THEIR DIETS?

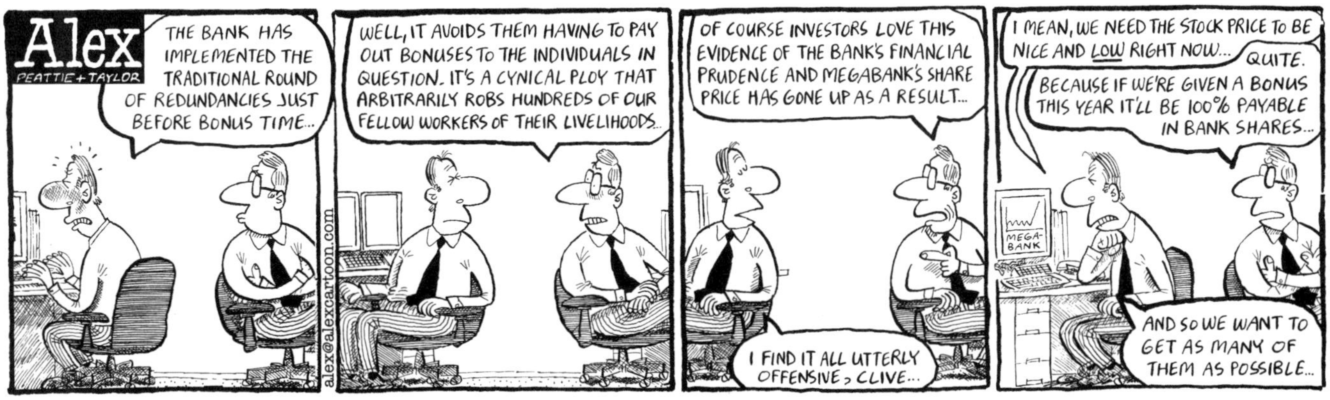
Alex
PEATTIE + TAYLOR
THE BANK HAS IMPLEMENTED THE TRADITIONAL ROUND OF REDUNDANCIES JUST BEFORE BONUS TIME...
WELL, IT AVOIDS THEM HAVING TO PAY OUT BONUSES TO THE INDIVIDUALS IN QUESTION. IT'S A CYNICAL PLOY THAT ARBITRARILY ROBS HUNDREDS OF OUR FELLOW WORKERS OF THEIR LIVELIHOODS...
alex@alexcartoon.com
OF COURSE INVESTORS LOVE THIS EVIDENCE OF THE BANK'S FINANCIAL PRUDENCE AND MEGABANK'S SHARE PRICE HAS GONE UP AS A RESULT...
I FIND IT ALL UTTERLY OFFENSIVE, CLIVE...
I MEAN, WE NEED THE STOCK PRICE TO BE NICE AND LOW RIGHT NOW...
QUITE. BECAUSE IF WE'RE GIVEN A BONUS THIS YEAR IT'LL BE 100% PAYABLE IN BANK SHARES...
MEGA-BANK
AND SO WE WANT TO GET AS MANY OF THEM AS POSSIBLE...

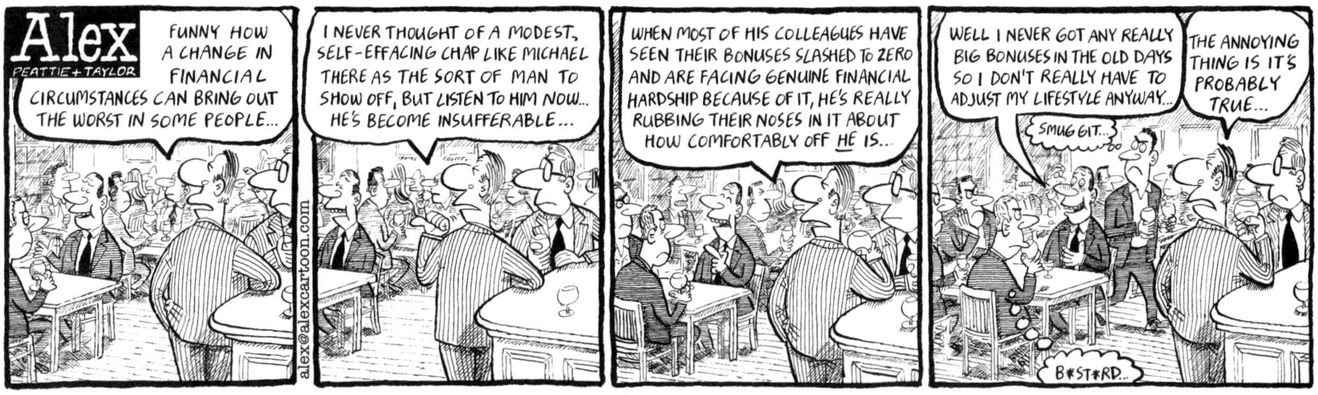
Alex
PEATTIE + TAYLOR
FUNNY HOW A CHANGE IN FINANCIAL CIRCUMSTANCES CAN BRING OUT THE WORST IN SOME PEOPLE...
I NEVER THOUGHT OF A MODEST, SELF-EFFACING CHAP LIKE MICHAEL THERE AS THE SORT OF MAN TO SHOW OFF, BUT LISTEN TO HIM NOW... HE'S BECOME INSUFFERABLE...
alex@alexcartoon.com
WHEN MOST OF HIS COLLEAGUES HAVE SEEN THEIR BONUSES SLASHED TO ZERO AND ARE FACING GENUINE FINANCIAL HARDSHIP BECAUSE OF IT, HE'S REALLY RUBBING THEIR NOSES IN IT ABOUT HOW COMFORTABLY OFF HE IS...
WELL I NEVER GOT ANY REALLY BIG BONUSES IN THE OLD DAYS SO I DON'T REALLY HAVE TO ADJUST MY LIFESTYLE ANYWAY...
THE ANNOYING THING IS IT'S PROBABLY TRUE...
SMUG GIT...
B*ST*RD...

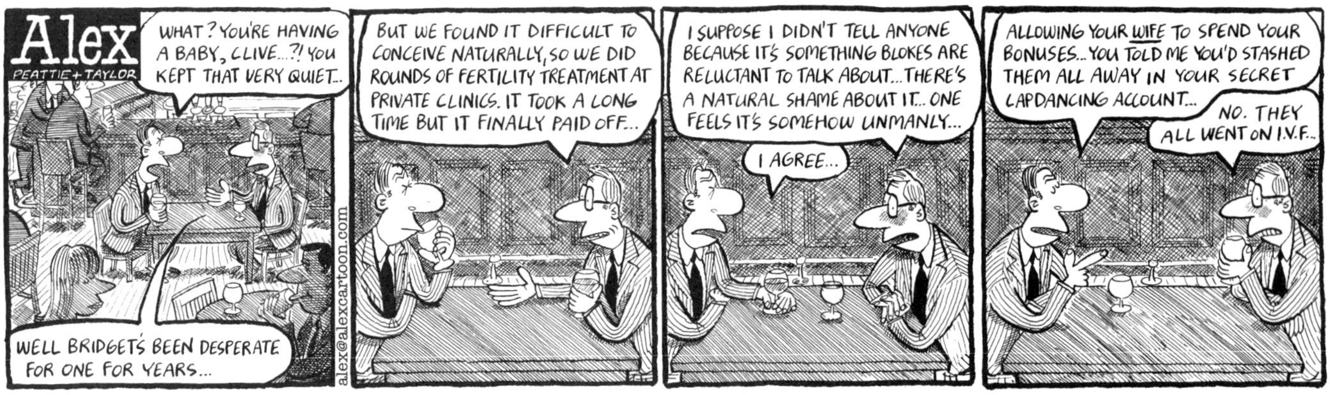
Alex
PEATTIE + TAYLOR
WHAT? YOU'RE HAVING A BABY, CLIVE...?! YOU KEPT THAT VERY QUIET...
WELL BRIDGET'S BEEN DESPERATE FOR ONE FOR YEARS...
alex@alexcartoon.com
BUT WE FOUND IT DIFFICULT TO CONCEIVE NATURALLY, SO WE DID ROUNDS OF FERTILITY TREATMENT AT PRIVATE CLINICS. IT TOOK A LONG TIME BUT IT FINALLY PAID OFF...
I SUPPOSE I DIDN'T TELL ANYONE BECAUSE IT'S SOMETHING BLOKES ARE RELUCTANT TO TALK ABOUT... THERE'S A NATURAL SHAME ABOUT IT... ONE FEELS IT'S SOMEHOW UNMANLY...
I AGREE...
ALLOWING YOUR WIFE TO SPEND YOUR BONUSES... YOU TOLD ME YOU'D STASHED THEM ALL AWAY IN YOUR SECRET LAPDANCING ACCOUNT...
NO. THEY ALL WENT ON I.V.F...

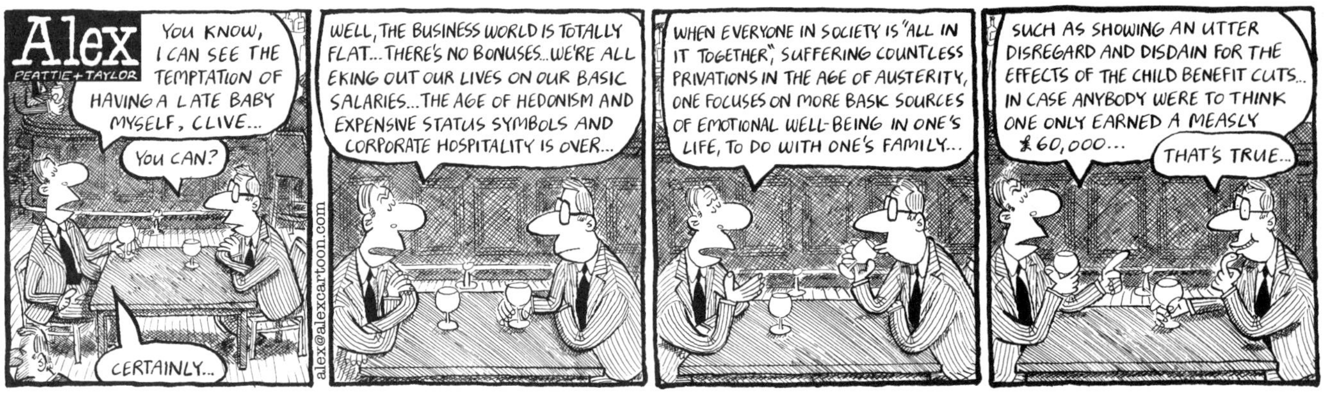
Alex
PEATTIE + TAYLOR
YOU KNOW, I CAN SEE THE TEMPTATION OF HAVING A LATE BABY MYSELF, CLIVE...
YOU CAN?
CERTAINLY...
alex@alexcartoon.com
WELL, THE BUSINESS WORLD IS TOTALLY FLAT... THERE'S NO BONUSES... WE'RE ALL EKING OUT OUR LIVES ON OUR BASIC SALARIES... THE AGE OF HEDONISM AND EXPENSIVE STATUS SYMBOLS AND CORPORATE HOSPITALITY IS OVER...
WHEN EVERYONE IN SOCIETY IS "ALL IN IT TOGETHER", SUFFERING COUNTLESS PRIVATIONS IN THE AGE OF AUSTERITY, ONE FOCUSES ON MORE BASIC SOURCES OF EMOTIONAL WELL-BEING IN ONE'S LIFE, TO DO WITH ONE'S FAMILY...
SUCH AS SHOWING AN UTTER DISREGARD AND DISDAIN FOR THE EFFECTS OF THE CHILD BENEFIT CUTS... IN CASE ANYBODY WERE TO THINK ONE ONLY EARNED A MEASLY £60,000...
THAT'S TRUE...

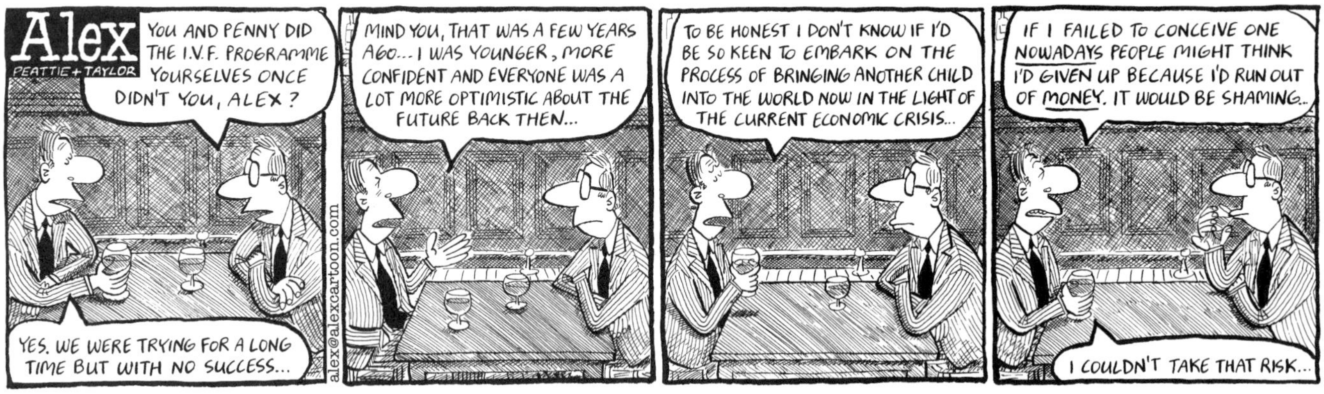
Alex
PEATTIE + TAYLOR
YOU AND PENNY DID THE I.V.F. PROGRAMME YOURSELVES ONCE DIDN'T YOU, ALEX?
YES. WE WERE TRYING FOR A LONG TIME BUT WITH NO SUCCESS...
alex@alexcartoon.com
MIND YOU, THAT WAS A FEW YEARS AGO... I WAS YOUNGER, MORE CONFIDENT AND EVERYONE WAS A LOT MORE OPTIMISTIC ABOUT THE FUTURE BACK THEN...
TO BE HONEST I DON'T KNOW IF I'D BE SO KEEN TO EMBARK ON THE PROCESS OF BRINGING ANOTHER CHILD INTO THE WORLD NOW IN THE LIGHT OF THE CURRENT ECONOMIC CRISIS...
IF I FAILED TO CONCEIVE ONE NOWADAYS PEOPLE MIGHT THINK I'D GIVEN UP BECAUSE I'D RUN OUT OF MONEY. IT WOULD BE SHAMING...
I COULDN'T TAKE THAT RISK...

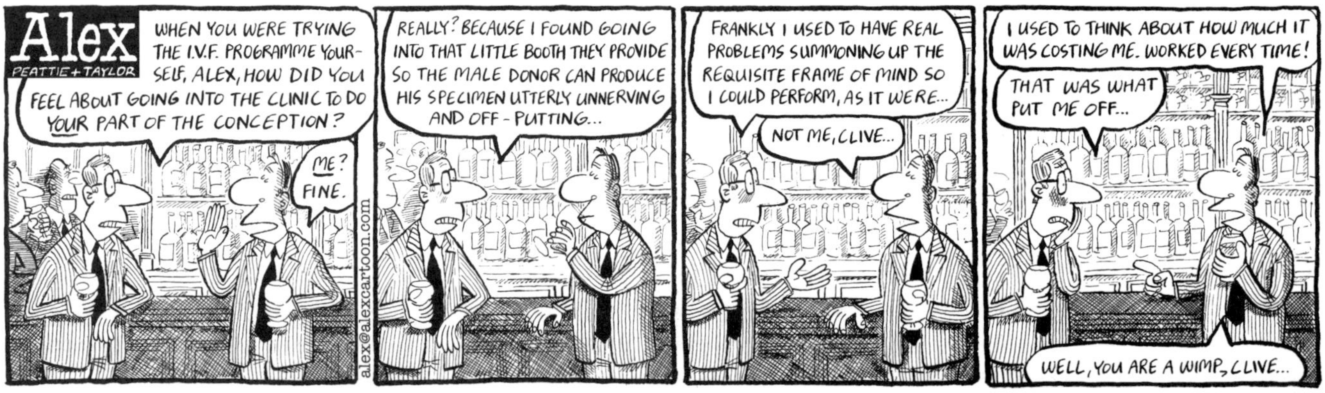
Alex
PEATTIE + TAYLOR
WHEN YOU WERE TRYING THE I.V.F. PROGRAMME YOURSELF, ALEX, HOW DID YOU FEEL ABOUT GOING INTO THE CLINIC TO DO YOUR PART OF THE CONCEPTION?
ME? FINE.
alex@alexcartoon.com
REALLY? BECAUSE I FOUND GOING INTO THAT LITTLE BOOTH THEY PROVIDE SO THE MALE DONOR CAN PRODUCE HIS SPECIMEN UTTERLY UNNERVING AND OFF-PUTTING...
FRANKLY I USED TO HAVE REAL PROBLEMS SUMMONING UP THE REQUISITE FRAME OF MIND SO I COULD PERFORM, AS IT WERE...
NOT ME, CLIVE...
I USED TO THINK ABOUT HOW MUCH IT WAS COSTING ME. WORKED EVERY TIME!
THAT WAS WHAT PUT ME OFF...
WELL, YOU ARE A WIMP, CLIVE...

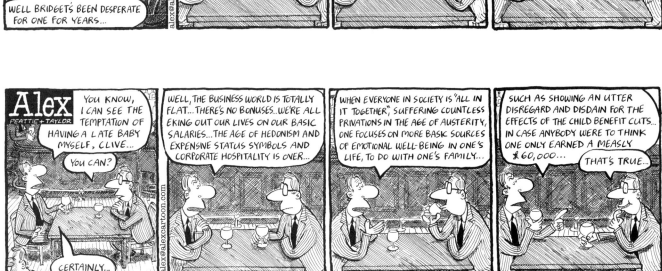

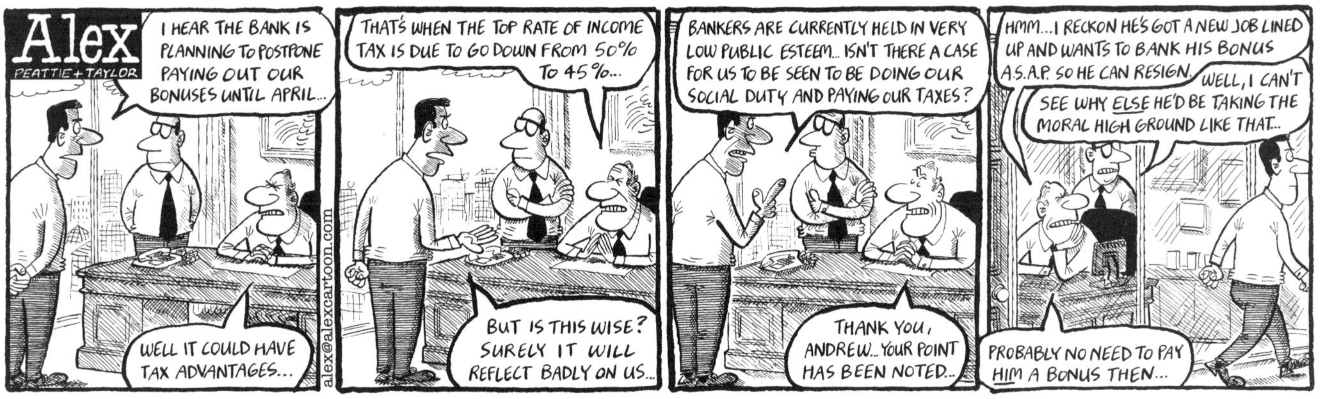
Alex
PEATTIE + TAYLOR
I HEAR THE BANK IS PLANNING TO POSTPONE PAYING OUT OUR BONUSES UNTIL APRIL...
WELL IT COULD HAVE TAX ADVANTAGES...
alex@alexcartoon.com
THAT'S WHEN THE TOP RATE OF INCOME TAX IS DUE TO GO DOWN FROM 50% TO 45%...
BUT IS THIS WISE? SURELY IT WILL REFLECT BADLY ON US...
BANKERS ARE CURRENTLY HELD IN VERY LOW PUBLIC ESTEEM... ISN'T THERE A CASE FOR US TO BE SEEN TO BE DOING OUR SOCIAL DUTY AND PAYING OUR TAXES?
THANK YOU, ANDREW... YOUR POINT HAS BEEN NOTED...
HMM... I RECKON HE'S GOT A NEW JOB LINED UP AND WANTS TO BANK HIS BONUS A.S.A.P. SO HE CAN RESIGN.
WELL, I CAN'T SEE WHY ELSE HE'D BE TAKING THE MORAL HIGH GROUND LIKE THAT...
PROBABLY NO NEED TO PAY HIM A BONUS THEN...

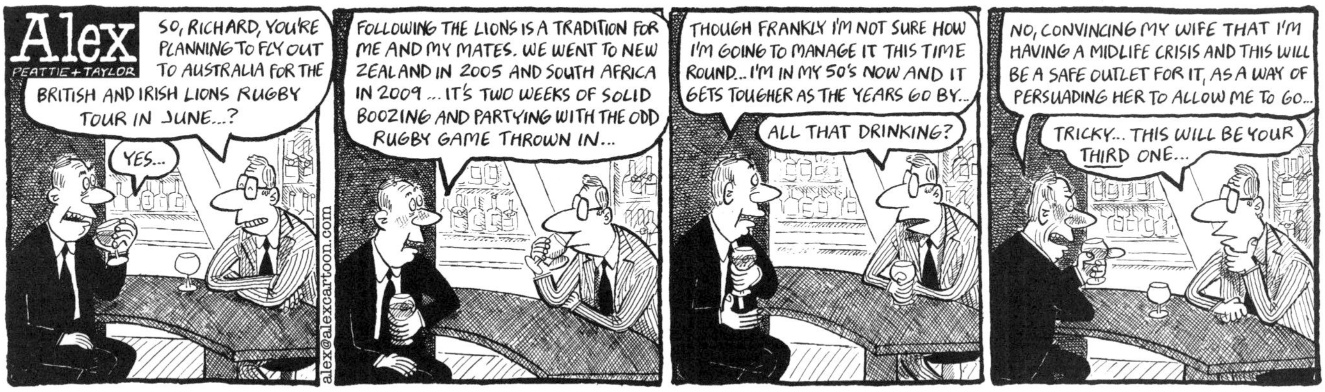
Alex
PEATTIE + TAYLOR
SO, RICHARD, YOU'RE PLANNING TO FLY OUT TO AUSTRALIA FOR THE BRITISH AND IRISH LIONS RUGBY TOUR IN JUNE...?
YES...
alex@alexcartoon.com
FOLLOWING THE LIONS IS A TRADITION FOR ME AND MY MATES. WE WENT TO NEW ZEALAND IN 2005 AND SOUTH AFRICA IN 2009 ... IT'S TWO WEEKS OF SOLID BOOZING AND PARTYING WITH THE ODD RUGBY GAME THROWN IN...
THOUGH FRANKLY I'M NOT SURE HOW I'M GOING TO MANAGE IT THIS TIME ROUND... I'M IN MY 50'S NOW AND IT GETS TOUGHER AS THE YEARS GO BY...
ALL THAT DRINKING?
NO, CONVINCING MY WIFE THAT I'M HAVING A MIDLIFE CRISIS AND THIS WILL BE A SAFE OUTLET FOR IT, AS A WAY OF PERSUADING HER TO ALLOW ME TO GO...
TRICKY... THIS WILL BE YOUR THIRD ONE...

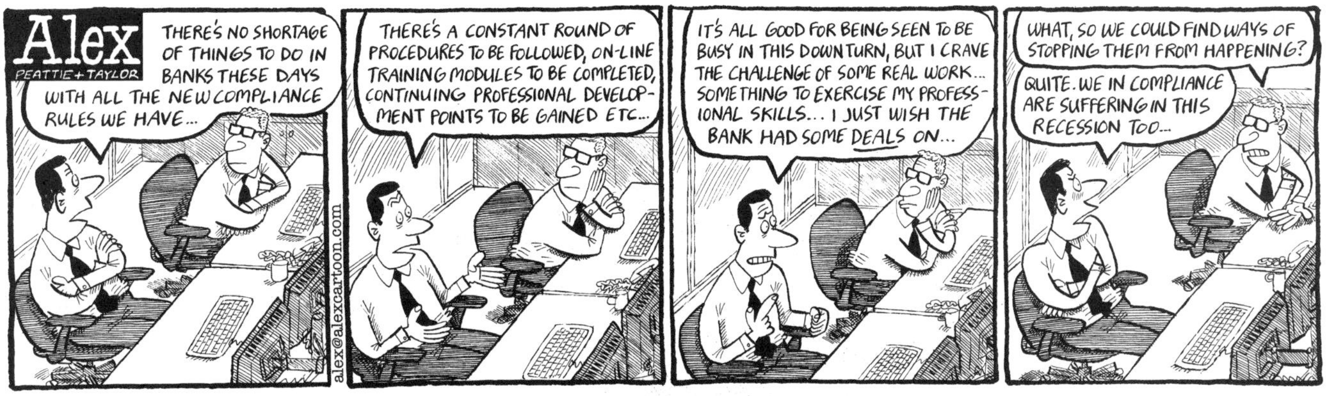
Alex
PEATTIE + TAYLOR
THERE'S NO SHORTAGE OF THINGS TO DO IN BANKS THESE DAYS WITH ALL THE NEW COMPLIANCE RULES WE HAVE...
alex@alexcartoon.com
THERE'S A CONSTANT ROUND OF PROCEDURES TO BE FOLLOWED, ON-LINE TRAINING MODULES TO BE COMPLETED, CONTINUING PROFESSIONAL DEVELOPMENT POINTS TO BE GAINED ETC...
IT'S ALL GOOD FOR BEING SEEN TO BE BUSY IN THIS DOWNTURN, BUT I CRAVE THE CHALLENGE OF SOME REAL WORK... SOMETHING TO EXERCISE MY PROFESSIONAL SKILLS... I JUST WISH THE BANK HAD SOME DEALS ON...
WHAT, SO WE COULD FIND WAYS OF STOPPING THEM FROM HAPPENING?
QUITE. WE IN COMPLIANCE ARE SUFFERING IN THIS RECESSION TOO...

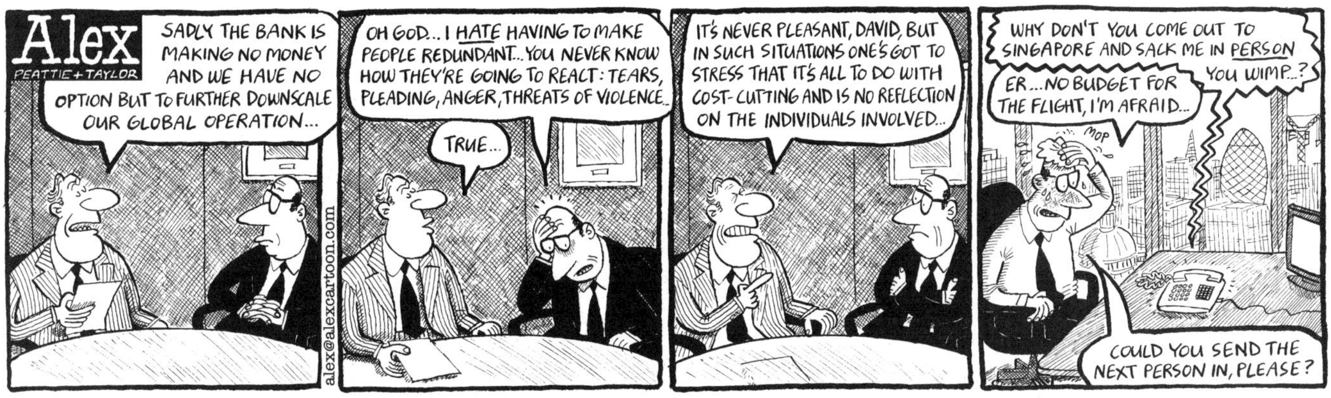
Alex
PEATTIE + TAYLOR
SADLY THE BANK IS MAKING NO MONEY AND WE HAVE NO OPTION BUT TO FURTHER DOWNSCALE OUR GLOBAL OPERATION...
alex@alexcartoon.com
OH GOD... I HATE HAVING TO MAKE PEOPLE REDUNDANT... YOU NEVER KNOW HOW THEY'RE GOING TO REACT: TEARS, PLEADING, ANGER, THREATS OF VIOLENCE...
TRUE...
IT'S NEVER PLEASANT, DAVID, BUT IN SUCH SITUATIONS ONE'S GOT TO STRESS THAT IT'S ALL TO DO WITH COST-CUTTING AND IS NO REFLECTION ON THE INDIVIDUALS INVOLVED...
WHY DON'T YOU COME OUT TO SINGAPORE AND SACK ME IN PERSON YOU WIMP...?
ER... NO BUDGET FOR THE FLIGHT, I'M AFRAID...
MOP
COULD YOU SEND THE NEXT PERSON IN, PLEASE?

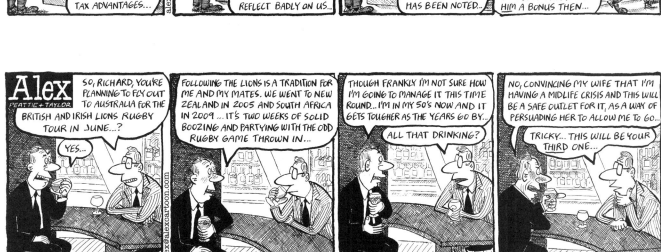

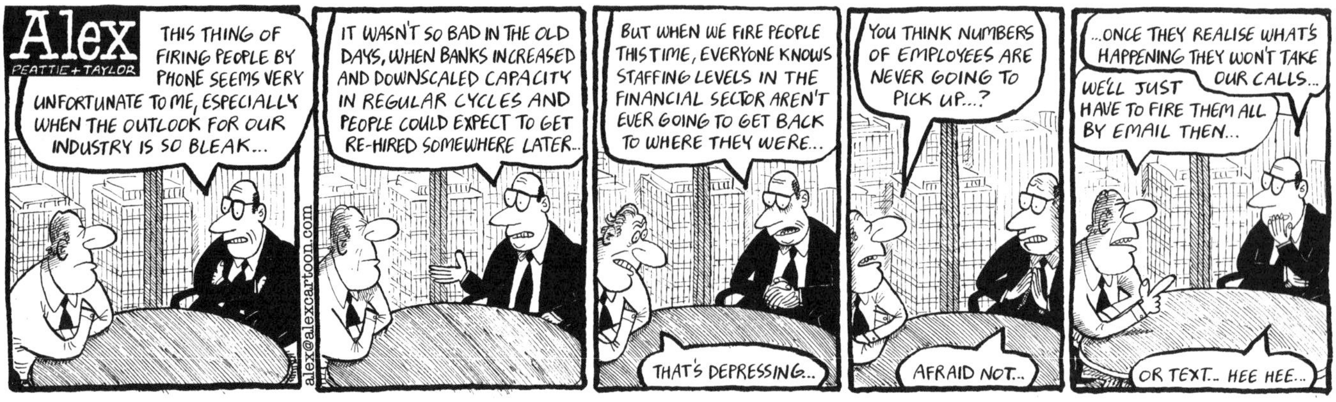
Alex
PEATTIE + TAYLOR
THIS THING OF FIRING PEOPLE BY PHONE SEEMS VERY UNFORTUNATE TO ME, ESPECIALLY WHEN THE OUTLOOK FOR OUR INDUSTRY IS SO BLEAK...
alex@alexcartoon.com
IT WASN'T SO BAD IN THE OLD DAYS, WHEN BANKS INCREASED AND DOWNSCALED CAPACITY IN REGULAR CYCLES AND PEOPLE COULD EXPECT TO GET RE-HIRED SOMEWHERE LATER...
BUT WHEN WE FIRE PEOPLE THIS TIME, EVERYONE KNOWS STAFFING LEVELS IN THE FINANCIAL SECTOR AREN'T EVER GOING TO GET BACK TO WHERE THEY WERE...
THAT'S DEPRESSING...
YOU THINK NUMBERS OF EMPLOYEES ARE NEVER GOING TO PICK UP...?
AFRAID NOT...
...ONCE THEY REALISE WHAT'S HAPPENING THEY WON'T TAKE OUR CALLS...
WE'LL JUST HAVE TO FIRE THEM ALL BY EMAIL THEN...
OR TEXT... HEE HEE...

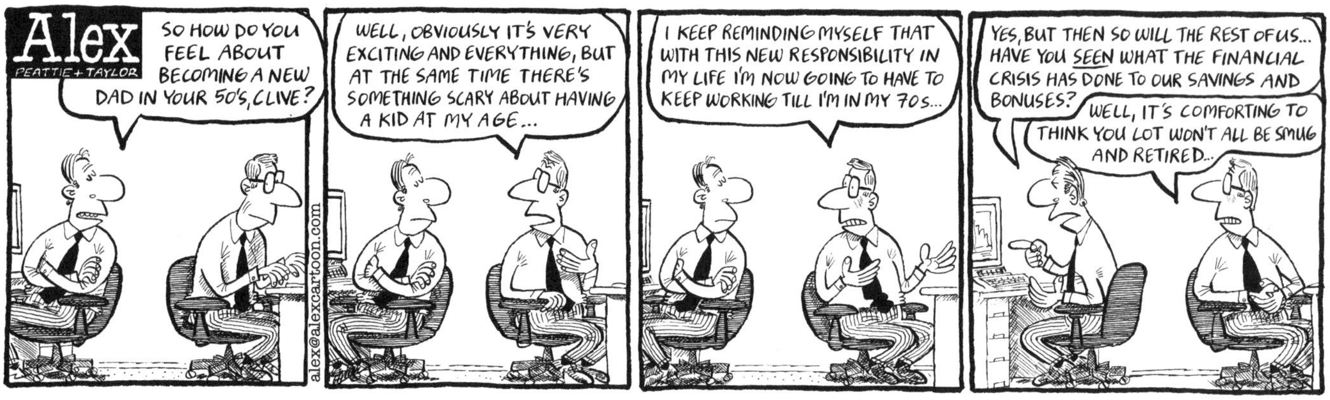
Alex
PEATTIE + TAYLOR
SO HOW DO YOU FEEL ABOUT BECOMING A NEW DAD IN YOUR 50'S, CLIVE?
alex@alexcartoon.com
WELL, OBVIOUSLY IT'S VERY EXCITING AND EVERYTHING, BUT AT THE SAME TIME THERE'S SOMETHING SCARY ABOUT HAVING A KID AT MY AGE...
I KEEP REMINDING MYSELF THAT WITH THIS NEW RESPONSIBILITY IN MY LIFE I'M NOW GOING TO HAVE TO KEEP WORKING TILL I'M IN MY 70S...
YES, BUT THEN SO WILL THE REST OF US... HAVE YOU SEEN WHAT THE FINANCIAL CRISIS HAS DONE TO OUR SAVINGS AND BONUSES?
WELL, IT'S COMFORTING TO THINK YOU LOT WON'T ALL BE SMUG AND RETIRED...

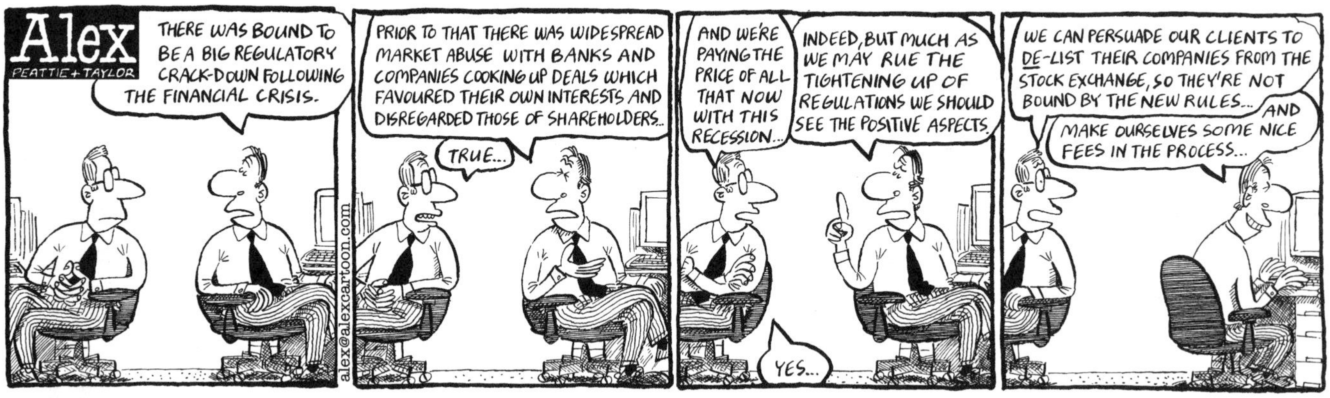
Alex
PEATTIE + TAYLOR
THERE WAS BOUND TO BE A BIG REGULATORY CRACK-DOWN FOLLOWING THE FINANCIAL CRISIS.
alex@alexcartoon.com
PRIOR TO THAT THERE WAS WIDESPREAD MARKET ABUSE WITH BANKS AND COMPANIES COOKING UP DEALS WHICH FAVOURED THEIR OWN INTERESTS AND DISREGARDED THOSE OF SHAREHOLDERS...
TRUE...
AND WE'RE PAYING THE PRICE OF ALL THAT NOW WITH THIS RECESSION...
INDEED, BUT MUCH AS WE MAY RUE THE TIGHTENING UP OF REGULATIONS WE SHOULD SEE THE POSITIVE ASPECTS.
YES...
WE CAN PERSUADE OUR CLIENTS TO DE-LIST THEIR COMPANIES FROM THE STOCK EXCHANGE, SO THEY'RE NOT BOUND BY THE NEW RULES...
AND MAKE OURSELVES SOME NICE FEES IN THE PROCESS...

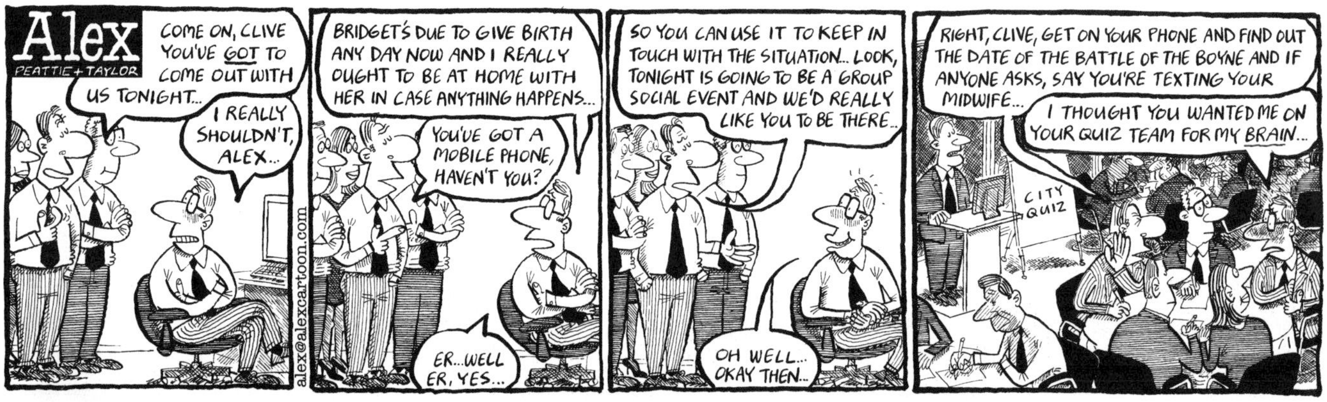
Alex
PEATTIE + TAYLOR
COME ON, CLIVE YOU'VE GOT TO COME OUT WITH US TONIGHT...
I REALLY SHOULDN'T, ALEX...
alex@alexcartoon.com
BRIDGET'S DUE TO GIVE BIRTH ANY DAY NOW AND I REALLY OUGHT TO BE AT HOME WITH HER IN CASE ANYTHING HAPPENS...
YOU'VE GOT A MOBILE PHONE, HAVEN'T YOU?
ER...WELL ER, YES...
SO YOU CAN USE IT TO KEEP IN TOUCH WITH THE SITUATION... LOOK, TONIGHT IS GOING TO BE A GROUP SOCIAL EVENT AND WE'D REALLY LIKE YOU TO BE THERE...
OH WELL... OKAY THEN...
RIGHT, CLIVE, GET ON YOUR PHONE AND FIND OUT THE DATE OF THE BATTLE OF THE BOYNE AND IF ANYONE ASKS, SAY YOU'RE TEXTING YOUR MIDWIFE...
I THOUGHT YOU WANTED ME ON YOUR QUIZ TEAM FOR MY BRAIN...
CITY QUIZ

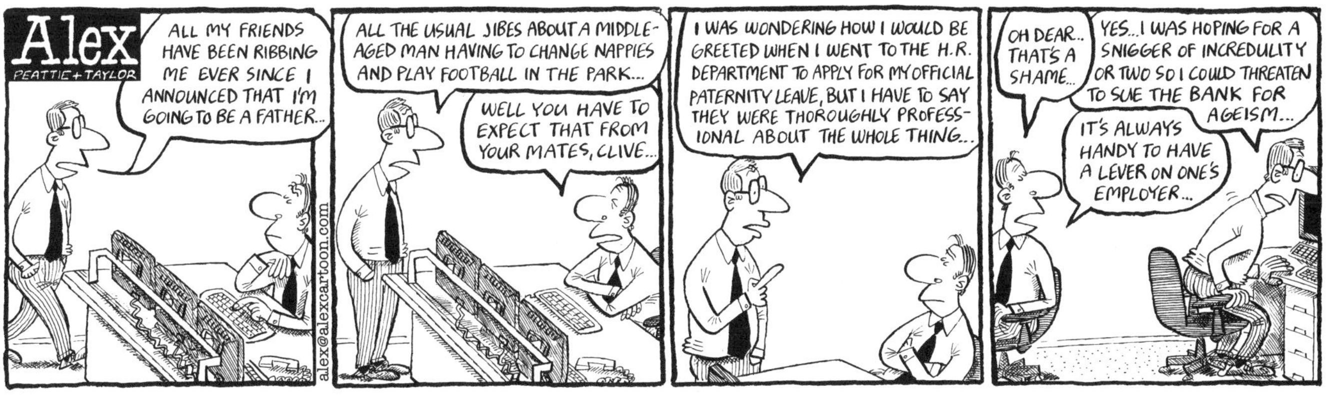
Alex
PEATTIE + TAYLOR
ALL MY FRIENDS HAVE BEEN RIBBING ME EVER SINCE I ANNOUNCED THAT I'M GOING TO BE A FATHER...
ALL THE USUAL JIBES ABOUT A MIDDLE-AGED MAN HAVING TO CHANGE NAPPIES AND PLAY FOOTBALL IN THE PARK...
WELL YOU HAVE TO EXPECT THAT FROM YOUR MATES, CLIVE...
I WAS WONDERING HOW I WOULD BE GREETED WHEN I WENT TO THE H.R. DEPARTMENT TO APPLY FOR MY OFFICIAL PATERNITY LEAVE, BUT I HAVE TO SAY THEY WERE THOROUGHLY PROFESS-IONAL ABOUT THE WHOLE THING...
OH DEAR.. THAT'S A SHAME...
YES...I WAS HOPING FOR A SNIGGER OF INCREDULITY OR TWO SO I COULD THREATEN TO SUE THE BANK FOR AGEISM...
IT'S ALWAYS HANDY TO HAVE A LEVER ON ONE'S EMPLOYER...
alex@alexcartoon.com

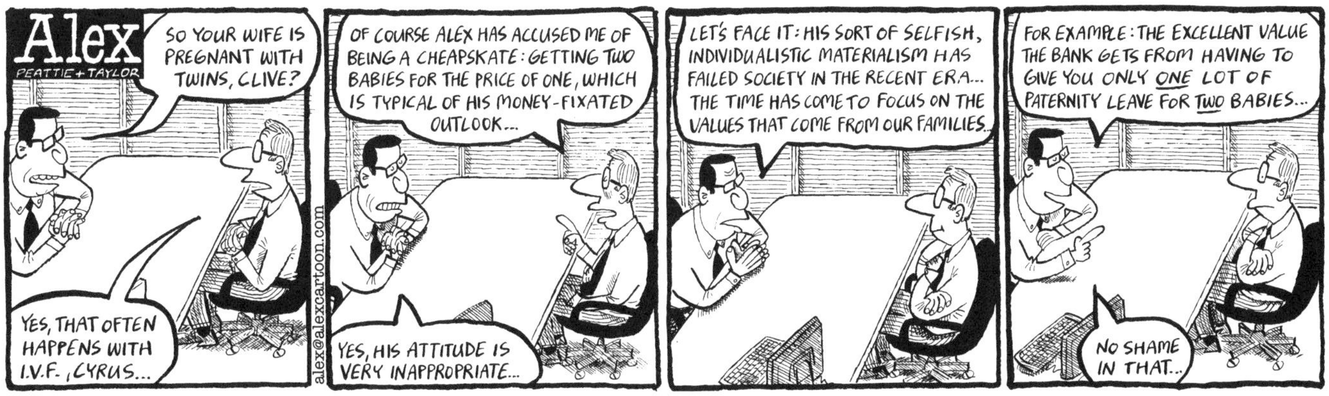
Alex
PEATTIE + TAYLOR
SO YOUR WIFE IS PREGNANT WITH TWINS, CLIVE?
YES, THAT OFTEN HAPPENS WITH I.V.F., CYRUS...
OF COURSE ALEX HAS ACCUSED ME OF BEING A CHEAPSKATE: GETTING TWO BABIES FOR THE PRICE OF ONE, WHICH IS TYPICAL OF HIS MONEY-FIXATED OUTLOOK...
YES, HIS ATTITUDE IS VERY INAPPROPRIATE...
LET'S FACE IT: HIS SORT OF SELFISH, INDIVIDUALISTIC MATERIALISM HAS FAILED SOCIETY IN THE RECENT ERA... THE TIME HAS COME TO FOCUS ON THE VALUES THAT COME FROM OUR FAMILIES...
FOR EXAMPLE: THE EXCELLENT VALUE THE BANK GETS FROM HAVING TO GIVE YOU ONLY ONE LOT OF PATERNITY LEAVE FOR TWO BABIES...
NO SHAME IN THAT...
alex@alexcartoon.com

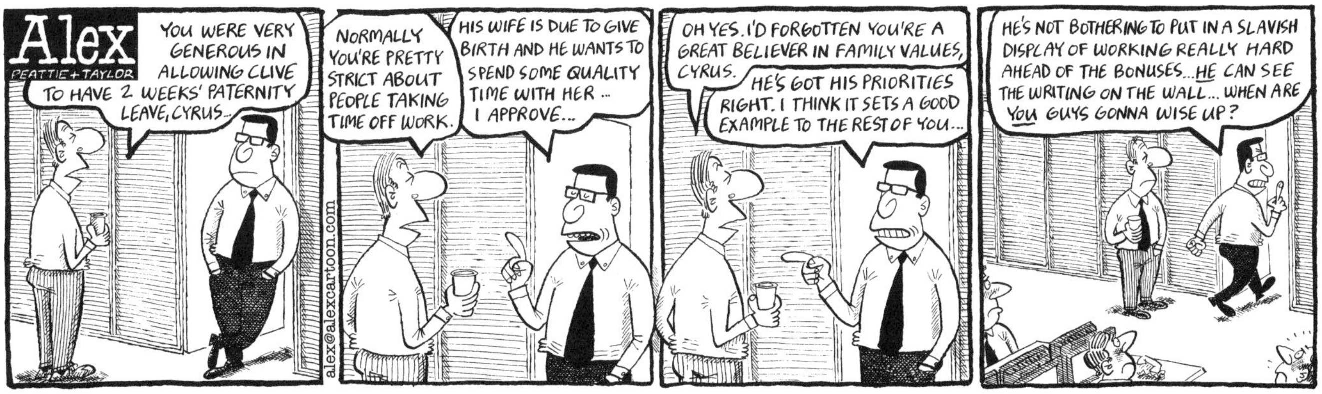
Alex
PEATTIE + TAYLOR
YOU WERE VERY GENEROUS IN ALLOWING CLIVE TO HAVE 2 WEEKS' PATERNITY LEAVE, CYRUS...
NORMALLY YOU'RE PRETTY STRICT ABOUT PEOPLE TAKING TIME OFF WORK.
HIS WIFE IS DUE TO GIVE BIRTH AND HE WANTS TO SPEND SOME QUALITY TIME WITH HER ... I APPROVE...
OH YES. I'D FORGOTTEN YOU'RE A GREAT BELIEVER IN FAMILY VALUES, CYRUS.
HE'S GOT HIS PRIORITIES RIGHT. I THINK IT SETS A GOOD EXAMPLE TO THE REST OF YOU...
HE'S NOT BOTHERING TO PUT IN A SLAVISH DISPLAY OF WORKING REALLY HARD AHEAD OF THE BONUSES...HE CAN SEE THE WRITING ON THE WALL... WHEN ARE YOU GUYS GONNA WISE UP?
alex@alexcartoon.com

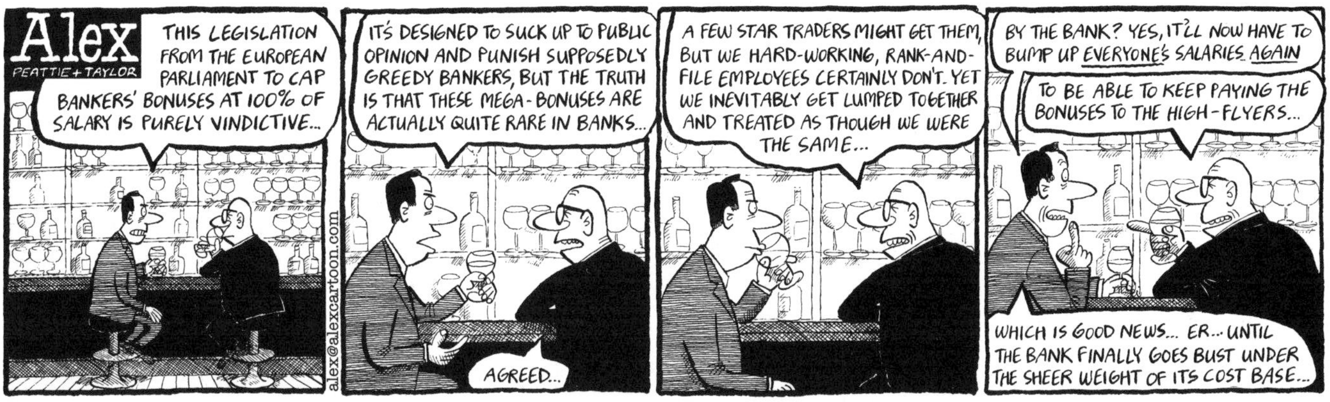
Alex
PEATTIE + TAYLOR
THIS LEGISLATION FROM THE EUROPEAN PARLIAMENT TO CAP BANKERS' BONUSES AT 100% OF SALARY IS PURELY VINDICTIVE...
IT'S DESIGNED TO SUCK UP TO PUBLIC OPINION AND PUNISH SUPPOSEDLY GREEDY BANKERS, BUT THE TRUTH IS THAT THESE MEGA-BONUSES ARE ACTUALLY QUITE RARE IN BANKS...
AGREED...
A FEW STAR TRADERS MIGHT GET THEM, BUT WE HARD-WORKING, RANK-AND-FILE EMPLOYEES CERTAINLY DON'T. YET WE INEVITABLY GET LUMPED TOGETHER AND TREATED AS THOUGH WE WERE THE SAME...
BY THE BANK? YES, IT'LL NOW HAVE TO BUMP UP EVERYONE'S SALARIES AGAIN
TO BE ABLE TO KEEP PAYING THE BONUSES TO THE HIGH-FLYERS...
WHICH IS GOOD NEWS... ER... UNTIL THE BANK FINALLY GOES BUST UNDER THE SHEER WEIGHT OF ITS COST BASE...
alex@alexcartoon.com

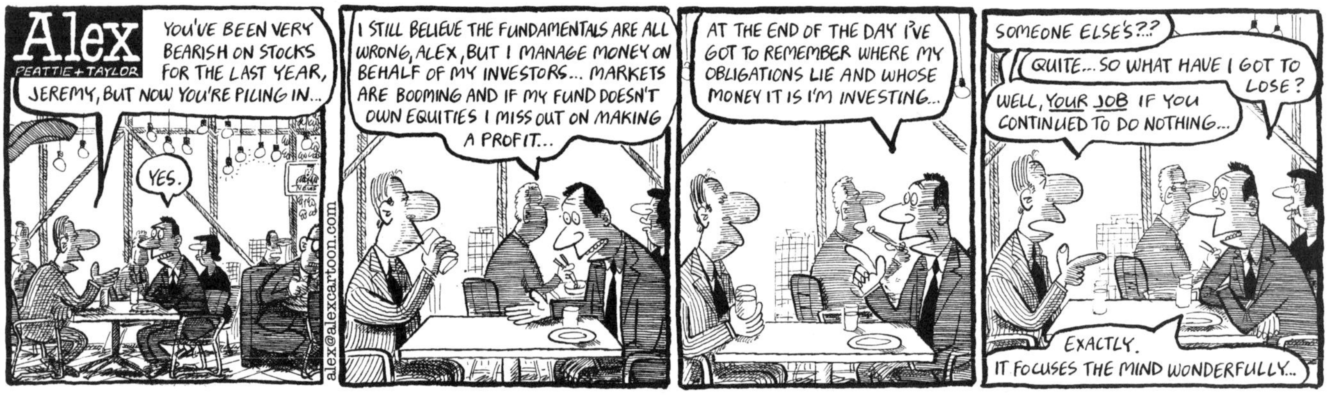
Alex
PEATTIE + TAYLOR
YOU'VE BEEN VERY BEARISH ON STOCKS FOR THE LAST YEAR, JEREMY, BUT NOW YOU'RE PILING IN...
YES.
I STILL BELIEVE THE FUNDAMENTALS ARE ALL WRONG, ALEX, BUT I MANAGE MONEY ON BEHALF OF MY INVESTORS... MARKETS ARE BOOMING AND IF MY FUND DOESN'T OWN EQUITIES I MISS OUT ON MAKING A PROFIT...
AT THE END OF THE DAY I'VE GOT TO REMEMBER WHERE MY OBLIGATIONS LIE AND WHOSE MONEY IT IS I'M INVESTING...
SOMEONE ELSE'S??
QUITE... SO WHAT HAVE I GOT TO LOSE?
WELL, YOUR JOB IF YOU CONTINUED TO DO NOTHING...
EXACTLY. IT FOCUSES THE MIND WONDERFULLY...
alex@alexcartoon.com

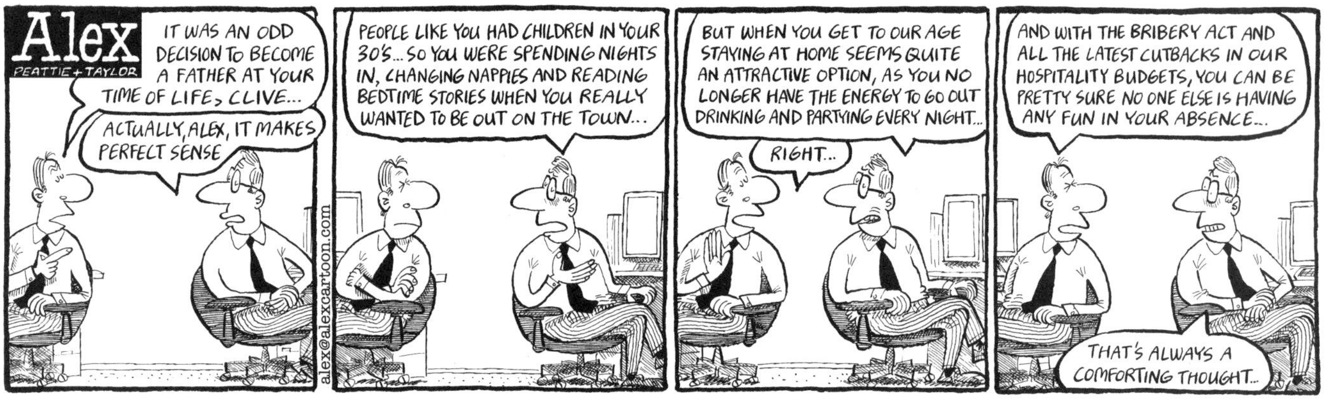
Alex
PEATTIE + TAYLOR
IT WAS AN ODD DECISION TO BECOME A FATHER AT YOUR TIME OF LIFE, CLIVE...
ACTUALLY, ALEX, IT MAKES PERFECT SENSE
PEOPLE LIKE YOU HAD CHILDREN IN YOUR 30'S... SO YOU WERE SPENDING NIGHTS IN, CHANGING NAPPIES AND READING BEDTIME STORIES WHEN YOU REALLY WANTED TO BE OUT ON THE TOWN...
BUT WHEN YOU GET TO OUR AGE STAYING AT HOME SEEMS QUITE AN ATTRACTIVE OPTION, AS YOU NO LONGER HAVE THE ENERGY TO GO OUT DRINKING AND PARTYING EVERY NIGHT...
RIGHT...
AND WITH THE BRIBERY ACT AND ALL THE LATEST CUTBACKS IN OUR HOSPITALITY BUDGETS, YOU CAN BE PRETTY SURE NO ONE ELSE IS HAVING ANY FUN IN YOUR ABSENCE...
THAT'S ALWAYS A COMFORTING THOUGHT...
alex@alexcartoon.com

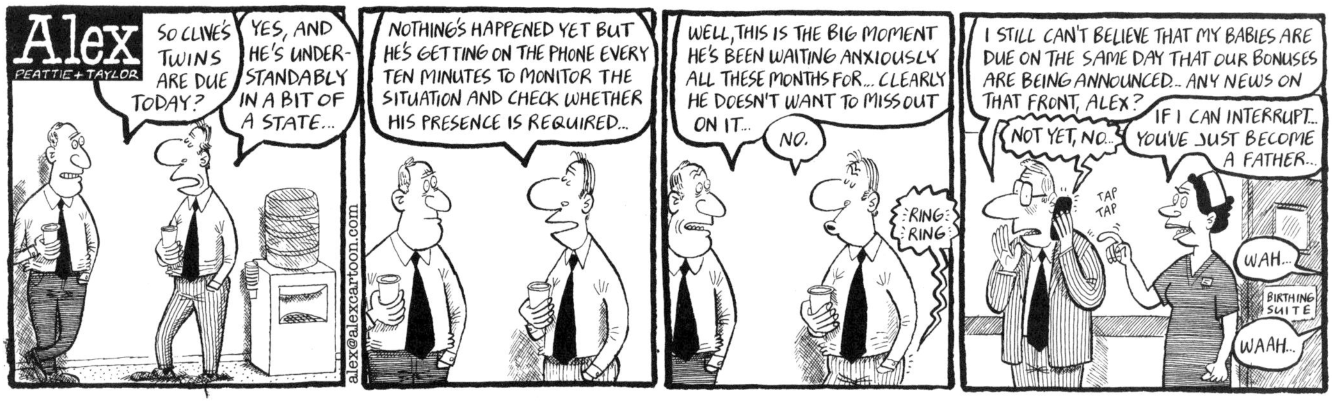
Alex
PEATTIE + TAYLOR
SO CLIVE'S TWINS ARE DUE TODAY?
YES, AND HE'S UNDER-STANDABLY IN A BIT OF A STATE...
NOTHING'S HAPPENED YET BUT HE'S GETTING ON THE PHONE EVERY TEN MINUTES TO MONITOR THE SITUATION AND CHECK WHETHER HIS PRESENCE IS REQUIRED...
WELL, THIS IS THE BIG MOMENT HE'S BEEN WAITING ANXIOUSLY ALL THESE MONTHS FOR... CLEARLY HE DOESN'T WANT TO MISS OUT ON IT...
NO.
RING RING
I STILL CAN'T BELIEVE THAT MY BABIES ARE DUE ON THE SAME DAY THAT OUR BONUSES ARE BEING ANNOUNCED... ANY NEWS ON THAT FRONT, ALEX?
NOT YET, NO...
TAP TAP
IF I CAN INTERRUPT... YOU'VE JUST BECOME A FATHER...
WAH...
BIRTHING SUITE
WAAH...
alex@alexcartoon.com

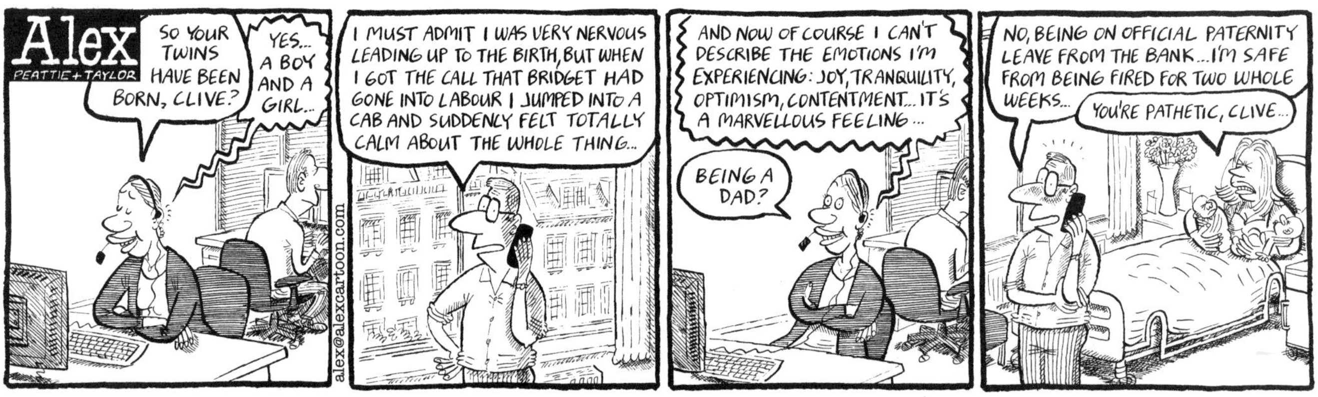
Alex
PEATTIE + TAYLOR
SO YOUR TWINS HAVE BEEN BORN, CLIVE?
YES... A BOY AND A GIRL...
I MUST ADMIT I WAS VERY NERVOUS LEADING UP TO THE BIRTH, BUT WHEN I GOT THE CALL THAT BRIDGET HAD GONE INTO LABOUR I JUMPED INTO A CAB AND SUDDENLY FELT TOTALLY CALM ABOUT THE WHOLE THING...
AND NOW OF COURSE I CAN'T DESCRIBE THE EMOTIONS I'M EXPERIENCING: JOY, TRANQUILITY, OPTIMISM, CONTENTMENT... IT'S A MARVELLOUS FEELING...
BEING A DAD?
NO, BEING ON OFFICIAL PATERNITY LEAVE FROM THE BANK... I'M SAFE FROM BEING FIRED FOR TWO WHOLE WEEKS...
YOU'RE PATHETIC, CLIVE...
alex@alexcartoon.com

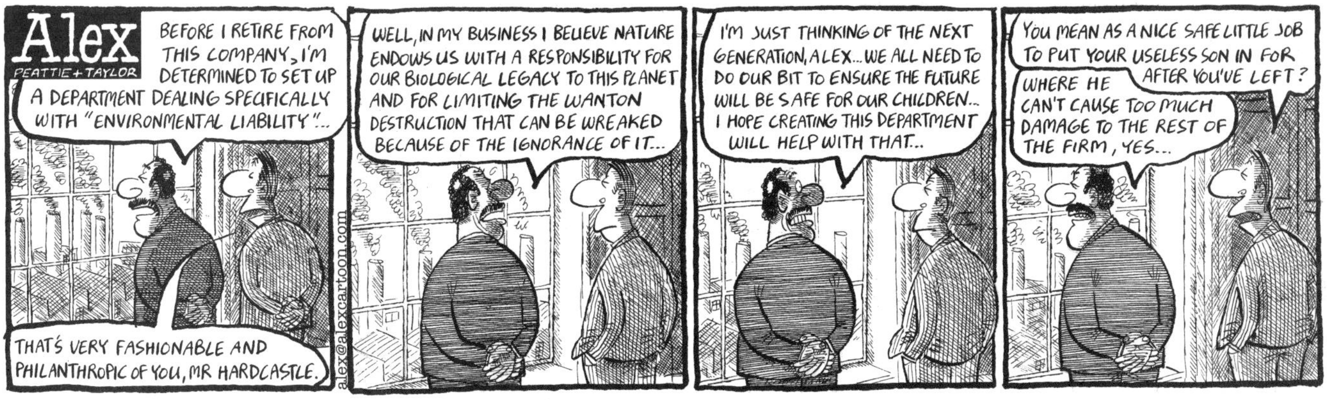
Alex
PEATTIE + TAYLOR
BEFORE I RETIRE FROM THIS COMPANY, I'M DETERMINED TO SET UP A DEPARTMENT DEALING SPECIFICALLY WITH "ENVIRONMENTAL LIABILITY"...
THAT'S VERY FASHIONABLE AND PHILANTHROPIC OF YOU, MR HARDCASTLE.
alex@alexcartoon.com
WELL, IN MY BUSINESS I BELIEVE NATURE ENDOWS US WITH A RESPONSIBILITY FOR OUR BIOLOGICAL LEGACY TO THIS PLANET AND FOR LIMITING THE WANTON DESTRUCTION THAT CAN BE WREAKED BECAUSE OF THE IGNORANCE OF IT...
I'M JUST THINKING OF THE NEXT GENERATION, ALEX... WE ALL NEED TO DO OUR BIT TO ENSURE THE FUTURE WILL BE SAFE FOR OUR CHILDREN... I HOPE CREATING THIS DEPARTMENT WILL HELP WITH THAT...
YOU MEAN AS A NICE SAFE LITTLE JOB TO PUT YOUR USELESS SON IN FOR AFTER YOU'VE LEFT?
WHERE HE CAN'T CAUSE TOO MUCH DAMAGE TO THE REST OF THE FIRM, YES...

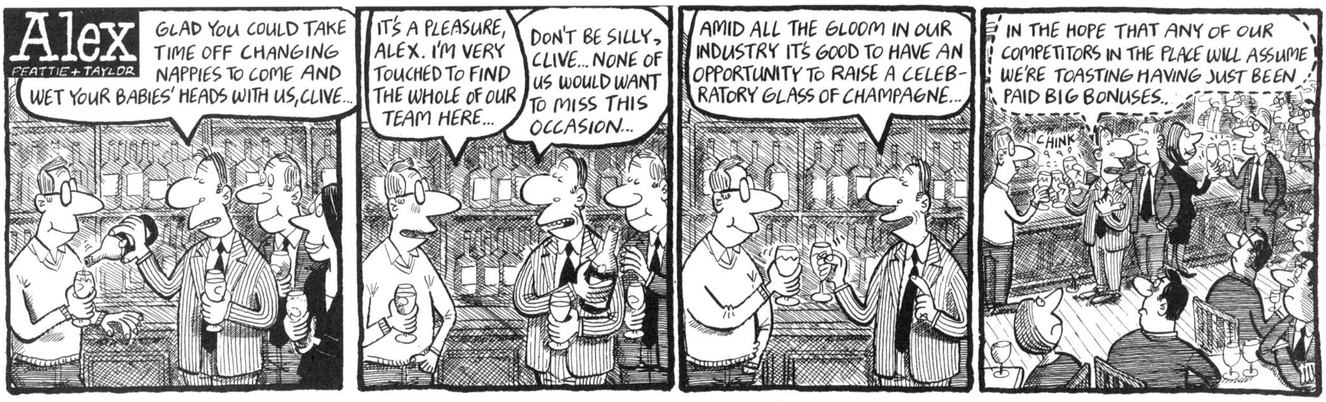
Alex
PEATTIE + TAYLOR
GLAD YOU COULD TAKE TIME OFF CHANGING NAPPIES TO COME AND WET YOUR BABIES' HEADS WITH US, CLIVE...
IT'S A PLEASURE, ALEX. I'M VERY TOUCHED TO FIND THE WHOLE OF OUR TEAM HERE...
DON'T BE SILLY, CLIVE... NONE OF US WOULD WANT TO MISS THIS OCCASION...
AMID ALL THE GLOOM IN OUR INDUSTRY IT'S GOOD TO HAVE AN OPPORTUNITY TO RAISE A CELEBRATORY GLASS OF CHAMPAGNE...
IN THE HOPE THAT ANY OF OUR COMPETITORS IN THE PLACE WILL ASSUME WE'RE TOASTING HAVING JUST BEEN PAID BIG BONUSES...
CHINK

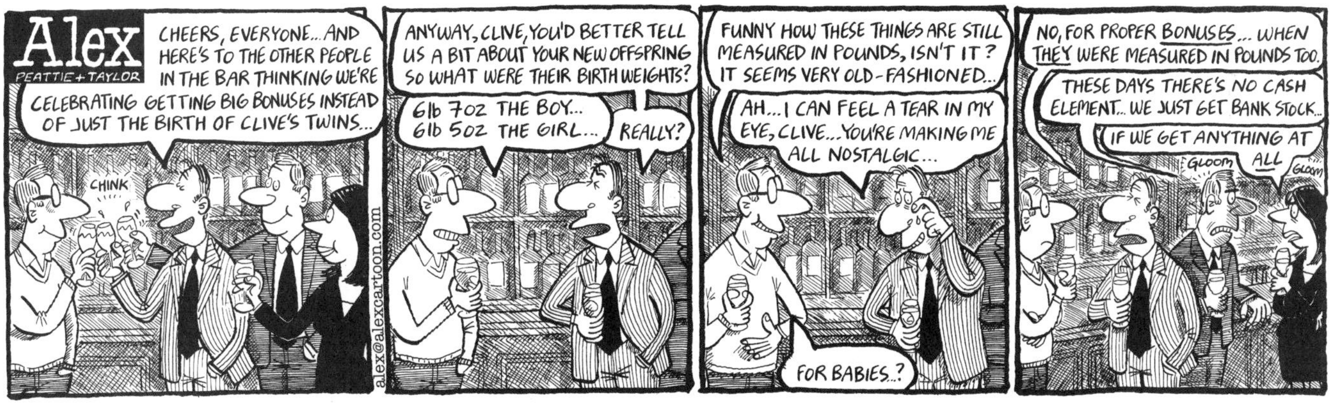
Alex
PEATTIE + TAYLOR
CHEERS, EVERYONE... AND HERE'S TO THE OTHER PEOPLE IN THE BAR THINKING WE'RE CELEBRATING GETTING BIG BONUSES INSTEAD OF JUST THE BIRTH OF CLIVE'S TWINS...
CHINK
alex@alexcartoon.com
ANYWAY, CLIVE, YOU'D BETTER TELL US A BIT ABOUT YOUR NEW OFFSPRING SO WHAT WERE THEIR BIRTH WEIGHTS?
6lb 7oz THE BOY... 6lb 5oz THE GIRL...
REALLY?
FUNNY HOW THESE THINGS ARE STILL MEASURED IN POUNDS, ISN'T IT? IT SEEMS VERY OLD-FASHIONED...
AH... I CAN FEEL A TEAR IN MY EYE, CLIVE... YOU'RE MAKING ME ALL NOSTALGIC...
FOR BABIES...?
NO, FOR PROPER BONUSES... WHEN THEY WERE MEASURED IN POUNDS TOO.
THESE DAYS THERE'S NO CASH ELEMENT... WE JUST GET BANK STOCK...
IF WE GET ANYTHING AT ALL
GLOOM
GLOOM

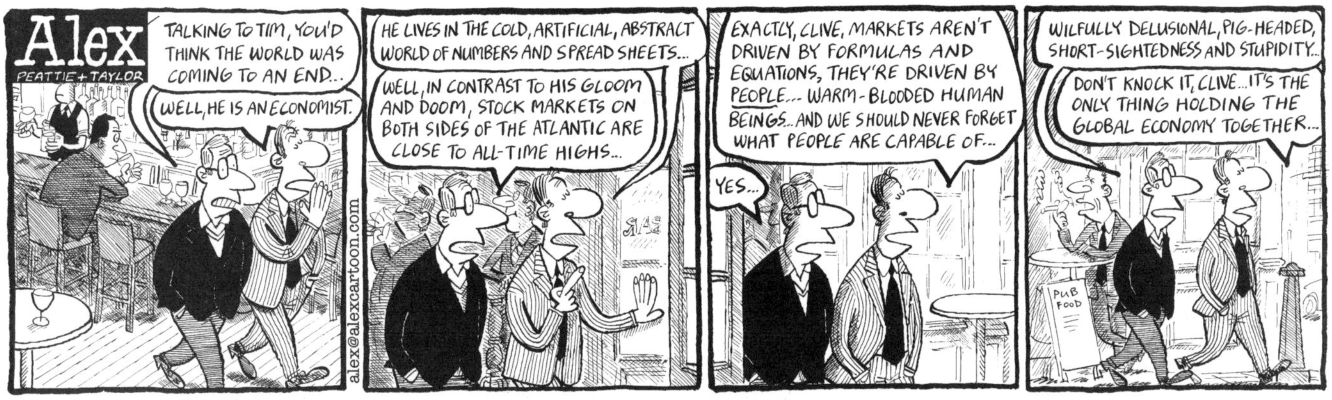
Alex
PEATTIE + TAYLOR
TALKING TO TIM, YOU'D THINK THE WORLD WAS COMING TO AN END...
WELL, HE IS AN ECONOMIST.
alex@alexcartoon.com
HE LIVES IN THE COLD, ARTIFICIAL, ABSTRACT WORLD OF NUMBERS AND SPREAD SHEETS...
WELL, IN CONTRAST TO HIS GLOOM AND DOOM, STOCK MARKETS ON BOTH SIDES OF THE ATLANTIC ARE CLOSE TO ALL-TIME HIGHS...
EXACTLY, CLIVE, MARKETS AREN'T DRIVEN BY FORMULAS AND EQUATIONS, THEY'RE DRIVEN BY PEOPLE... WARM-BLOODED HUMAN BEINGS... AND WE SHOULD NEVER FORGET WHAT PEOPLE ARE CAPABLE OF...
YES...
WILFULLY DELUSIONAL, PIG-HEADED, SHORT-SIGHTEDNESS AND STUPIDITY...
DON'T KNOCK IT, CLIVE... IT'S THE ONLY THING HOLDING THE GLOBAL ECONOMY TOGETHER...
PUB FOOD

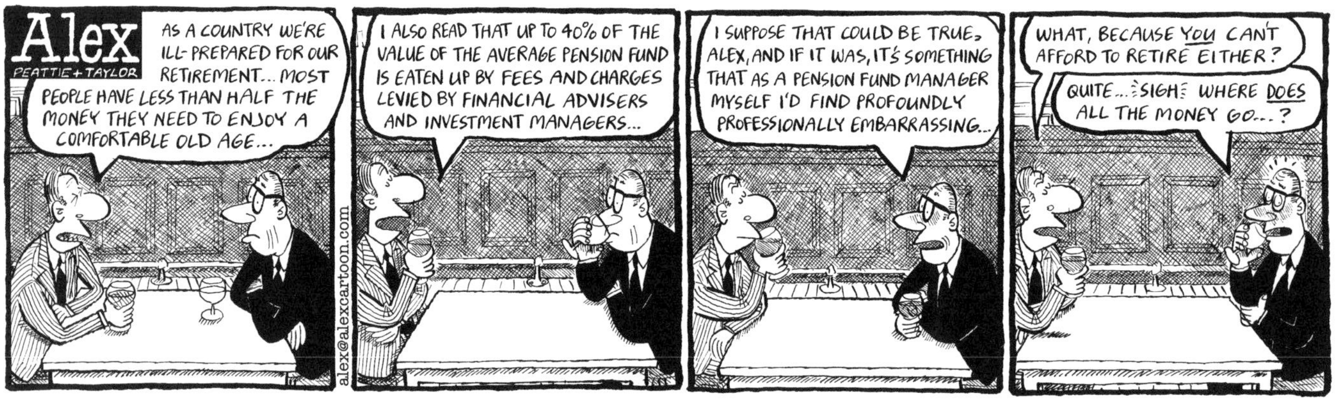
Alex
PEATTIE + TAYLOR
AS A COUNTRY WE'RE ILL-PREPARED FOR OUR RETIREMENT... MOST PEOPLE HAVE LESS THAN HALF THE MONEY THEY NEED TO ENJOY A COMFORTABLE OLD AGE...
alex@alexcartoon.com
I ALSO READ THAT UP TO 40% OF THE VALUE OF THE AVERAGE PENSION FUND IS EATEN UP BY FEES AND CHARGES LEVIED BY FINANCIAL ADVISERS AND INVESTMENT MANAGERS...
I SUPPOSE THAT COULD BE TRUE, ALEX, AND IF IT WAS, IT'S SOMETHING THAT AS A PENSION FUND MANAGER MYSELF I'D FIND PROFOUNDLY PROFESSIONALLY EMBARRASSING...
WHAT, BECAUSE YOU CAN'T AFFORD TO RETIRE EITHER?
QUITE... SIGH WHERE DOES ALL THE MONEY GO...?

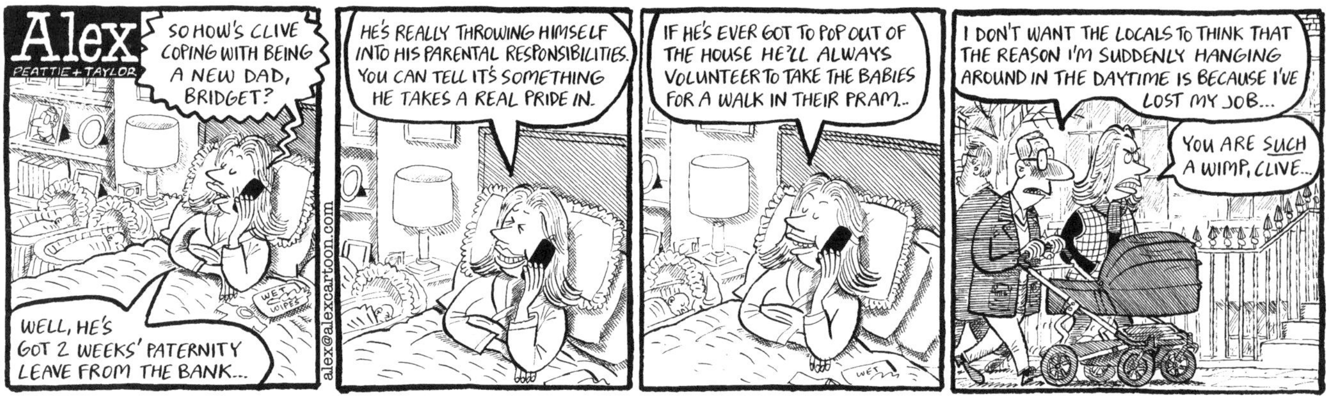
Alex
PEATTIE + TAYLOR
SO HOW'S CLIVE COPING WITH BEING A NEW DAD, BRIDGET?
WELL, HE'S GOT 2 WEEKS' PATERNITY LEAVE FROM THE BANK...
alex@alexcartoon.com
HE'S REALLY THROWING HIMSELF INTO HIS PARENTAL RESPONSIBILITIES. YOU CAN TELL IT'S SOMETHING HE TAKES A REAL PRIDE IN.
IF HE'S EVER GOT TO POP OUT OF THE HOUSE HE'LL ALWAYS VOLUNTEER TO TAKE THE BABIES FOR A WALK IN THEIR PRAM...
I DON'T WANT THE LOCALS TO THINK THAT THE REASON I'M SUDDENLY HANGING AROUND IN THE DAYTIME IS BECAUSE I'VE LOST MY JOB...
YOU ARE SUCH A WIMP, CLIVE...

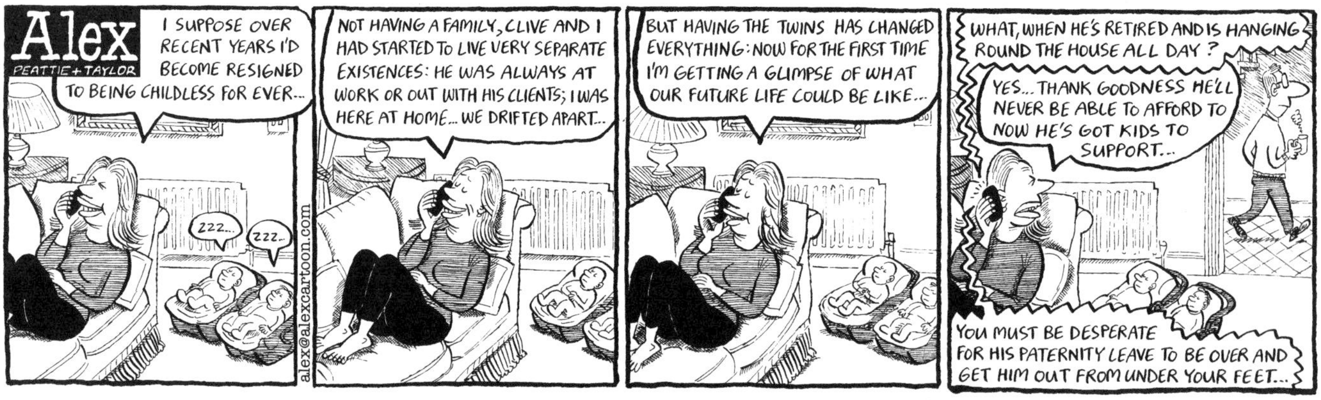
Alex
PEATTIE + TAYLOR
I SUPPOSE OVER RECENT YEARS I'D BECOME RESIGNED TO BEING CHILDLESS FOR EVER...
ZZZ...
ZZZ...
alex@alexcartoon.com
NOT HAVING A FAMILY, CLIVE AND I HAD STARTED TO LIVE VERY SEPARATE EXISTENCES: HE WAS ALWAYS AT WORK OR OUT WITH HIS CLIENTS; I WAS HERE AT HOME... WE DRIFTED APART...
BUT HAVING THE TWINS HAS CHANGED EVERYTHING: NOW FOR THE FIRST TIME I'M GETTING A GLIMPSE OF WHAT OUR FUTURE LIFE COULD BE LIKE...
WHAT, WHEN HE'S RETIRED AND IS HANGING ROUND THE HOUSE ALL DAY?
YES... THANK GOODNESS HE'LL NEVER BE ABLE TO AFFORD TO NOW HE'S GOT KIDS TO SUPPORT...
YOU MUST BE DESPERATE FOR HIS PATERNITY LEAVE TO BE OVER AND GET HIM OUT FROM UNDER YOUR FEET...

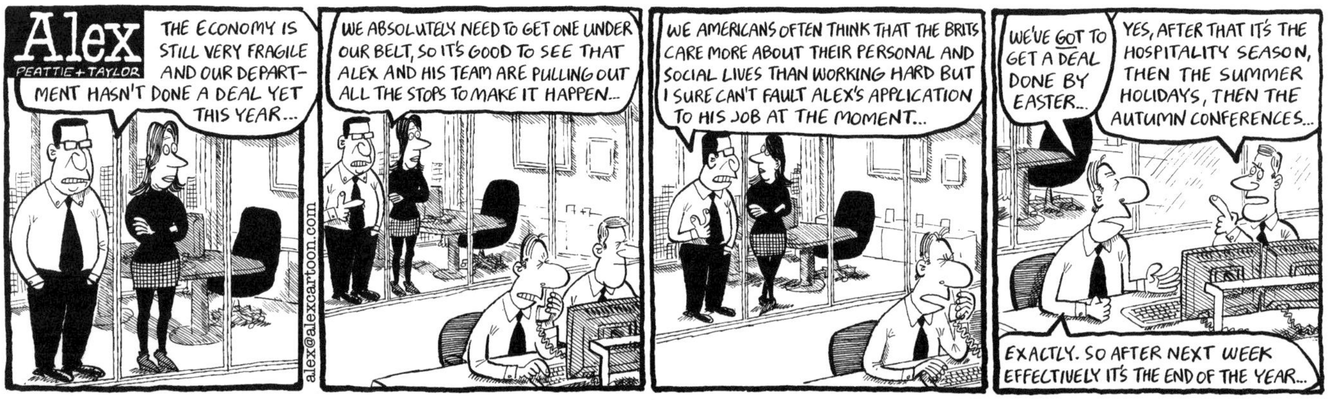
Alex
PEATTIE + TAYLOR
THE ECONOMY IS STILL VERY FRAGILE AND OUR DEPARTMENT HASN'T DONE A DEAL YET THIS YEAR...
alex@alexcartoon.com
WE ABSOLUTELY NEED TO GET ONE UNDER OUR BELT, SO IT'S GOOD TO SEE THAT ALEX AND HIS TEAM ARE PULLING OUT ALL THE STOPS TO MAKE IT HAPPEN...
WE AMERICANS OFTEN THINK THAT THE BRITS CARE MORE ABOUT THEIR PERSONAL AND SOCIAL LIVES THAN WORKING HARD BUT I SURE CAN'T FAULT ALEX'S APPLICATION TO HIS JOB AT THE MOMENT...
WE'VE GOT TO GET A DEAL DONE BY EASTER...
YES, AFTER THAT IT'S THE HOSPITALITY SEASON, THEN THE SUMMER HOLIDAYS, THEN THE AUTUMN CONFERENCES...
EXACTLY. SO AFTER NEXT WEEK EFFECTIVELY IT'S THE END OF THE YEAR...

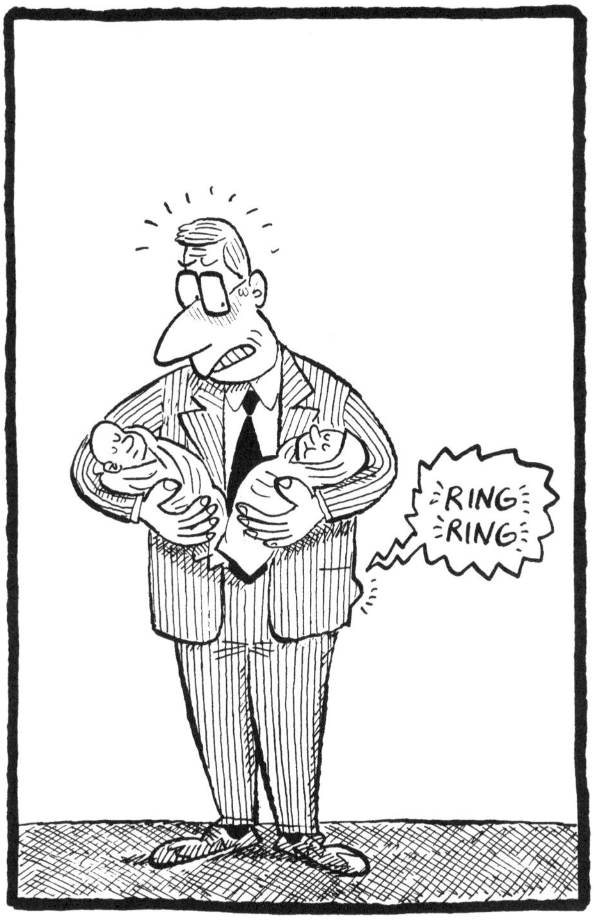
RING
RING

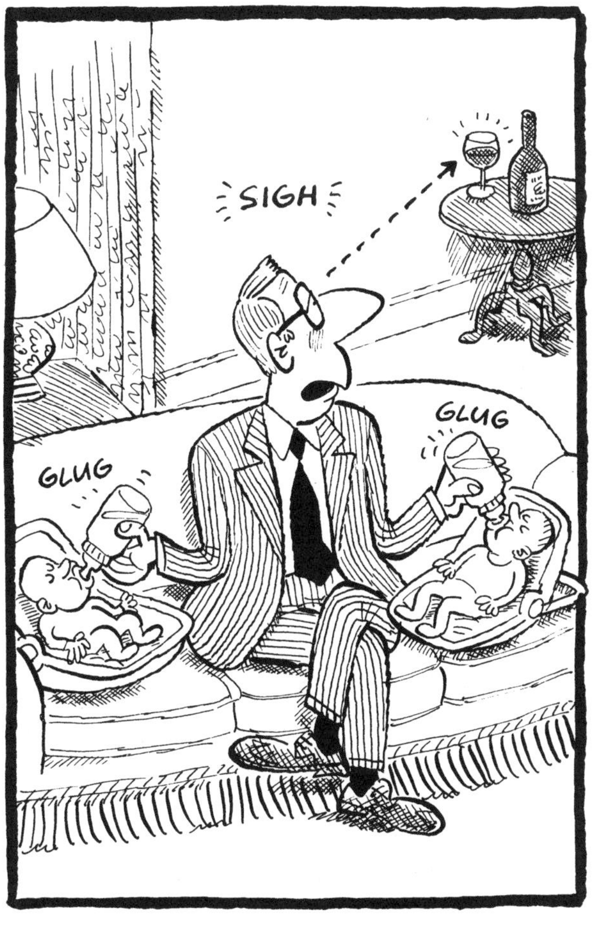
SIGH
GLUG
GLUG

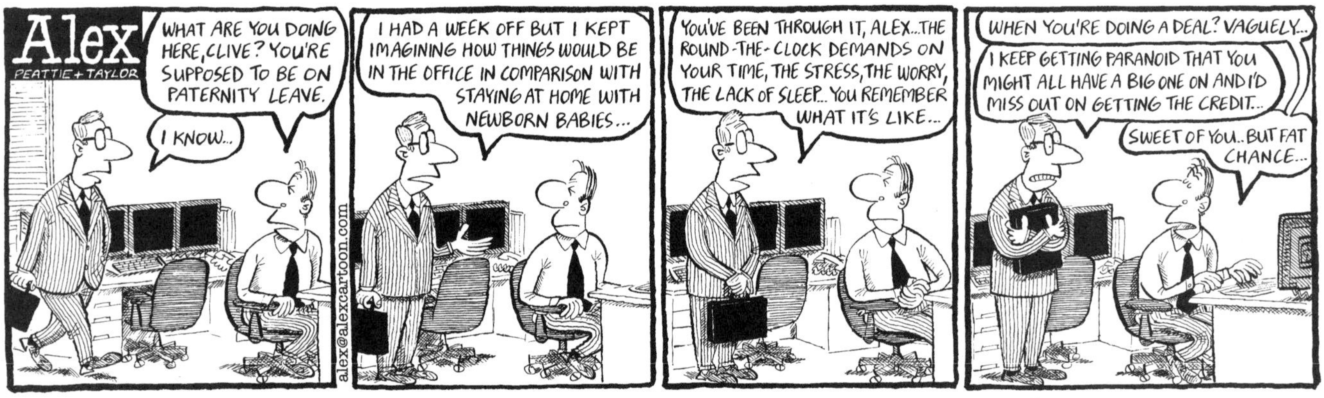
Alex
PEATTIE + TAYLOR
WHAT ARE YOU DOING HERE, CLIVE? YOU'RE SUPPOSED TO BE ON PATERNITY LEAVE.
I KNOW...
I HAD A WEEK OFF BUT I KEPT IMAGINING HOW THINGS WOULD BE IN THE OFFICE IN COMPARISON WITH STAYING AT HOME WITH NEWBORN BABIES...
alex@alexcartoon.com
YOU'VE BEEN THROUGH IT, ALEX...THE ROUND-THE-CLOCK DEMANDS ON YOUR TIME, THE STRESS, THE WORRY, THE LACK OF SLEEP... YOU REMEMBER WHAT IT'S LIKE...
WHEN YOU'RE DOING A DEAL? VAGUELY...
I KEEP GETTING PARANOID THAT YOU MIGHT ALL HAVE A BIG ONE ON AND I'D MISS OUT ON GETTING THE CREDIT...
SWEET OF YOU.. BUT FAT CHANCE...

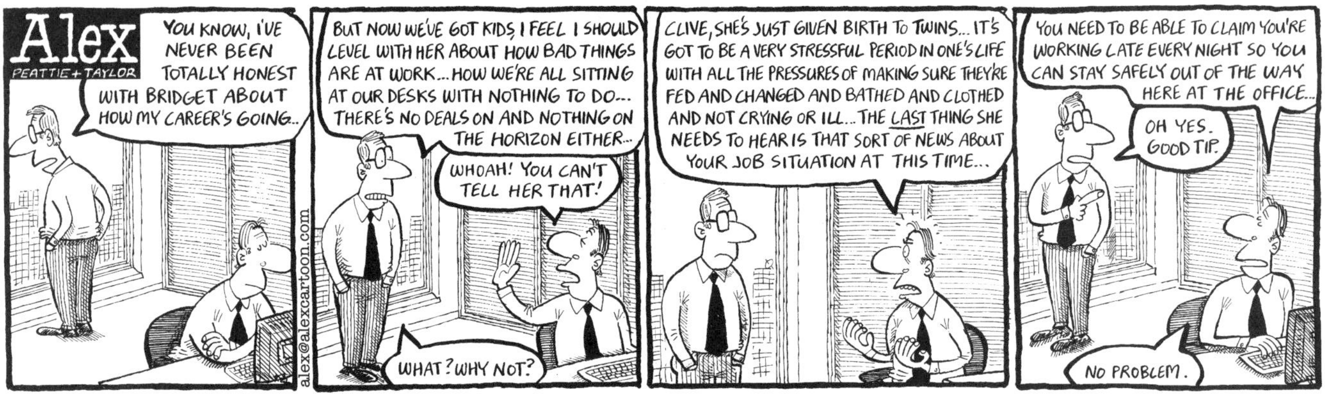
Alex
PEATTIE + TAYLOR
YOU KNOW, I'VE NEVER BEEN TOTALLY HONEST WITH BRIDGET ABOUT HOW MY CAREER'S GOING...
alex@alexcartoon.com
BUT NOW WE'VE GOT KIDS I FEEL I SHOULD LEVEL WITH HER ABOUT HOW BAD THINGS ARE AT WORK... HOW WE'RE ALL SITTING AT OUR DESKS WITH NOTHING TO DO... THERE'S NO DEALS ON AND NOTHING ON THE HORIZON EITHER...
WHOAH! YOU CAN'T TELL HER THAT!
WHAT? WHY NOT?
CLIVE, SHE'S JUST GIVEN BIRTH TO TWINS... IT'S GOT TO BE A VERY STRESSFUL PERIOD IN ONE'S LIFE WITH ALL THE PRESSURES OF MAKING SURE THEY'RE FED AND CHANGED AND BATHED AND CLOTHED AND NOT CRYING OR ILL... THE LAST THING SHE NEEDS TO HEAR IS THAT SORT OF NEWS ABOUT YOUR JOB SITUATION AT THIS TIME...
YOU NEED TO BE ABLE TO CLAIM YOU'RE WORKING LATE EVERY NIGHT SO YOU CAN STAY SAFELY OUT OF THE WAY HERE AT THE OFFICE...
OH YES. GOOD TIP.
NO PROBLEM.

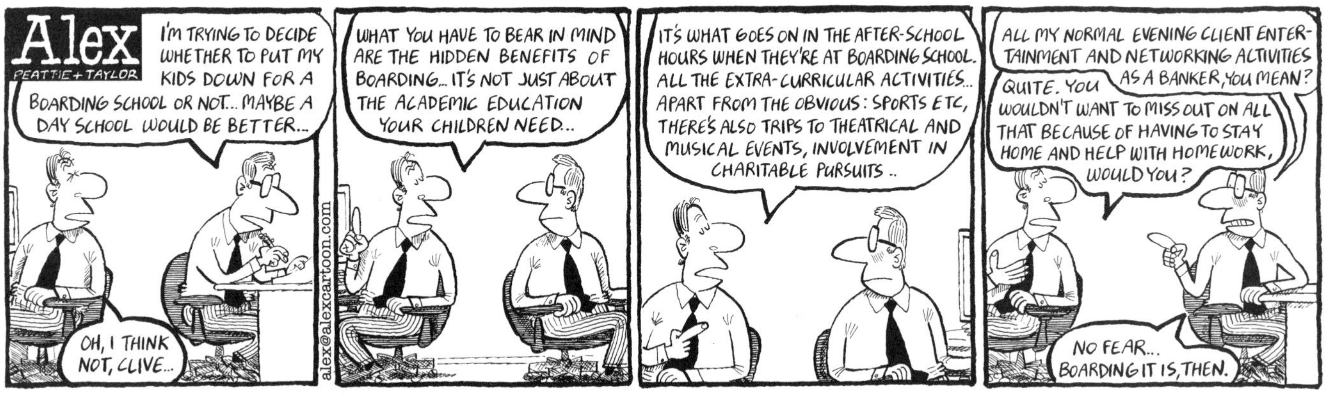
Alex
PEATTIE + TAYLOR
I'M TRYING TO DECIDE WHETHER TO PUT MY KIDS DOWN FOR A BOARDING SCHOOL OR NOT... MAYBE A DAY SCHOOL WOULD BE BETTER...
OH, I THINK NOT, CLIVE...
alex@alexcartoon.com
WHAT YOU HAVE TO BEAR IN MIND ARE THE HIDDEN BENEFITS OF BOARDING... IT'S NOT JUST ABOUT THE ACADEMIC EDUCATION YOUR CHILDREN NEED...
IT'S WHAT GOES ON IN THE AFTER-SCHOOL HOURS WHEN THEY'RE AT BOARDING SCHOOL. ALL THE EXTRA-CURRICULAR ACTIVITIES... APART FROM THE OBVIOUS: SPORTS ETC, THERE'S ALSO TRIPS TO THEATRICAL AND MUSICAL EVENTS, INVOLVEMENT IN CHARITABLE PURSUITS..
ALL MY NORMAL EVENING CLIENT ENTERTAINMENT AND NETWORKING ACTIVITIES AS A BANKER, YOU MEAN?
QUITE. YOU WOULDN'T WANT TO MISS OUT ON ALL THAT BECAUSE OF HAVING TO STAY HOME AND HELP WITH HOMEWORK, WOULD YOU?
NO FEAR... BOARDING IT IS, THEN.

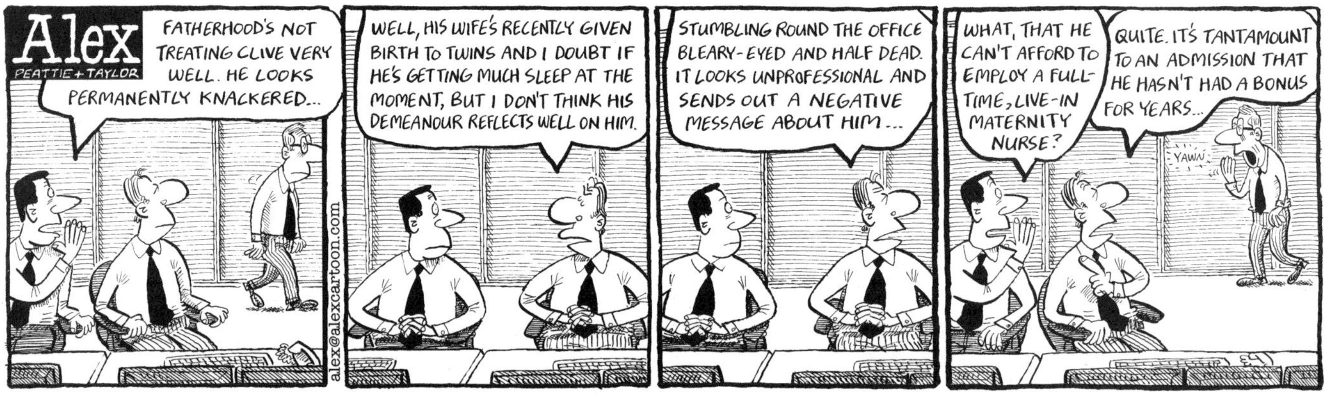
Alex
PEATTIE + TAYLOR
FATHERHOOD'S NOT TREATING CLIVE VERY WELL. HE LOOKS PERMANENTLY KNACKERED...
alex@alexcartoon.com
WELL, HIS WIFE'S RECENTLY GIVEN BIRTH TO TWINS AND I DOUBT IF HE'S GETTING MUCH SLEEP AT THE MOMENT, BUT I DON'T THINK HIS DEMEANOUR REFLECTS WELL ON HIM.
STUMBLING ROUND THE OFFICE BLEARY-EYED AND HALF DEAD. IT LOOKS UNPROFESSIONAL AND SENDS OUT A NEGATIVE MESSAGE ABOUT HIM...
WHAT, THAT HE CAN'T AFFORD TO EMPLOY A FULL-TIME, LIVE-IN MATERNITY NURSE?
QUITE. IT'S TANTAMOUNT TO AN ADMISSION THAT HE HASN'T HAD A BONUS FOR YEARS...
YAWN

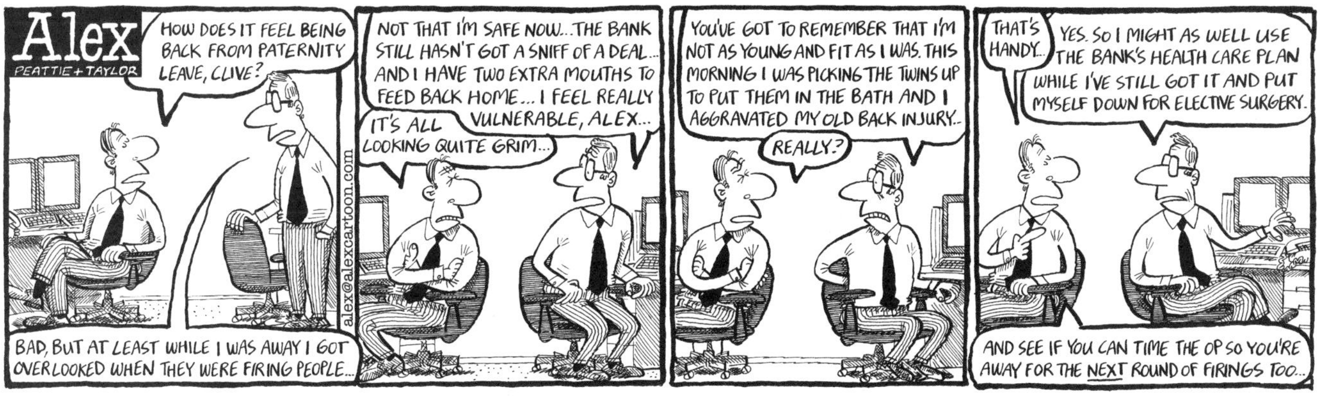
Alex
PEATTIE + TAYLOR
HOW DOES IT FEEL BEING BACK FROM PATERNITY LEAVE, CLIVE?
BAD, BUT AT LEAST WHILE I WAS AWAY I GOT OVERLOOKED WHEN THEY WERE FIRING PEOPLE...
alex@alexcartoon.com
NOT THAT I'M SAFE NOW... THE BANK STILL HASN'T GOT A SNIFF OF A DEAL... AND I HAVE TWO EXTRA MOUTHS TO FEED BACK HOME... I FEEL REALLY VULNERABLE, ALEX...
IT'S ALL LOOKING QUITE GRIM...
YOU'VE GOT TO REMEMBER THAT I'M NOT AS YOUNG AND FIT AS I WAS. THIS MORNING I WAS PICKING THE TWINS UP TO PUT THEM IN THE BATH AND I AGGRAVATED MY OLD BACK INJURY...
REALLY?
THAT'S HANDY...
YES. SO I MIGHT AS WELL USE THE BANK'S HEALTH CARE PLAN WHILE I'VE STILL GOT IT AND PUT MYSELF DOWN FOR ELECTIVE SURGERY.
AND SEE IF YOU CAN TIME THE OP SO YOU'RE AWAY FOR THE NEXT ROUND OF FIRINGS TOO...

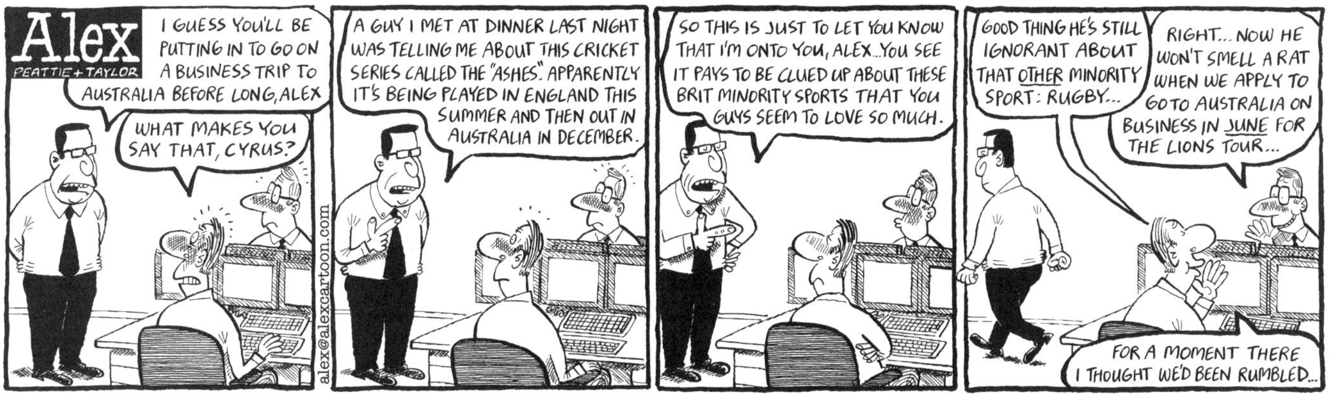
Alex
PEATTIE + TAYLOR
I GUESS YOU'LL BE PUTTING IN TO GO ON A BUSINESS TRIP TO AUSTRALIA BEFORE LONG, ALEX
WHAT MAKES YOU SAY THAT, CYRUS?
alex@alexcartoon.com
A GUY I MET AT DINNER LAST NIGHT WAS TELLING ME ABOUT THIS CRICKET SERIES CALLED THE "ASHES". APPARENTLY IT'S BEING PLAYED IN ENGLAND THIS SUMMER AND THEN OUT IN AUSTRALIA IN DECEMBER.
SO THIS IS JUST TO LET YOU KNOW THAT I'M ONTO YOU, ALEX... YOU SEE IT PAYS TO BE CLUED UP ABOUT THESE BRIT MINORITY SPORTS THAT YOU GUYS SEEM TO LOVE SO MUCH.
GOOD THING HE'S STILL IGNORANT ABOUT THAT OTHER MINORITY SPORT: RUGBY...
RIGHT... NOW HE WON'T SMELL A RAT WHEN WE APPLY TO GO TO AUSTRALIA ON BUSINESS IN JUNE FOR THE LIONS TOUR...
FOR A MOMENT THERE I THOUGHT WE'D BEEN RUMBLED...

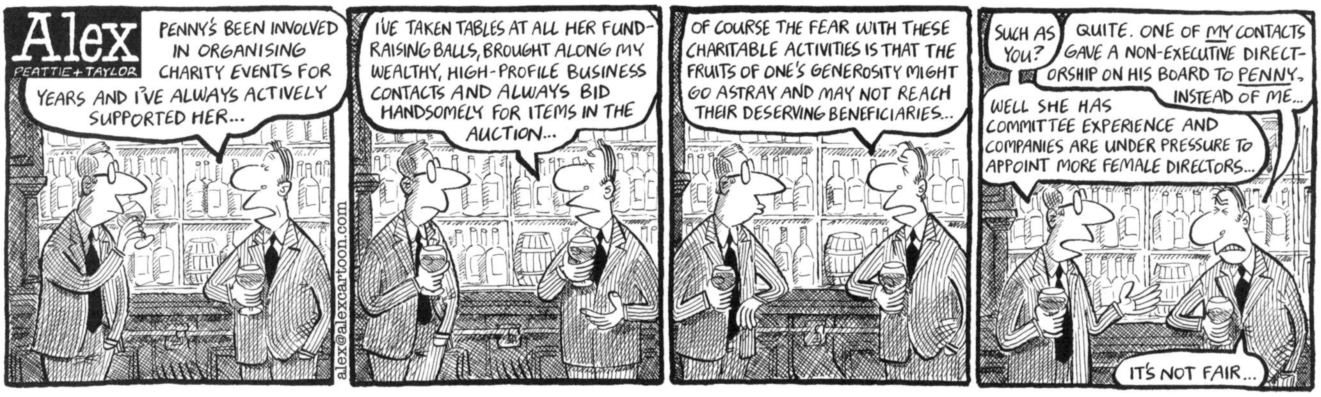
Alex
PEATTIE + TAYLOR
PENNY'S BEEN INVOLVED IN ORGANISING CHARITY EVENTS FOR YEARS AND I'VE ALWAYS ACTIVELY SUPPORTED HER...
alex@alexcartoon.com
I'VE TAKEN TABLES AT ALL HER FUND-RAISING BALLS, BROUGHT ALONG MY WEALTHY, HIGH-PROFILE BUSINESS CONTACTS AND ALWAYS BID HANDSOMELY FOR ITEMS IN THE AUCTION...
OF COURSE THE FEAR WITH THESE CHARITABLE ACTIVITIES IS THAT THE FRUITS OF ONE'S GENEROSITY MIGHT GO ASTRAY AND MAY NOT REACH THEIR DESERVING BENEFICIARIES...
SUCH AS YOU?
QUITE. ONE OF MY CONTACTS GAVE A NON-EXECUTIVE DIRECTORSHIP ON HIS BOARD TO PENNY, INSTEAD OF ME...
WELL SHE HAS COMMITTEE EXPERIENCE AND COMPANIES ARE UNDER PRESSURE TO APPOINT MORE FEMALE DIRECTORS...
IT'S NOT FAIR...

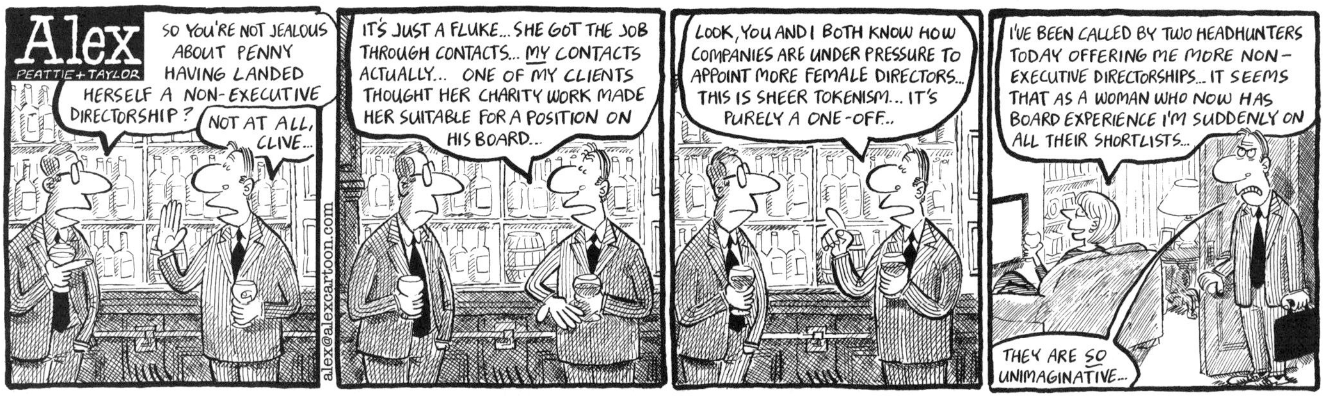
Alex
PEATTIE + TAYLOR
SO YOU'RE NOT JEALOUS ABOUT PENNY HAVING LANDED HERSELF A NON-EXECUTIVE DIRECTORSHIP?
NOT AT ALL, CLIVE...
alex@alexcartoon.com
IT'S JUST A FLUKE... SHE GOT THE JOB THROUGH CONTACTS... MY CONTACTS ACTUALLY... ONE OF MY CLIENTS THOUGHT HER CHARITY WORK MADE HER SUITABLE FOR A POSITION ON HIS BOARD...
LOOK, YOU AND I BOTH KNOW HOW COMPANIES ARE UNDER PRESSURE TO APPOINT MORE FEMALE DIRECTORS... THIS IS SHEER TOKENISM... IT'S PURELY A ONE-OFF...
I'VE BEEN CALLED BY TWO HEADHUNTERS TODAY OFFERING ME MORE NON-EXECUTIVE DIRECTORSHIPS... IT SEEMS THAT AS A WOMAN WHO NOW HAS BOARD EXPERIENCE I'M SUDDENLY ON ALL THEIR SHORTLISTS...
THEY ARE SO UNIMAGINATIVE...

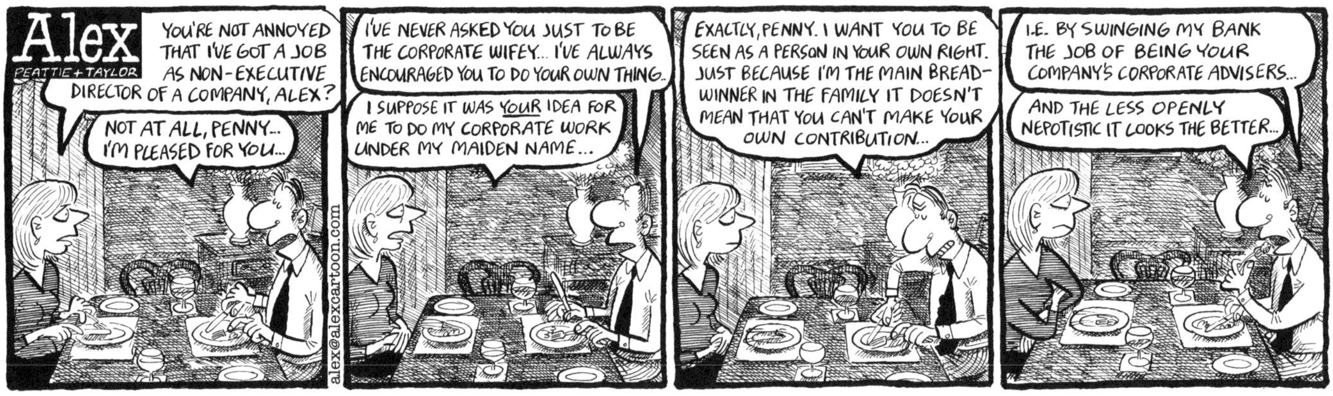
Alex
PEATTIE+TAYLOR
YOU'RE NOT ANNOYED THAT I'VE GOT A JOB AS NON-EXECUTIVE DIRECTOR OF A COMPANY, ALEX?
NOT AT ALL, PENNY... I'M PLEASED FOR YOU...
alex@alexcartoon.com
I'VE NEVER ASKED YOU JUST TO BE THE CORPORATE WIFEY... I'VE ALWAYS ENCOURAGED YOU TO DO YOUR OWN THING.
I SUPPOSE IT WAS YOUR IDEA FOR ME TO DO MY CORPORATE WORK UNDER MY MAIDEN NAME...
EXACTLY, PENNY. I WANT YOU TO BE SEEN AS A PERSON IN YOUR OWN RIGHT. JUST BECAUSE I'M THE MAIN BREAD-WINNER IN THE FAMILY IT DOESN'T MEAN THAT YOU CAN'T MAKE YOUR OWN CONTRIBUTION...
I.E. BY SWINGING MY BANK THE JOB OF BEING YOUR COMPANY'S CORPORATE ADVISERS...
AND THE LESS OPENLY NEPOTISTIC IT LOOKS THE BETTER...

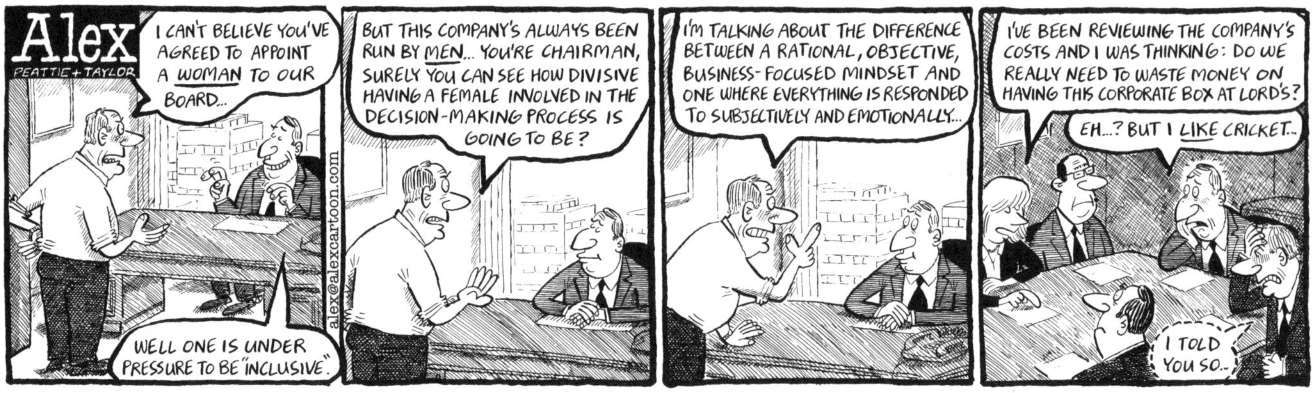
Alex
PEATTIE+TAYLOR
I CAN'T BELIEVE YOU'VE AGREED TO APPOINT A WOMAN TO OUR BOARD...
WELL ONE IS UNDER PRESSURE TO BE "INCLUSIVE".
alex@alexcartoon.com
BUT THIS COMPANY'S ALWAYS BEEN RUN BY MEN... YOU'RE CHAIRMAN, SURELY YOU CAN SEE HOW DIVISIVE HAVING A FEMALE INVOLVED IN THE DECISION-MAKING PROCESS IS GOING TO BE?
I'M TALKING ABOUT THE DIFFERENCE BETWEEN A RATIONAL, OBJECTIVE, BUSINESS-FOCUSED MINDSET AND ONE WHERE EVERYTHING IS RESPONDED TO SUBJECTIVELY AND EMOTIONALLY...
I'VE BEEN REVIEWING THE COMPANY'S COSTS AND I WAS THINKING: DO WE REALLY NEED TO WASTE MONEY ON HAVING THIS CORPORATE BOX AT LORD'S?
EH...? BUT I LIKE CRICKET...
I TOLD YOU SO...

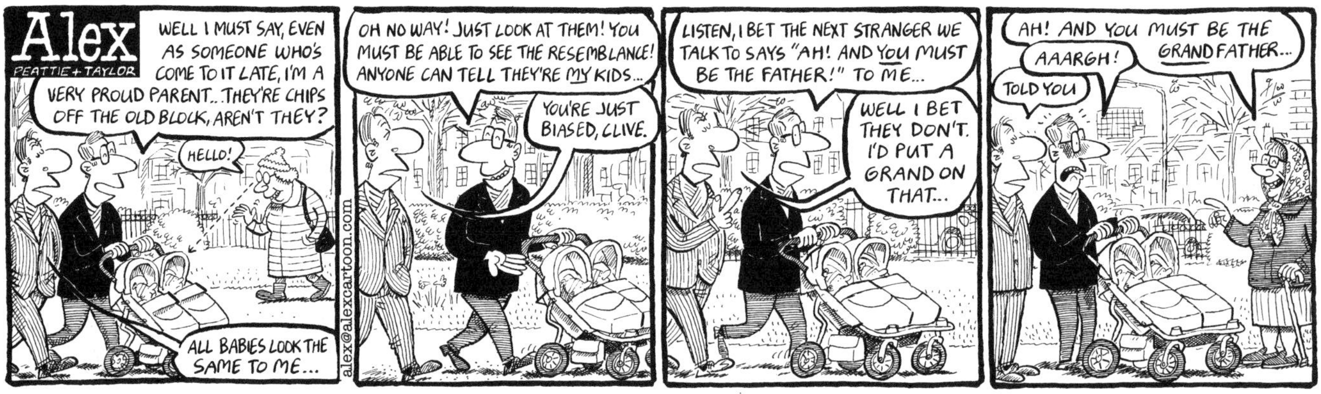
Alex
PEATTIE+TAYLOR
WELL I MUST SAY, EVEN AS SOMEONE WHO'S COME TO IT LATE, I'M A VERY PROUD PARENT... THEY'RE CHIPS OFF THE OLD BLOCK, AREN'T THEY?
HELLO!
ALL BABIES LOOK THE SAME TO ME...
alex@alexcartoon.com
OH NO WAY! JUST LOOK AT THEM! YOU MUST BE ABLE TO SEE THE RESEMBLANCE! ANYONE CAN TELL THEY'RE MY KIDS...
YOU'RE JUST BIASED, CLIVE.
LISTEN, I BET THE NEXT STRANGER WE TALK TO SAYS "AH! AND YOU MUST BE THE FATHER!" TO ME...
WELL I BET THEY DON'T. I'D PUT A GRAND ON THAT...
AH! AND YOU MUST BE THE GRANDFATHER...
AAARGH!
TOLD YOU

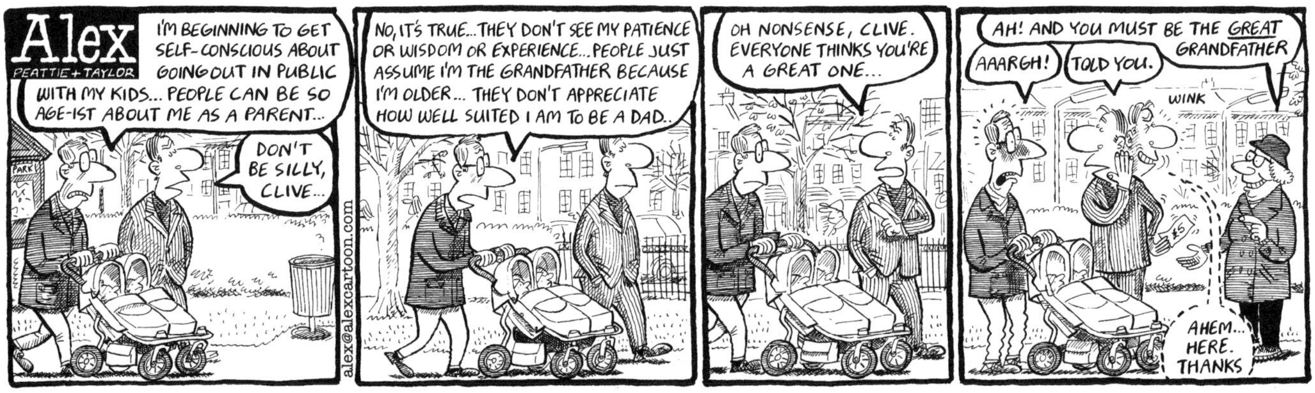
Alex
PEATTIE+TAYLOR
I'M BEGINNING TO GET SELF-CONSCIOUS ABOUT GOING OUT IN PUBLIC WITH MY KIDS... PEOPLE CAN BE SO AGE-IST ABOUT ME AS A PARENT...
DON'T BE SILLY, CLIVE...
PARK
alex@alexcartoon.com
NO, IT'S TRUE... THEY DON'T SEE MY PATIENCE OR WISDOM OR EXPERIENCE... PEOPLE JUST ASSUME I'M THE GRANDFATHER BECAUSE I'M OLDER... THEY DON'T APPRECIATE HOW WELL SUITED I AM TO BE A DAD...
OH NONSENSE, CLIVE. EVERYONE THINKS YOU'RE A GREAT ONE...
AH! AND YOU MUST BE THE GREAT GRANDFATHER
AAARGH!
TOLD YOU.
WINK
AHEM... HERE. THANKS

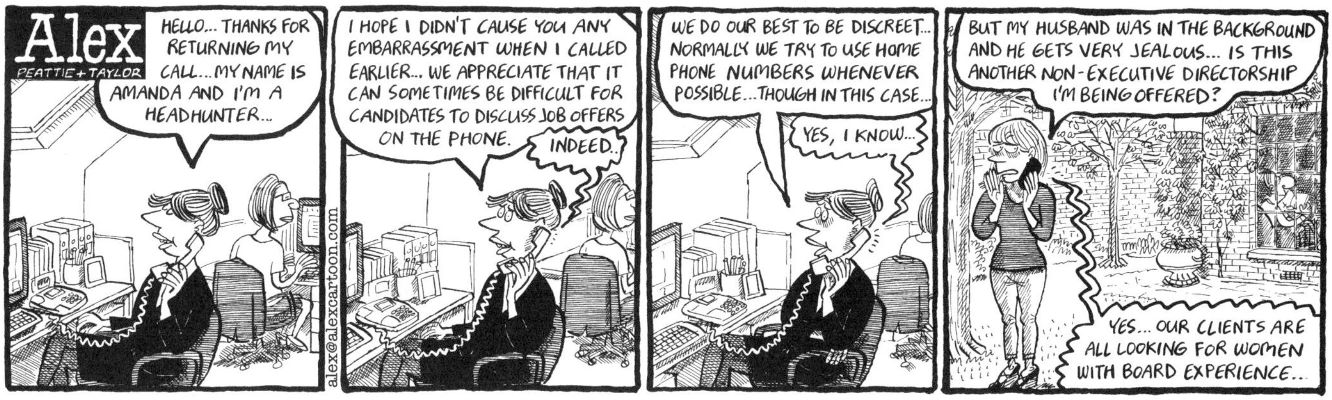
Alex
PEATTIE + TAYLOR
HELLO... THANKS FOR RETURNING MY CALL... MY NAME IS AMANDA AND I'M A HEADHUNTER...
I HOPE I DIDN'T CAUSE YOU ANY EMBARRASSMENT WHEN I CALLED EARLIER... WE APPRECIATE THAT IT CAN SOMETIMES BE DIFFICULT FOR CANDIDATES TO DISCUSS JOB OFFERS ON THE PHONE.
INDEED..
alex@alexcartoon.com
WE DO OUR BEST TO BE DISCREET... NORMALLY WE TRY TO USE HOME PHONE NUMBERS WHENEVER POSSIBLE... THOUGH IN THIS CASE...
YES, I KNOW...
BUT MY HUSBAND WAS IN THE BACKGROUND AND HE GETS VERY JEALOUS... IS THIS ANOTHER NON-EXECUTIVE DIRECTORSHIP I'M BEING OFFERED?
YES... OUR CLIENTS ARE ALL LOOKING FOR WOMEN WITH BOARD EXPERIENCE...

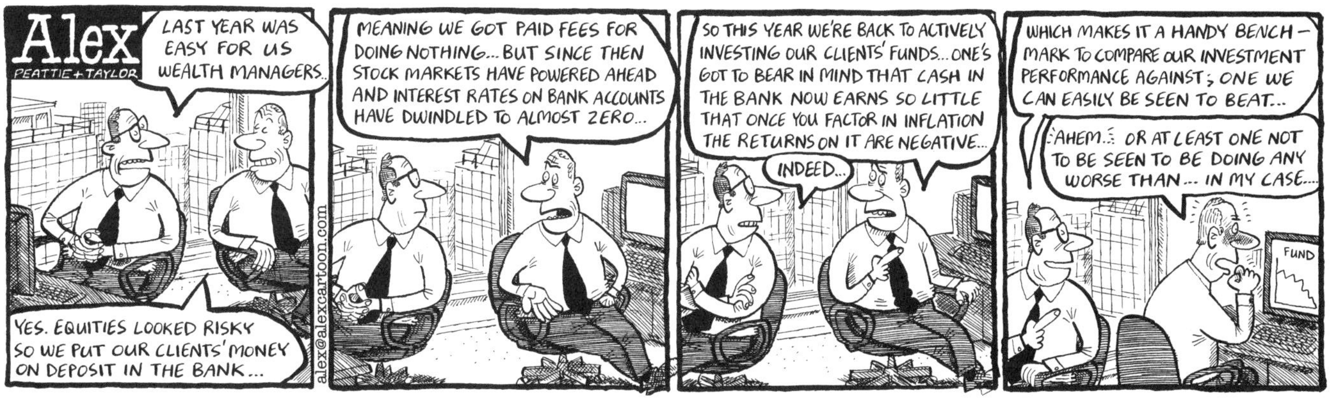
Alex
PEATTIE + TAYLOR
LAST YEAR WAS EASY FOR US WEALTH MANAGERS.
YES. EQUITIES LOOKED RISKY SO WE PUT OUR CLIENTS' MONEY ON DEPOSIT IN THE BANK...
alex@alexcartoon.com
MEANING WE GOT PAID FEES FOR DOING NOTHING... BUT SINCE THEN STOCK MARKETS HAVE POWERED AHEAD AND INTEREST RATES ON BANK ACCOUNTS HAVE DWINDLED TO ALMOST ZERO...
SO THIS YEAR WE'RE BACK TO ACTIVELY INVESTING OUR CLIENTS' FUNDS... ONE'S GOT TO BEAR IN MIND THAT CASH IN THE BANK NOW EARNS SO LITTLE THAT ONCE YOU FACTOR IN INFLATION THE RETURNS ON IT ARE NEGATIVE...
INDEED...
WHICH MAKES IT A HANDY BENCH-MARK TO COMPARE OUR INVESTMENT PERFORMANCE AGAINST; ONE WE CAN EASILY BE SEEN TO BEAT...
AHEM... OR AT LEAST ONE NOT TO BE SEEN TO BE DOING ANY WORSE THAN... IN MY CASE...
FUND

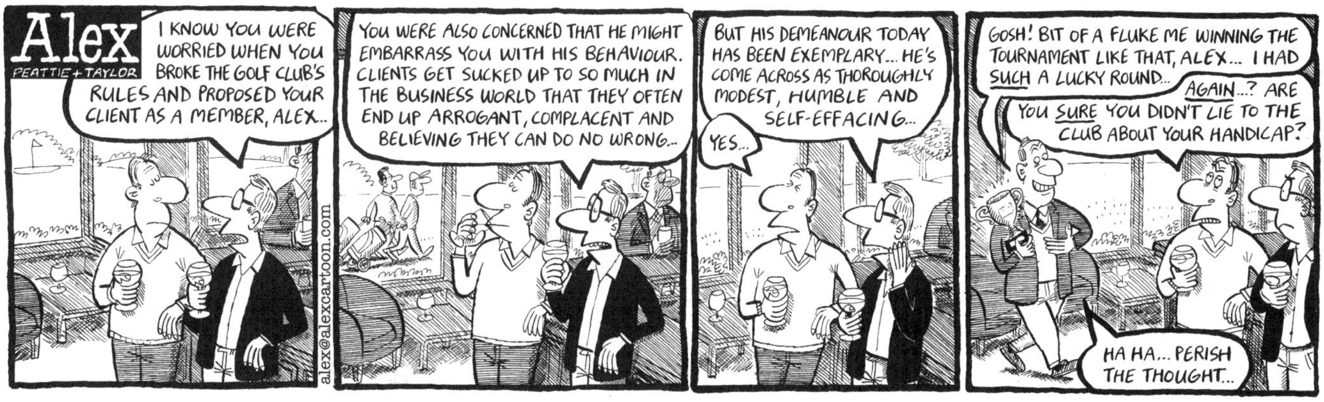
Alex
PEATTIE + TAYLOR
I KNOW YOU WERE WORRIED WHEN YOU BROKE THE GOLF CLUB'S RULES AND PROPOSED YOUR CLIENT AS A MEMBER, ALEX...
alex@alexcartoon.com
YOU WERE ALSO CONCERNED THAT HE MIGHT EMBARRASS YOU WITH HIS BEHAVIOUR. CLIENTS GET SUCKED UP TO SO MUCH IN THE BUSINESS WORLD THAT THEY OFTEN END UP ARROGANT, COMPLACENT AND BELIEVING THEY CAN DO NO WRONG...
BUT HIS DEMEANOUR TODAY HAS BEEN EXEMPLARY... HE'S COME ACROSS AS THOROUGHLY MODEST, HUMBLE AND SELF-EFFACING...
YES...
GOSH! BIT OF A FLUKE ME WINNING THE TOURNAMENT LIKE THAT, ALEX... I HAD SUCH A LUCKY ROUND...
AGAIN...? ARE YOU SURE YOU DIDN'T LIE TO THE CLUB ABOUT YOUR HANDICAP?
HA HA... PERISH THE THOUGHT...

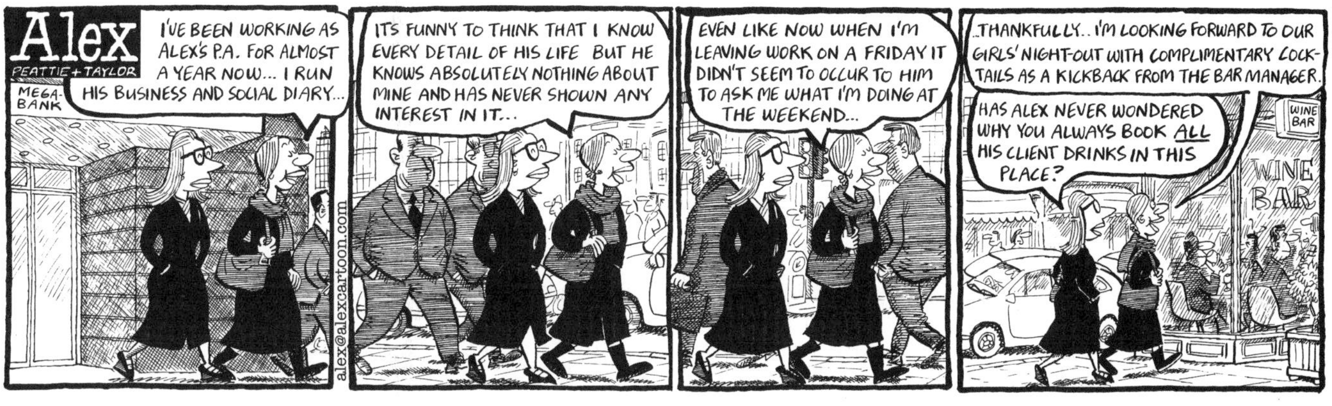
Alex
PEATTIE + TAYLOR
I'VE BEEN WORKING AS ALEX'S P.A. FOR ALMOST A YEAR NOW... I RUN HIS BUSINESS AND SOCIAL DIARY...
MEGA-BANK
alex@alexcartoon.com
IT'S FUNNY TO THINK THAT I KNOW EVERY DETAIL OF HIS LIFE BUT HE KNOWS ABSOLUTELY NOTHING ABOUT MINE AND HAS NEVER SHOWN ANY INTEREST IN IT...
EVEN LIKE NOW WHEN I'M LEAVING WORK ON A FRIDAY IT DIDN'T SEEM TO OCCUR TO HIM TO ASK ME WHAT I'M DOING AT THE WEEKEND...
..THANKFULLY.. I'M LOOKING FORWARD TO OUR GIRLS' NIGHT-OUT WITH COMPLIMENTARY COCK-TAILS AS A KICKBACK FROM THE BAR MANAGER.
HAS ALEX NEVER WONDERED WHY YOU ALWAYS BOOK ALL HIS CLIENT DRINKS IN THIS PLACE?
WINE BAR
WINE BAR

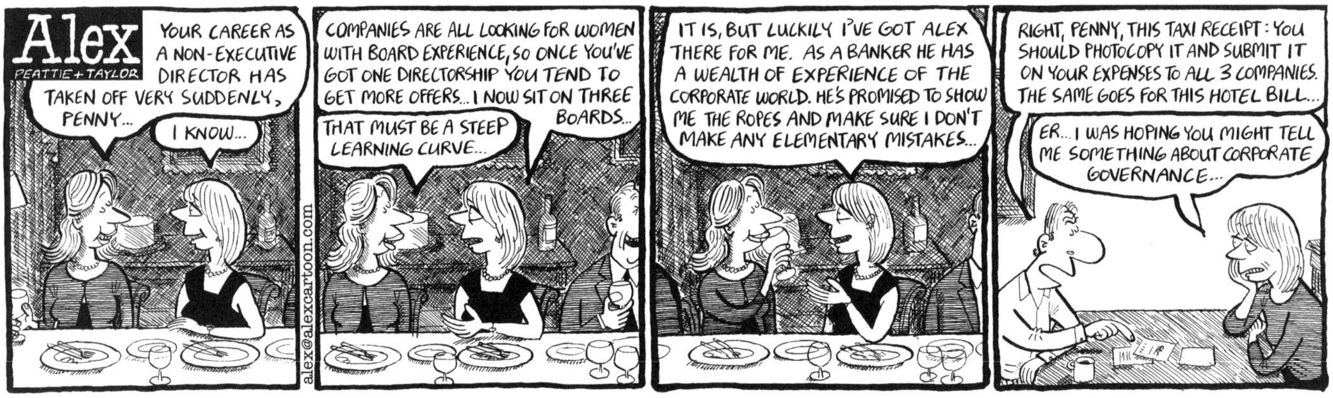
Alex
PEATTIE + TAYLOR
YOUR CAREER AS A NON-EXECUTIVE DIRECTOR HAS TAKEN OFF VERY SUDDENLY, PENNY...
I KNOW...
alex@alexcartoon.com
COMPANIES ARE ALL LOOKING FOR WOMEN WITH BOARD EXPERIENCE, SO ONCE YOU'VE GOT ONE DIRECTORSHIP YOU TEND TO GET MORE OFFERS... I NOW SIT ON THREE BOARDS...
THAT MUST BE A STEEP LEARNING CURVE...
IT IS, BUT LUCKILY I'VE GOT ALEX THERE FOR ME. AS A BANKER HE HAS A WEALTH OF EXPERIENCE OF THE CORPORATE WORLD. HE'S PROMISED TO SHOW ME THE ROPES AND MAKE SURE I DON'T MAKE ANY ELEMENTARY MISTAKES...
RIGHT, PENNY, THIS TAXI RECEIPT: YOU SHOULD PHOTOCOPY IT AND SUBMIT IT ON YOUR EXPENSES TO ALL 3 COMPANIES. THE SAME GOES FOR THIS HOTEL BILL...
ER... I WAS HOPING YOU MIGHT TELL ME SOMETHING ABOUT CORPORATE GOVERNANCE...

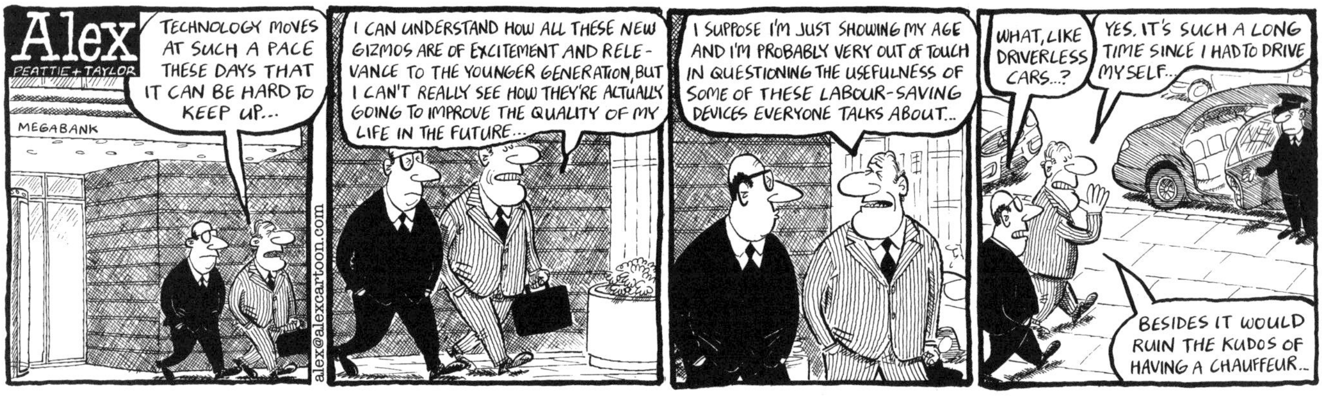
Alex
PEATTIE + TAYLOR
TECHNOLOGY MOVES AT SUCH A PACE THESE DAYS THAT IT CAN BE HARD TO KEEP UP...
MEGABANK
alex@alexcartoon.com
I CAN UNDERSTAND HOW ALL THESE NEW GIZMOS ARE OF EXCITEMENT AND RELEVANCE TO THE YOUNGER GENERATION, BUT I CAN'T REALLY SEE HOW THEY'RE ACTUALLY GOING TO IMPROVE THE QUALITY OF MY LIFE IN THE FUTURE...
I SUPPOSE I'M JUST SHOWING MY AGE AND I'M PROBABLY VERY OUT OF TOUCH IN QUESTIONING THE USEFULNESS OF SOME OF THESE LABOUR-SAVING DEVICES EVERYONE TALKS ABOUT...
WHAT, LIKE DRIVERLESS CARS...?
YES. IT'S SUCH A LONG TIME SINCE I HAD TO DRIVE MYSELF...
BESIDES IT WOULD RUIN THE KUDOS OF HAVING A CHAUFFEUR...

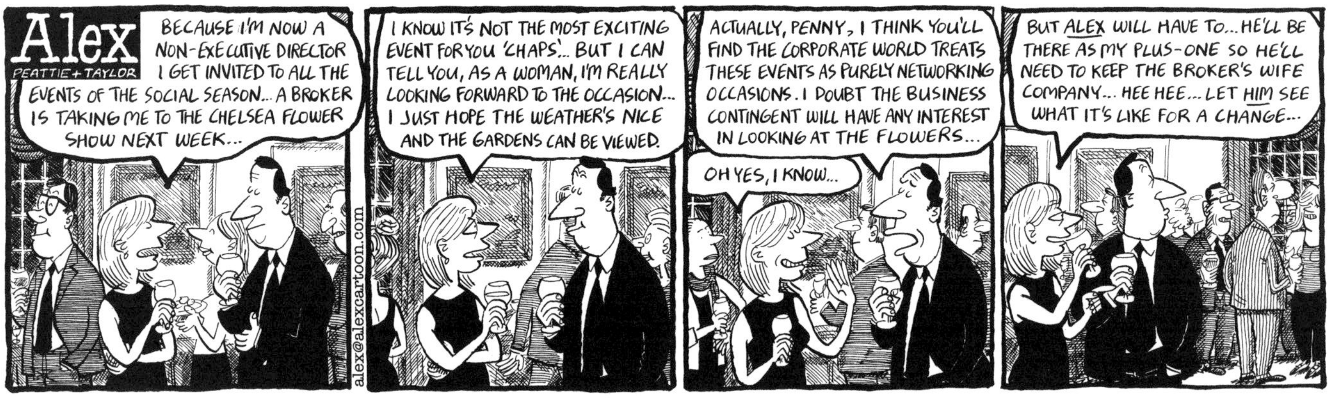
Alex
PEATTIE + TAYLOR
BECAUSE I'M NOW A NON-EXECUTIVE DIRECTOR I GET INVITED TO ALL THE EVENTS OF THE SOCIAL SEASON... A BROKER IS TAKING ME TO THE CHELSEA FLOWER SHOW NEXT WEEK...
alex@alexcartoon.com
I KNOW IT'S NOT THE MOST EXCITING EVENT FOR YOU 'CHAPS'... BUT I CAN TELL YOU, AS A WOMAN, I'M REALLY LOOKING FORWARD TO THE OCCASION... I JUST HOPE THE WEATHER'S NICE AND THE GARDENS CAN BE VIEWED.
ACTUALLY, PENNY, I THINK YOU'LL FIND THE CORPORATE WORLD TREATS THESE EVENTS AS PURELY NETWORKING OCCASIONS. I DOUBT THE BUSINESS CONTINGENT WILL HAVE ANY INTEREST IN LOOKING AT THE FLOWERS...
OH YES, I KNOW...
BUT ALEX WILL HAVE TO... HE'LL BE THERE AS MY PLUS-ONE SO HE'LL NEED TO KEEP THE BROKER'S WIFE COMPANY... HEE HEE... LET HIM SEE WHAT IT'S LIKE FOR A CHANGE...

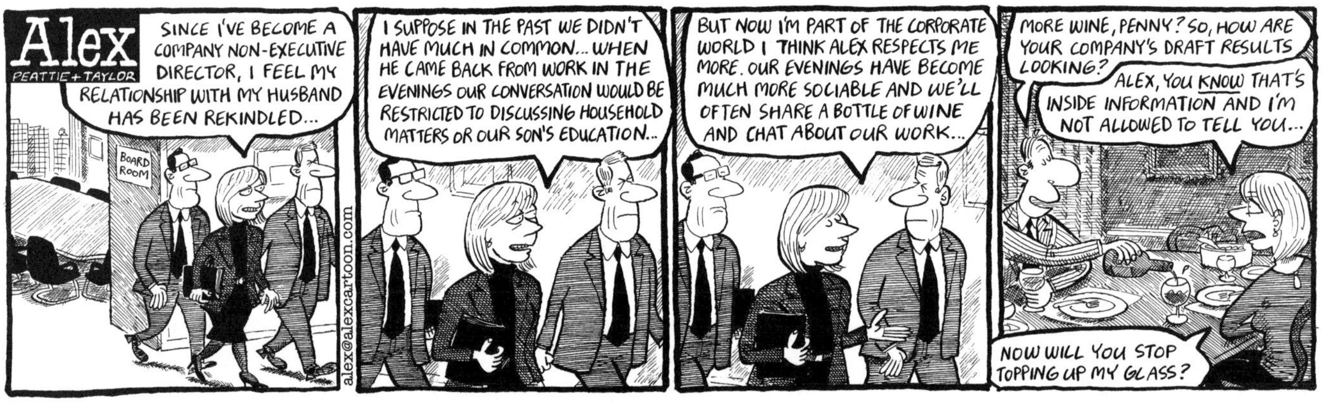
Alex
PEATTIE + TAYLOR
SINCE I'VE BECOME A COMPANY NON-EXECUTIVE DIRECTOR, I FEEL MY RELATIONSHIP WITH MY HUSBAND HAS BEEN REKINDLED...
BOARD ROOM
alex@alexcartoon.com
I SUPPOSE IN THE PAST WE DIDN'T HAVE MUCH IN COMMON... WHEN HE CAME BACK FROM WORK IN THE EVENINGS OUR CONVERSATION WOULD BE RESTRICTED TO DISCUSSING HOUSEHOLD MATTERS OR OUR SON'S EDUCATION...
BUT NOW I'M PART OF THE CORPORATE WORLD I THINK ALEX RESPECTS ME MORE. OUR EVENINGS HAVE BECOME MUCH MORE SOCIABLE AND WE'LL OFTEN SHARE A BOTTLE OF WINE AND CHAT ABOUT OUR WORK...
MORE WINE, PENNY? SO, HOW ARE YOUR COMPANY'S DRAFT RESULTS LOOKING?
ALEX, YOU KNOW THAT'S INSIDE INFORMATION AND I'M NOT ALLOWED TO TELL YOU...
NOW WILL YOU STOP TOPPING UP MY GLASS?

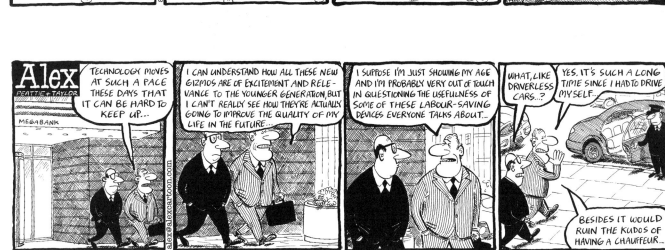

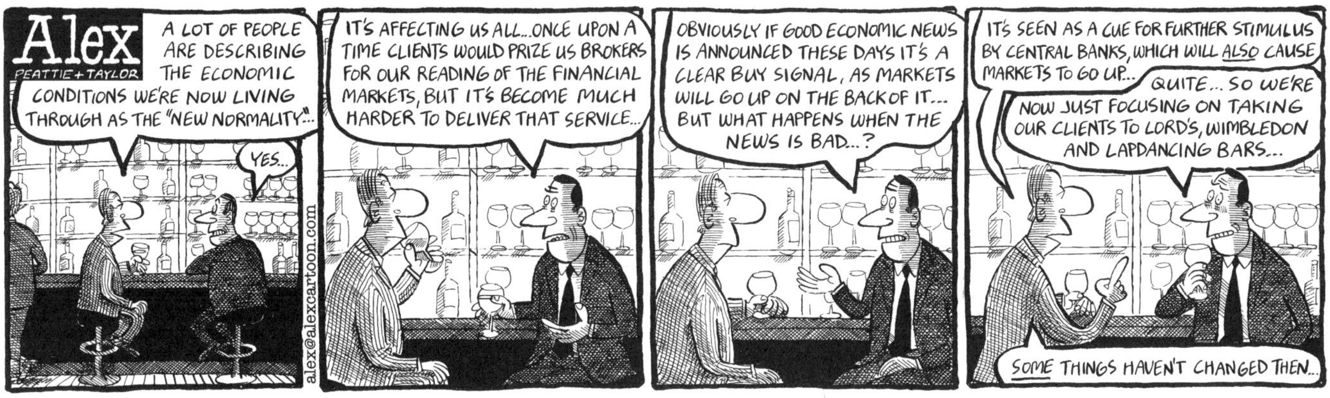
Alex
PEATTIE + TAYLOR
A LOT OF PEOPLE ARE DESCRIBING THE ECONOMIC CONDITIONS WE'RE NOW LIVING THROUGH AS THE "NEW NORMALITY"...
YES...
IT'S AFFECTING US ALL...ONCE UPON A TIME CLIENTS WOULD PRIZE US BROKERS FOR OUR READING OF THE FINANCIAL MARKETS, BUT IT'S BECOME MUCH HARDER TO DELIVER THAT SERVICE...
OBVIOUSLY IF GOOD ECONOMIC NEWS IS ANNOUNCED THESE DAYS IT'S A CLEAR BUY SIGNAL, AS MARKETS WILL GO UP ON THE BACK OF IT... BUT WHAT HAPPENS WHEN THE NEWS IS BAD...?
IT'S SEEN AS A CUE FOR FURTHER STIMULUS BY CENTRAL BANKS, WHICH WILL ALSO CAUSE MARKETS TO GO UP...
QUITE... SO WE'RE NOW JUST FOCUSING ON TAKING OUR CLIENTS TO LORD'S, WIMBLEDON AND LAPDANCING BARS...
SOME THINGS HAVEN'T CHANGED THEN...
alex@alexcartoon.com

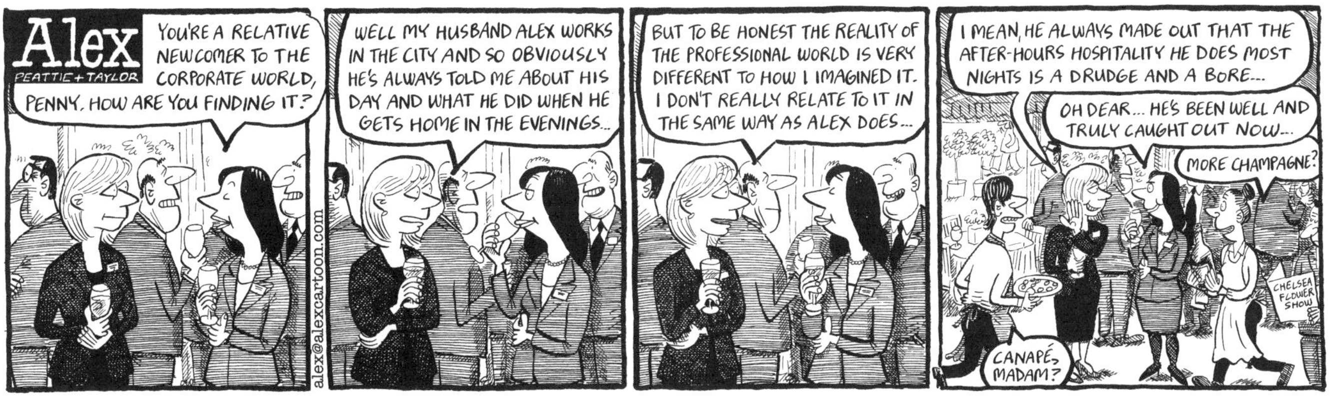
Alex
PEATTIE + TAYLOR
YOU'RE A RELATIVE NEWCOMER TO THE CORPORATE WORLD, PENNY. HOW ARE YOU FINDING IT?
WELL MY HUSBAND ALEX WORKS IN THE CITY AND SO OBVIOUSLY HE'S ALWAYS TOLD ME ABOUT HIS DAY AND WHAT HE DID WHEN HE GETS HOME IN THE EVENINGS...
BUT TO BE HONEST THE REALITY OF THE PROFESSIONAL WORLD IS VERY DIFFERENT TO HOW I IMAGINED IT. I DON'T REALLY RELATE TO IT IN THE SAME WAY AS ALEX DOES...
I MEAN, HE ALWAYS MADE OUT THAT THE AFTER-HOURS HOSPITALITY HE DOES MOST NIGHTS IS A DRUDGE AND A BORE...
OH DEAR... HE'S BEEN WELL AND TRULY CAUGHT OUT NOW...
MORE CHAMPAGNE?
CHELSEA FLOWER SHOW
CANAPÉ, MADAM?
alex@alexcartoon.com

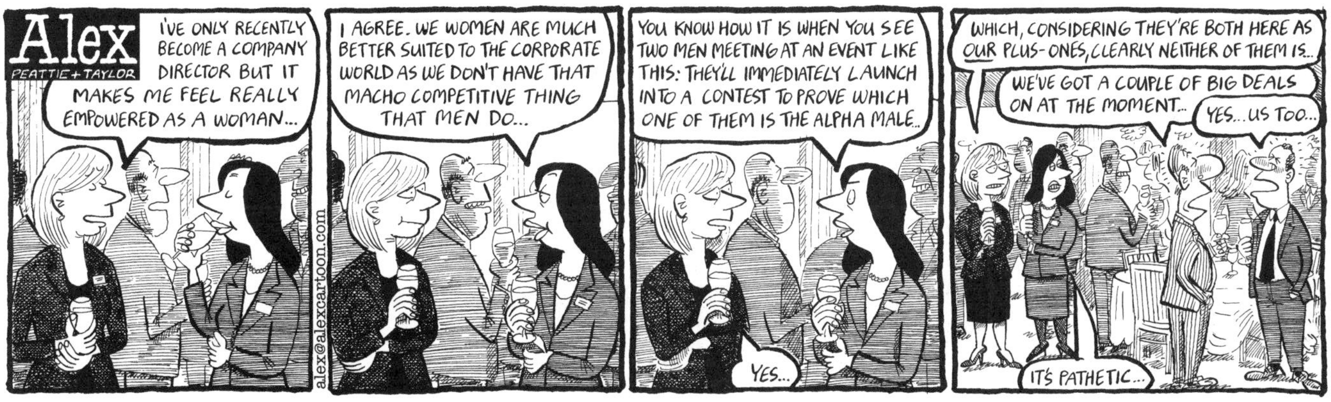
Alex
PEATTIE + TAYLOR
I'VE ONLY RECENTLY BECOME A COMPANY DIRECTOR BUT IT MAKES ME FEEL REALLY EMPOWERED AS A WOMAN...
I AGREE. WE WOMEN ARE MUCH BETTER SUITED TO THE CORPORATE WORLD AS WE DON'T HAVE THAT MACHO COMPETITIVE THING THAT MEN DO...
YOU KNOW HOW IT IS WHEN YOU SEE TWO MEN MEETING AT AN EVENT LIKE THIS: THEY'LL IMMEDIATELY LAUNCH INTO A CONTEST TO PROVE WHICH ONE OF THEM IS THE ALPHA MALE...
YES...
WHICH, CONSIDERING THEY'RE BOTH HERE AS OUR PLUS-ONES, CLEARLY NEITHER OF THEM IS...
WE'VE GOT A COUPLE OF BIG DEALS ON AT THE MOMENT...
YES... US TOO...
IT'S PATHETIC...
alex@alexcartoon.com

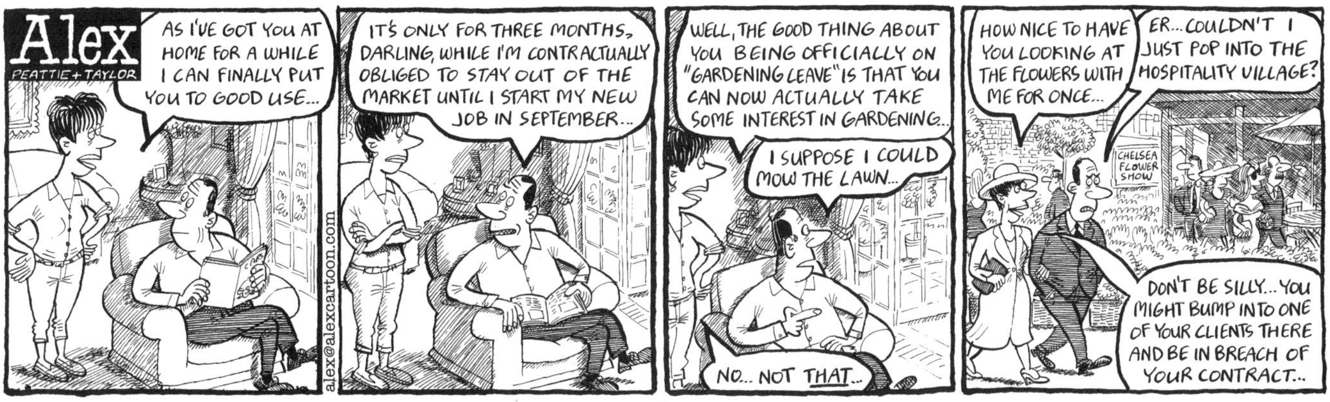
Alex
PEATTIE + TAYLOR
AS I'VE GOT YOU AT HOME FOR A WHILE I CAN FINALLY PUT YOU TO GOOD USE...
IT'S ONLY FOR THREE MONTHS, DARLING, WHILE I'M CONTRACTUALLY OBLIGED TO STAY OUT OF THE MARKET UNTIL I START MY NEW JOB IN SEPTEMBER...
WELL, THE GOOD THING ABOUT YOU BEING OFFICIALLY ON "GARDENING LEAVE" IS THAT YOU CAN NOW ACTUALLY TAKE SOME INTEREST IN GARDENING...
I SUPPOSE I COULD MOW THE LAWN...
NO... NOT THAT...
HOW NICE TO HAVE YOU LOOKING AT THE FLOWERS WITH ME FOR ONCE...
ER... COULDN'T I JUST POP INTO THE HOSPITALITY VILLAGE?
CHELSEA FLOWER SHOW
DON'T BE SILLY... YOU MIGHT BUMP INTO ONE OF YOUR CLIENTS THERE AND BE IN BREACH OF YOUR CONTRACT...
alex@alexcartoon.com

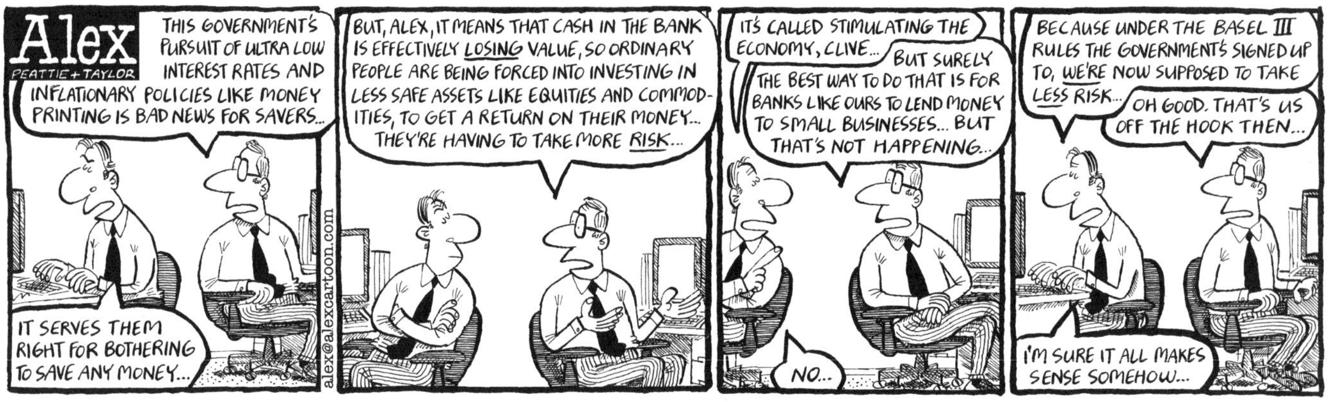
Alex
PEATTIE + TAYLOR
THIS GOVERNMENT'S PURSUIT OF ULTRA LOW INTEREST RATES AND INFLATIONARY POLICIES LIKE MONEY PRINTING IS BAD NEWS FOR SAVERS...
IT SERVES THEM RIGHT FOR BOTHERING TO SAVE ANY MONEY...
alex@alexcartoon.com
BUT, ALEX, IT MEANS THAT CASH IN THE BANK IS EFFECTIVELY LOSING VALUE, SO ORDINARY PEOPLE ARE BEING FORCED INTO INVESTING IN LESS SAFE ASSETS LIKE EQUITIES AND COMMODITIES, TO GET A RETURN ON THEIR MONEY... THEY'RE HAVING TO TAKE MORE RISK...
IT'S CALLED STIMULATING THE ECONOMY, CLIVE...
BUT SURELY THE BEST WAY TO DO THAT IS FOR BANKS LIKE OURS TO LEND MONEY TO SMALL BUSINESSES... BUT THAT'S NOT HAPPENING...
NO...
BECAUSE UNDER THE BASEL III RULES THE GOVERNMENT'S SIGNED UP TO, WE'RE NOW SUPPOSED TO TAKE LESS RISK...
OH GOOD. THAT'S US OFF THE HOOK THEN...
I'M SURE IT ALL MAKES SENSE SOMEHOW...

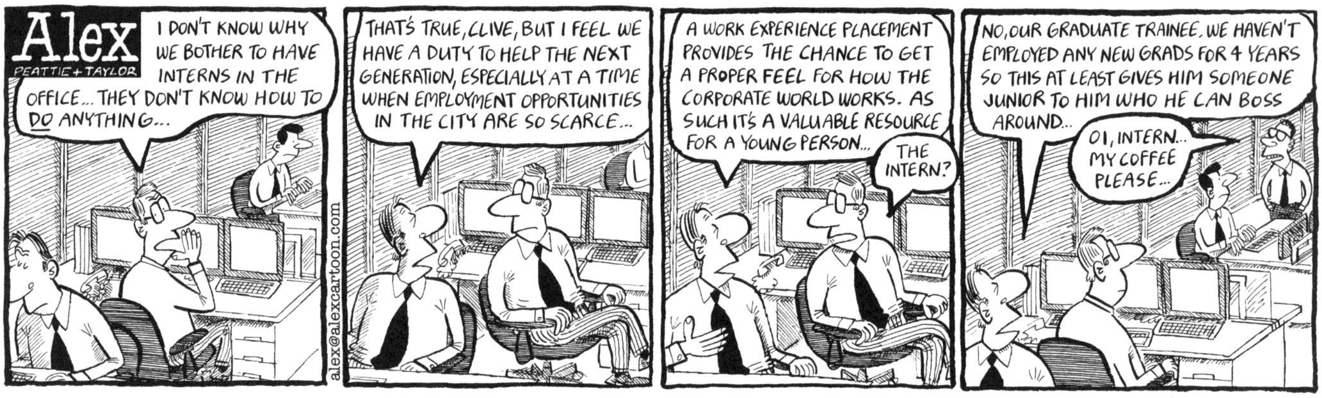
Alex
PEATTIE + TAYLOR
I DON'T KNOW WHY WE BOTHER TO HAVE INTERNS IN THE OFFICE... THEY DON'T KNOW HOW TO DO ANYTHING...
alex@alexcartoon.com
THAT'S TRUE, CLIVE, BUT I FEEL WE HAVE A DUTY TO HELP THE NEXT GENERATION, ESPECIALLY AT A TIME WHEN EMPLOYMENT OPPORTUNITIES IN THE CITY ARE SO SCARCE...
A WORK EXPERIENCE PLACEMENT PROVIDES THE CHANCE TO GET A PROPER FEEL FOR HOW THE CORPORATE WORLD WORKS. AS SUCH IT'S A VALUABLE RESOURCE FOR A YOUNG PERSON...
THE INTERN?
NO, OUR GRADUATE TRAINEE. WE HAVEN'T EMPLOYED ANY NEW GRADS FOR 4 YEARS SO THIS AT LEAST GIVES HIM SOMEONE JUNIOR TO HIM WHO HE CAN BOSS AROUND...
OI, INTERN... MY COFFEE PLEASE...

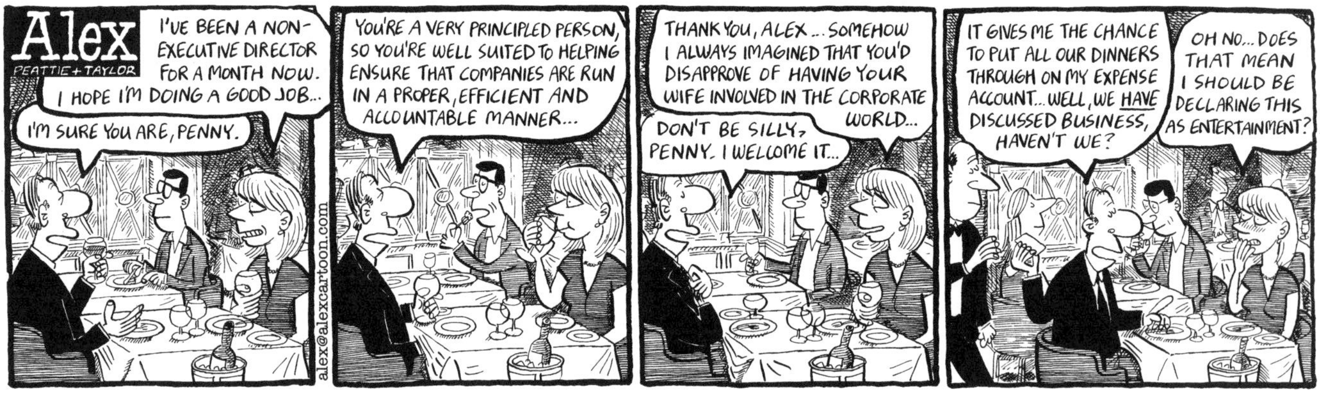
Alex
PEATTIE + TAYLOR
I'VE BEEN A NON-EXECUTIVE DIRECTOR FOR A MONTH NOW. I HOPE I'M DOING A GOOD JOB...
I'M SURE YOU ARE, PENNY.
alex@alexcartoon.com
YOU'RE A VERY PRINCIPLED PERSON, SO YOU'RE WELL SUITED TO HELPING ENSURE THAT COMPANIES ARE RUN IN A PROPER, EFFICIENT AND ACCOUNTABLE MANNER...
THANK YOU, ALEX... SOMEHOW I ALWAYS IMAGINED THAT YOU'D DISAPPROVE OF HAVING YOUR WIFE INVOLVED IN THE CORPORATE WORLD...
DON'T BE SILLY, PENNY. I WELCOME IT...
IT GIVES ME THE CHANCE TO PUT ALL OUR DINNERS THROUGH ON MY EXPENSE ACCOUNT... WELL, WE HAVE DISCUSSED BUSINESS, HAVEN'T WE?
OH NO... DOES THAT MEAN I SHOULD BE DECLARING THIS AS ENTERTAINMENT?

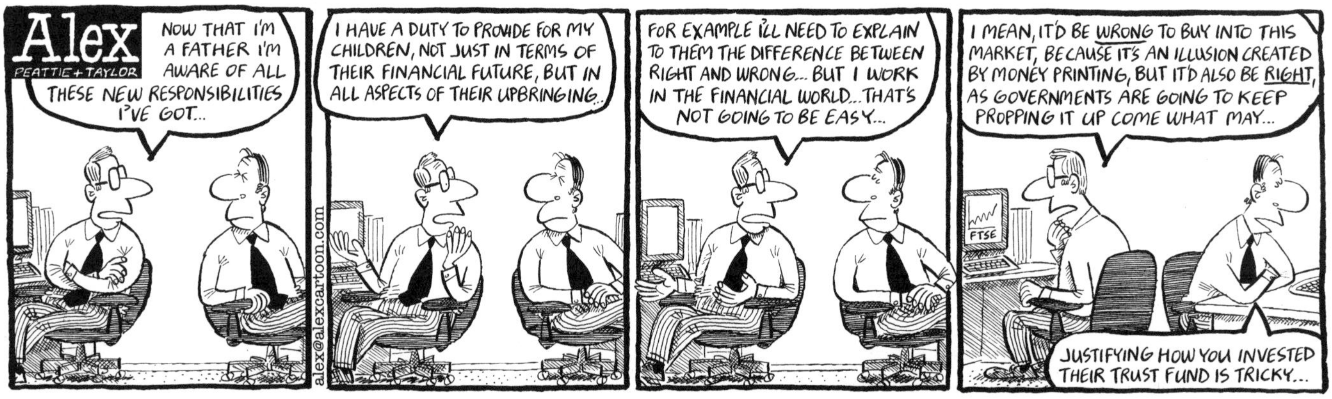
Alex
PEATTIE + TAYLOR
NOW THAT I'M A FATHER I'M AWARE OF ALL THESE NEW RESPONSIBILITIES I'VE GOT...
alex@alexcartoon.com
I HAVE A DUTY TO PROVIDE FOR MY CHILDREN, NOT JUST IN TERMS OF THEIR FINANCIAL FUTURE, BUT IN ALL ASPECTS OF THEIR UPBRINGING...
FOR EXAMPLE I'LL NEED TO EXPLAIN TO THEM THE DIFFERENCE BETWEEN RIGHT AND WRONG... BUT I WORK IN THE FINANCIAL WORLD... THAT'S NOT GOING TO BE EASY...
I MEAN, IT'D BE WRONG TO BUY INTO THIS MARKET, BECAUSE IT'S AN ILLUSION CREATED BY MONEY PRINTING, BUT IT'D ALSO BE RIGHT, AS GOVERNMENTS ARE GOING TO KEEP PROPPING IT UP COME WHAT MAY...
FTSE
JUSTIFYING HOW YOU INVESTED THEIR TRUST FUND IS TRICKY...

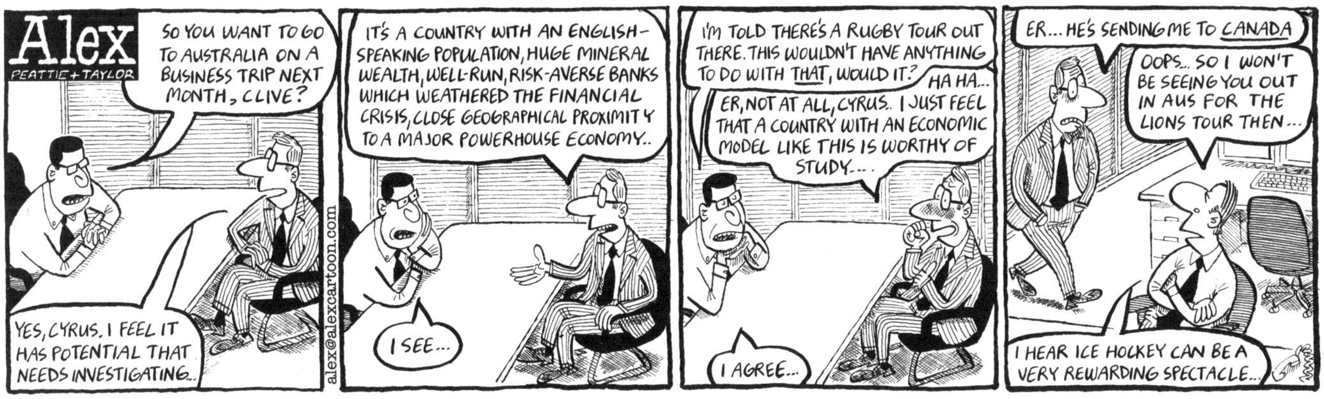
Alex
PEATTIE + TAYLOR
SO YOU WANT TO GO TO AUSTRALIA ON A BUSINESS TRIP NEXT MONTH, CLIVE?
YES, CYRUS. I FEEL IT HAS POTENTIAL THAT NEEDS INVESTIGATING...
alex@alexcartoon.com
IT'S A COUNTRY WITH AN ENGLISH-SPEAKING POPULATION, HUGE MINERAL WEALTH, WELL-RUN, RISK-AVERSE BANKS WHICH WEATHERED THE FINANCIAL CRISIS, CLOSE GEOGRAPHICAL PROXIMITY TO A MAJOR POWERHOUSE ECONOMY..
I SEE...
I'M TOLD THERE'S A RUGBY TOUR OUT THERE. THIS WOULDN'T HAVE ANYTHING TO DO WITH THAT, WOULD IT?
HA HA... ER, NOT AT ALL, CYRUS.. I JUST FEEL THAT A COUNTRY WITH AN ECONOMIC MODEL LIKE THIS IS WORTHY OF STUDY....
I AGREE...
ER... HE'S SENDING ME TO CANADA
OOPS.. SO I WON'T BE SEEING YOU OUT IN AUS FOR THE LIONS TOUR THEN...
I HEAR ICE HOCKEY CAN BE A VERY REWARDING SPECTACLE...

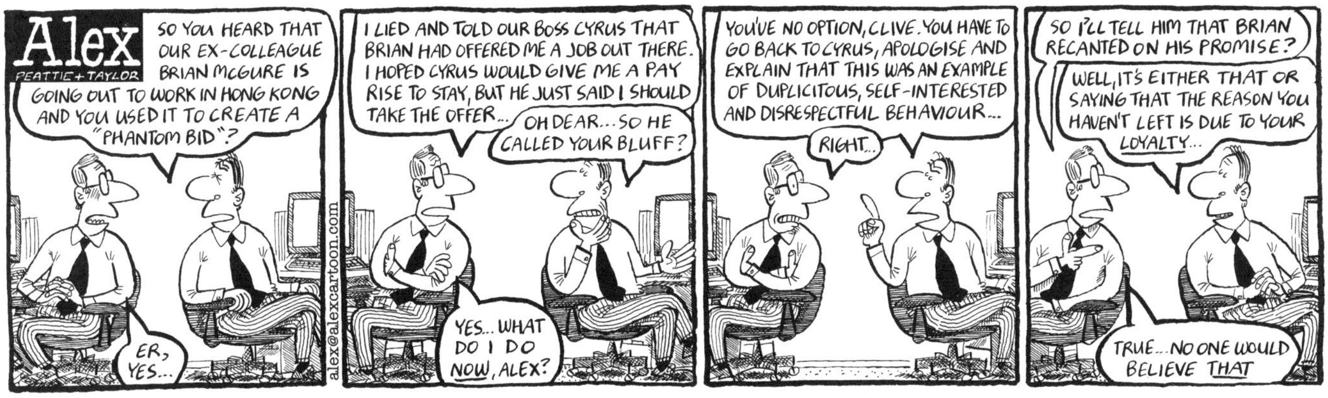
Alex
PEATTIE + TAYLOR
SO YOU HEARD THAT OUR EX-COLLEAGUE BRIAN MCGURE IS GOING OUT TO WORK IN HONG KONG AND YOU USED IT TO CREATE A "PHANTOM BID"?
ER, YES...
alex@alexcartoon.com
I LIED AND TOLD OUR BOSS CYRUS THAT BRIAN HAD OFFERED ME A JOB OUT THERE. I HOPED CYRUS WOULD GIVE ME A PAY RISE TO STAY, BUT HE JUST SAID I SHOULD TAKE THE OFFER...
OH DEAR... SO HE CALLED YOUR BLUFF?
YES... WHAT DO I DO NOW, ALEX?
YOU'VE NO OPTION, CLIVE. YOU HAVE TO GO BACK TO CYRUS, APOLOGISE AND EXPLAIN THAT THIS WAS AN EXAMPLE OF DUPLICITOUS, SELF-INTERESTED AND DISRESPECTFUL BEHAVIOUR...
RIGHT...
SO I'LL TELL HIM THAT BRIAN RECANTED ON HIS PROMISE?
WELL, IT'S EITHER THAT OR SAYING THAT THE REASON YOU HAVEN'T LEFT IS DUE TO YOUR LOYALTY...
TRUE... NO ONE WOULD BELIEVE THAT

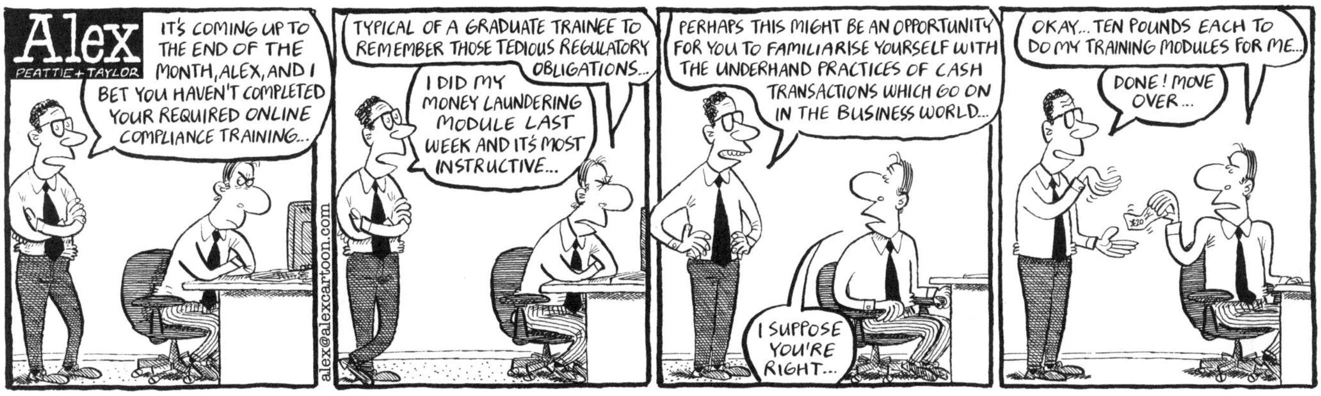
Alex
PEATTIE + TAYLOR
IT'S COMING UP TO THE END OF THE MONTH, ALEX, AND I BET YOU HAVEN'T COMPLETED YOUR REQUIRED ONLINE COMPLIANCE TRAINING...
alex@alexcartoon.com
TYPICAL OF A GRADUATE TRAINEE TO REMEMBER THOSE TEDIOUS REGULATORY OBLIGATIONS...
I DID MY MONEY LAUNDERING MODULE LAST WEEK AND IT'S MOST INSTRUCTIVE...
PERHAPS THIS MIGHT BE AN OPPORTUNITY FOR YOU TO FAMILIARISE YOURSELF WITH THE UNDERHAND PRACTICES OF CASH TRANSACTIONS WHICH GO ON IN THE BUSINESS WORLD...
I SUPPOSE YOU'RE RIGHT...
OKAY... TEN POUNDS EACH TO DO MY TRAINING MODULES FOR ME...
DONE! MOVE OVER...

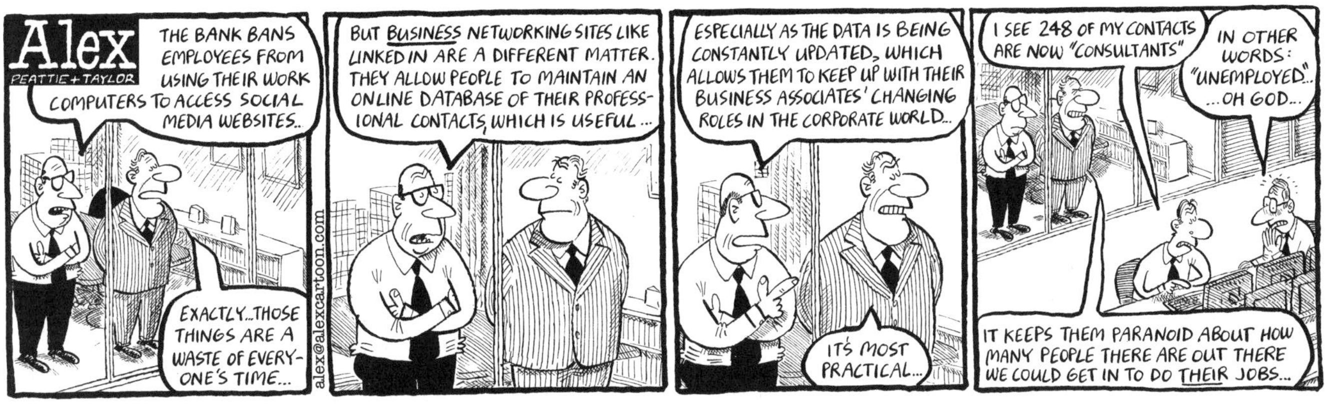
Alex
PEATTIE + TAYLOR
THE BANK BANS EMPLOYEES FROM USING THEIR WORK COMPUTERS TO ACCESS SOCIAL MEDIA WEBSITES..
EXACTLY...THOSE THINGS ARE A WASTE OF EVERY-ONE'S TIME...
alex@alexcartoon.com
BUT BUSINESS NETWORKING SITES LIKE LINKEDIN ARE A DIFFERENT MATTER. THEY ALLOW PEOPLE TO MAINTAIN AN ONLINE DATABASE OF THEIR PROFESS-IONAL CONTACTS, WHICH IS USEFUL...
ESPECIALLY AS THE DATA IS BEING CONSTANTLY UPDATED, WHICH ALLOWS THEM TO KEEP UP WITH THEIR BUSINESS ASSOCIATES' CHANGING ROLES IN THE CORPORATE WORLD...
IT'S MOST PRACTICAL...
I SEE 248 OF MY CONTACTS ARE NOW "CONSULTANTS"
IN OTHER WORDS: "UNEMPLOYED"... ...OH GOD...
IT KEEPS THEM PARANOID ABOUT HOW MANY PEOPLE THERE ARE OUT THERE WE COULD GET IN TO DO THEIR JOBS...

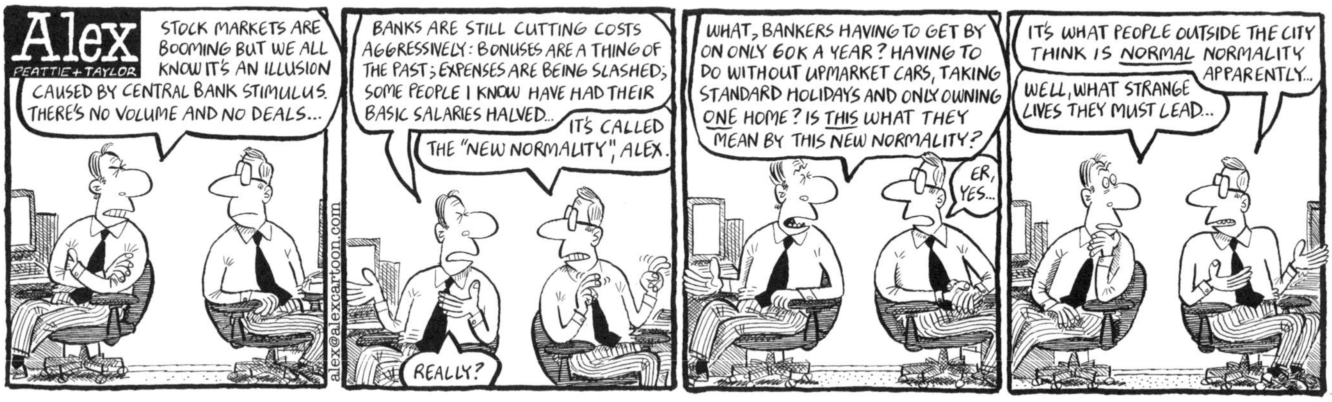
Alex
PEATTIE+TAYLOR
STOCK MARKETS ARE BOOMING BUT WE ALL KNOW IT'S AN ILLUSION CAUSED BY CENTRAL BANK STIMULUS. THERE'S NO VOLUME AND NO DEALS...
BANKS ARE STILL CUTTING COSTS AGGRESSIVELY: BONUSES ARE A THING OF THE PAST; EXPENSES ARE BEING SLASHED; SOME PEOPLE I KNOW HAVE HAD THEIR BASIC SALARIES HALVED...
IT'S CALLED THE "NEW NORMALITY", ALEX.
REALLY?
alex@alexcartoon.com
WHAT, BANKERS HAVING TO GET BY ON ONLY 60K A YEAR? HAVING TO DO WITHOUT UPMARKET CARS, TAKING STANDARD HOLIDAYS AND ONLY OWNING ONE HOME? IS THIS WHAT THEY MEAN BY THIS NEW NORMALITY?
ER, YES...
IT'S WHAT PEOPLE OUTSIDE THE CITY THINK IS NORMAL NORMALITY APPARENTLY...
WELL, WHAT STRANGE LIVES THEY MUST LEAD...

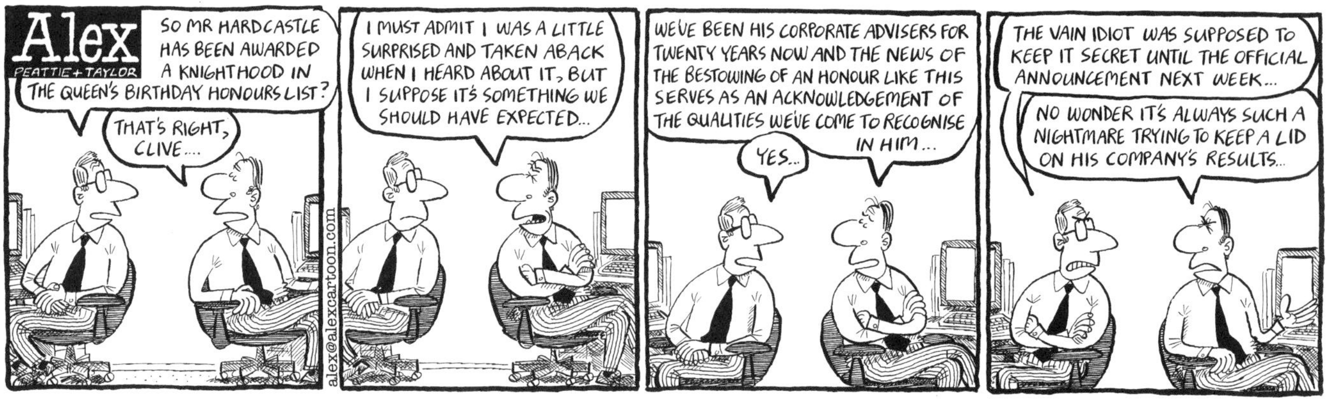
Alex
PEATTIE+TAYLOR
SO MR HARDCASTLE HAS BEEN AWARDED A KNIGHTHOOD IN THE QUEEN'S BIRTHDAY HONOURS LIST?
THAT'S RIGHT, CLIVE....
I MUST ADMIT I WAS A LITTLE SURPRISED AND TAKEN ABACK WHEN I HEARD ABOUT IT, BUT I SUPPOSE IT'S SOMETHING WE SHOULD HAVE EXPECTED...
alex@alexcartoon.com
WE'VE BEEN HIS CORPORATE ADVISERS FOR TWENTY YEARS NOW AND THE NEWS OF THE BESTOWING OF AN HONOUR LIKE THIS SERVES AS AN ACKNOWLEDGEMENT OF THE QUALITIES WE'VE COME TO RECOGNISE IN HIM...
YES...
THE VAIN IDIOT WAS SUPPOSED TO KEEP IT SECRET UNTIL THE OFFICIAL ANNOUNCEMENT NEXT WEEK...
NO WONDER IT'S ALWAYS SUCH A NIGHTMARE TRYING TO KEEP A LID ON HIS COMPANY'S RESULTS...

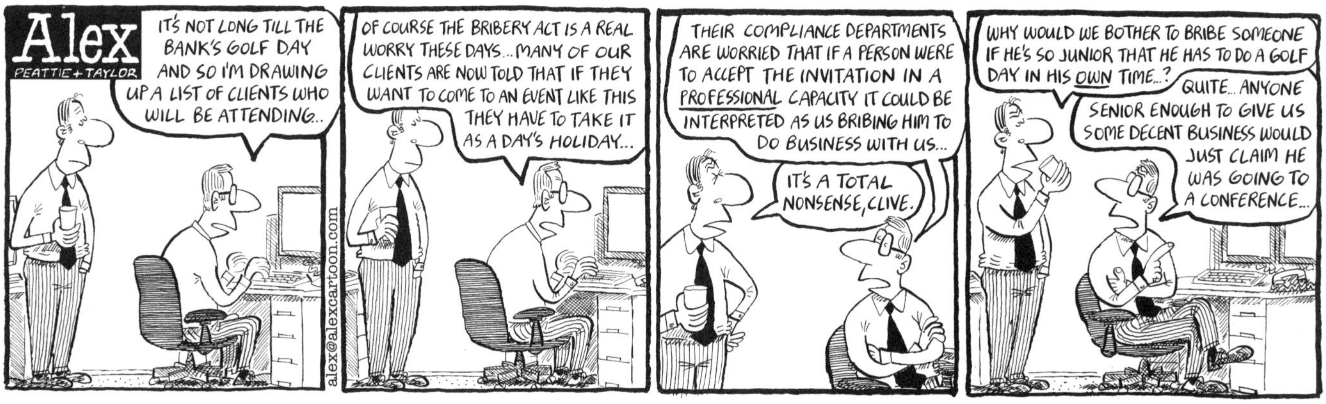
Alex
PEATTIE+TAYLOR
IT'S NOT LONG TILL THE BANK'S GOLF DAY AND SO I'M DRAWING UP A LIST OF CLIENTS WHO WILL BE ATTENDING...
OF COURSE THE BRIBERY ACT IS A REAL WORRY THESE DAYS... MANY OF OUR CLIENTS ARE NOW TOLD THAT IF THEY WANT TO COME TO AN EVENT LIKE THIS THEY HAVE TO TAKE IT AS A DAY'S HOLIDAY...
alex@alexcartoon.com
THEIR COMPLIANCE DEPARTMENTS ARE WORRIED THAT IF A PERSON WERE TO ACCEPT THE INVITATION IN A PROFESSIONAL CAPACITY IT COULD BE INTERPRETED AS US BRIBING HIM TO DO BUSINESS WITH US...
IT'S A TOTAL NONSENSE, CLIVE.
WHY WOULD WE BOTHER TO BRIBE SOMEONE IF HE'S SO JUNIOR THAT HE HAS TO DO A GOLF DAY IN HIS OWN TIME...?
QUITE... ANYONE SENIOR ENOUGH TO GIVE US SOME DECENT BUSINESS WOULD JUST CLAIM HE WAS GOING TO A CONFERENCE...

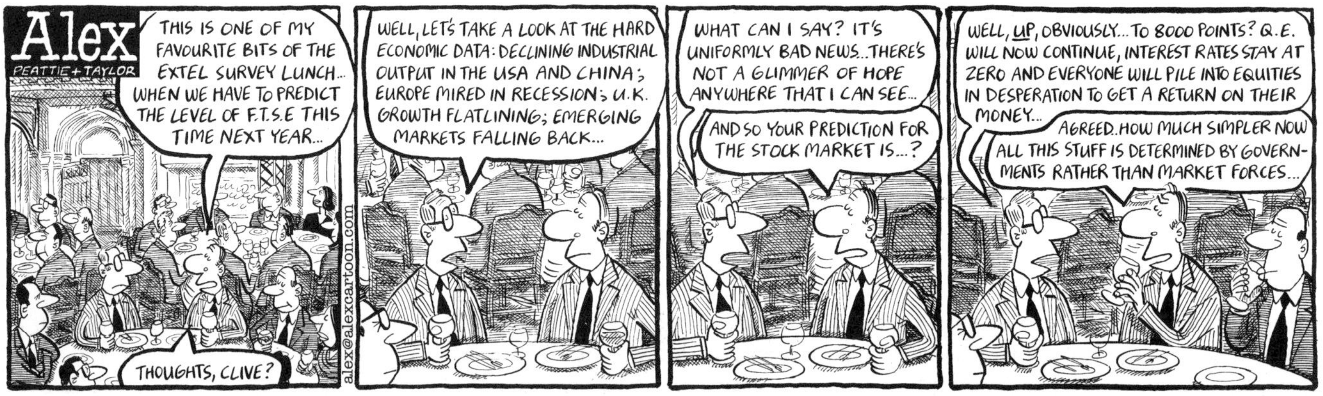
Alex
PEATTIE+TAYLOR
THIS IS ONE OF MY FAVOURITE BITS OF THE EXTEL SURVEY LUNCH... WHEN WE HAVE TO PREDICT THE LEVEL OF F.T.S.E THIS TIME NEXT YEAR...
THOUGHTS, CLIVE?
alex@alexcartoon.com
WELL, LET'S TAKE A LOOK AT THE HARD ECONOMIC DATA: DECLINING INDUSTRIAL OUTPUT IN THE USA AND CHINA; EUROPE MIRED IN RECESSION; U.K. GROWTH FLATLINING; EMERGING MARKETS FALLING BACK...
WHAT CAN I SAY? IT'S UNIFORMLY BAD NEWS... THERE'S NOT A GLIMMER OF HOPE ANYWHERE THAT I CAN SEE...
AND SO YOUR PREDICTION FOR THE STOCK MARKET IS...?
WELL, UP, OBVIOUSLY... TO 8000 POINTS? Q.E. WILL NOW CONTINUE, INTEREST RATES STAY AT ZERO AND EVERYONE WILL PILE INTO EQUITIES IN DESPERATION TO GET A RETURN ON THEIR MONEY...
AGREED. HOW MUCH SIMPLER NOW ALL THIS STUFF IS DETERMINED BY GOVERNMENTS RATHER THAN MARKET FORCES...

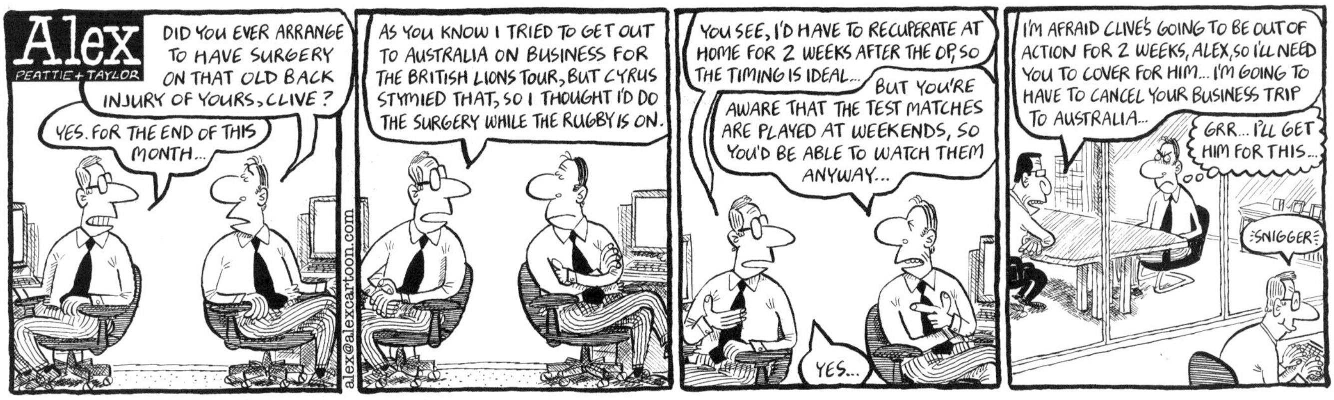
Alex
PEATTIE + TAYLOR
DID YOU EVER ARRANGE TO HAVE SURGERY ON THAT OLD BACK INJURY OF YOURS, CLIVE?
YES. FOR THE END OF THIS MONTH...
AS YOU KNOW I TRIED TO GET OUT TO AUSTRALIA ON BUSINESS FOR THE BRITISH LIONS TOUR, BUT CYRUS STYMIED THAT, SO I THOUGHT I'D DO THE SURGERY WHILE THE RUGBY IS ON.
alex@alexcartoon.com
YOU SEE, I'D HAVE TO RECUPERATE AT HOME FOR 2 WEEKS AFTER THE OP, SO THE TIMING IS IDEAL...
BUT YOU'RE AWARE THAT THE TEST MATCHES ARE PLAYED AT WEEKENDS, SO YOU'D BE ABLE TO WATCH THEM ANYWAY...
YES...
I'M AFRAID CLIVE'S GOING TO BE OUT OF ACTION FOR 2 WEEKS, ALEX, SO I'LL NEED YOU TO COVER FOR HIM... I'M GOING TO HAVE TO CANCEL YOUR BUSINESS TRIP TO AUSTRALIA...
GRR... I'LL GET HIM FOR THIS...
SNIGGER

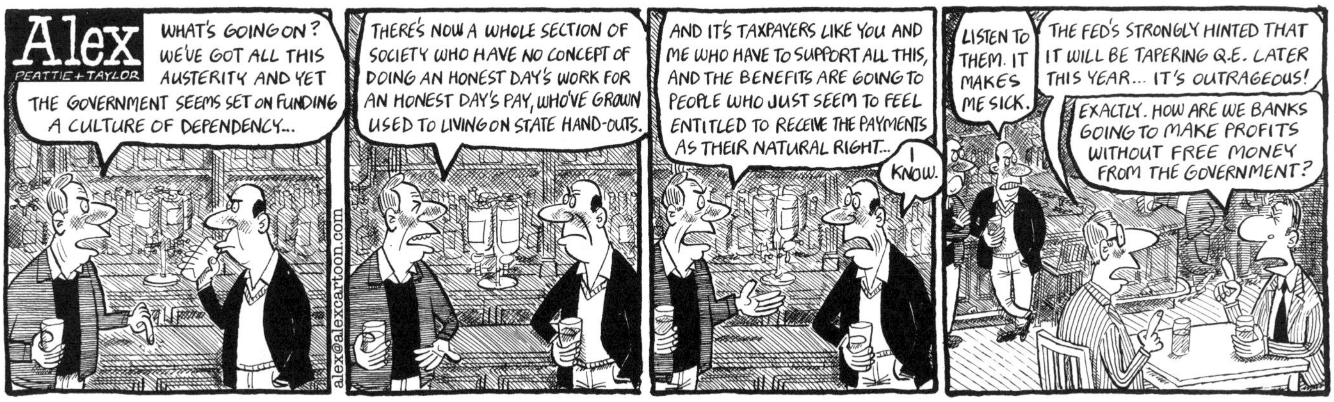
Alex
PEATTIE + TAYLOR
WHAT'S GOING ON? WE'VE GOT ALL THIS AUSTERITY AND YET THE GOVERNMENT SEEMS SET ON FUNDING A CULTURE OF DEPENDENCY...
THERE'S NOW A WHOLE SECTION OF SOCIETY WHO HAVE NO CONCEPT OF DOING AN HONEST DAY'S WORK FOR AN HONEST DAY'S PAY, WHO'VE GROWN USED TO LIVING ON STATE HAND-OUTS.
alex@alexcartoon.com
AND IT'S TAXPAYERS LIKE YOU AND ME WHO HAVE TO SUPPORT ALL THIS, AND THE BENEFITS ARE GOING TO PEOPLE WHO JUST SEEM TO FEEL ENTITLED TO RECEIVE THE PAYMENTS AS THEIR NATURAL RIGHT...
I KNOW.
LISTEN TO THEM. IT MAKES ME SICK.
THE FED'S STRONGLY HINTED THAT IT WILL BE TAPERING Q.E. LATER THIS YEAR... IT'S OUTRAGEOUS!
EXACTLY. HOW ARE WE BANKS GOING TO MAKE PROFITS WITHOUT FREE MONEY FROM THE GOVERNMENT?

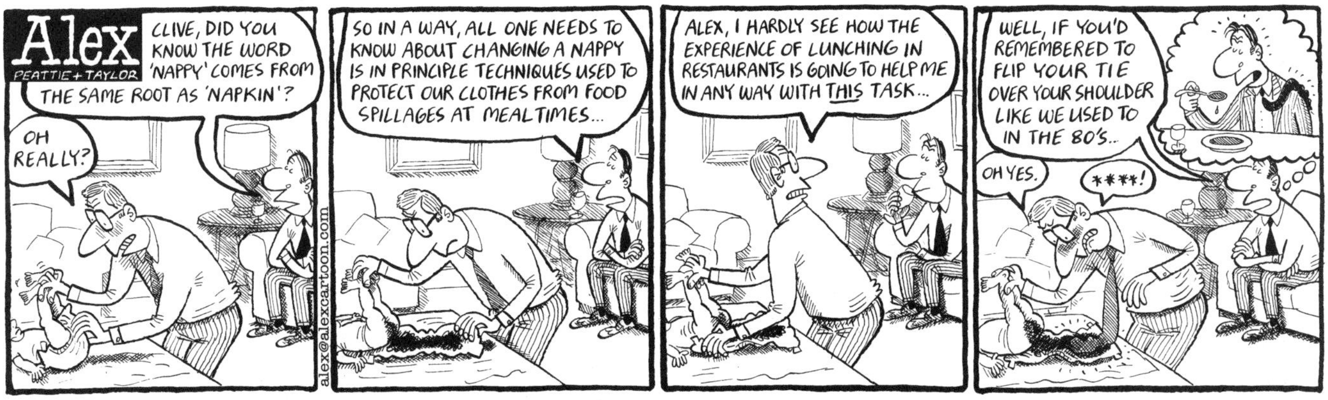
Alex
PEATTIE + TAYLOR
CLIVE, DID YOU KNOW THE WORD 'NAPPY' COMES FROM THE SAME ROOT AS 'NAPKIN'?
OH REALLY?
alex@alexcartoon.com
SO IN A WAY, ALL ONE NEEDS TO KNOW ABOUT CHANGING A NAPPY IS IN PRINCIPLE TECHNIQUES USED TO PROTECT OUR CLOTHES FROM FOOD SPILLAGES AT MEALTIMES...
ALEX, I HARDLY SEE HOW THE EXPERIENCE OF LUNCHING IN RESTAURANTS IS GOING TO HELP ME IN ANY WAY WITH THIS TASK...
WELL, IF YOU'D REMEMBERED TO FLIP YOUR TIE OVER YOUR SHOULDER LIKE WE USED TO IN THE 80'S...
OH YES.
****!

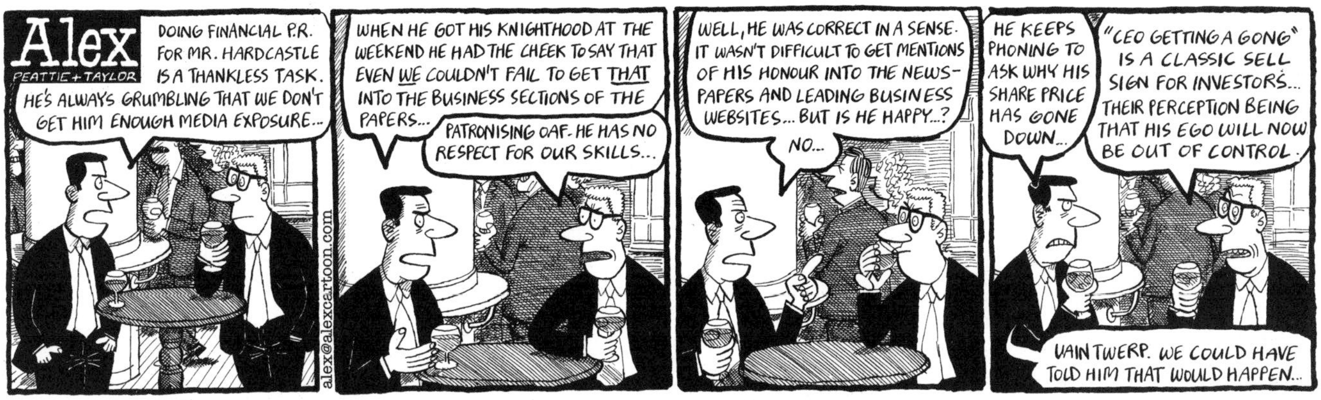
Alex
PEATTIE + TAYLOR
DOING FINANCIAL P.R. FOR MR. HARDCASTLE IS A THANKLESS TASK. HE'S ALWAYS GRUMBLING THAT WE DON'T GET HIM ENOUGH MEDIA EXPOSURE...
alex@alexcartoon.com
WHEN HE GOT HIS KNIGHTHOOD AT THE WEEKEND HE HAD THE CHEEK TO SAY THAT EVEN WE COULDN'T FAIL TO GET THAT INTO THE BUSINESS SECTIONS OF THE PAPERS...
PATRONISING OAF. HE HAS NO RESPECT FOR OUR SKILLS...
WELL, HE WAS CORRECT IN A SENSE. IT WASN'T DIFFICULT TO GET MENTIONS OF HIS HONOUR INTO THE NEWS-PAPERS AND LEADING BUSINESS WEBSITES... BUT IS HE HAPPY...?
NO...
HE KEEPS PHONING TO ASK WHY HIS SHARE PRICE HAS GONE DOWN...
"CEO GETTING A GONG" IS A CLASSIC SELL SIGN FOR INVESTORS... THEIR PERCEPTION BEING THAT HIS EGO WILL NOW BE OUT OF CONTROL.
VAIN TWERP. WE COULD HAVE TOLD HIM THAT WOULD HAPPEN...

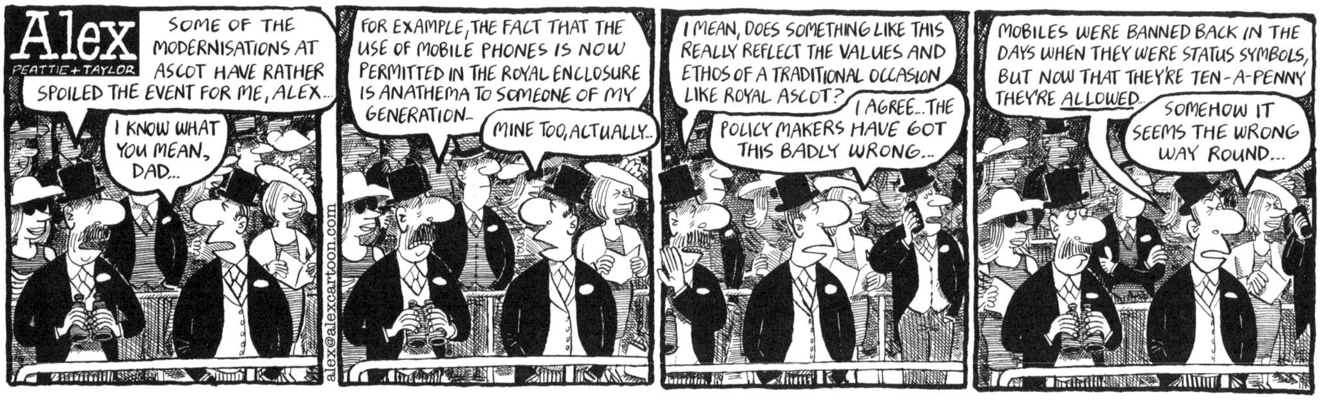
Alex
PEATTIE + TAYLOR
SOME OF THE MODERNISATIONS AT ASCOT HAVE RATHER SPOILED THE EVENT FOR ME, ALEX...
I KNOW WHAT YOU MEAN, DAD...
alex@alexcartoon.com
FOR EXAMPLE, THE FACT THAT THE USE OF MOBILE PHONES IS NOW PERMITTED IN THE ROYAL ENCLOSURE IS ANATHEMA TO SOMEONE OF MY GENERATION...
MINE TOO, ACTUALLY...
I MEAN, DOES SOMETHING LIKE THIS REALLY REFLECT THE VALUES AND ETHOS OF A TRADITIONAL OCCASION LIKE ROYAL ASCOT?
I AGREE... THE POLICY MAKERS HAVE GOT THIS BADLY WRONG...
MOBILES WERE BANNED BACK IN THE DAYS WHEN THEY WERE STATUS SYMBOLS, BUT NOW THAT THEY'RE TEN-A-PENNY THEY'RE ALLOWED...
SOMEHOW IT SEEMS THE WRONG WAY ROUND...

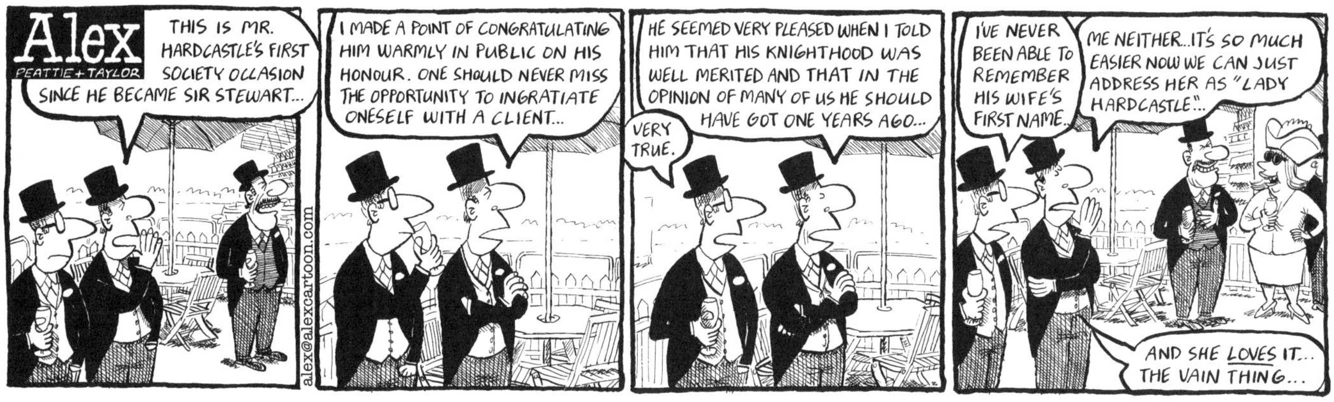
Alex
PEATTIE + TAYLOR
THIS IS MR. HARDCASTLE'S FIRST SOCIETY OCCASION SINCE HE BECAME SIR STEWART...
alex@alexcartoon.com
I MADE A POINT OF CONGRATULATING HIM WARMLY IN PUBLIC ON HIS HONOUR. ONE SHOULD NEVER MISS THE OPPORTUNITY TO INGRATIATE ONESELF WITH A CLIENT...
HE SEEMED VERY PLEASED WHEN I TOLD HIM THAT HIS KNIGHTHOOD WAS WELL MERITED AND THAT IN THE OPINION OF MANY OF US HE SHOULD HAVE GOT ONE YEARS AGO...
VERY TRUE.
I'VE NEVER BEEN ABLE TO REMEMBER HIS WIFE'S FIRST NAME...
ME NEITHER... IT'S SO MUCH EASIER NOW WE CAN JUST ADDRESS HER AS "LADY HARDCASTLE"...
AND SHE LOVES IT... THE VAIN THING...

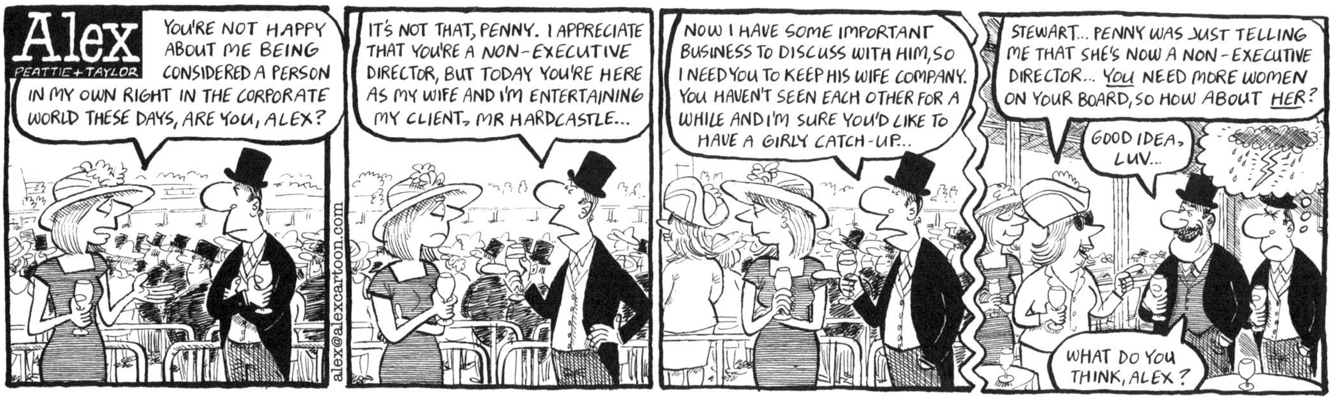
Alex
PEATTIE + TAYLOR
YOU'RE NOT HAPPY ABOUT ME BEING CONSIDERED A PERSON IN MY OWN RIGHT IN THE CORPORATE WORLD THESE DAYS, ARE YOU, ALEX?
alex@alexcartoon.com
IT'S NOT THAT, PENNY. I APPRECIATE THAT YOU'RE A NON-EXECUTIVE DIRECTOR, BUT TODAY YOU'RE HERE AS MY WIFE AND I'M ENTERTAINING MY CLIENT, MR HARDCASTLE...
NOW I HAVE SOME IMPORTANT BUSINESS TO DISCUSS WITH HIM, SO I NEED YOU TO KEEP HIS WIFE COMPANY. YOU HAVEN'T SEEN EACH OTHER FOR A WHILE AND I'M SURE YOU'D LIKE TO HAVE A GIRLY CATCH-UP...
STEWART... PENNY WAS JUST TELLING ME THAT SHE'S NOW A NON-EXECUTIVE DIRECTOR... YOU NEED MORE WOMEN ON YOUR BOARD, SO HOW ABOUT HER?
GOOD IDEA, LUV...
WHAT DO YOU THINK, ALEX?

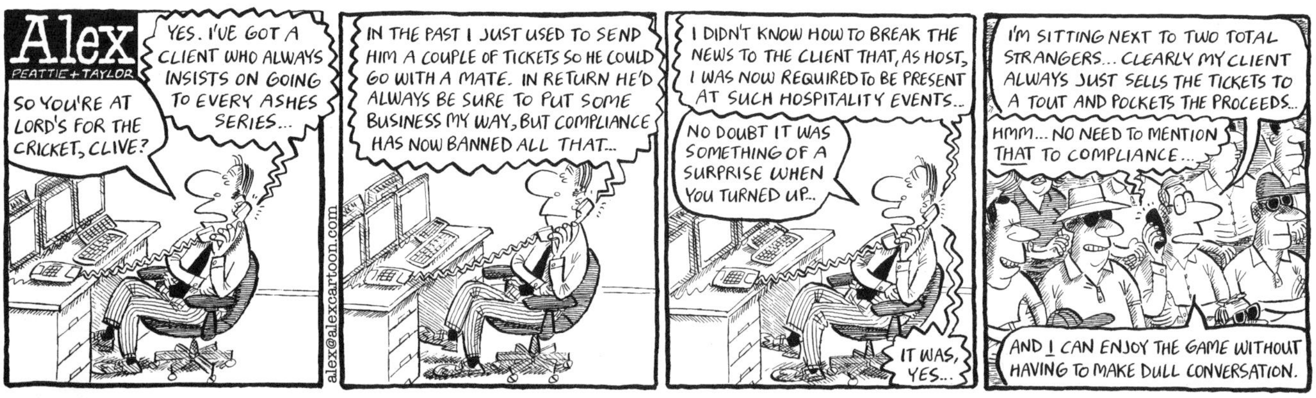
Alex
PEATTIE + TAYLOR
SO YOU'RE AT LORD'S FOR THE CRICKET, CLIVE?
YES. I'VE GOT A CLIENT WHO ALWAYS INSISTS ON GOING TO EVERY ASHES SERIES...
alex@alexcartoon.com
IN THE PAST I JUST USED TO SEND HIM A COUPLE OF TICKETS SO HE COULD GO WITH A MATE. IN RETURN HE'D ALWAYS BE SURE TO PUT SOME BUSINESS MY WAY, BUT COMPLIANCE HAS NOW BANNED ALL THAT...
I DIDN'T KNOW HOW TO BREAK THE NEWS TO THE CLIENT THAT, AS HOST, I WAS NOW REQUIRED TO BE PRESENT AT SUCH HOSPITALITY EVENTS...
NO DOUBT IT WAS SOMETHING OF A SURPRISE WHEN YOU TURNED UP...
IT WAS, YES...
I'M SITTING NEXT TO TWO TOTAL STRANGERS... CLEARLY MY CLIENT ALWAYS JUST SELLS THE TICKETS TO A TOUT AND POCKETS THE PROCEEDS...
HMM... NO NEED TO MENTION THAT TO COMPLIANCE...
AND I CAN ENJOY THE GAME WITHOUT HAVING TO MAKE DULL CONVERSATION.

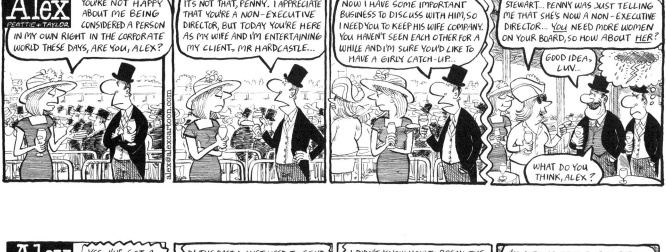

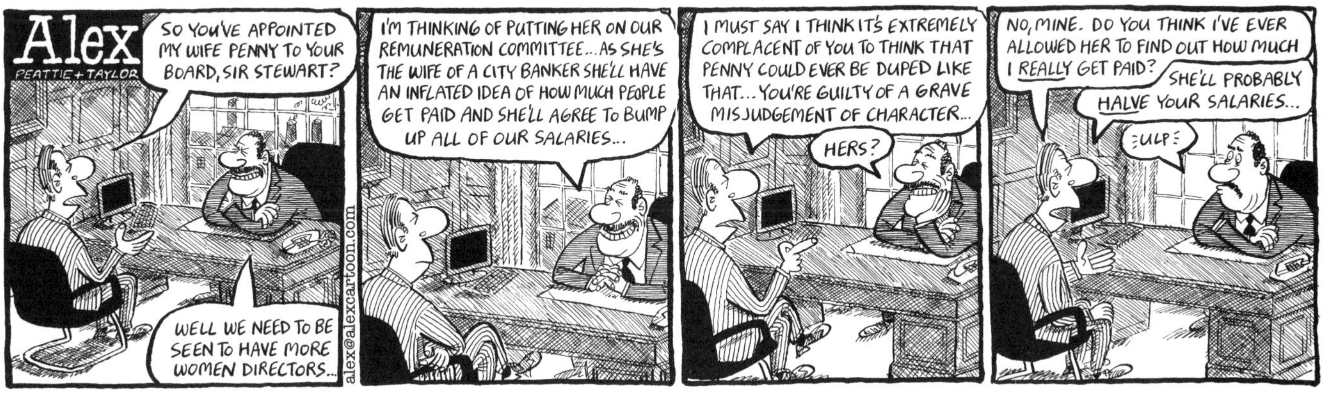
Alex
PEATTIE + TAYLOR
SO YOU'VE APPOINTED MY WIFE PENNY TO YOUR BOARD, SIR STEWART?
WELL WE NEED TO BE SEEN TO HAVE MORE WOMEN DIRECTORS...
alex@alexcartoon.com
I'M THINKING OF PUTTING HER ON OUR REMUNERATION COMMITTEE... AS SHE'S THE WIFE OF A CITY BANKER SHE'LL HAVE AN INFLATED IDEA OF HOW MUCH PEOPLE GET PAID AND SHE'LL AGREE TO BUMP UP ALL OF OUR SALARIES...
I MUST SAY I THINK IT'S EXTREMELY COMPLACENT OF YOU TO THINK THAT PENNY COULD EVER BE DUPED LIKE THAT... YOU'RE GUILTY OF A GRAVE MISJUDGEMENT OF CHARACTER...
HERS?
NO, MINE. DO YOU THINK I'VE EVER ALLOWED HER TO FIND OUT HOW MUCH I REALLY GET PAID?
SHE'LL PROBABLY HALVE YOUR SALARIES...
ULP

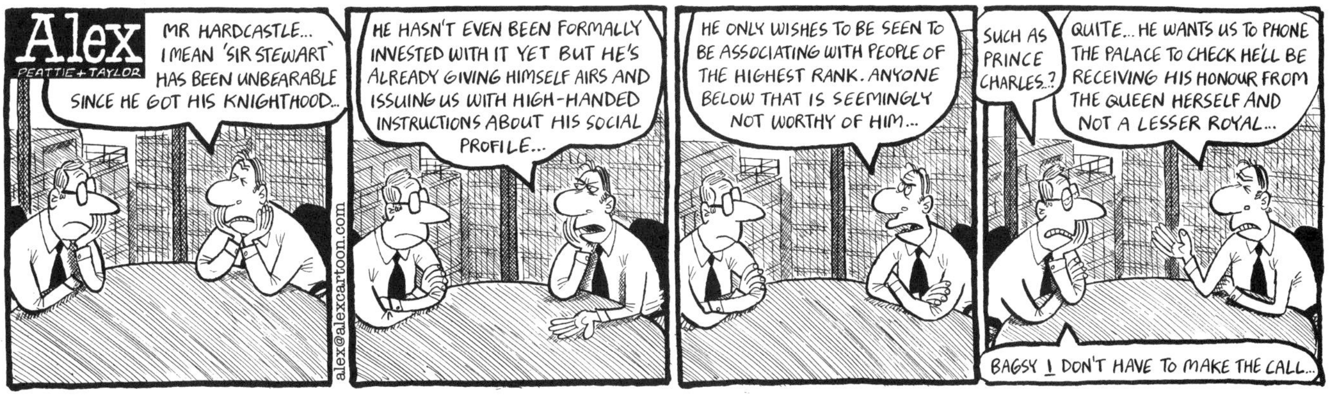
Alex
PEATTIE + TAYLOR
MR HARDCASTLE... I MEAN 'SIR STEWART' HAS BEEN UNBEARABLE SINCE HE GOT HIS KNIGHTHOOD...
alex@alexcartoon.com
HE HASN'T EVEN BEEN FORMALLY INVESTED WITH IT YET BUT HE'S ALREADY GIVING HIMSELF AIRS AND ISSUING US WITH HIGH-HANDED INSTRUCTIONS ABOUT HIS SOCIAL PROFILE...
HE ONLY WISHES TO BE SEEN TO BE ASSOCIATING WITH PEOPLE OF THE HIGHEST RANK. ANYONE BELOW THAT IS SEEMINGLY NOT WORTHY OF HIM...
SUCH AS PRINCE CHARLES..?
QUITE... HE WANTS US TO PHONE THE PALACE TO CHECK HE'LL BE RECEIVING HIS HONOUR FROM THE QUEEN HERSELF AND NOT A LESSER ROYAL...
BAGSY I DON'T HAVE TO MAKE THE CALL...

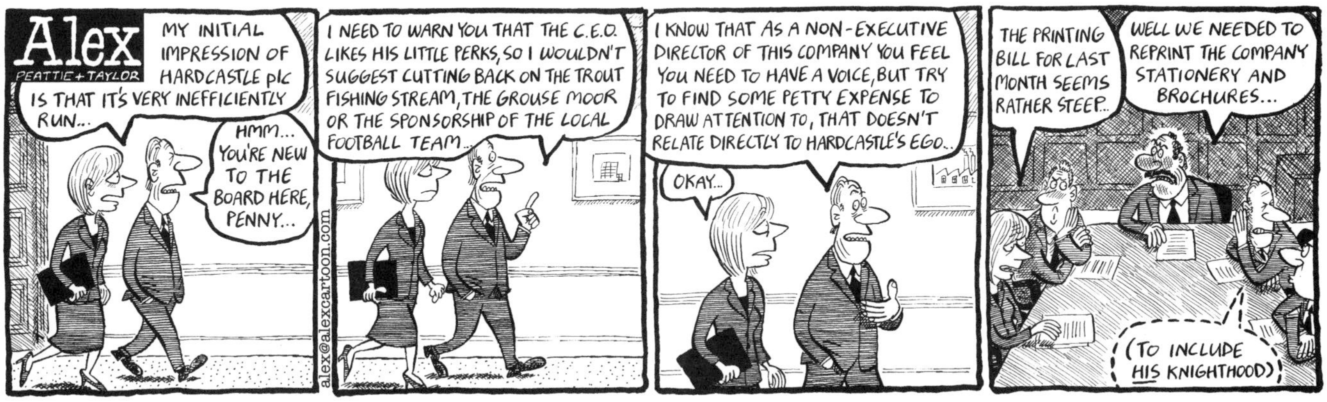
Alex
PEATTIE + TAYLOR
MY INITIAL IMPRESSION OF HARDCASTLE plc IS THAT IT'S VERY INEFFICIENTLY RUN...
HMM... YOU'RE NEW TO THE BOARD HERE, PENNY...
alex@alexcartoon.com
I NEED TO WARN YOU THAT THE C.E.O. LIKES HIS LITTLE PERKS, SO I WOULDN'T SUGGEST CUTTING BACK ON THE TROUT FISHING STREAM, THE GROUSE MOOR OR THE SPONSORSHIP OF THE LOCAL FOOTBALL TEAM...
I KNOW THAT AS A NON-EXECUTIVE DIRECTOR OF THIS COMPANY YOU FEEL YOU NEED TO HAVE A VOICE, BUT TRY TO FIND SOME PETTY EXPENSE TO DRAW ATTENTION TO, THAT DOESN'T RELATE DIRECTLY TO HARDCASTLE'S EGO...
OKAY...
THE PRINTING BILL FOR LAST MONTH SEEMS RATHER STEEP...
WELL WE NEEDED TO REPRINT THE COMPANY STATIONERY AND BROCHURES...
(TO INCLUDE HIS KNIGHTHOOD)

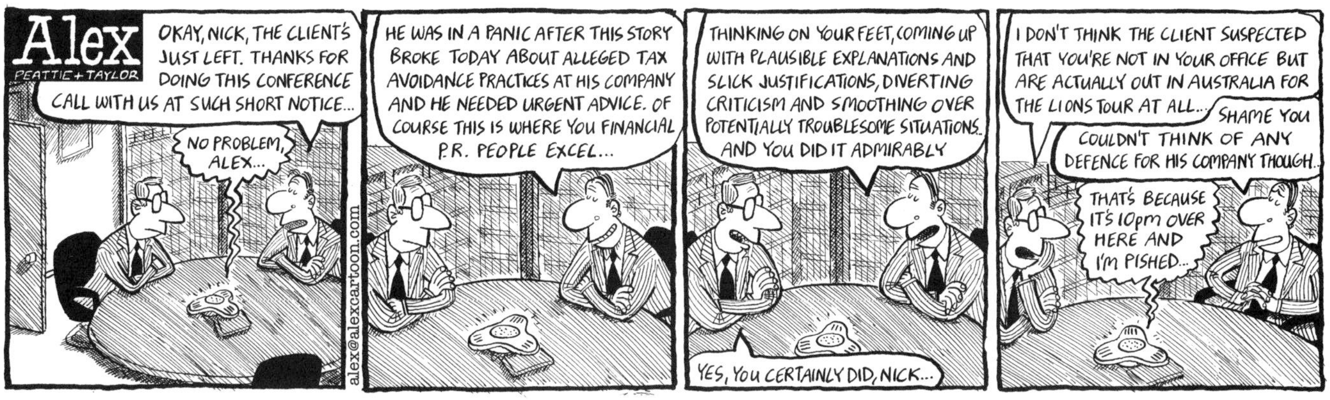
Alex
PEATTIE + TAYLOR
OKAY, NICK, THE CLIENT'S JUST LEFT. THANKS FOR DOING THIS CONFERENCE CALL WITH US AT SUCH SHORT NOTICE...
NO PROBLEM, ALEX...
alex@alexcartoon.com
HE WAS IN A PANIC AFTER THIS STORY BROKE TODAY ABOUT ALLEGED TAX AVOIDANCE PRACTICES AT HIS COMPANY AND HE NEEDED URGENT ADVICE. OF COURSE THIS IS WHERE YOU FINANCIAL P.R. PEOPLE EXCEL...
THINKING ON YOUR FEET, COMING UP WITH PLAUSIBLE EXPLANATIONS AND SLICK JUSTIFICATIONS, DIVERTING CRITICISM AND SMOOTHING OVER POTENTIALLY TROUBLESOME SITUATIONS... AND YOU DID IT ADMIRABLY
YES, YOU CERTAINLY DID, NICK...
I DON'T THINK THE CLIENT SUSPECTED THAT YOU'RE NOT IN YOUR OFFICE BUT ARE ACTUALLY OUT IN AUSTRALIA FOR THE LIONS TOUR AT ALL...
SHAME YOU COULDN'T THINK OF ANY DEFENCE FOR HIS COMPANY THOUGH...
THAT'S BECAUSE IT'S 10pm OVER HERE AND I'M PISHED...

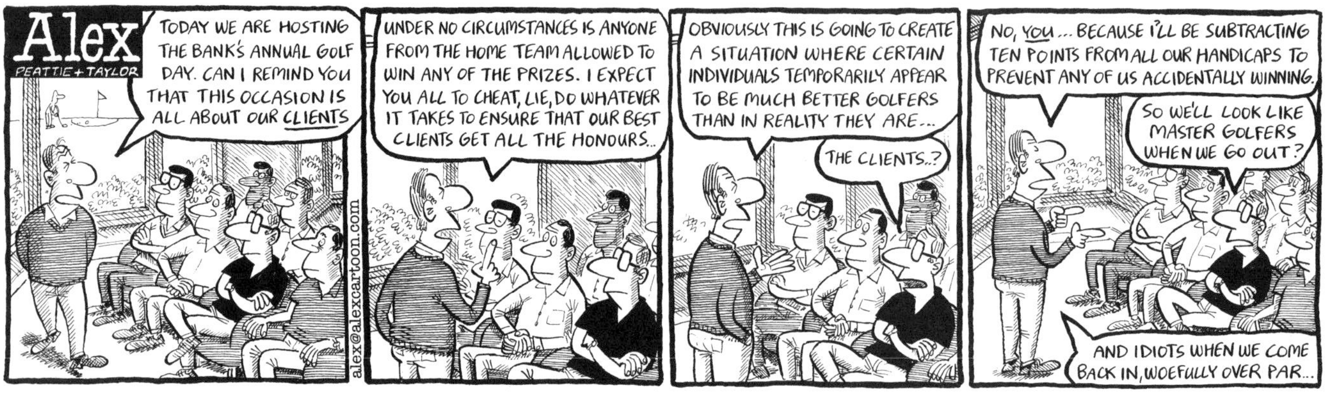
Alex
PEATTIE + TAYLOR
TODAY WE ARE HOSTING THE BANK'S ANNUAL GOLF DAY. CAN I REMIND YOU THAT THIS OCCASION IS ALL ABOUT OUR CLIENTS
UNDER NO CIRCUMSTANCES IS ANYONE FROM THE HOME TEAM ALLOWED TO WIN ANY OF THE PRIZES. I EXPECT YOU ALL TO CHEAT, LIE, DO WHATEVER IT TAKES TO ENSURE THAT OUR BEST CLIENTS GET ALL THE HONOURS...
alex@alexcartoon.com
OBVIOUSLY THIS IS GOING TO CREATE A SITUATION WHERE CERTAIN INDIVIDUALS TEMPORARILY APPEAR TO BE MUCH BETTER GOLFERS THAN IN REALITY THEY ARE...
THE CLIENTS..?
NO, YOU... BECAUSE I'LL BE SUBTRACTING TEN POINTS FROM ALL OUR HANDICAPS TO PREVENT ANY OF US ACCIDENTALLY WINNING.
SO WE'LL LOOK LIKE MASTER GOLFERS WHEN WE GO OUT?
AND IDIOTS WHEN WE COME BACK IN, WOEFULLY OVER PAR...

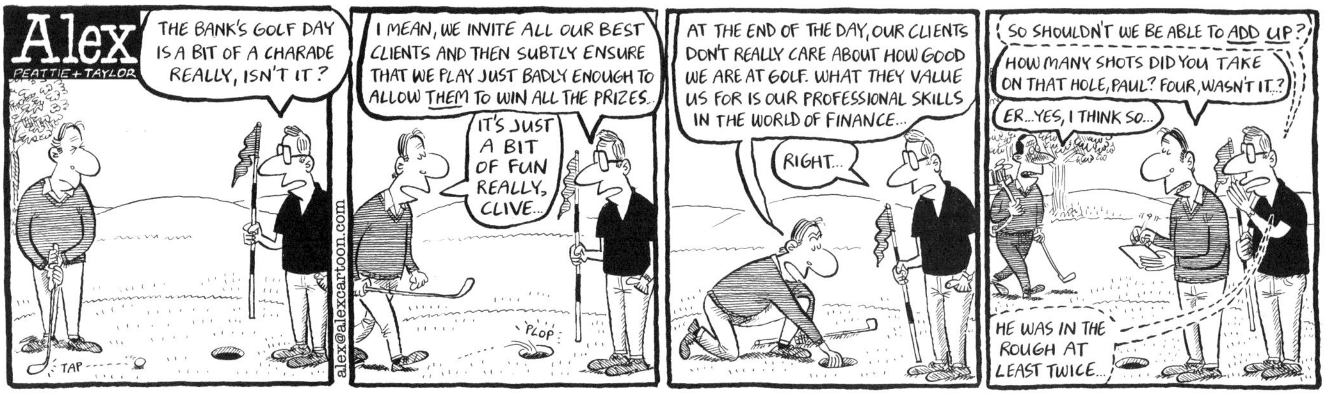
Alex
PEATTIE + TAYLOR
THE BANK'S GOLF DAY IS A BIT OF A CHARADE REALLY, ISN'T IT?
TAP
alex@alexcartoon.com
I MEAN, WE INVITE ALL OUR BEST CLIENTS AND THEN SUBTLY ENSURE THAT WE PLAY JUST BADLY ENOUGH TO ALLOW THEM TO WIN ALL THE PRIZES.
IT'S JUST A BIT OF FUN REALLY, CLIVE...
PLOP
AT THE END OF THE DAY, OUR CLIENTS DON'T REALLY CARE ABOUT HOW GOOD WE ARE AT GOLF. WHAT THEY VALUE US FOR IS OUR PROFESSIONAL SKILLS IN THE WORLD OF FINANCE...
RIGHT...
SO SHOULDN'T WE BE ABLE TO ADD UP?
HOW MANY SHOTS DID YOU TAKE ON THAT HOLE, PAUL? FOUR, WASN'T IT..?
ER...YES, I THINK SO...
HE WAS IN THE ROUGH AT LEAST TWICE...

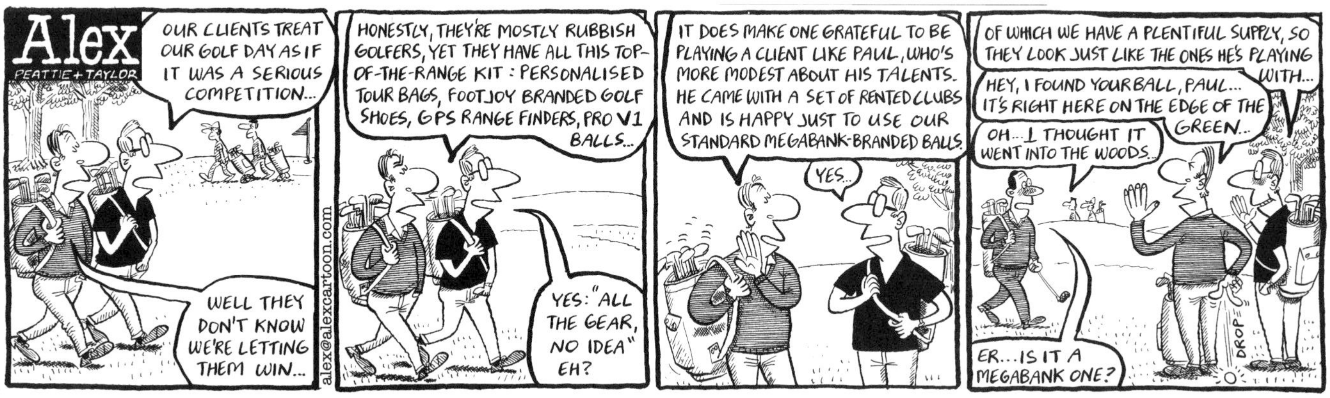
Alex
PEATTIE + TAYLOR
OUR CLIENTS TREAT OUR GOLF DAY AS IF IT WAS A SERIOUS COMPETITION...
WELL THEY DON'T KNOW WE'RE LETTING THEM WIN...
alex@alexcartoon.com
HONESTLY, THEY'RE MOSTLY RUBBISH GOLFERS, YET THEY HAVE ALL THIS TOP-OF-THE-RANGE KIT: PERSONALISED TOUR BAGS, FOOTJOY BRANDED GOLF SHOES, GPS RANGE FINDERS, PRO V1 BALLS...
YES: "ALL THE GEAR, NO IDEA" EH?
IT DOES MAKE ONE GRATEFUL TO BE PLAYING A CLIENT LIKE PAUL, WHO'S MORE MODEST ABOUT HIS TALENTS. HE CAME WITH A SET OF RENTED CLUBS AND IS HAPPY JUST TO USE OUR STANDARD MEGABANK-BRANDED BALLS.
YES...
OF WHICH WE HAVE A PLENTIFUL SUPPLY, SO THEY LOOK JUST LIKE THE ONES HE'S PLAYING WITH...
HEY, I FOUND YOUR BALL, PAUL... IT'S RIGHT HERE ON THE EDGE OF THE GREEN...
OH... I THOUGHT IT WENT INTO THE WOODS...
DROP
ER... IS IT A MEGABANK ONE?

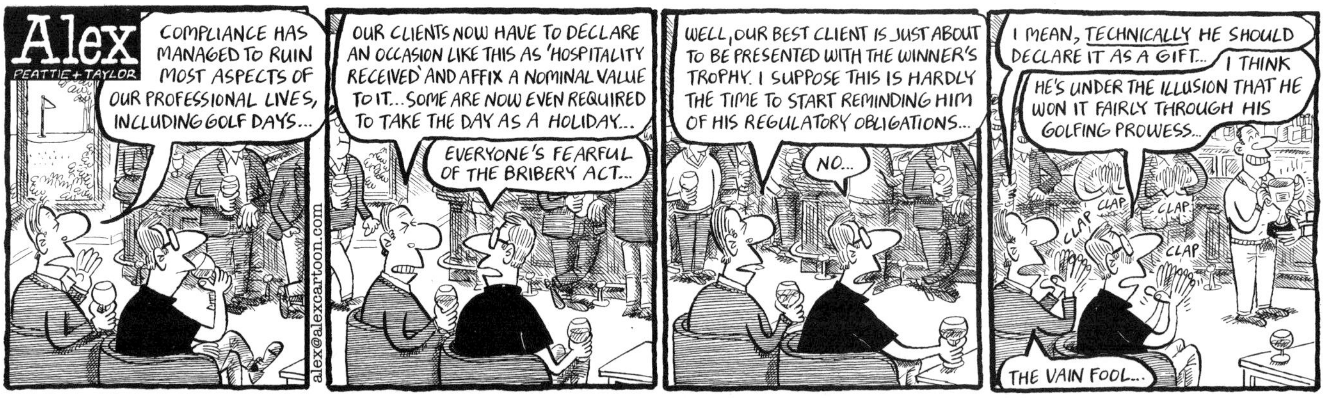
Alex
PEATTIE + TAYLOR
COMPLIANCE HAS MANAGED TO RUIN MOST ASPECTS OF OUR PROFESSIONAL LIVES, INCLUDING GOLF DAYS...
alex@alexcartoon.com
OUR CLIENTS NOW HAVE TO DECLARE AN OCCASION LIKE THIS AS 'HOSPITALITY RECEIVED' AND AFFIX A NOMINAL VALUE TO IT... SOME ARE NOW EVEN REQUIRED TO TAKE THE DAY AS A HOLIDAY...
EVERYONE'S FEARFUL OF THE BRIBERY ACT...
WELL, OUR BEST CLIENT IS JUST ABOUT TO BE PRESENTED WITH THE WINNER'S TROPHY. I SUPPOSE THIS IS HARDLY THE TIME TO START REMINDING HIM OF HIS REGULATORY OBLIGATIONS...
NO...
I MEAN, TECHNICALLY HE SHOULD DECLARE IT AS A GIFT...
I THINK HE'S UNDER THE ILLUSION THAT HE WON IT FAIRLY THROUGH HIS GOLFING PROWESS...
CLAP CLAP CLAP CLAP
THE VAIN FOOL...

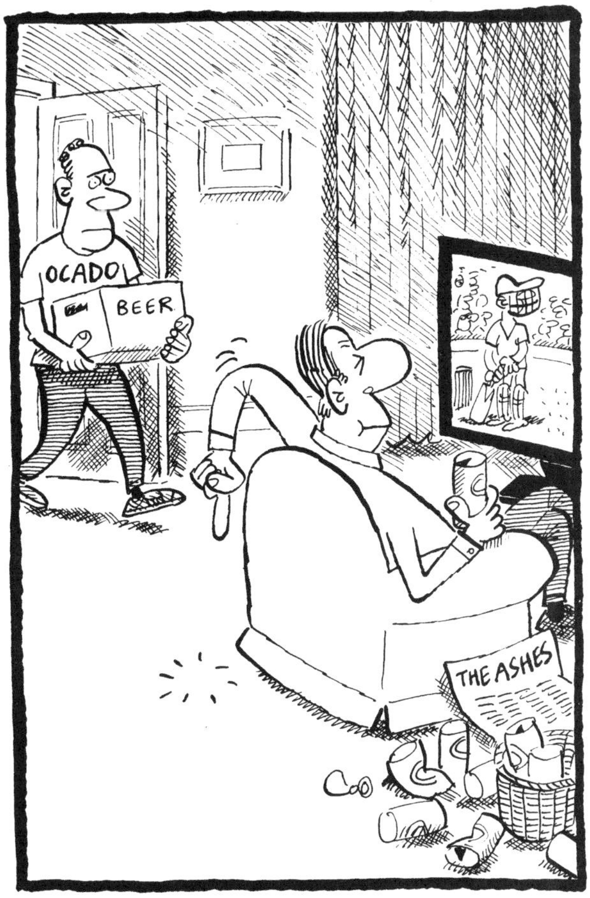
OCADO
BEER
THE ASHES

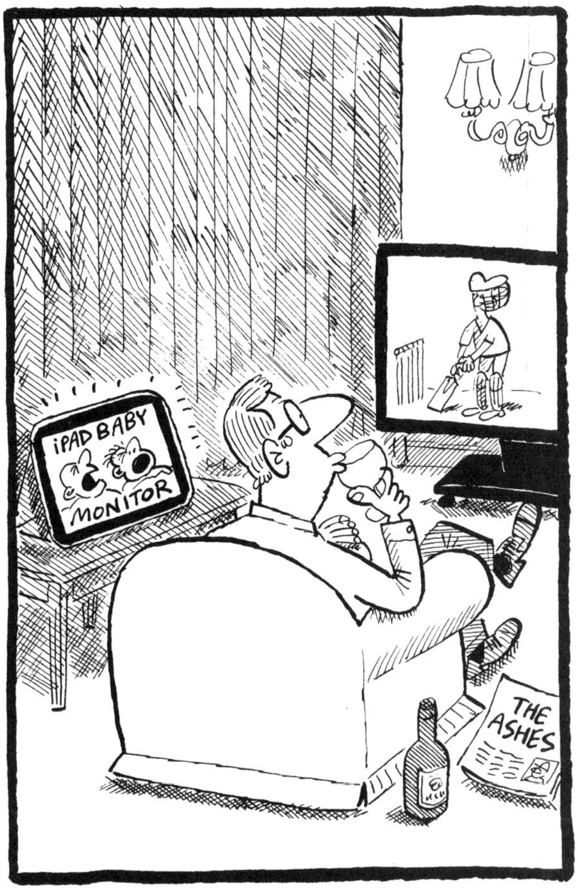
iPAD BABY
MONITOR
THE ASHES

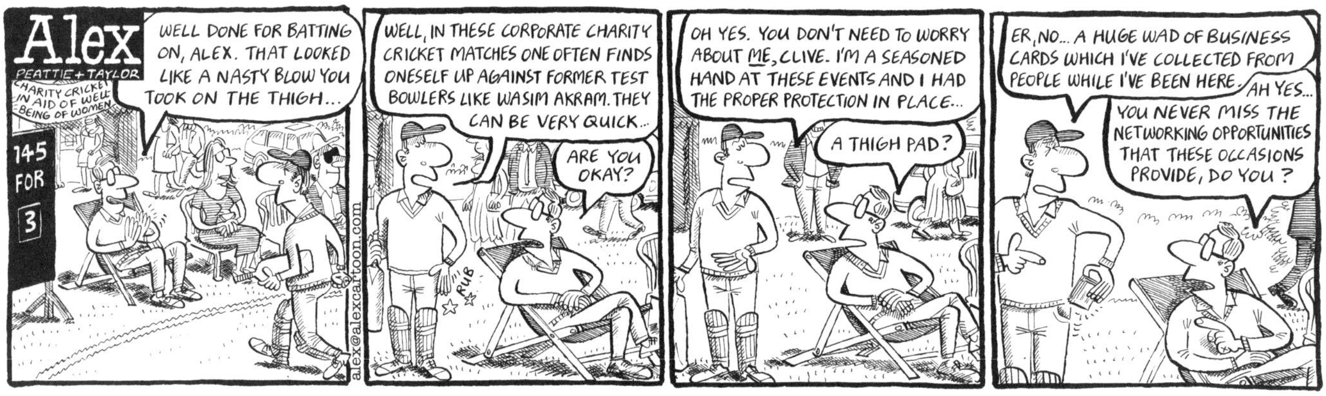
Alex
PEATTIE + TAYLOR
CHARITY CRICKET IN AID OF WELL BEING OF WOMEN
145 FOR 3
WELL DONE FOR BATTING ON, ALEX. THAT LOOKED LIKE A NASTY BLOW YOU TOOK ON THE THIGH...
alex@alexcartoon.com
WELL, IN THESE CORPORATE CHARITY CRICKET MATCHES ONE OFTEN FINDS ONESELF UP AGAINST FORMER TEST BOWLERS LIKE WASIM AKRAM. THEY CAN BE VERY QUICK...
ARE YOU OKAY?
OH YES. YOU DON'T NEED TO WORRY ABOUT ME, CLIVE. I'M A SEASONED HAND AT THESE EVENTS AND I HAD THE PROPER PROTECTION IN PLACE...
A THIGH PAD?
ER, NO... A HUGE WAD OF BUSINESS CARDS WHICH I'VE COLLECTED FROM PEOPLE WHILE I'VE BEEN HERE.
AH YES... YOU NEVER MISS THE NETWORKING OPPORTUNITIES THAT THESE OCCASIONS PROVIDE, DO YOU?

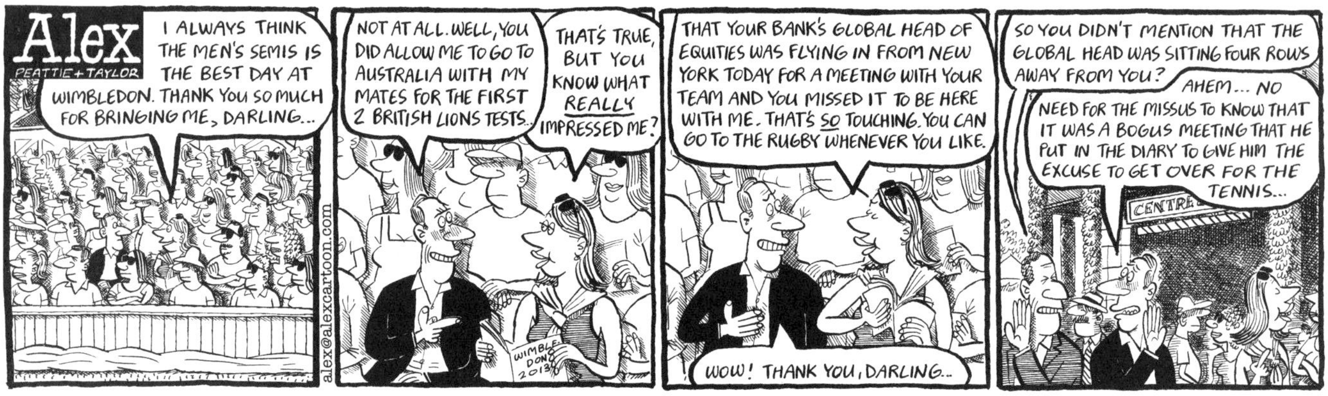
Alex
PEATTIE + TAYLOR
I ALWAYS THINK THE MEN'S SEMIS IS THE BEST DAY AT WIMBLEDON. THANK YOU SO MUCH FOR BRINGING ME, DARLING...
alex@alexcartoon.com
NOT AT ALL. WELL, YOU DID ALLOW ME TO GO TO AUSTRALIA WITH MY MATES FOR THE FIRST 2 BRITISH LIONS TESTS...
THAT'S TRUE, BUT YOU KNOW WHAT REALLY IMPRESSED ME?
WIMBLEDON 2013
THAT YOUR BANK'S GLOBAL HEAD OF EQUITIES WAS FLYING IN FROM NEW YORK TODAY FOR A MEETING WITH YOUR TEAM AND YOU MISSED IT TO BE HERE WITH ME. THAT'S SO TOUCHING. YOU CAN GO TO THE RUGBY WHENEVER YOU LIKE.
WOW! THANK YOU, DARLING...
SO YOU DIDN'T MENTION THAT THE GLOBAL HEAD WAS SITTING FOUR ROWS AWAY FROM YOU?
AHEM... NO NEED FOR THE MISSUS TO KNOW THAT IT WAS A BOGUS MEETING THAT HE PUT IN THE DIARY TO GIVE HIM THE EXCUSE TO GET OVER FOR THE TENNIS...
CENTRE

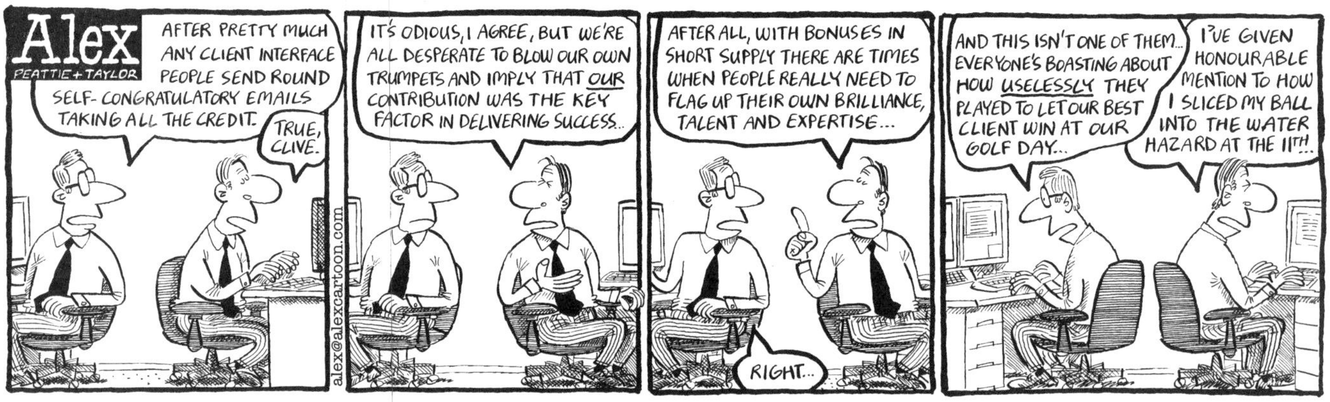
Alex
PEATTIE + TAYLOR
AFTER PRETTY MUCH ANY CLIENT INTERFACE PEOPLE SEND ROUND SELF-CONGRATULATORY EMAILS TAKING ALL THE CREDIT.
TRUE, CLIVE.
alex@alexcartoon.com
IT'S ODIOUS, I AGREE, BUT WE'RE ALL DESPERATE TO BLOW OUR OWN TRUMPETS AND IMPLY THAT OUR CONTRIBUTION WAS THE KEY FACTOR IN DELIVERING SUCCESS...
AFTER ALL, WITH BONUSES IN SHORT SUPPLY THERE ARE TIMES WHEN PEOPLE REALLY NEED TO FLAG UP THEIR OWN BRILLIANCE, TALENT AND EXPERTISE...
RIGHT...
AND THIS ISN'T ONE OF THEM... EVERYONE'S BOASTING ABOUT HOW USELESSLY THEY PLAYED TO LET OUR BEST CLIENT WIN AT OUR GOLF DAY...
I'VE GIVEN HONOURABLE MENTION TO HOW I SLICED MY BALL INTO THE WATER HAZARD AT THE 11TH!!

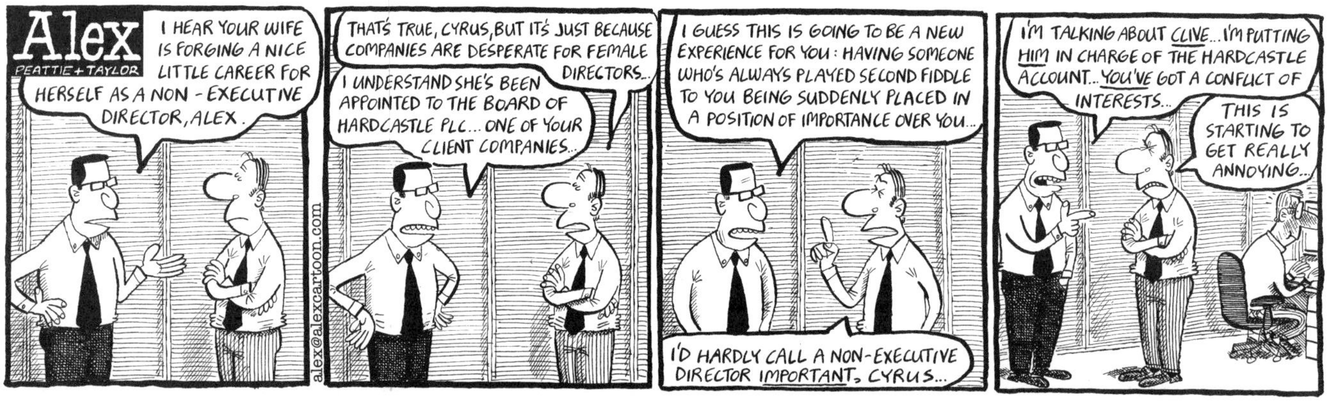
Alex
PEATTIE + TAYLOR
I HEAR YOUR WIFE IS FORGING A NICE LITTLE CAREER FOR HERSELF AS A NON-EXECUTIVE DIRECTOR, ALEX.
alex@alexcartoon.com
THAT'S TRUE, CYRUS, BUT IT'S JUST BECAUSE COMPANIES ARE DESPERATE FOR FEMALE DIRECTORS...
I UNDERSTAND SHE'S BEEN APPOINTED TO THE BOARD OF HARDCASTLE PLC... ONE OF YOUR CLIENT COMPANIES...
I GUESS THIS IS GOING TO BE A NEW EXPERIENCE FOR YOU: HAVING SOMEONE WHO'S ALWAYS PLAYED SECOND FIDDLE TO YOU BEING SUDDENLY PLACED IN A POSITION OF IMPORTANCE OVER YOU...
I'D HARDLY CALL A NON-EXECUTIVE DIRECTOR IMPORTANT, CYRUS...
I'M TALKING ABOUT CLIVE... I'M PUTTING HIM IN CHARGE OF THE HARDCASTLE ACCOUNT... YOU'VE GOT A CONFLICT OF INTERESTS...
THIS IS STARTING TO GET REALLY ANNOYING...

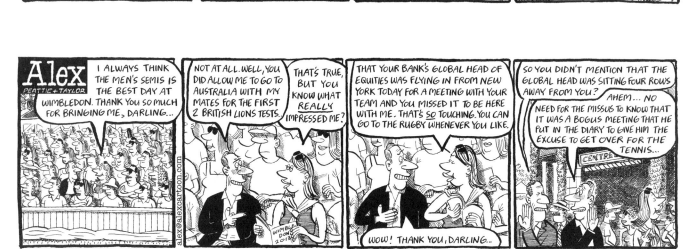

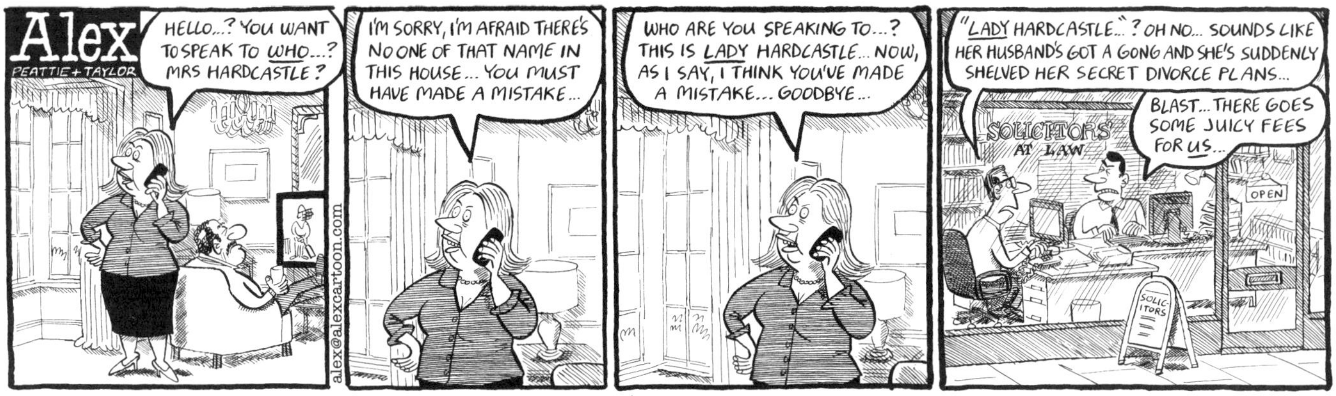
Alex
PEATTIE + TAYLOR
HELLO...? YOU WANT TO SPEAK TO WHO...? MRS HARDCASTLE?
I'M SORRY, I'M AFRAID THERE'S NO ONE OF THAT NAME IN THIS HOUSE... YOU MUST HAVE MADE A MISTAKE...
WHO ARE YOU SPEAKING TO...? THIS IS LADY HARDCASTLE... NOW, AS I SAY, I THINK YOU'VE MADE A MISTAKE... GOODBYE...
"LADY HARDCASTLE..."? OH NO... SOUNDS LIKE HER HUSBAND'S GOT A GONG AND SHE'S SUDDENLY SHELVED HER SECRET DIVORCE PLANS...
BLAST... THERE GOES SOME JUICY FEES FOR US...
SOLICITORS AT LAW
OPEN
SOLICITORS
alex@alexcartoon.com

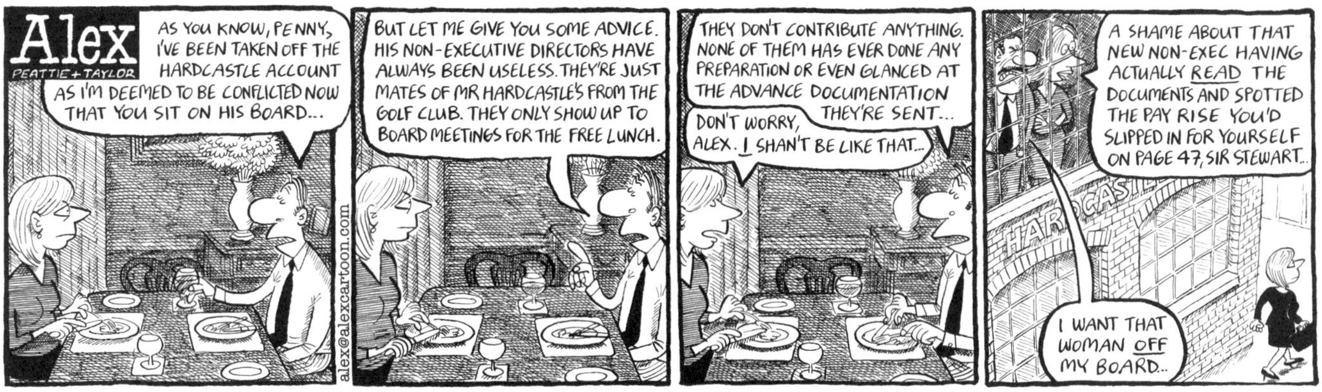
Alex
PEATTIE + TAYLOR
AS YOU KNOW, PENNY, I'VE BEEN TAKEN OFF THE HARDCASTLE ACCOUNT AS I'M DEEMED TO BE CONFLICTED NOW THAT YOU SIT ON HIS BOARD...
BUT LET ME GIVE YOU SOME ADVICE. HIS NON-EXECUTIVE DIRECTORS HAVE ALWAYS BEEN USELESS. THEY'RE JUST MATES OF MR HARDCASTLE'S FROM THE GOLF CLUB. THEY ONLY SHOW UP TO BOARD MEETINGS FOR THE FREE LUNCH.
THEY DON'T CONTRIBUTE ANYTHING. NONE OF THEM HAS EVER DONE ANY PREPARATION OR EVEN GLANCED AT THE ADVANCE DOCUMENTATION THEY'RE SENT...
DON'T WORRY, ALEX. I SHAN'T BE LIKE THAT...
A SHAME ABOUT THAT NEW NON-EXEC HAVING ACTUALLY READ THE DOCUMENTS AND SPOTTED THE PAY RISE YOU'D SLIPPED IN FOR YOURSELF ON PAGE 47, SIR STEWART...
I WANT THAT WOMAN OFF MY BOARD...
HARDCASTLE
alex@alexcartoon.com

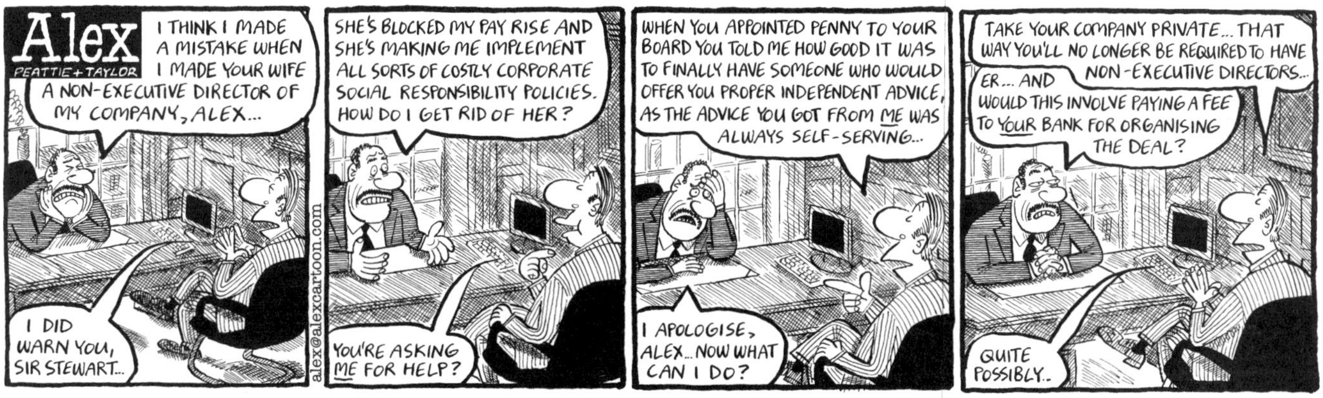
Alex
PEATTIE + TAYLOR
I THINK I MADE A MISTAKE WHEN I MADE YOUR WIFE A NON-EXECUTIVE DIRECTOR OF MY COMPANY, ALEX...
I DID WARN YOU, SIR STEWART...
SHE'S BLOCKED MY PAY RISE AND SHE'S MAKING ME IMPLEMENT ALL SORTS OF COSTLY CORPORATE SOCIAL RESPONSIBILITY POLICIES. HOW DO I GET RID OF HER?
YOU'RE ASKING ME FOR HELP?
WHEN YOU APPOINTED PENNY TO YOUR BOARD YOU TOLD ME HOW GOOD IT WAS TO FINALLY HAVE SOMEONE WHO WOULD OFFER YOU PROPER INDEPENDENT ADVICE, AS THE ADVICE YOU GOT FROM ME WAS ALWAYS SELF-SERVING...
I APOLOGISE, ALEX... NOW WHAT CAN I DO?
TAKE YOUR COMPANY PRIVATE... THAT WAY YOU'LL NO LONGER BE REQUIRED TO HAVE NON-EXECUTIVE DIRECTORS...
ER... AND WOULD THIS INVOLVE PAYING A FEE TO YOUR BANK FOR ORGANISING THE DEAL?
QUITE POSSIBLY..
alex@alexcartoon.com

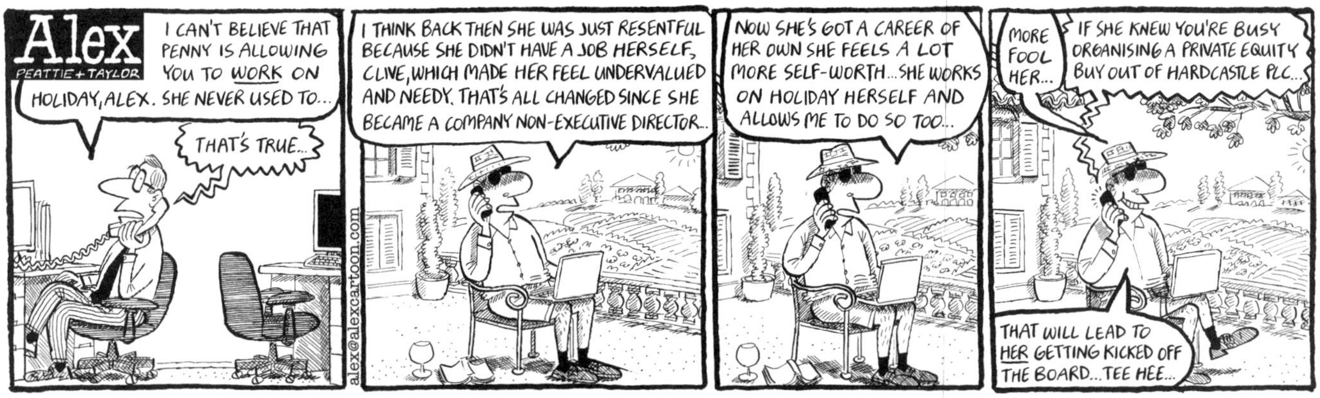
Alex
PEATTIE + TAYLOR
I CAN'T BELIEVE THAT PENNY IS ALLOWING YOU TO WORK ON HOLIDAY, ALEX. SHE NEVER USED TO...
THAT'S TRUE...
I THINK BACK THEN SHE WAS JUST RESENTFUL BECAUSE SHE DIDN'T HAVE A JOB HERSELF, CLIVE, WHICH MADE HER FEEL UNDERVALUED AND NEEDY. THAT'S ALL CHANGED SINCE SHE BECAME A COMPANY NON-EXECUTIVE DIRECTOR...
NOW SHE'S GOT A CAREER OF HER OWN SHE FEELS A LOT MORE SELF-WORTH... SHE WORKS ON HOLIDAY HERSELF AND ALLOWS ME TO DO SO TOO...
MORE FOOL HER...
IF SHE KNEW YOU'RE BUSY ORGANISING A PRIVATE EQUITY BUY OUT OF HARDCASTLE PLC...
THAT WILL LEAD TO HER GETTING KICKED OFF THE BOARD... TEE HEE...
alex@alexcartoon.com

FOLLOW ALEX ON TWITTER

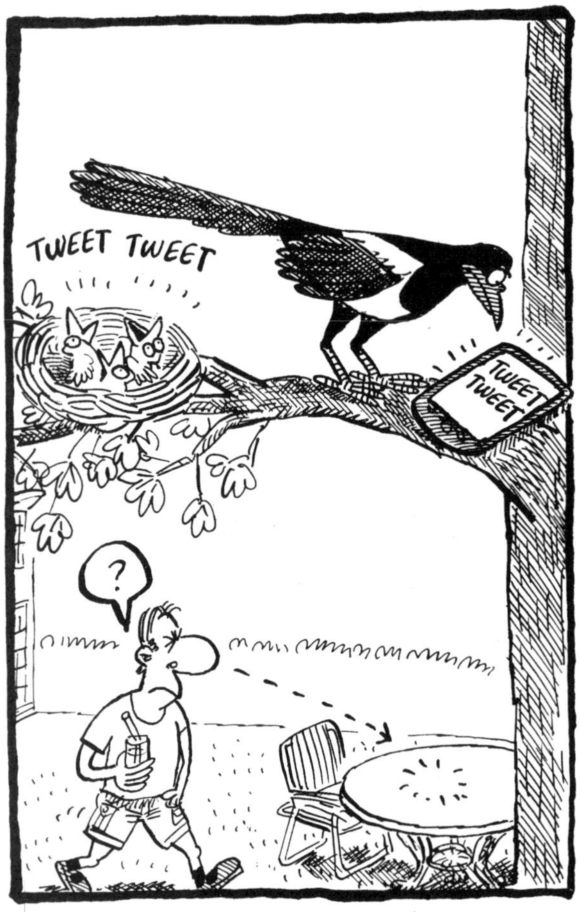
TWEET TWEET
TWEET TWEET
?

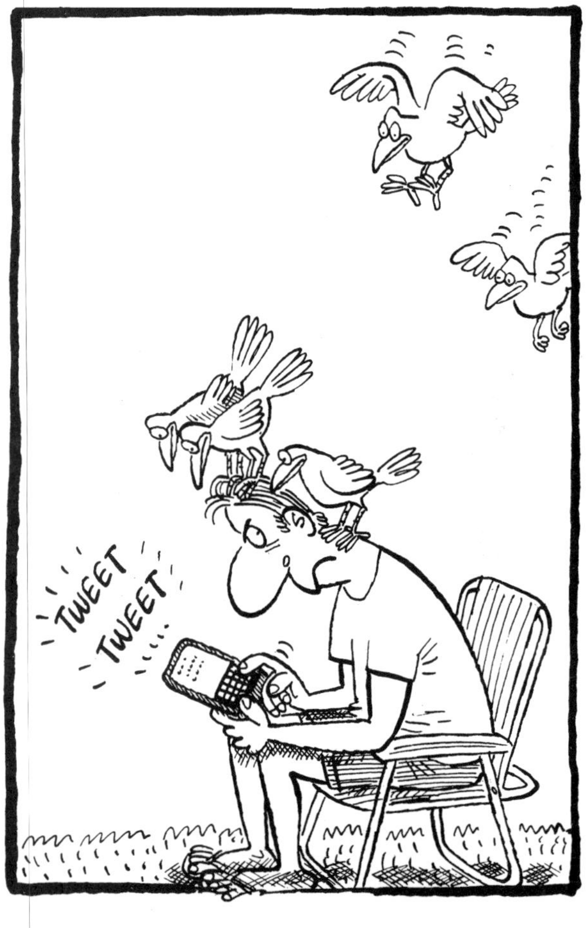
TWEET TWEET